An Architectural Travel Guide to Utah

An Architectural Travel Guide to

Utah

MARTHA BRADLEY EVANS

The University of Utah Press | Salt Lake City

Utah Division of
State History
A DIVISION OF THE UTAH
DEPARTMENT OF HERITAGE & ARTS

Copublished in partnership with the Utah State Historical Society

Copyright © 2021 by The University of Utah Press. All rights reserved.

Library of Congress Cataloging-in-Publication Data

Names: Bradley Evans, Martha, author.
Title: An architectural travel guide to Utah / Martha Bradley Evans.
Description: Salt Lake City : The University of Utah Press : The Utah State Historical
    Society, [2020] | Includes bibliographical references and index.
Identifiers: LCCN 2020014596 (print) | LCCN 2020014597 (ebook) | ISBN
    9781647690083 (paperback) | ISBN 9781647690090 (ebook)
Subjects: LCSH: Architecture—Utah—Guidebooks. | LCGFT: Guidebooks.
Classification: LCC NA730.U8 B73 2020 (print) | LCC NA730.U8 (ebook) | DDC
    720.9792—dc23
LC record available at https://lccn.loc.gov/2020014596
LC ebook record available at https://lccn.loc.gov/2020014597

All photographs by Martha Bradley Evans unless otherwise noted.

Errata and further information on this and other titles available at UofUpress.com

Printed and bound in the United States of America.

Contents

Preface

There is nothing like a great building. Buildings evoke a sense of the human experience. They are living, breathing voices of the past and hold clues as to what we most hope for in life. A state's architecture is a dynamic documentary of values and history, of real lives that played out in a physical world.

For a painter like Utah's LeConte Stewart, buildings contribute to the spirit of a place and are key elements in an indigenous landscape. Unlike the proverbial "geography of nowhere" of franchise buildings and anonymous architecture that could be found anywhere, the buildings Stewart studied in rural landscapes bring stones and sky, building technologies and cultural expectations into a uniquely Utah blend. They are of this place.

For decades Stewart planted himself in agricultural fields at the base of the foothills along the eastern edge of Davis County. From there the seasons ran across the hills like clouds blocking the sun, changing the land beneath them. Like Monet with his famous Rouen Cathedral series, Stewart studied the effects of light and color and texture on form and indelibly imprinted the foothills of Davis County on our collective consciousness. But Stewart's paintings, like those of many Utah landscape painters, inspire a sense of the built past. The small rural homestead that forms the focal point of countless paintings suggests a life we remember—a collective identity spelled out in wooden barns, zigzag fences, and adobe buildings.

Places carve out identities for us as individuals but also as members of communities with shared histories and present lives. Cultural critic Dolores Hayden suggests this collective memory is embedded in architecture. She writes, "Identity is intimately tied to memory: both our personal memories (where we have come from and where we have dwelt) and the collective or social memories interconnected with the histories of our families, neighbors, fellow workers, and ethnic communities. Urban landscapes are storehouses for these social memories, because natural features such as hills or harbors, as well as streets, buildings, and patterns of settlement, frame the lives of many people and often outlast many lives." Hayden describes the "power of place" as "the power of ordinary landscapes to nurture citizens' public memory."[1]

So where do we begin? If we think of built landscapes instead of single buildings, we start with the big picture, a larger frame. As with a landscape painting, this reflects a conscious choice by the artist. In our effort to understand this landscape—the built and natural environment of Utah—we can start with the big picture and acknowledge that it is unabashedly subjective but engaging, a proposition as potentially as expansive and unlimited as the sky. As we dig in and begin to search for a sense of this place—at least the spatial context of Utah's buildings—we need to commit to real effort. We need to get to the absolutely perfect place.

Many of the best places are on top of private or secure buildings. The American Towers, the Wells Fargo and Walker Bank buildings, the One Utah Center, and the LDS Church Office tower each provides spectacular and informative views of Salt Lake City. They present the best opportunity we have for seeing the big picture, the sprawling view, the way space stretches beyond what we can see unless we hike to the top of Ensign Peak or Mount Olympus. When we are lucky enough to have such a view, we are teased by the meanings the space seems to suggest. We can see the tension between the built landscape and the natural world beyond. Although it is not the only important place, Salt Lake City is a starting point, a sort of center point not all that different from the town square at the center of most Utah towns and cities. The mountains bordering the line of settlements that snake their way through Utah from north to south provide countless opportunities to see from above what we have built.

When my children were younger we used to go up to Fortuna Elementary School on the east bench of the city above Wasatch Boulevard, before it made way for more suburban development. We would lie down, prop ourselves up on our elbows, and face the city and its night lights as if it were a huge drive-in movie screen, and we would talk about what we saw. We never really knew for sure whether this cluster of lights or that one really was the former Cottonwood Mall or the baseball field or whatever. It didn't seem to matter. It seemed incredibly complex, beautiful, and infinitely interesting (at least to me).

One of the very best views of downtown Salt Lake City is from the top of Ensign Peak, just north of the State Capitol. A short and not too difficult hike, it provides the best vantage point of the grid of streets that stretches out in every direction from the city center. You get a sense of commercial centers, where stores and office buildings blend into industrial zones of warehouses and light industries or into residential areas of houses and apartment buildings. You also can feel the expanse of the valley, the way it sweeps from side to side, and the way the mountains form an edge but also an ever-present backdrop, the principal figure on this landscape. You cannot understand Utah's built environment without getting a handle on the mountains—they sustained settlement with water from streams running down their slopes, with stone quarried from their canyons, and with timber cut from their forests. Distant in view is the Great Salt Lake, appearing to be more mirage than reality. The sublime stretch of islands that rise up out of the lake, and the changing hues of earth and water and sky again speak to relationships, systems, and patterns on the landscape.

Every chance you get to go somewhere tall or high—the viewing rooms at the Rice-Eccles Stadium, the steps in front of the State Capitol, the top of the Exchange Place parking garage, the top of the Walker Bank building, anywhere along the Shoreline Trail, or vantage points along roads near the canyons—you have a special opportunity to know and understand more. These places provide moments of enlightenment and vision, and they can help illuminate things we don't notice when we are at street level looking up, or in a car restricted by a window frame, or on a tour being instructed by a guide.

If asked for a list of my favorite buildings in Utah, I wouldn't hesitate with a few—the Pine Valley Meetinghouse, the Spring City Tabernacle, the Cathedral of the Madeleine, Peery's Egyptian Theater—but many of them would be names you wouldn't recognize. Much biased toward the vernacular or most commonplace, I find the simple pioneer hall-parlor houses to be a poignant statement about faith and courage, sacrifice and endurance. And I love them in either stone or adobe. The best way to experience these buildings is to walk inside and close the door behind you. Be patient and be quiet. Experience them. Touch an adobe or plaster-covered wall. I wish I could say drag your tongue across its surface (though you might think I was nuts), but be sure to smell it. It will remind you that it came from the earth, that the line between that building and the natural world that gave birth to it is fine. The relationship is direct and tangible. The best way to understand our cities and towns, our buildings, is to experience them, to walk around them and through them and take time to hear what they're saying.

Maybe it is not possible to catch the essence of a place, but it is worth trying. Once while doing research at the Huntington Library, I sat for a few minutes for a break and then took time to stretch and walk around the grounds a bit. I walked past an orange tree in full bloom. I smelled it long before I saw it, and it was the most beautiful fragrance I had ever smelled. I still remember it. I don't remember what I was working on, or the "important topics" I was researching, but I remember, decades later, that smell. Perhaps that is what it is like to catch the essence of a place. To use all our senses, maybe even our logic, to understand a place more fully. More than what can be comprehended at a glance, this type of understanding runs deep and stays with us, is imprinted on us in a different way.

If like me you sincerely want to experience this place, it helps if you get out of your car and stop and talk to people who are standing in their front yard or on the sidewalk outside their store. Ask them to tell you the names of things and how they fit together into a community. Ask for stories and what they remember about the history of storms and the age of trees, who kept their house up and who didn't. You can get from them the real sense of a place, the authentic geography, and take some measure of the love of it. There is no way around it—if you want to understand, you must take the time. Books help. But this type of geographical understanding, of comprehending place, can be sought out and borrowed.

The nineteenth-century settlers of what Leonard Arrington called the Great Basin Kingdom sought to make ideas about religion and community tangible. They came to a land already inhabited by native peoples. In each case, on a largely unconscious level, they were seeking to make their lives meaningful and understandable by creating spaces that kept and transmitted meanings.[2] Bolstered by the belief that the Mormons had been mandated to do this by God, they built temples, tabernacles, meetinghouses, and strict, orderly towns that were the living expression of the power of religious ideas.

The dusty towns of the Mormon white settlers seemed more like frontier visions of future growth rather than kingdoms of God, but they aspired to much more. They wanted nothing less than to be a suitable central place colored by millennial expectations of the world made anew. An understanding of a city or a place requires attention to its structure, its character, and its meaning, all functioning in a system that orients visitors or inhabitants to place.

This is a perfect characterization of the way the early temples in Salt Lake City, St. George, Manti, and Logan; the Kol Ami or B'nai Israel synagogues; and the Cathedral of the Madeleine functioned as pieces in a system of orientation.

Anyone who takes time to drive by a childhood home understands the way places make memories cohere in complex ways. Our attachments to places are material, social, and imaginative. Places contain memories and contribute to our ability to remember. The temple reminded the Mormons what to remember, what was most significant, what a believer's relationship was with God.

The power that comes with place is a sort of cultural citizenship, an identity that is formed not out of legal membership but out of a sense of cultural belonging. In Utah it reaches beyond individual or sometimes conflicting identities to encompass larger common themes such as the exodus west, persecution, restoration, truth, and the kingdom of God. Each of these narrative events shared by the Mormon people was embedded in the spaces of their city. Therefore, identity was intimately tied to the interconnection of collective and social memories.

In recalling the landscapes of my past, I remember the rooms lining up along a central hall of our ranch-style home. I remember the compartments and corners of my grandmother's Victorian cottage, and the textures, shadows, and spaces I glided through as a young girl. This landscape of the imagination has no absolute meaning, but an interpretation formed through our living of those spaces. Buildings evoke memory. The sense of haunting, or the way spaces such as those in our homes or public buildings are being inhabited by memory suggests ways memory is inscribed on the public consciousness.

Acknowledgments

I have to believe that the dozens of individuals who have produced National Register of Historic Places nominations, county histories, local walking tours, and family histories have done their good work largely for the love it. I am grateful to them for their determined efforts to help us remember this wonderful place. As always, I acknowledge the profound good fortune it has been to be the mother to six wonderful children: Jason, Elizabeth, Rachael, Emily, Katelyn, and Patrick, and a stepmother to four more: Sean, Scott, Jake, and Aly. Together with their partners—Sharley, Mark, Jerry, Alisa, Malisa, Naiomi—and my grandchildren—Aspen, Krissie, Dylan, Stella, Ruby, Jaxon, Aliya, Akolea, Toshiro, Noe, Chloe Mags, Simone, Riden, and Oliver—they have given my life meaning, filled my days with happiness and joy, and blessed me beyond measure.

I get emotional when I think about this project coming to a close because I have worked on it periodically over a very long time. I really love this state. Driving from one end of the state to another, photographing and exploring its buildings, towns, and vast open spaces has been a source of immense joy. I will keep doing it, and I hope you will join me in the search for meaning in this beautiful place.

Context for the Guide

Several prominent themes run through the selection of sites in this guide: the buildings represent the state's ethnic, social, religious, and cultural diversity; they reveal the original settlement by Native people, the colonization of the region settled by the Latter-day Saints; and they portray the settlers' economic development and relationship with the land. Although the architecture is similar to that in other parts of the country, many of these buildings are built with indigenous materials that are particular to Utah.

Overview of Utah History

The traditional narrative of Utah's history begins with the historic trek of the Mormon pioneers into the Salt Lake Valley and Brigham Young's statement: "This is the place." But the earliest inhabitants of this region and the earliest ones who came here from elsewhere moved into the area by eleven thousand years ago. Paleo-Indian hunters came south into the area that would be called Utah in pursuit of large game. It is estimated that until about two thousand years ago, Great Basin and Plateau Archaic peoples hunted and also gathered or planted seeds on this land. Remnants of residence and harvesting sites and examples of their tools and other artifacts have survived. Two more sedentary cultures—the Ancestral Pueblo (Anasazi) and the Fremont—built pit houses and aboveground structures out of adobe brick or stone; marked rock walls with art depicting what they experienced and believed; and constructed a range of artifacts, such as pottery and tools, that archaeologists have found in the ruins of their villages, storage cists, and other sites. In Utah between two thousand and seven hundred years ago, Ancestral Puebloans lived primarily in the south, especially the southeast, while the Fremont occupied much of the northern two-thirds of the present state. Subsequently and perhaps even earlier, the Shoshones, Utes, Paiutes, Goshutes, and Navajos resided across Utah. Pushed by white settlers from most of their ancestral lands, they continue to live in and contribute to Utah's culture.

When the Mormon pioneers entered Utah on July 24, 1847, they benefited from exploration by both fur trappers such as Étienne Provost and Antoine Robidoux and explorers such as Francisco Atanasio Domínguez and Francisco Vélez de Escalante, who had identified key transportation routes in the region, detected resources, and painted a picture of a country that was vast, varied, and dramatic. The Latter-day Saints came to Utah as a place of refuge after a failed attempt at building the "City of Zion," first in Missouri and then in Nauvoo, Illinois.[1]

State Map of Utah

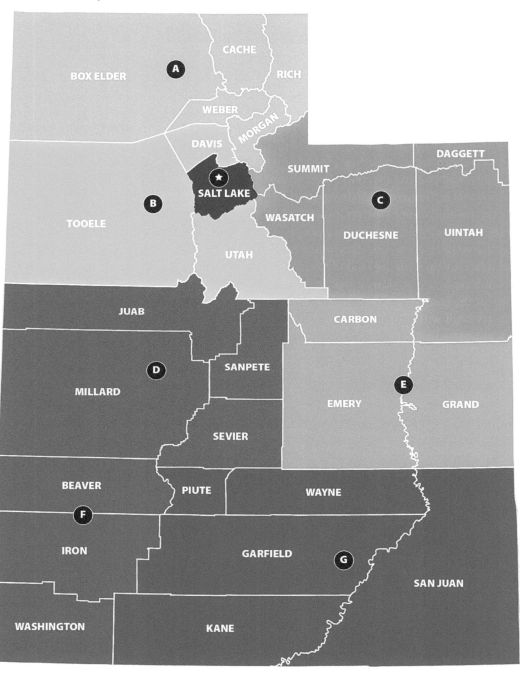

Mormon prophet and president Brigham Young's strong leadership of colonization originated at church headquarters in Salt Lake City, designing what one historian called the "Great Basin Kingdom" with an eye toward the settlement of a region, proximity to water from mountain foothills, movement from town to town in a day's journey by wagon, and expansion of the physical footprint of the church through a series of towns based on the Plat of the City of Zion.[2] By the second decade of the twentieth century, more than four hundred of these towns had been carved out in the Utah landscape.[3] This first wave of immigration to Utah included primarily white settlers from the East Coast, Great Britain, and Scandinavia.

Besides what would eventually become Utah Territory, Brigham Young proposed that his new State of Deseret include southwestern Nevada, northwestern New Mexico, the upper half of Arizona, and part of Southern California. The U.S. Congress designed a different plan with the Compromise of 1850, carving out Utah Territory rather than Deseret, which included parts of Nevada, Colorado, and Wyoming and was further reduced in size by 1868.

The story of Utah has always been one of migrations—of the most ancient peoples moving through the area who built homes and other structures into the side of a canyon wall or drilled down into the earth; of wagon trains of white settlers who came from the eastern United States, Scandinavia, and the British Isles; of the Greek, Welsh, and Scottish immigrants who came to Utah at the end of the nineteenth century to work in Utah's mines in Summit County; and of the Greeks, Italians, and immigrants from Slavic countries who at the turn of the nineteenth century, came first to Salt Lake City and then dispersed

in search of jobs in Utah mines near towns like Helper, Eureka, or Frisco. Chinese immigrants came to Utah to work on the railroad, and many Japanese immigrants stayed in Utah after relocation at the end of World War II. Twentieth- and twenty-first-century immigration included increasing numbers of people from Mexico and Central and South America. Each population of men and women who came to Utah and decided to stay left traces in the physical landscape of their building heritage, living patterns, and aspirations for a new life in a new place.

The Mormons had intentionally distanced themselves from the rest of the United States, hoping to practice their religion without persecution of the kind they had experienced in the Midwest. Regardless, their practice of plural marriage, which was publicly announced in 1852, and the tension over church and state were continual irritants to mainstream America. Federal troops came to Utah in 1857 under the direction of Sidney Johnston, and then again in 1861 to bring Brigham Young's Utah Territory into compliance with federal law and practice. Utah applied for statehood six times before it succeeded in 1896, and then only after the Mormon Church had issued the 1890 Manifesto ending the official practice of taking plural wives.

The completion of the transcontinental railroad on May 10, 1869, at Promontory Summit had a profound impact on Utah's history. Again, people as well as goods and services started to flow in and out of the area, promoting commerce, mining, agricultural production, stock raising, and importantly, greater diversity.

From the first, a steady stream of people explored, exploited, developed, and visited Utah, mapping, studying, identifying resources, and communicating what they saw to the world outside. Major John Wesley Powell's journey along the Green and Colorado Rivers identified water resources, so critical to survival in this arid landscape. By the 1960s, with the construction of Lake Powell and Flaming Gorge Reservoir, both rivers became significant in regional planning for water reclamation and attractive as recreational destinations.

Utah's economy dipped in the early 1920s, in part a response to changes in the national demand for agricultural and mining products during World War I. Unemployment rates reached 33 percent between 1932 and 1940, and only three states experienced a more serious decline than Utah.[4] But the state benefited significantly from the New Deal.[5] FDR's New Deal offered a combination of programs to help states recover from the Depression, at the same time offering the opportunity for reform. According to authors Brian Q. Cannon and Jessie Embry, "Over the course of the first six years of the New Deal (1933–39), Utah received 156.6 percent of the nationwide average per-capita aid on a statewide basis."[6] Among the many New Deal programs that benefited Utah's economy and residents were five that resulted in Utah buildings: the Civil Works Administration (CWA), Federal Emergency Relief Administration (FERA), National Youth Administration (NYA), Works Progress Administration (WPA), and Public Works Administration (PWA). In total, these programs produced 233 public buildings in Utah,[7] several of which are described in this guide.

A similar infusion of capital came to Utah during World War II with the expansion of the Ogden Arsenal along with the construction of four significant military installations, including the Defense Depot Ogden, Tooele Army Depot, Hill Air Force Base, and the U.S. Naval Supply Depot at Clearfield. These have continued to be important contributors to Utah's economy, employing thousands and inspiring economic prosperity in Davis and Weber Counties.

Utah in the twenty-first century has an identity beyond that of the center of a world religion and includes an emphasis on health, access to the natural world, and a reputation for innovation. The natural landscape is always present in the story of Utah's architecture, reflected in the orientation or placement of buildings near accessible water or the amenities offered by canyons, in building materials, and in the metaphoric quality of shapes conjured by architects inspired by the majestic landscape that surrounds them. Utah has seven national parks, which attract 23.5 million visitors annually according to the *Deseret News*.[8] Towns bordering the parks, such as Springdale, Moab, and Kanab, have capitalized on the opportunity this presents and have built their economy around tourism. Besides this type of tourism, Utah is known for its ski industry, with world-class resorts at Park City, Alta, Snowbird, Brighton, Snow Basin, and Cedar Breaks. Utah has a rich history of native peoples and rugged white settlers. It is a religious center with a forward-thinking tradition of healthy living in the context of one of the most varied and dramatic natural landscapes in the world.

Selection of Buildings

I chose buildings for this handbook that are exemplary, that represent various trends, styles, or building technologies, or that illuminate particular themes. For example, as the Latter-day Saints settled Utah Territory and moved into Nevada, California, and Idaho they laid out towns according to the guidelines of the Plat of the City of Zion, but they also built predictable building types. There is a recognizable materiality and physical form to a Mormon village that is partly about the way streets are laid out and houses are oriented to the lot, but also about building types, forms, and functions. Depending on the size of the community, the LDS ward meetinghouse might have been humble and shaped like a simple *I*, with the short end of the rectangle facing the street, or grander in scale and ornamentation if the town was a more important population center. An LDS tithing office, a granary, or a Relief Society hall might have been built nearby, suggesting complex economic arrangements between residents of a young community. Homes built with adobe bricks are found across the state, with bricks reflecting the color and texture of the native soil.

In a similar way, the impact of the New Deal can be seen throughout the state in public buildings built under the auspices of the WPA, built elements constructed by the Civilian Conservation Corps, and murals funded by the Federal Art Project.

Buildings were selected for inclusion for the same reasons they might be nominated for the National Register of Historic Places: primarily, they have architectural integrity and significance; they are associated with individuals, events, or activities that contributed to the state's history; they illuminate the state's social, economic, political, or historical development; and they tell the story of this place through physical, tangible, and material remains. Most of these buildings come from the historic period as defined by the National Park Service. Prominent exceptions to this informal rule are buildings such as Abravanel (Symphony) Hall in Salt Lake City, the First Security Bank Building (Ken Garff Building), and the

Leonardo (Salt Lake City Public Library), which represent modern trends and are landmark buildings that significantly altered urban environments; or landscape features such as Hoover Dam that express a unique moment in Utah's history. National Register nominations produced by individual preservation consultants, Certified Local Government (CLG) groups, or local historical societies have been enormously important in the research for this book. I am tremendously grateful for the quiet, but important, work they have done.

Sources and Readings on Utah Architecture

This architectural guidebook includes representative buildings from across the state. A significant number of them are listed on the National Register of Historic Places or are National Historic Landmarks. The nomination forms for these designations include architectural descriptions, historical narratives, site maps, and other pertinent information and provided a treasure trove of material for the descriptions of buildings in this text. Nominations produced by consultants, homeowners, CLG groups, or other individuals reflect the widely held respect in this state for historic properties. These forms are readily available through the National Park Service website or can be accessed through the Utah State Historical Society's website.

In addition, dozens of local historical associations, CLG groups, and Daughters of Utah Pioneers or Sons of Utah Pioneers groups have produced local histories, guidebooks, walking tours, pamphlets, or websites about local resources. Hundreds of these informally produced materials capture local history and make it accessible for a broad audience of residents, tourists, and those interested in history. The website of the Utah State Historical Society, as well as that of Preservation Utah, provide historical overviews, walking tours, photograph archives, and other valuable information used for this book. Upon completion of this publication, my extensive collection of these materials will be located at the Marriott Library at the University of Utah

Several excellent articles have been published in the *Utah Historical Quarterly* about the state's architecture over the past forty years. But two issues in particular provide a wealth of information and interpretation of Utah's built landscape. The first—volume 43, number 3 (Summer 1975)—includes the following articles: "The Architectural History of Utah," by Peter Goss; "William Harrison Folsom: Pioneer Architect," by Paul L. Anderson; "Spring City: A Look at a Nineteenth-Century Mormon Village," by Cindy Rice; "Stone Buildings of Beaver City," by Richard C. Poulsen; "A Heritage of Stone in Willard," by Teddy Griffith; and "Religious Architecture of the LDS Church: Influences and Changes since 1847," by Allen D. Roberts. Particularly important, the work of Goss and Roberts defined the field and laid out the framework for the study of Utah's architecture for the next several years. The second issue—volume 54, number 2 (Winter 1986)—includes the following articles: "Further Investigations: Architecture at the Turn of the Century," by Peter L. Goss; "Frederic Albert Hale, Architect," by Judith Brunvand; "The 'Unrivalled Perkins' Addition': Portrait of a Streetcar Subdivision," by Roger V. Roper; "William Allen, Architect-Builder, and His Contribution to the Built Environment of Davis County," by Peter L. Goss; "William Allen's Clients: A Socio-Economic Inquiry," by Glen M.

Leonard; and "'The Best of Its Kind and Grade': Rebuilding the Sanpete Valley, 1890–1910," by Thomas Carter.

Each of the following four books helps illuminate different aspects of Utah's architectural heritage.[9] Richard Jackson's *Places of Worship: 150 Years of Latter-day Saint Architecture* describes the religious architecture of the Latter-day Saints in a sweeping study of meetinghouse, stake house, tabernacle, and temple architecture throughout the region. Published through the Religious Studies Center at Brigham Young University, it focuses on the built traditions of the Latter-day Saints.

While Tom Carter's book *Building Zion: The Material World of Mormon Settlement* also centers on the experience of the Latter-day Saints, it focuses on one region—Sanpete County—and is in a way like a case study, using the material culture of this part of the state to reveal much that is rich about the church's experience. The result of a lifetime of thoughtful analysis, drawing, study, reflection, and interpretation, this important book makes a unique contribution to both Mormon studies and the study of vernacular architecture. No other book uses the cultural landscape and material culture as a lens through which to interpret the Mormon experience.

Tom Carter and Peter Goss's *Utah's Historic Architecture* is the go-to study about Utah's architecture. Although the authors spend considerable time helping the reader understand style and historical context, their strongest contribution is in their analysis of typology, helping us understand the architecture of the state through a different lens.

Allen Roberts's *Salt Lake City's Historic Architecture* is also useful for understanding the state's building traditions. Arcadia Publishing's local or city volumes feature photographs of key buildings and other built features with informative captions. Many valuable contributions to architectural history like those of Allen Roberts have also been made through formal reports or publications in the context of preservation or architectural projects.

Two important books produced during the surge of excellent scholarship originating in the Utah State Historical Society in the 1980s are key texts in understanding specific buildings in Salt Lake City but also provide the historical context for the growth and development of the state's

capital city.[10] John McCormick analyzed the commercial architecture of downtown Salt Lake City in *The Historic Buildings of Downtown Salt Lake City*, adding insightful descriptions and historical details. Karl T. Haglund and Philip Notarianni did the same kind of analysis for a single neighborhood or part of the city in *The Avenues of Salt Lake City*, creating a lively historical narrative and including an important photographic record and maps that help illuminate the ways the Avenues were both similar to and different from other parts of the city.

Utah's Architectural History

The concept of the built landscape helps us think in holistic ways about the space that human beings conceptualize, build, and inhabit. A built landscape is more than a collection of buildings and other built structures; it also includes farm fields where we work, parks where we congregate, and streets that move us through space but also define relationships. The concept of built landscapes illuminates the relationship of residents to place, their relationships with each other, and the ways they interact with the land. It is at the same time a collective of ideas and artifacts, as well as people and natural formations. In Utah's built landscapes, men and women constructed buildings with rocks and timber harvested from the land, rooting their homes, places of worship, schools, and institutions in a particular geography that challenged them, nurtured them, and distinguished their efforts in place making.

Ancient Inhabitants

The earliest remnants of built landscape in this region are the ruins of the Ancestral Puebloans. These prehistoric Native American peoples inhabited the Four Corners area of southeastern Utah, northeastern Arizona, southwestern Colorado, and northwestern New Mexico between approximately 700 BC and the arrival of the Spaniards in the Southwest. Their ancestors migrated to the Western Hemisphere from Asia on a land bridge across the Bering Strait between Siberia and Alaska.

When they moved from being a semi-nomadic people to one identified with a fixed place, the Ancestral Puebloans built more permanent dwellings instead of living in caves or brush shelters. Easily the most distinctive feature of their culture was their architecture. When one looks at an aerial photograph of an Ancestral Puebloan settlement, it looks strikingly like the floor plan of a single building. The relationship between the separate pit houses, granaries, and other structures is implicit, like a web. One can see the physical manifestation of community that was about survival, kinship, and a support system. The village settlement was another significant principle of organization. Ancestral Puebloan buildings were usually found in clusters. Rarely did a single structure constitute a community.

White Settlement

There are hints in Utah's buildings of the origins of its first white settlers, who came as a group. What we call Utah's vernacular architecture, or architecture built by common folk with indigenous materials and with little pretense in style, has its roots on the East Coast or in Europe. Seen wherever the Latter-day Saints lived—first in Kirtland, Ohio; then in Missouri and in Nauvoo, Illinois; and later in the Great Basin—the simple forms of rectangular houses with floor plans shaped like an *I*, an *H*, or a *T* were built broadside to the street with moderately pitched gabled roofs, doors at the center, and simple decor faintly influenced by a Classical consciousness. A rudimentary awareness of the golden mean and proportions similarly expressed an awareness of appropriate relationships between squares and rectangles and the ordered placement of windows and doors. Built of log, adobe, or kiln-dried bricks, these house types were repeated hundreds of times throughout the territory that extended north to Idaho, west to what is today Nevada, and as far south as San Bernardino, California. When the short end of the rectangle faced the street, it was almost always a public building—a church, a schoolhouse, a cooperative, or a city hall.

Because colonization in Utah proceeded quickly after 1847 along the lines drawn by the mountain ranges to the north and east, and Brigham Young had deployed groups of settlers from Salt Lake City to claim the region, it was often necessary to erect temporary shelters while more permanent buildings were under construction. Dugouts were one type of temporary dwelling that required substantial effort in terms of muscle power but not much in terms of specialized tools or materials. Dugouts were often nearly square and were sunk into the earth to capitalize on the shelter provided by dirt walls and makeshift roofs made of wood, branches, and sod or dirt. Sidewalls rose a couple of feet above the pit and were usually built with logs, stones, or adobe bricks. Dugouts were often used as storage sheds after the pioneers built more permanent log or brick buildings.[1]

Perhaps the most characteristic element of Mormon colonization was its group orientation. Individual fur trappers and explorers had first identified the area as prime and fertile ground for settlement, but when the Mormons came into the area they came in groups. Essentially well-rounded, stratified, and in some sense self-sufficient communities emerged within a few years. Solidified by their common goals, groups of Mormon settlers created communities dedicated to the prospect of building orderly, stable, and thriving towns.

Moreover, unlike in the mythic West, a group settled this state, a community of believers in the same religion. As a result, from the start it was a place with a strong sense of exclusivity. Salt Lake City was conceived of as a sacred city, the very building of which became ritual, a demonstration of faith. For the Mormons, the Great Basin was Zion, the proverbial garden, the "Land of Bountiful" promised in scripture.

From the start, Zion was a central place from which the church president directed the colonization of the region; it was a model city, a prototype repeated hundreds of times throughout the region. As a model, it embodied religious ideas in tangible, physical form. Salt Lake City was an intentional center, the metaphorical nexus of literal ideas about the centrality of religion in the lives of its first settlers. The strict cardinality of the way this version of Zion was mapped extended that center in each direction from the sacred to the profane, endowing space with new meaning and connection to this essential core idea. Distinctive doctrines such as consecration or cooperation wove a web—a city that mapped ideas about community in space.

With the 1833 revelation that LDS prophet Joseph Smith called "The Plat of the City of Zion," he demonstrated his belief in the symbolic power of a city as an image imbued with theological content. With the plat, Smith presented an idea about how to build the cities of what the Latter-day Saints thought would be the kingdom of God on the earth. In its ideal form the city of Zion was both an idea about urban design and a formula for a distinctive pattern of living as a community of believers.

Geography defined the pattern of the mining town. Towns like Park City and Eureka nestled at the edges of mountain ranges that provided mineral wealth. Service industries lined the streets, serving transient populations of miners and mine owners until men brought their families to town and planted roots.

It would be easy to look at pioneer buildings and assume they are all the same, but in fact there is remarkable diversity in building materials, floor plans, and design. They express diversity that has not been noted among the Mormon settlers of this region.

Because Utah's settlers moved so quickly toward permanent settlements and more stable types of housing, log cabins have received less attention than the more well-known adobe hall-parlor houses. More impermanent and seemingly transient in their construction, these early structures were common in most Utah communities. Moreover, for some ethnic groups, log construction was considered an appropriate choice for a family home, and it could be more technically complex than it might appear at first glance. Each ethnic group had its own log construction traditions including building forms, timber-fitting techniques, and corner-timbering types.

The Scandinavians built timber walls with tightly fitted logs with grooves in the tops that produced snug, gapless joints. Others built with gaps, or interstices

between the log tiers that were filled with chinking of clay, mortar, stone, or shingles. Log granaries with Swedish-style double-notched corners, Norwegian-style barns built with stone and timber, and the Scandinavian *parstuga* houses, known as pair houses, suggest more ethnic and cultural diversity than might be assumed.[2]

Variations can be attributed to ethnicity, but also to available natural resources, the building skills of the early settlers (which varied dramatically), geographical location, and economics. Most men had at least some basic knowledge of how to build a house. This can be seen in a range of vernacular structures from houses to outbuildings, all constructed without written plans and using traditional skills and knowledge.

Forts

In the settlement of the region, the pioneers battled the desert environment, competed for natural resources, and disturbed ancestral lands of the Native Americans. Conflict with the landscape was perhaps inevitable as these newcomers claimed the land as their own. Contrasting value systems and cultures as well as opposing claims to the land resulted in periodic warfare between the native and new inhabitants of this place. During the escalation of the Walker War in the spring and summer of 1853, the small isolated towns of rural Utah were particularly vulnerable. To protect themselves as they divided up property, dug irrigation ditches, and planted fields, they left their new homes to live instead in the safety of a community fort.

The fort, the space most associated with the mythic settlement of the western frontier, was often where a community began to emerge. Built briefly because of the threat of attack by native peoples, forts were also a critical communal building effort that allowed settlers to pool their resources and come together for both safety and shelter, and they were usually built at the heart of a community. Forts were almost always square or rectangular and were built of whatever materials were available—adobe, logs, or stone. Cabin row forts, detached wall forts, and contiguous compartment forts were the most common among the thirty-five or so forts built in Utah. The old pioneer fort in Salt Lake City filled first one and eventually two city blocks and had nine-foot-tall adobe brick walls that were wider at the bottom than the top.

Log Buildings

Cottonwood trees lined creeks throughout the state and provided a ready source of wood for early log construction. Although their trunks were not as straight or as long as those of coniferous trees, cottonwoods were nevertheless available for log buildings. However, chinking or filling the interstices between the logs was time consuming and very difficult, so the straighter the logs, the better. The top and bottom edges of the logs were not hewn in the first generation of log buildings, so chinking was critical in creating a tight, weatherproof interior. Log buildings in Utah display the most common types of notching found elsewhere in the United States. The log buildings that weathered well usually used the half or full dovetail notch, although barns and other outbuildings often had saddle notches, which were simpler to construct. Both created tight corners and strengthened the structure of the building.

Utah's climate posed unusual problems in terms of dealing with the elements.

Severe winters and dry, hot summers necessitated well-insulated walls. Sometimes builders would fill stud-frame walls with adobe brick, concrete made of mud, or rubble stone, much like the half-timber construction methods of Great Britain in the Tudor period. One prominent example of this building technique was the St. George office of Brigham Young, found due east of his home in St. George, Utah, built in 1874.

Adobe

One of the most unusual features of pioneer architecture is the frequent and original use of adobe for bricks. Although Utah's pioneer adobe structures did not resemble the pueblos of the Southwest in its use (in Utah adobe was molded into standard-sized brick molds), adobe played a prominent and key role in the physical growth of the territory during the first four decades of settlement. Driven by the scarcity of wood for building, the Mormon pioneers adapted adobe to their own needs. With adobe bricks they mimicked what they had known and built traditional rectangular houses with gabled roofs, not unlike those built of frame or bricks in other parts of the country.

When travelers came through Utah Territory, they often commented on this unique use of adobe, noting this combination of the familiar and the exotic. Some of the most interesting descriptions of nineteenth-century Utah are in the accounts of visitors traveling through the area. Jacob Heinrich Schiel, a German geologist working for the Gunnison geological expedition in 1853, reported that in Salt Lake City "everything bears the mark of poverty and makeshift.... The houses are constructed chiefly of so-called adobe (air dried brick), one-story high and covered with shingles. Log cabins are relatively scarce since wood must be brought a distance of thirty to forty miles from the Wasatch Mountains and consequently must be used sparingly."[3] Journalist Horace Greeley visited Salt Lake City in 1859 and observed, "The houses generally small and of one-story—are all built of adobe (sun hardened brick), and have a neat and quiet look."[4] Perhaps the most colorful writer and explorer to pass through the region was Richard Burton, who visited Utah Territory in 1860. Burton saw the similarity between "thick sundried adobe" in Utah and materials "common to all parts of the Eastern World," so much so that at a "distance the aspect was somewhat oriental."[5]

Nineteenth-century builders occasionally noted in their journals the technique for producing adobe bricks. Most had firsthand experience with the production of adobe bricks. Nearly everyone, including women and children, joined in the community dance, raising skirts precariously high as they stomped in the wet clay and straw, helped mold bricks in homemade molds, or carried and laid the mud bricks to bake in the sun or be placed in the walls. Adobe was used for homes but also for barns, granaries, chicken coops, sheds, and other outbuildings. In the same way that neighbors joined to help each other produce bricks for their homes, they united in the production of bricks for schools, meetinghouses, forts, and other public buildings. Adobe making contributed to community building. Adobe houses were built for members of all social classes and adobe was used indiscriminately by different ethnic groups.

The size and quality of adobe bricks varied according to region, different soil qualities, humidity, and experience. In Parowan,

for instance, adobe bricks were reddish brown and measured ten by five by three inches. In St. George, the bricks were a yellow buff and measured twelve by six by four inches. The best adobes were made from loam or clay-loam soil. Soil with too much clay caused the bricks to shrink or crack while drying, and too much sand caused them to crumble and fail to bond properly.

No skilled labor was required for the manufacture of adobe bricks, and they could be made quickly. Rather than being laid with a special mortar or lime, adobe bricks were laid with the same mud they were made of. Because it was not as strong a building material as wood or brick, the walls of an adobe house had to be very thick, usually two or three withes (vertical bricks) thick. But these thick walls produced a well-insulated interior, warm in winter and cool in summer. Adobe walls were resistant to fire, another advantage over a wooden building. The natural deterioration was reduced with a cover of stucco or plaster. Many adobe buildings had decorative veneered exteriors—asphalt sheets nailed to the bricks, either plain or scored stucco to resemble brickwork or stonework, or wooden sheathing.

Although brick had been popular in Nauvoo before the Latter-day Saints came to Utah, it was not widely used until the 1860s, when more communities established brickyards of their own.[6] Used initially as a veneer to cover adobe bricks, it was later used for load-bearing walls. Unlike in Illinois or on the East Coast, brick was usually not used in decorative patterning or bonds, although there are prominent exceptions from the nineteenth century in Fountain Green and Panguitch, where expert brick masons transformed even the smallest vernacular houses into fanciful and intricately decorated beauties.

Regional variety in building materials and technology was nowhere in better evidence than in the beautiful vernacular stone buildings constructed in Willard, Utah, or in Beaver and Sanpete Counties, each with its own indigenous material. While there were several techniques for laying stone walls, the method that was sure evidence of a stonemason in town was ashlar masonry. Ashlar walls were created by cutting the stones into precise rectangles laid in evenly rising horizontal courses. Builders often used a different technique known as rubble masonry, with irregularly cut stones. Random rubble masonry consisted of unevenly shaped and sized stones that were laid indiscriminately. Some effort was made to shape the stones into horizontal courses. Even rougher, coursed rubble walls often had an overlay of mortar that was smoothed into an almost plaster-like finish, which obscured some of the irregularities of the stone.

We could easily exaggerate the effect of the social and religious homogeneity of the territory. Instead, there was considerable variation in buildings and in the arrangement of private residences on town lots. The prevailing individual unit of settlement was the homestead. In town, houses were located on lots large enough for outbuildings—smokehouses, barns, outhouses, granaries—as well as small orchards and a household garden. Although the configuration varied, the basic components were the same. This became the domain of the women, who managed production of food for the family and maintenance of the home.

Some of Utah's most beautiful buildings are stone variations of the standard pioneer forms. Despite the difficulty of building with stone—it was time consuming and required special skills and tools—it was the preferred material for high-style public and religious buildings and homes when the owner could afford it. While most men knew something about building a house or barn, few knew much about the craft of stonemasonry. Moreover, stone was costly to transport and cut. Unless there was a ready supply of stone nearby, a builder would more likely choose a less complicated solution to constructing his family's house. Far more common after the initial stage of settlement, an impressive group of European stonemasons had immigrated to Utah with the Mormons. Scandinavians in Sanpete County used the beautiful cream-colored oolite limestone from the nearby San Pitch Mountains, sometimes with smooth ashlar or cut-stone surfaces, which contrasted greatly with the stone found in Willard to the north. Shadrach Jones, a Welsh stonemason in Weber County, built a range of houses from the simple two-story cottage his own family occupied in Willard to the more extravagant homes of wealthy customers nearby. When brick and lumber became more readily available for construction, stone buildings were far less frequently built.

Traces of ethnicity were more rarely and subtly expressed in building techniques and massing. Because of the powerful urge to unify, newcomers from Scandinavia or Great Britain built as those already here had built—sturdy, formal, rationally proportioned houses based on variations of rectangular boxes. More important were the restrictions placed on builders by available materials, tools, and technologies, and the great distance between Utah and other national urban centers.

Although Brigham Young modeled types of building materials, desirable building styles, and building essentials, no official statements dictated house design. His references to building were pragmatic and quality oriented rather than prescriptive as to technique or specific materials. He said in 1860: "Good houses are comfortable and very convenient, and please our feelings, and are tolerably healthful when properly ventilated. If we cannot raise grain, raise houses, and build the best houses we can think of. If you are going to do a good deed, do as good a one as you can think of. If you wish to build a house, build as good a one as you can imagine."[7]

The prevailing message was to build "good houses," houses that were metaphors for the kingdom. They were stable, permanent, dignified, and orderly, a mirror of the value system of church members. Good workmanship, the best materials, and practical design were basic ideals driving most building projects. For the first generation, the resulting design aesthetic was overwhelmingly a simple geometric block, symmetrical organization, and a sense of style. Wherever they came from, these nineteenth-century builders held deep assumptions about what a building should be. Those ideas shaped form. Size, materials, and techniques varied according to location and builder. Even those who billed themselves as architects were usually carpenters first. They were masons or contractors who were not professionally trained and were certainly only slightly skilled at draftsmanship.

Ecclesiastical Architecture, Public Meeting Spaces, and Secular Activities

As soon as a group of settlers laid out their town plan, distributed lots to families, and began plowing fields, they joined forces to raise a meetinghouse. Built during the same season as the first houses, meetinghouses expressed the community ethic and the cooperative lifestyle of the Mormon people and were built during the first five years after settlement. The earliest extant meetinghouses were simple rectangular structures undistinguished by reference to style or sophisticated technology. Similar to their domestic counterparts, they were often built of logs, adobe bricks, or some other indigenous material, sometimes in or part of a fort. Limited by available tools brought by the pioneers in their wagons across the plains, these buildings were erected communally and quickly, sometimes in a single day.

The first generation of churches served as a location for schools, town or county government meetings, and most social activities like dances or theatricals. They were not technically or exclusively churches. Their multipurpose nature was perfectly in sync with the broad-based approach to religion taken by the Latter-day Saints. Only a blurred line existed between the temporal and the spiritual. The meetinghouse served as the backdrop for both. There was no difference in design or conception between the typical residence and the meetinghouse in the early settlement period.

After the initial attempt at survival, a measure of stability allowed settlers to build irrigation and road systems, sawmills and gristmills, and other local industries and businesses. As communities became more permanent, more durable meetinghouses replaced the earliest ones. In this building phase, pioneer builders attempted to build higher-quality buildings that were slightly larger and utilized better craftsmanship. A stronger attention to style led to more Classical detailing, including cornices, pediments, bracket motifs, pilasters, quoins, and belfries that were added to the basic rectangular form of the buildings. This helped distinguish them from houses and public buildings.

The Impact of the Railroad

Regardless of where they were in the settlement process, all Utah towns were affected by the coming of the railroad in 1869. Certainly all local industries were impacted, but building in particular benefited from a wider selection of materials, new technologies, and exposure to outside styles and trends. Increasing numbers of non-Mormons also influenced building trends.

The railroad brought into Utah Territory new influences, new people, new technologies, and new commercial entities that started to change the sacred city into a secular city more like other western cities. The railroad mapped the west side of Salt Lake City, Ogden, and other Utah towns with spurs that ran east and west, with related industries and enterprises, and with immigrant populations who lived on the west side near the depots and created ethnic enclaves that contrasted with the Mormon Anglo-Saxon hegemony of the east side.

Although the railroad brought new goods for sale, the impact was not necessarily as immediate on building as might be assumed. In terms of style, building technology, and outside exposure, Utah lagged behind national trends for the next several decades. In fact, it would be well into the twentieth century before the gap narrowed significantly. Regardless, such national events as the 1893 World's Columbian Exposition in Chicago affected local building. Utah men and women attended and exhibited at the fair, including a display of silk produced by the sericulture movement of the Mormon Relief Society. Publications

such as builders' guides and books, as well as travel and the influx of newcomers with expectations of duplicating the worlds they left behind, changed both the look and methods of construction.

Although Utah builders would build Classical-style buildings throughout the first fifty years, the churches they built in the decades after the arrival of the railroad finally looked like religious buildings, with engaged central towers, Gothic and stained-glass windows, and buttresses and pinnacles as well as other recognizable Gothic Revival elements. Together they created buildings that spoke to a new level of sophistication, community-wide stability and permanence, and the special character of the building efforts of this particular group.

More than any other single factor, the group orientation of the Utah pioneers shaped their religious buildings. In the Midwest, church meetings were often held outdoors at the "stand" in Nauvoo, so an open-air tradition was familiar to them. In the Salt Lake Valley, the first large-scale gathering place was under a bower that was hastily constructed out of timber, with tree branches for a roof and simple log benches. In the spring of 1849, the original bower was replaced by a larger, more carefully constructed one that was one hundred feet long and sixty feet wide. More than one hundred posts supported the roof, which was composed of boughs with dirt piled on top.

Not long after the pioneers' arrival, Salt Lake City increased in size and complexity. Important early on as a supply station for wagon trains traveling farther west and as a regional center for trade, it was also the center of the LDS Church and seemed the perfect location for a large building for church conferences. During the spring of

1851, the church decided to build a tabernacle, a large building for its General Conference and other public meetings. Funded by a subscription drive, almost as soon as this building designed by Truman O. Angell Sr. was built, it was deemed too small for the crowds who gathered to hear their church leaders speak. The next year, Angell designed yet another tabernacle, this one with a distinctive elliptically arched roof 150 feet wide and 250 feet long.

Historically the tabernacle played a particular role in Mormon communities and religious life. Each ward had its own meetinghouse, the multipurpose center of its religious and secular activities. But after the 1830s, members came together for larger meetings in yet another ecclesiastical unit called the stake. Stake meetings were the scene of instruction where Mormons received advice from their leaders on virtually every topic ranging from town building to family organization. No sacred rituals took place in the Mormon tabernacle. Instead, its sole purpose was for large-scale meetings. Therefore the principal focus was the assembly room, which was almost always elaborately decorated. In many cases, the tabernacle included no other rooms of significance. These buildings were also the scene of some public gatherings, but not parties, dances, plays, or other social activities.

Tabernacles were built with the most impressive indigenous materials available locally and had elaborately designed interiors as well. Single-axis plans varied in some examples, with side wings in a cruciform shape. The most tangible physical evidence of regional hegemony, the tabernacle was also a clear statement that the church was a substantial presence. In the hierarchy of Mormon church buildings, the tabernacle occupied a position between that of the meetinghouse and the temple. It was a public building, and no secret or sacred ceremonies were performed within, but it was dignified and formal, and a higher type of religious discourse proceeded within its walls.

Besides the meetinghouse and tabernacle, local communities built other buildings related to their religious activities, including temples, Relief Society halls and granaries, tithing offices or bishop's storehouses, and tithing barns, all of which were important to identity, the building of community, and the survival of the pioneers in the harsh environment of the American West.

In the hierarchy of Mormon buildings, temples have a special place. Not public places of worship, and used only by righteous Latter-day Saints, temples form the backdrop to sacred rituals and ordinances. Performances of the Mormon endowment for the living and the dead, baptisms and sealings (marriage ceremonies that have significance beyond death), are performed in separate rooms designed for different purposes. The interior of the temple has a hierarchy of rooms, increasing in importance to the celestial room, the "Holy of Holies," sealing rooms, and a baptismal font, usually a pool mounted on the backs of sculpted oxen.

The first Mormon temples in Kirtland and then Nauvoo reflected current styles and national influences, as well as a search for functional integrity in space and its relationship to liturgy. Temples in both places were often the locale of public meetings besides religious activities. When temples were built in Utah Territory, their use was restricted to only the most faithful, and they therefore became sacred interiors that formed a boundary between insiders and outsiders. Furthermore, the interior symbolized the transitional state between this world and the next, where the faithful communed with God.

It is perhaps ironic that when the Mormons first came to Utah Territory they were trying to escape religious persecution and seeking refuge. In their own community-building efforts, however, they made no effort to embrace outsiders but fortified themselves against the exigencies of both nature and the world outside. Their economic policies facilitated unity and self-sufficiency for the church. This hegemony was read as an offense and challenge by other religious groups watching the growth of the church from outside the area.

An integral part of "kingdom" building was providing a setting for secular as well as religious activities. Cultural, educational, and civic structures appeared during the first decades after settlement. By the 1850s and 1860s, other buildings besides churches and houses were built throughout the territory. At first overwhelmingly practical and functional, this first generation of public buildings addressed the commitment to building a community that was orderly, stable, enduring, and respectable.

Located just half a block away from Brigham Young's home, the Church dedicated Salt Lake City's Social Hall on January 1, 1853. Fully in line with the Mormon tradition of staging theatricals, dances, banquets, musicals, and other social activities, the Social Hall became the scene of public gatherings. Truman O. Angell Sr. designed this simple thirty-three by seventy-three-foot rectangular structure, and William Ward (Angell's assistant on the Salt Lake Temple) supervised the stonecutters. The building was divided into five bays; the main floor level was constructed with adobe brick. Both levels had multipane sash windows, and there was a medium-pitched

roof with a continuous cornice and cornice returns. When it was first constructed, the main floor walls were left unstuccoed and without decorative quoins at the corners. But later, quoins and a formal entrance were added, resulting in a more dignified and finished look. The hall's main chamber often held as many as three hundred to five hundred people. Two elegant chandeliers provided lighting from an elliptical ceiling. A stage along the east end featured a bust of Shakespeare in the center of the proscenium.

It has been convincingly suggested by architectural historian Tom Carter that the pioneers were familiar with the "Genteel" city, or the city of culture and proper society. Besides reflecting faith and belief, the Genteel city demonstrated civility and the desire to create a good society in tangible, physical terms.[8]

Not long after the first settlement, Brigham Young felt the saints needed a grander setting for theatrical performances. When it was completed, the Salt Lake Theater was considered one of the most architecturally significant buildings constructed during Brigham Young's lifetime. Young encouraged his people to live righteous lives but also to enjoy themselves. Theater, dance, and music became popular escapes from the unending cycle of community building. The Salt Lake Theater was located a block south of President Young's Beehive House. Financed in part by the sale of surplus goods acquired from Johnston's Army when it vacated the territory, the adobe and stone structure was by far the largest in the territory at the time, measuring 80 by 144 feet. Designed by church architect William Folsom, it was completed and opened in March 1862. Architect and British convert E. L. T. Harrison designed the interior in the best tradition of contemporary English styling. The theater was consistent with the Greek Revival style, complete with a tripartite facade, freestanding fluted Doric columns, and a peripheral design with pilasters around the central block. Beneath the cornice, there was an entablature with metope and triglyph motifs, and a low-pitched hipped roof capped by an attic clerestory window provided lighting for the interior.

The center of governmental and other public functions was the Council Hall. Designed by Truman O. Angell Sr. in 1849, this important territorial building was on the southwest corner of South Temple and Main Street.

First the Council Hall and then the Territorial Capitol in 1852 were early efforts to house the activities of civil government. Regional governmental buildings mirrored the styled structures built in Salt Lake City but on a much smaller scale.

Within months of the completion of the railroad in 1869, Brigham Young began plans for a church-wide economic system that would combat competition from the non-Mormon businesses that promised to soon enter the territory. Already bristling from local competition that he thought was draining the resources of his people, Young and others saw an opportunity to combine their interests into a "cooperative" merchandising enterprise that would bolster their strength against competition. Young and other business leaders like Horace Eldredge and George Q. Cannon met in the Council Hall in 1868 to discuss the formation of Zion's Cooperative Mercantile Institution (ZCMI). A Salt Lake City–based department store and wholesale entity would supply a system of local branches, owned and operated by stockholders. As a result, a number of cooperative buildings were built in communities throughout the territory.

LDS Buildings Evolve

The Mormon Church's building program changed dramatically during the twentieth century. After the first decades, the auxiliary functions of the church were brought under one roof. Churches again became multipurpose buildings with offices, classrooms, cultural halls, and chapels all in the same structure. Also because of the regional growth of the church, building activities were centralized in the Building Department, which increasingly relied on the use of standard plans for new church buildings. Standardization was favored because it was believed to be more efficient and economical, provided homogeneity in terms of style, and was well suited to church programs.

The earliest standard-plan buildings were the tithing offices built during the first decade of the twentieth century. Three basic plans and configurations were available, each basically the same size but varying somewhat in roof shape, window placement, and facade arrangement.

Joseph Don Carlos Young designed a group of Mormon churches in the 1920s that were colloquially called "Colonel's Twins" because of their two main rectangular forms, which were standard in the plans and approach to church building. In these buildings, two rectangular shapes are connected toward the back, forming an *H* shape. The chapel is on one side and the cultural hall on the other. Classrooms and offices are typically in the vestibule section or at the back of each wing. Typically built with red brick, Colonel's Twins also feature Colonial Revival detailing that is painted white to form an interesting contrast with the wall surface. Theodore Pope designed a group of Colonial-style buildings in the 1930s and 1940s that also had Classical detailing but included towers with steeples like those typically found on Congregational churches in New England. Pope experimented liberally with the arrangement of rooms, linking chapel and cultural hall spaces for greater flexibility for large meetings.

After the 1950s and the church's Building Missionary Program, standard planning began in earnest. The 1960s correlation programs supported the use of standard plans, and correlated buildings related directly to the function of church programs—worship, education, and recreation. Ward meetinghouses, stake centers, and eventually temples were designed and built under the auspices of the church Building Department.

The End of Mormon Hegemony

Not long after the Latter-day Saints made Utah their home, other churches sent missionaries to the area. Businessmen saw Utah as a market ripe for exploitation, and many came to Utah Territory to make a quick profit off the Mormon settlers.

These people helped Utah's economy thrive. Utah's mine, farm, and business workers came from other parts of the United States but more importantly from Europe and the Far East, drawn to Utah by the promise of work, opportunities unavailable in their homelands, and the chance to start life anew. Despite their importance to the story of the state, the voices of this population have not been heard or written into official narratives. They have been disregarded or perhaps devalued, and the history of the state for generations has been told as if it had one kind of resident, one kind of neighborhood, and one culture, religion, and set of traditions.

In 1857, Johnston's Army, all of whom were non-Mormons, entered the valley and set up camp twenty-five miles southwest of Salt Lake City in Cedar Valley. Colonel Patrick E. Connor's troops, who were Catholics and Protestants, entered the valley in 1862 along with a huge crowd of camp followers—merchants, artisans, and other workers again drawn by the potential market in this isolated location in the West.

When the railroad and federal troops came to Utah, they were accompanied by non-Mormon miners, merchants, and travelers who brought their own religions, attitudes about family and social life, and businesses. Gradually, Utah became more diverse. By 1896, most major religions had established congregations in the state. The churches they built are compelling reminders of the religious diversity that helped enrich this community.

Independence Hall in Salt Lake City represented the religious diversity that emerged in Utah Territory after federal troops arrived to restore order in the 1860s. It also demonstrated a powerful coalition of marginalized religious congregations who co-opted space for worship activities. Independence Hall was at the same time a church, a school, a convention center, and a social club for more than twenty-five years. Built on the south side of 300 South between West Temple and East Temple (which is now State Street), this multiuse building provided the backdrop for Jewish, Methodist, Episcopalian, and Congregational religious services and meetings of a Masonic order established by merchant James Ellis. Eventually each of these religious groups would build its own distinctive, high-style building. John Titus, P. Edward Connor, William Sloan, W. Kerr, Howard Livingston, Samuel Kahn, J. Mechling, Dr. Griswald, and George W. Carlson formed the core group of the Young Men's Literary Association, a nondenominational group seeking self-improvement through book discussion and speech. They purchased the land for the building for $2,500. The adobe building was thirty-three feet wide and fifty-seven feet long and comfortably sat two hundred people. Buggies pulled into a space between the building and the street. One contemporary description helps us imagine what the interior looked like: "You entered a vestibule, where overshoes and rubbers were often deposited. Then into the rear of the main hall, where stood a great potbelly stove with quite a gathering space around it before you came to the benches or pews. The pulpit was on a platform at the east end of the hall, with the organ just below on the right, and a door on the left leading to the Primary Department."[9]

In the decades after the railroad came to Utah, the era of Mormon isolation and independence came to an end. By the end of the century, the state's economy was blatantly capitalistic, and growth and development were manifested in a growing sophistication typified by a new variety of buildings. Exposure to national styles and trends in building increased in part because of magazines, pattern books, and other style guides that circulated among local architects and builders. Private owners became familiar with national styles in social intercourse with the world outside Utah.

Also important to understanding this period are Utah Territory's successive bids at statehood and the requisite accommodations—what one historian called the "Americanization of Utah for statehood" requirements.[10] Utah catered to national markets and made the effort to meet America competitively, mirroring physical changes in other cities nationwide. Thus began the process of accommodation and assimilation, in which the territory became more acceptable, joined national parties, and dumped unpopular doctrines and practices.

The city's original large lots and blocks were subdivided over time and new streets and courts were cut into them. Brigham Young's Beehive House and Lion House, as well as his family school and orchard, the White House on the hill, and Amelia's Palace or Gardo House, were all within a block of the Salt Lake Theater, the Council Hall, the Social Hall, and Zion's Cooperative Mercantile. This area of just a few blocks was more than a traditional city center; it was the power center of the church, an incredible advantage for Young, his family, and other church leaders.

Nearby as well was evidence of the changing times—Brigham Street became a boulevard of mansions as non-Mormon millionaires and outsiders advertised both their wealth and their determination to make a permanent mark on this place. The railroad tracks and stations created an industrial sphere identified by warehouses, loading docks, and factories, and the tracks also became a marker between the working-class neighborhoods on the west side and a growing non-Mormon ethnic population on the east side.

Salt Lake City's Main Street looked much like those in other frontier towns by the 1860s. One- or two-level commercial buildings built up against each other, dusty streets that had to be sprinkled to keep the dust down, and animals pulling wagons and tied up at hitching posts in front of businesses were all common features. But over the next few decades this would change. Buildings would become increasingly larger and more diverse and would be built with fancier materials—brick, frame, and adobe buildings would line each side of the street, followed by stores with cast-iron fronts, and by the end of the century tall steel-frame buildings would rival those in other western American cities.

Buildings make it easy to track the change from the settlement period to a more stratified and progressive city. Although visible reminders of the utopian dream of the original settlers—the tabernacle, Social Hall, and ZCMI—were prominent landmarks from the communitarian era, increasingly commercial images replaced earlier ones. Salt Lake City became an environment as much based on capitalism as any other city in the country.

Keeping pace with the Progressive Era, Utah's cities shaped their amenities after national models of the "City Beautiful." City parks, boulevards, and other City Beautiful efforts made this a beautiful and efficient landscape. In the same way that Utah's politics became more mainstream, Utah's cities became more American—buildings, street systems, and patterns of use are cultural artifacts that ordered daily life and reveal for us its contours. Shifting from early dreams to present realities, the city at the turn of the century included large-scale public buildings, major recreational facilities, and a substantial commercial downtown district in each of the state's largest cities.

With the increase in local trade and the organization of civil society, central places emerged, towns placed strategically on the land. These central places tended to be located a predictable distance from each other—the same thirty-five-mile pattern established early on by Brigham Young held constant. These towns interacted in a complicated system of exchange and formed integral links in a network system. Salt Lake City served as the gateway to the larger network, the principal city in the system.

Importantly, Salt Lake City was not the only city to grow. Ogden, Provo, and Logan each built new theaters, city halls, and other large-scale public projects. The first decade of the twentieth century brought civic improvements to each—the extension of streetcar lines and the decision to place transmission lines in conduits under the streets changed the appearance of downtown areas. Transportation improvements led to new suburbs expanding to the periphery of town, connected by streetcar systems and eventually by bus routes, so that towns spread in virtually every direction.

Twentieth Century

Buildings in Utah during the twentieth century were marked by diversity. Mirroring national trends and styles in a process similar to tape delay, the century began in the Victorian mode, bungalows and Period Revival houses followed in the next decade, and then came World War II cottages in the wake of the war. The state was impacted by federal programs of the New Deal, the Federal Housing Administration, and Veterans Administration loans in the same ways as other western states. These programs had the intended effect—they pumped money into rural Utah and funded the building of roads, schools, and public buildings, as well as countless middle-class subdivisions for returning veterans and their young families. In important ways, they changed the pattern of Utah's physical fabric.

Utah has had an active and significant architectural community since the late nineteenth century, professionally trained and familiar with national styles and the latest technology. First founded in 1921, the Utah branch of the American Institute of Architects, like its parent organization, the

AIA, advocates for the value of architecture. The organization's agenda combines representing the interests of architects in their professional development, community service, and government affairs and recognizing architectural achievement. Historically, however, the AIA has been the professional organization for Utah's architects, providing them with a forum for community activities and in-service education.

Historic Preservation

During the mid-1970s preservation became an important part of the building effort in the state. However, historic preservation began much earlier with a grassroots organization—the newly organized Daughters of Utah Pioneers (DUP) and Sons of Utah Pioneers stepped forward in 1899 to save the Isaac Chase / Brigham Young Flour Mill and Home in Liberty Park from demolition. Many Utahns lamented and in fact protested the loss of the old Bishop's Storehouse in 1909 in preparation for building the Hotel Utah. During the first half of the twentieth century the Social Hall, Salt Lake Theater, and Gardo House were all torn down to make way for new buildings. The DUP responded to this with a new awareness of the value of historic properties by obtaining log cabins and old meetinghouses throughout the state and converting them to "relic" halls for the display of DUP-collected materials. Few, however, underwent restoration or interpretation. As a result, these one-room log cabins often sit on a concrete slab near a bronze marker and are made unobtainable by a chain-link fence. They are nevertheless ubiquitous parts of the Utah town landscape.

The first significant preservation efforts in Utah were undertaken in the early 1960s,

in part thanks to the enthusiasm spawned by the restoration of historic Nauvoo, Illinois, by the LDS Church and the commotion over the planned destruction of the Lion and Beehive Houses. Instead, Mormon leaders chose to restore the two houses and create museums in them before the passage of the National Historic Preservation Act of 1966. The state of Utah obtained and restored sites such as the Jacob Hamblin House, Council Hall (near the capitol), Territorial Statehouse, and Fairfield Stage Station, which are administered by State Parks and Recreation. Since then, the church and the state have had inconsistent track records in preservation—destroying some sites while saving others. Important losses include Salt Lake's Louis Sullivan Building, the Dooly Building, the Hotel Newhouse, and the Coalville Tabernacle, all landmark buildings worth saving.

Important leaders in preservation in Utah include the State Historic Preservation Office (SHPO) and Utah Heritage Foundation, now known as Preservation Utah. In the past two decades the SHPO has made a significant effort to document the historical resources of this state. Preservation Utah is an eloquent advocate for preservation of Utah's buildings. Privately funded, Preservation Utah works with state and federal agencies to provide education, funding, and experience in preservation efforts.

Graduate School of Architecture, University of Utah

Architectural education at the University of Utah began with the son of Brigham Young, Joseph Don Carlos Young, one of Utah's first professionally trained architects, who taught courses at the school in the 1880s.

Young left Utah for a time to study architecture at Rensselaer Polytechnic Institute in Troy, New York. When he returned he taught architectural and mechanical drawing and was appointed church architect for the LDS Church to succeed Truman O. Angell. When the Department of Art was organized in 1888–89, Young taught classes there and in 1889 William Ward, a stonecutter and architect who worked on the Nauvoo Temple and Lion House among other projects, succeeded him. During the late nineteenth century, architecture students studied for three years before they began working in local architects' offices. The Department of Art closed in 1891–92 and students left the state to study elsewhere. Some even took correspondence courses from schools like the International Correspondence School of Scranton, Pennsylvania.

Under President A. Ray Olpin, the fine arts curriculum resurfaced at the University of Utah as the School of Fine Arts in 1946 with leadership from Dean Avard Fairbanks, a well-known sculptor. In 1948, the American Institute of Architects met in Salt Lake City for its annual conference. At those meetings, Olpin met Galen Oman, an architect from Columbus, Ohio. Olpin asked him to start a department of architecture at the University of Utah. That same summer architect Roger Bailey met Olpin and encouraged the idea as well.

It would be Roger Bailey who would head the new department after 1949, a program housed in army barracks left over after World War II. In 1963, Robert L. Bliss was appointed head of the department, and he was dean from 1974 to 1986. During his administration the school began offering a master of architecture professional degree. Carl Inoway became dean in 1986 and served until 1992. In 1990,

the program offered a bachelor of science degree in architectural studies, and master of science degrees in architectural studies, historic preservation, and computers in architecture. William C. Miller came to Utah from Kansas State in 1992 to become the new dean until 2002. The first female dean, Brenda Scheer, took the College of Architecture and Planning to new heights, establishing an accredited urban planning undergraduate and graduate program and creating the new position of director of the School of Architecture, first held by Professor Patrick Tripeny, then well-known local architect Prescott Muir, and in 2014 Professor Mimi Locher. Keith Diaz Moore became dean in 2013.

The Art and Architecture Complex (AAC) is a cluster of forms in the same sense as a grouping of buildings. The art wing and the architecture wing of the building are connected by a covered passageway on the first level and a hallway on the second. They are twin sisters in a sense, each providing a neutral backdrop to the creative endeavor. To the east, architectural students meet in studio spaces, and faculty offices on the second floor radiate around a central faculty lounge. The Bailey exhibition space is a two-story expanse with a huge window that at one time looked out at the Wasatch Range but today frames the business building next door. To the west, the art wing does much the same. Gallery space southeast of the main office provides a display area for student work and visiting shows. Studios are found on each of the upper levels, with an open courtyard at the top. The Utah Museum of Fine Arts was housed in the west wing, which extends from the art side of the building, until it moved into its new home to the east in the Marcia and John Price Building. With a style termed Brutalism for its exposed structural materials—in this case reinforced concrete and cedar paneling—and its heavy, raw forms, the AAC uses dark spaces and an intriguing system of paths and staircases to create a challenging and, for some, welcome space apart from the rest of campus for the exploration of space, light, color, and form by future architects and designers.

Conclusion

There are many different ways to try to understand buildings and cities. Places have distinct boundaries or borders—the edges where they change from one reality to another. After World War II, like many American cities, Utah's cities grew on the periphery. Suburban neighborhoods had roads that defied the grids and meandered in new configurations, representing for many a new version of the American Dream. Strip malls became more common than town greens, and the utopian dream of Utah's founders was only vaguely evident behind new layers of shifting identities.

After midcentury, a prescribed list of amenities rather than a genuine or authentic identification with place and space marked lifestyles. The proverbial good life, displayed in stuccoed shopping centers and franchised restaurants, could be anywhere or nowhere—as architectural critic James Kunstler calls it, "The Geography of Nowhere." Bland and lacking in character, place often became an empty cultural barrier for future generations to read, a reaction to potential profit instead of a genuine concern for context.

Utah was preoccupied with the Olympics for almost two decades—first securing the Olympic bid, and finally preparing for what might prove to be a two-week party. Physical change in our cities and towns is an act of collective will, as well as an art form that communicates what we as citizens value. Together we either knowingly or unknowingly participate in a continuing dialectic, an evolutionary process that never reaches a conclusion. In the twenty-first century, Utah is poised at a threshold that can determine its place among American communities in the future. We are faced with the choice to model the good life in the unique context of our history and our natural environment, or to become like any other place in the United States.

Utah is definitely a place in flux, of shifting identities. What the state was ten years ago and what it is now are different. What it will represent to the world in the future is still up for grabs. When a crowd throws confetti up into the air on New Year's Eve, it looks beautiful catching the light, but when it lands it can potentially end up a big mess. How and what we build matters greatly.

The boundaries between the Mormon settlers and outsiders were in part intentional and in part circumstantial. At the turn of the century those boundaries seemed to blur as Utah became a state and attempted to pull toward the mainstream. But boundaries serve us well in definition—we understand some things and some places better if we hold them up against what they are not.

The mountains have always been the most prominent figures in the Utah landscape—certainly a boundary, they are the most unique natural amenity we can offer. The line of settlements tracking alongside them looks like a shadow from the north to the south. For each generation the mountains have provided shelter, refuge, and protection. They drew the Olympics, they promised refuge to the pioneers, they entertain outdoor enthusiasts. They will be here after we are gone. Perhaps what we represent will be not what we can duplicate but what others cannot achieve. Perhaps we will be known for the care we give the landscape that feeds us. Perhaps not.

The nineteenth-century histories of this place are not the only history worth keeping. Somehow I hope we'll remember to track the movement from then to now. When I was a girl, my friends and I babysat all week to earn enough money to take the bus downtown to State Street and 300 South. We would walk through Auerbach's and the Paris department store, cross at the half street and walk through Kress's, eat lunch at the soda bar at Walgreen's, and walk through ZCMI's maze of wooden columns and slanting floors. On special occasions, my grandmother would treat me to lunch at the Mayflower Café, requiring only that I wear crisp white gloves that made me feel like Minnie Mouse.

I never made the connection between Temple Square and Auerbach's. I doubt that I even knew how close they were. What mattered instead was the pattern of streets and experiences that I had mastered and valued. They extended my world from Holladay, Utah, to downtown. I felt powerful and special because of it. And it was a place that gave that to me.

We must understand the changing forces at work, the unique resources at our command as well as the special character of our place in developing a new vision that reflects the values we share as a community. As it is said, we should "make no small plans for they have no magic to stir men's souls." The power of places is immense. They matter. And if they are better, our lives are better. We have torn down too many Coalville Tabernacles. We have failed to remember and respect the ancient inhabitants of this place. We have erected too many monuments to mediocrity. We have built as if it doesn't matter. But it does.

Salt Lake City

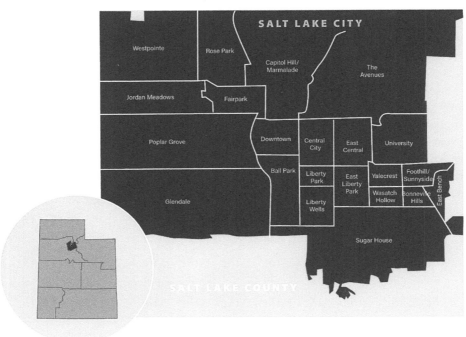

Salt Lake City and Salt Lake County

Introduction to Salt Lake City

Salt Lake City is best known as the headquarters of the Church of Jesus Christ of Latter-day Saints, but it is also routinely listed as one of the healthiest cities to raise a family and one of the best places to start a new business, and it is recommended for its convenient access to canyons for hiking, skiing, and other mountain sports. Salt Lake City is not just a single entity but a thriving urban environment with a growing diversity of people, institutions, opportunities, and ideas. Before white settlers moved into the Salt Lake Valley, Ute Indians lived to the south in what is now Utah County, and Shoshones lived to the north. The valley, framed by two mountain ranges and an extensive saltwater lake to the northwest, was a place in between, with evidence of camps the Indians occasionally used as they traveled to adjacent valleys.

The Mormon pioneers came to the Salt Lake Valley on July 24, 1847, and laid out a city according to the guidelines of the Plat of the City of Zion, a prescription given to them in the form of a revelation by their prophet Joseph Smith in 1833. Although the Mormons never built a city exactly as delineated in the plat but produced variations on the theme, Salt Lake City had its wide streets, orientation toward the cardinal points of the compass, a central block reserved for the principal religious buildings, and an emphasis on community, what the Mormons called "Zion." Although Temple Square was not at the literal center of the city, it was the symbolic and visual center, and the street numbering system began on its southeast corner.

Salt Lake City became a sort of prototype for cities that would be created throughout Utah Territory, a constructed formula for the Mormon version of the good life. Beyond the patterns suggested by the Plat of the City of Zion, the emphasis on community embodied in the Deseret Storehouse and tithing yard, and the architecture that provided cultural amenities such as the Salt Lake Theater, the Social Hall, and the types of house ubiquitous throughout the region, were modeled in Salt Lake City and imitated in most Mormon towns across the region.

After the 1850s, Main Street became the center of commerce, with small single-story commercial block buildings lining both sides of the street. After 1868 and the organization of Zion's Cooperative Mercantile Institution (ZCMI), several of these individual businesses became part of a cooperative association and were marked as LDS businesses by a masthead with an all-seeing eye and the words "Holiness to the Lord." With

Marmalade District / Capitol Hill Neighborhood.
Photograph by Elizabeth Cotter. Used with permission of photographer.

the coming of the railroad in 1870 and the increasing diversification of the city's commercial scene, non-Mormon and Mormon businessmen faced off along Main Street, with Exchange Place on 400 South as the mainstay of mining wealth, and the top of Main Street with businesses owned by or related to the Mormon church. Salt Lake City was important as a religious headquarters, a supply station for wagon trains moving toward Oregon and California, and the center of colonization of Utah Territory and surrounding areas.

At the turn of the twentieth century, Salt Lake City's urban neighborhoods began spreading beyond the strict confines of downtown because of the streetcar system. The Rapid Transit Company laid lines that moved through the Avenues from west to east and to the Ninth and Ninth area, and lines that inspired new subdivisions like Westminster Heights to the southeast.

Besides being home to a world religion, Salt Lake City is the seat of state, local, and county government, best exemplified by the Utah State Capitol in its prominent location at the top of State Street, where it is visible from across the valley. Both the City and County Building and the Scott Matheson Courthouse are landmark buildings that speak to the importance of government, democratic processes, and the common ground they produce for residents of the state and city.

The City

Marmalade District / Capitol Hill Neighborhood
Area between North Temple, 600 North, State Street, and 300 West
Late 1800s and early 1900s

Narrow, steep streets veering off from the strict grid of the city to the south signal the contrast between the Marmalade / Capitol Hill neighborhoods and the rest of downtown Salt Lake City. Within a few years after white settlement, Orson Pratt's survey of the city established Temple Square as the symbolic center of town. One- and two-room log and adobe houses appeared on the hillside to the north. Some are still extant and are among the oldest houses in the valley. The oldest neighborhood of the two, the Marmalade, features streets named for fruit jellies like Apricot, Almond, and Quince. Perfectly located with proximity to both the Utah State Capitol and downtown commercial and religious districts, the area was first home to working-class families who needed to live close to where they earned a living. Diversity more than any other characteristic distinguishes this urban neighborhood—diversity of buildings, people, and terrain. Like pioneer-era houses throughout the region, the first generation of houses were simple rectangular structures with hints of Greek Revival detailing. When the railroad came to the city in 1870, charming Victorian cottages adorned with gingerbread, shingled wall surfaces, and multiple roof pitches were built close to the street, in contrast to the usual twenty-foot setback of other neighborhoods nearby. In the early twentieth century, a stately street of substantial Craftsman houses lined the upper section of Main Street on the eastern edge of the district. The homes built in the Capitol Hill neighborhood—between North Temple and 600 North and between State Street and 300 West—are much more substantial and architecturally distinctive; several, like the McCune Mansion, were the homes of some of the wealthiest inhabitants of the city.

East of Capitol Hill, City Creek Canyon is an important defining element in this part of the city. In advance of the first party of Latter-day Saint pioneers who descended into the valley in 1847, scouts identified City Creek as a good supply of water for the valley below. Because of the diversity of the Capitol Hill neighborhood in terms of

architectural style as well as its population, its distinctive history, and its contribution to the city, it was nominated to the National Register of Historic Places as a historic district in 1980.

Salt Lake City Public Library
400 South 200 East
2003
Moshe Safdie

It is rare that a single building has such a profound impact on a place as the Salt Lake City Public Library at 400 South and 200 East. This is a building that inspires a love of architecture. Each generation of public libraries sums up the architectural tastes and technologies of the day. The late nineteenth-century Beaux Arts–style Salt Lake City Public Library is grand and elegant, impressing the importance of literacy on a city new on the national stage. The 1960s library on 500 South and 200 East

Salt Lake City Public Library.
Photograph by Elizabeth Cotter. Used with permission of photographer.

captures the fascination with sophisticated new building materials—New Formalism expressed through concrete panels and simple geometric space. Similarly, the Safdie library displays a new idea about space and form. Distinctive mostly in the way it challenges the strict regularity of the grid, the building's form cuts a swath in the air with a long, crescent-shaped wall that wraps around the north and east sides of the main building. A wall emerges from the ground level at the outdoor piazza and moves both up and around until it reaches a fifth level, creating a grand urban room, the equivalent of a streetscape. Stairs trace the upward curve of the wall to a rooftop plaza over the main library space, adding to accessibility and offering an interesting vantage point for the library itself.

Visitors have many opportunities to sit and enjoy the space, whether at one of the tables in the stone-paved urban room or at one of the upstairs reading rooms or galleries that look out at the Wasatch Range and are connected to the main building by a sky bridge. Throughout the year public lectures are held in the auditorium, which has a seating capacity of three hundred and provides meeting space for community-wide events. The library's exterior is triangular, with one wall facing the mountains and acting like a lens, resulting in a transparency

that opens the building up to the beautiful natural environment. According to Nancy Tessman, library director in 2006, "Moshe Safdie was really sensitive . . . to the idea that the library intended to create common ground and that the building should display that. . . . The building reflects the idea of an open mind. There are 360-degree views of the city from it. You can look outward in every direction."[1] What's more, a large public piazza, outdoor amphitheater, and rooftop garden and terrace provide space where the natural and the built worlds come together and provide ample opportunity for library patrons to relax and reflect.

In every way, the library is a public project. In fact, voters approved an $84 million bond to fund the new library, which required dramatic reshaping of Block 37, home to the circuit and district courts, the jail, the Metropolitan Hall of Justice, and public safety buildings, all of which vacated the site and moved to new facilities. The library board selected the internationally renowned Moshe Safdie and Associates, who worked in conjunction with a local firm, Valentiner Crane Brunjes Onyon Architects. Safdie was born in Israel, studied architecture in Canada, and has offices in Boston, Montreal, Toronto, and Jerusalem.

The Avenues
Area between A Street, South Temple, Virginia Street, and Eleventh Avenue
1853

Although the Plat of the City of Zion created a powerful template for settlement mirrored in the orthogonal streets of more than four hundred cities settled by the Latter-day Saints in Utah Territory, in Salt Lake City within five years after first settlement, development deviated from the original grid. The first neighborhood to do

The Avenues

so was the Avenues, the city's first suburb, which stretched up the sides of the foothills and was platted in 1853. Although there are a number of bungalows and even apartment buildings lining streets in the Avenues, it is the Victorian-style house more than any other that created a distinctive stamp on this urban neighborhood. The full range of expression is here, from tiny Victorian cross-wing cottages to elaborate mansions at the eastern top of First and Second Avenues. Known for their picturesque diversity, color, and texture, these Victorian ladies sit on streets designated from east to west by the letters of the alphabet and from north to south by numbers. These are densely built neighborhoods with houses right up against each other, with small back and front yards but expressive of a proud attitude. An exuberant celebration of financial success seems to be the bottom line here. At the southern edge of the Avenues district, some of the wealthiest mining entrepreneurs and successful businessmen built mansions along South Temple. Expressing a diversity of people similar to the architectural diversity so characteristic of the neighborhood, working-class people, professionals, and eventually university professors chose to make their homes there. As would be true of neighborhoods formed on the east bench, water limited what was possible and was a perpetual problem. Streetcar lines provided transportation downtown along First, Third, and Sixth Avenues, which were slightly wider than the others.

During the late 1960s and 1970s the Avenues went through significant revitalization, with restoration efforts under way on every block. Homeowners began to see the benefit of owning and preserving historic properties. The neighborhood's distinctive historic character became its most significant drawing power.

Trinity African Methodist Episcopal Church
239 East 600 South
1909
Hurley Howell

Speaking to the ethnic diversity that emerged after the railroad came to Salt Lake City in 1870, Utah's first black congregation, the Trinity African Methodist Episcopal Church, organized in the 1880s. Long before there were enough members to warrant building their own church, loyal parishioners shared their homes with each other for worship. In the late 1880s they secured a lot

Trinity African Methodist Episcopal Church

and began to build a church on 400 West below 600 South in 1891. Not long after construction began, the congregation had to put the project on hold because they had failed to raise enough money to complete it. In 1907, they tried again. This time they bought a lot at 230 East 600 South with funds donated by Mary Bright, a black cook who had made her fortune cooking for miners in Leadville, Colorado. Two years later the building—designed by member Hurley Howell and built with the generous donations of members—was done.

Although modest and perhaps a bit provincial, the style of Trinity AME church is familiar to traditional Protestant architecture and is definitely recognizable as a church—a modest-sized brick building making veiled references to the Gothic style. It has a split-level plan and moves in a rectangle toward the rear of the lot. A brick addition obscures the entrance to the church and runs across part of the facade. Contrasting with the original building, the addition has a flat roof, rusticated brick, square window bays with metal-framed sliding windows, and plain doors. The exterior brick of the main building is painted a rich dark brownish red. On the southwest corner of the front facade is a square tower with a spiked steeple, creating asymmetry but signaling "church."

Leaded art-glass windows are found on the front and side bays and have various colorful foliated and geometric patterns, topped by segmented bays and corbeled brick arches. In the center of the front gable is a corbeled brick cross, and a simple molded cornice runs along the roofline.

Most important is what the church represents about the power of religious community. It is a symbol of the black community and the focus of African American social, educational, and religious activity in

Utah that spanned more than one hundred years. Offering important social cohesion for the black community, the church provided refuge and strength in an environment that was dominated by one religious group and had a particular racial and ethnic homogeneity.

Tenth Ward Square
Southwest corner of 400 South and 800 East
1873 (meetinghouse); 1887 (district schoolhouse); 1909 (chapel)
Richard K. A. Kletting (district schoolhouse); Ashton Brothers (chapel)

The three historic structures of the Salt Lake Tenth Ward Square provide a sort of guidebook to LDS architecture between the 1870s and the present, certainly the evolution of church approaches to providing for the needs of church members. Each structure addressed the religious, temporal, and educational needs of ward members. The earliest building on the site, a one-story adobe church built in 1849, was a multipurpose structure that served at various times as a meetinghouse and a school—virtually all community gatherings would have been held within. Four years after they built the adobe meetinghouse, the congregation replaced it with a larger, two-story adobe building that was demolished in 1898. The second-story rooms were used for plays—Maude Adams, a nationally known actress, performed in various theatricals there. The Tenth Ward Brass Band, the first ward band in the city, was organized there in 1868. Capturing the spirit of the multiple uses of the church, the saying that graced the lintel over the entryway (which was saved and incorporated into the design of the 1909 chapel) read: "Education forms the mind, but the soul makes the man."

In 1873, the Tenth Ward built a Greek Revival brick meetinghouse, the oldest

Tenth Ward Square

of the remaining buildings on the block. A Gothic Revival chapel was built in 1909 south of the 1873 building, complete with two square towers that mark the facade at the corners. Designed and built by Ashton Brothers, a local construction firm, this church featured pointed Gothic-arched and colored glass windows. Morgan and Mary Davies donated the principal window, which portrays Jesus Christ knocking at the door. Gothic details continue through the interior, including a beautiful wrought-iron railing for the stairway that leads up from the front door, as well as oak woodwork throughout with foliated patterns.

The ward built a district schoolhouse on the corner of the lot at 800 East and 400 South in 1887. When ward school districts were consolidated in 1890, Webster School was built across the street and the "Old Red Building" was used for ward classrooms. It was designed by Richard

Kletting, and a second floor provided additional classroom space. Dormer windows provided light for these rooms where Sunday School classes were held after the city school system was revamped in 1890.

The LDS Church began an extensive renovation of the complex in 1997 to preserve its unique nineteenth-century history.

Gilgal Garden
749 East 500 South
1945
Thomas Child

When I was a little girl I once got lost walking home from Hamilton School and found myself in Gilgal. Scared to death by the strange sculptures and otherworldly atmosphere of the gardens, I was sure I had stumbled upon hell. I hadn't, although I had mistakenly entered one of the most eccentrically unique spaces in Salt Lake City. Mormon bishop Thomas Battersby

Gilgal Garden

Child and sculptor Maurice Brooks built the garden and its granite and quartz statues of a sphinx with Joseph Smith's face, a roughly hewn Captain of the Lord's Host, and scriptures inscribed on stepping-stones and garden walls. It was forgotten for decades except for occasional visitors and curiosity seekers, but today the Friends of Gilgal Garden have raised enough money to save it from destruction in the path of development.

Tucked away behind houses on both 500 South and 800 East, the sculpture garden contains twelve sculptures, including a larger than life-size sculpture of Child himself, and stones engraved with Mormon scriptures, philosophical sayings, and references from world literature. Eccentric but weirdly wonderful, Gilgal is an anomaly in the midst of a traditional working-class neighborhood.

Trolley Square
Block between 600 East and 700 East, 500 South and 600 South
Early 1900s

At the turn of the century, trolleys were an important form of transportation around town, opening new "streetcar" neighborhoods with access to work a distance from one's home. E. H. Harriman acquired a controlling interest in the Utah Light and Traction Railway Company in 1906 and attempted to provide Salt Lake City with an electric trolley system on par with those of other cities in the nation. He put millions of dollars behind his good idea, bought the most up-to-date trolley cars, and built a large, and at the time modern, facility to house a garage and maintenance activities.

Before the 1960s, preservation largely isolated historic properties from the contemporary life of cities, in a way rendering them obsolete. Trolley Square's developers saw the value of "putting a new building inside an old shell" and came up with something new instead. They saved this important historic landmark and gave it new relevancy in the urban fabric, weaving it into the life of the city in a new way. It was featured in articles that appeared in the *New York Times, Washington Post, Los Angeles Times, Time, Fortune,* and *Better Homes and Gardens*; developer Wallace A. Wright Jr. and his eight business partners who bought the site were hailed for their vision in recognizing the value of giving new life to an aging neighborhood.

It is likely that Harriman would appreciate the innovative and adaptive reuse of the property by developer Wally Wright, who bedecked the trolley barn interior with parts of historic Victorian houses and the urban landscape, along with new store fronts in line with this historic theme to create a lively, enclosed shopping

Trolley Square

environment. Trolley Square opened as a shopping center in 1972 and is still going strong. Important as well for its influence on historic preservation in Utah, Trolley Square established the value of the past as an innovative and creative marketing device. Salt Lake City's early twentieth-century historic texture provides an interesting and delightful backdrop to the more traditional activities of shopping and dining in restaurants.

LDS First Ward Meetinghouse
760 South 800 East
1910–1914
Harold Burton and Hyrum Pope

The designers of the LDS First Ward Meetinghouse, Harold Burton and Hyrum Pope, were recognized during their own time as innovators and talented architects who helped bring Frank Lloyd Wright's distinctive ideas about building mass and form to Utah. This building is one of the earliest and best examples of the early modern Prairie school style of architecture in the western

United States and reflects in particular the influence of Wright's Unity Temple in its geometric masses, stylized linear decoration, and tiered elevations. In what was hardly the most avant-garde architectural environment, the First Ward Meetinghouse became the prototype for more than two dozen Mormon buildings, including churches, tabernacles, and eventually temples, in the United States and Canada.

The main space of the First Ward Meetinghouse accommodates the chapel, with the long axis facing the street, but overall the plan is shaped like a *T*. The building has two stories and two entrances, with a monumental staircase. The geometry of the Prairie style is articulated with pilasters that flank tall, narrow, leaded art-glass windows. The fine geometric cast-stone ornamentation illustrates the architect's familiarity with Wrightian aesthetics as articulated in the Larkin Building in Oak Park, Illinois. The central portion of the facade rises to a low-pitched parapet, although the roof is flat.

LDS First Ward Meetinghouse

The chapel continues with the Prairie style and is a simple, well-proportioned space with a high central nave lit by clerestory windows. Oak ornamentation mirrors the lines that follow the exterior masses with wooden banding in ornamental patterns. The floor slopes slightly in the central section, with pews to the sides elevated a few steps to provide good visibility from each part of the chapel. Prairie-style light fixtures add to the abundant natural light that floods the interior space.

LDS Fifth Ward Meetinghouse
740 South 300 West
1910
Lewis Telle Cannon and John Fetzer

One reason the settlement of the Great Basin was so efficiently managed was the Mormon ward. More than a congregation, the ward was a geographical unit of the LDS Church that was led by a lay minister, a bishop, who administered religious services, donations to the poor, and in many cases the distribution of land and organization of irrigation and construction projects. The ward's home, called a meetinghouse in the nineteenth century, was a multipurpose facility that housed religious rituals and services, political meetings, gatherings of the church's auxiliary organizations, and virtually every type of social activity that brought members together. The Fifth Ward is one of Salt Lake City's oldest wards.

First organized in 1853 in the southwest section of the city for an agricultural community, the ward met in a series of adobe buildings before it decided to build a more permanent church. As was true of so many revival-style churches built at the turn of the century, the choice of the Tudor Gothic style for this ward was about status, permanence, and perhaps a little competition to create a ward meetinghouse that best represented who they thought they were, or at least what they wanted the rest of the city to see.

Because it was in the heart of the Gateway neighborhood, the congregation had a distinctly immigrant feel and was more diverse than wards to the east. This population shifted over time. At the turn of the century, most members were of European ancestry; toward the middle of the twentieth century they were Hispanic; and for a time the Fifth Ward became the Lamanite Ward, serving the city's Indian population.

Although the principal style of this T-shaped church is Tudor Gothic, massing reveals the influence of the Prairie style. The flat-roofed building has a strong, dominant central mass with recessed sections that move forward or backward. Subtly pitched parapets, delineated with concrete contrasting with the red brick walls, move upward from the forward sections. At the same time, in line with the Tudor Gothic style, the church has window bays with corbeled arches and gabled facades decorated with bands of alternating white and red brick, concrete-capped buttresses at the corners of the building that mirror the ancient buttresses that held vertical walls that soared to unprecedented heights, and deeply recessed windows with thick mullions and splayed casings. An addition to the front of the building, constructed in 1937 in harmony with the original style, modified the impact of the large Gothic window over the main entrance.

Ballpark Trax Station
1300 South 180 West
1999
Phillips Associate Multidisciplinary Team
Although light rail stops are primarily about business—providing shelter and marking a destination—the Phillips

Associate Multidisciplinary Team, located at Salt Lake City's Phillips Gallery, brought together a collaborative team of ten painters, photographers, writers, sculptors, and landscape architects to design the Ballpark Station at 1300 South. They chose to create a visual memory of the neighborhood (at one point known as the People's Freeway) with various media, marking its residential, commercial, recreational, and industrial history in photographs, poetry, and sculpture.

Franklin Quest / Smith's Field
77 West 1300 South
1994
Valentiner Crane Brunjes Onyon Architects
There is a long tradition of stadium design that captures the perfect combination of enclosure, view, and history. Replacing the historic Derks Field, Franklin Quest and today, Smith's Field includes all the elements of a major league baseball park—a double-deck grandstand and luxury suites—and the quaint down-home feel of a minor league field. The city dedicated the field on April 8, 1994, for a total cost of $21 million. Salt Lake City Corporation owns the field, but a series of AAA professional baseball teams—the Salt Lake Buzz or the Salt Lake Bees, among others—have played there beneath summer skies in front of loyal fans. In the sentimental home of local baseball, the location has been the perfect draw for fans long accustomed to heading to the corner of 1300 South and West Temple for long summer evenings of baseball. In total, this open-air facility comfortably seats 12,650 in the lower and upper decks extending down each baseline. The field itself creates berm seating for 3,000 additional spectators who prefer to sit on picnic blankets during the game rather than seats.

Liberty Park

Smith's Field provides old-time stadium design with the most up-to-date comforts desired by both players and spectators. The field is right up against the street, reflecting its urban orientation, but opens to a breathtaking view of the mountains—the larger contextual environment. Oriented toward the east to maximize the view and reduce discomfort from the setting sun, and featuring an uninterrupted view of the Wasatch Range, the location seems perfectly suited for a sports facility. Stepping up gradually in height and back from the street, the field also mitigates the neighborhood scale of the surrounding area.

The Utah AIA recognized the success of the project with the 1996 Award for Excellence in Architecture.

Liberty Park
500 East to 700 East, 900 South to 1300 South
1881

The imposing shade and pine trees of Liberty Park line paths and roads traveled by generations of joggers, skaters, and walkers with strollers. This historic landscaping that matured more than one hundred years ago speaks to the age and tradition of this community gathering place. First established on the site of the Isaac Chase House and Mill that Chase had received in the original Big Field Survey of 1847, the site became locally known before long as Forest Park, the Locust Patch, and the Mill Farm. Brigham Young bought the farm property from Chase in 1860, trading Chase for property in Davis County. But Young's long-term plan was that the city purchase the land "for the lowest price" after his death. On April 20, 1881, the city bought the farm from the Brigham Young estate for $27,500, a purchase that made the local newspapers.

The city dedicated Liberty Park on July 17, 1882, as part of the annual celebration of the anniversary of the Battle of Bunker Hill and dedicated it for the use of the city's citizens. Like Central Park in New York City, which was designed in the 1850s, Liberty Park provides important open space in a densely populated part of the city. One of the earliest parks in Utah and certainly the largest, it reflects the Progressive Era belief in environmental determinism and the city's potential to redeem the moral character of its inhabitants. A small road circles the park on the periphery and connects with the interior at various points along the way. At the center of the park are the Tracy Aviary, an amusement park, tennis courts, a swimming pool, and a large pond. Also of interest are the Isaac Chase House and Mill.

Isaac Chase House
Center of Liberty Park, 600 East 900 South
1853–1854

Near the site of his mill, designed by Frederick Kesler, Isaac Chase built his home between 1853 and 1854. He used adobe bricks for both the mill and his home, made in the adobe pits called "Church Farm," an adobe yard on the site of the Forest Dale Golf Club. Pioneer-era builders used bricks from the yard for houses all over town. Expanding beyond the extreme restrictions of the modest single-room house they had been living in before their new home was completed, Chase's family lived in the house until 1860, when they moved to a house on State Street where Chase died the next year.

Dedicated in 1881, the Chase House was home to a groundskeeper until it became a relic hall for the DUP, and eventually the home of the state Folk Arts program.

Chase Mill
Liberty Park, 600 East 900 South
1852
Frederick Kesler

Sawmills and gristmills were important to the growth of new settlements in Utah Territory, and virtually every new community had one that fed off streams that cascaded down from the mountains nearby. Although many of these mills took on simple vernacular forms and were barely distinguishable from domestic dwellings or larger public buildings like schoolhouses, in some instances they took on a distinctive, characteristic form dictated in part by the type of machinery housed within.

Chase Mill.
Photograph by Elizabeth Cotter. Used with permission of photographer.

The Chase Mill in Salt Lake City is an example of a mid-nineteenth-century industrial complex. Originally known as the Mill Farm, it functioned in coordination with the Mormon tithing and public works system. The building itself is significant for the way it completes a picture of nineteenth-century life in the valley, but also for its creator. Mill designer and builder Frederick Kesler designed and engineered the Chase Mill. Kesler installed an innovative milling operation that utilized the most advanced machinery and techniques known in the mid-nineteenth century, including center-vent wheels, Oliver Evans–type automated equipment, and later, turbine waterwheels. His daughter freighted the irons and millstones when she immigrated in September 1847. Other Kesler mills include Heber C. Kimball's North Canyon flour mill, built in Bountiful in 1852–54; Franklin D. Richard's flour mill, built in 1860–62 in Farmington; and Samuel P. Hoyt's mill, built in Hoytsville in 1860–63. The clerestory roofline of the Chase Mill became the trademark of the Kesler mills. Chase built his family home nearby.

Isaac Chase hoped to bring water to fuel the mill from distant tributaries of Red Butte, Parley's, and Emigration Canyons, securing the deed to the property in 1847 and another fifteen acres soon after. Eventually he owned one hundred acres in total. The first story of the mill was made of stone, and construction of the upper stories began with either stone or adobe. The first mill he built on his property was an upright sawmill to cut lumber for his home and mill, and the next year he built a small crackling mill. Horizontal waterwheels powered the mill at Brigham Young's insistence; water ran through three arched openings near the bottom of the present foundation, passed over two horizontal wheels, and moved along a stone raceway that went out of the mill through a large arch to the west. After it spilled into a wood-floored tailrace outside the mill, it traveled to the creek flowing along the north side of the mill.

When he redesigned the Chase Mill in 1852, Kesler had spent the past five years in the East and was familiar with the most up-to-date innovations in mill design. Brigham Young bought into the mill in 1854, and his son Brigham Young Jr. managed the mill in 1859, producing flour that was important during the famine of 1856–57. The mill operated until 1882, when Salt Lake City bought the land from the Brigham Young estate for Liberty Park. After sitting vacant for decades, the mill was restored in 2006.

Tower Theatre
876 East 900 South
1921

One of two homes of the Utah Film Society, the Tower Theatre has historically held its own as the independent theater in town, showing art films, foreign films, and alternative entertainment. It is a Salt Lake venue of the Sundance Film Festival each January. Those familiar with the Tower today would be surprised at its historic appearance, which resembled a crenellated English castle. Significant as Salt Lake City's oldest freestanding theater, it was completed in 1921, with battlements and twin corner towers evoking an ancient British fortress. It was the first theater with air conditioning, and in the 1920s it was also known for the "Tower Talkies." In the spirit of equating progressiveness with modernism, when it was remodeled in 1953, the distinctive tower facade was covered over and modernized according to contemporary standards, and the interior was completely redesigned.

Tower Theatre

East Bench

Charles F. and Nan Little House
87 U Street
1910s
Ware and Treganza
The architects of the Commercial Club building, Walter Ware and Alberto Treganza, designed this Craftsman home for Charles F. and Nan Little. Mirroring the architectural style, distinctive size, and sophisticated design more typical of the Federal Heights neighborhood than of the Avenues to the west, this two-story brick and shingle house reflects the Prairie style, similar to the architects' design for the Ladies' Literary Club. This example's horizontal bands run around the structure;

a hipped roof and brackets support large overhanging eaves. Ware and Treganza designed a number of Craftsman houses in the city that similarly used shingles, sleeping porches, and these distinctive, sweeping eaves.

Owen Herrick Gray House
74 Virginia Street
1915
Owen Herrick Gray
One of Salt Lake City's most distinctive neighborhoods is Federal Heights, just north of the University of Utah campus and east of the Avenues, a place inhabited primarily by professionals. The owner of this home, Owen Herrick Gray, was an electrical engineer who moved to Salt Lake City in

1902. Virginia Street defines the western edge of Federal Heights, and the Avenues stretch west from there. The front porch of the Owen Herrick Gray House provides a welcoming and gracious entry to the street. This one-and-a-half-story brick and shingle Craftsman bungalow was built in 1915 and combines natural materials in a rich, earthy, and textural mix, contrasting wood and brick, shingles, and other decorative surfaces made of wood. Above the porch, a sleeping porch capitalized on the cool breezes coming out of the canyon on hot summer nights. When the family built this house in the early twentieth century, it was widely believed that sleeping outdoors would prevent tuberculosis. Braced wooden columns on both levels run across the front of the house.

Federal Heights
Virginia Street and South Temple to the northeast
1909
Federal Heights is nestled between the university district to the south, the Avenues to

the west, and the foothills of the Wasatch Range to the east. The Telluride Realty Company developed the neighborhood, in part from sections of Fort Douglas deeded to the city in 1874, on land that had originally been used by Charles Popper for his home, corral, and slaughterhouse. The company platted the neighborhood in November 1909, but work had started some time before. Advertisements for this exclusive neighborhood promoted a lifestyle that escaped the noise, traffic, and pollution of the city to the west. Fully in line with the most luxurious suburban neighborhoods nationally, stone pillars signaled entrance into a space characterized by wealth, beauty, and extravagance. The local newspaper, the *Salt Lake Tribune*, reported that $50,000 had been spent on extras, or what it called "high-class restrictions." In Salt Lake City, when coal was the principal material used for heating homes and in industry, pollution was a significant problem. Federal Heights offered an escape from the coal smoke that hovered over the city.

Federal Heights.
Photograph by Elizabeth Cotter. Used with permission of photographer.

Several of the architecturally distinctive homes in Federal Heights are listed on the National Register of Historic Places, with styles that range from Colonial or Mediterranean Revival to Prairie- or International-style mansions. Lushly landscaped with historic trees and gardens, and with stone walls or foundations, the neighborhood includes homes set farther back than in other parts of the city, with larger lots and more space in between. Ads marketing what was first known as Popperton and later as Federal Heights described the picturesque qualities of the neighborhood along with modern amenities like paved streets, cement sidewalks complete with curbs and gutters, and a convenient location near downtown Salt Lake City. At four key intersections, the neighborhood featured miniparks with grassy spaces.

Salt Lake City Cemetery
Between N and U Streets and between Fourth and Eleventh Avenues
1847–present

The Salt Lake City Cemetery's first burial was a little girl, Mary Wallace, who was buried on September 27, 1847. Since then, more than 120,000 people have been buried there. Surveyed two years after the pioneers arrived in the Salt Lake Valley, the cemetery originally included 20 acres and now includes more than 250. Numerous religious, governmental, and local leaders are buried here, including Senators Frank Moss and Wallace Bennett, and Mormon church leaders from George Q. Cannon to J. Reuben Clark. Joseph Fielding Smith is also buried in this cemetery.

But the cemetery tells the story of more than dignitaries who have died. It includes sections for certain religious groups such as Catholics and Jews, as well as sections for various ethnic groups such as Chinese and Japanese. Headstones suggest occupations or fraternal associations as well as beliefs, family relationships, or hope for life after death.

Part of the cemetery is laid out in a grid, reflecting the larger urban environment around it, and to the northeast the lanes start to meander, not unlike the way the street system changes once one enters the suburbs.

Fire Station No. 8
(Market Street Broiler / Porcupine Pub and Grille)
258 South 1300 East
1930 (original); 1980s (reuse)
Albert White (original); Gastronomy Inc. (adaptive reuse)

An excellent trailblazing example of adaptive reuse, Fire Station No. 8 took on a new life in the 1980s as a popular local eatery. In some ways, the fire station resembles a Gothic Revival church more than a public building, with its steeply pitched gabled roof, arched windows and doors, and asymmetrical facade. Built in 1930, this Period Revival, one-and-a-half-story building is a narrow rectangle that stretches from 1300 East toward the back of the lot, which is a little more than twice as long as it is wide. Other interesting details include cast-stone quoins accenting the brick exterior walls as well as light stone trim around the doors and windows. Hexagonal shingles on the roof contribute to the style as well.

During the first few decades of the twentieth century, Period Revival styles were popular in Utah. Although there are numerous examples of historical styles such as English Tudor, Spanish Colonial Revival, and French Norman, the English Revival styles were by far the most popular, particularly for churches.

Fire Station No. 8 / Market Street Broiler / Porcupine Pub and Grille

When first built in the 1930s, the fire station served the city's east bench, the University of Utah, and adjacent residential areas. Because both houses and the University of Utah surrounded it, the city worked with local builder Albert White to create a building that was aesthetically pleasing as well as functional. Set back the same distance from the street and conforming to the height and size of buildings nearby, the fire station was compatible with its larger environment.

In 1982, John Williams of Gastronomy Inc., known for his commitment to important historic preservation projects, bought the property to convert it into a restaurant through an adaptive reuse project that left the exterior intact but significantly reconfigured the interior space for use as a restaurant. Narrow bands of windows in the lower areas of the roof slopes and a

solid, cedar-sided railing wall about three feet high were added to the front to create an outdoor dining space. In 2016, the restaurant opened under new ownership as the Porcupine Pub and Grille.

Language and Communication Building
North Campus Drive and Central
Campus Drive
University of Utah
1990s
Brixen & Christopher

The Utah AIA gave this project an Award for Excellence in Architecture in 1996, an acknowledgment from the architectural community that LNCO is a well-designed building. From the air, LNCO would look like a gigantic zigzag, maximizing available window space for offices and meeting rooms and providing virtually every office with its own view of exterior or interior space. As one of the homes to the College of Humanities on the University of Utah campus, LNCO houses six departments and programs: English, Communication, Languages and Literature, Linguistics, Writing, and the College of Humanities administrative offices.

Built adjacent to an existing classroom building in the center of campus, formerly Orson Spencer Hall, LNCO is also oriented toward a pleasant interior plaza, a threshold to the complex as a whole and an outdoor teaching space. Designed with the intention of providing natural lighting for most offices and interior light courts for others, offices are grouped in subdivisions with casual gathering spaces at regular intervals for the various schools. The site slopes twenty-two feet from east to west, creating a multilevel building that reduces the effect of its significant mass despite its size. The building moves across the landscape in a provocative and interesting way. In terms of material and form, the building embraces the existing campus fabric, but in terms of interior space it creates a distinctively different orientation to the natural world.

Huntsman Cancer Institute
2000 Circle of Hope
2001
Jensen Haslam Architects

Besides the architectural design ambition to create a beautiful building that will make a powerful statement with its form and substance, a more complex vision drove the conceptualization of the Huntsman Cancer Institute. Everyone involved hoped the building would contribute to the process of healing by providing a supportive environment for families, patients, and medical staff in the sensitive endeavor of cancer research and treatment. The building itself had to become a symbol of hope.

This hyperconsciousness of the experience of patients and of the caregivers who support them drove the design of interior spaces in the original 673,000-square-foot building. Windows of chemotherapy suites overlook a hillside often covered with wildflowers or the valley below to the west, and interior materials have a textural richness and color mirroring the natural world. Limestone, granite, maple, and cherry wood on both interior and exterior features was used to create a feel more like that of a five-star hotel than the institutional setting more typical of a hospital. HCI founder Jon M. Huntsman's commitment to fighting cancer is exemplified in the dramatic structure. He said, "From an empty hillside to one of the world's leading cancer research and treatment facilities, our vision has always been to improve cancer outcomes for children and adults through innovative research."[2]

Fort Douglas
2000 East 300 South
1862
U.S. Army

When President Abraham Lincoln sent the Third California Volunteer Infantry to Utah in 1862, the government's stated goal was to protect the Overland Trail from conflict with Native Americans, but a broader intent was to bring the Mormon kingdom in Utah under federal control. Led by Colonel Patrick E. Connor, the Third California Volunteer Infantry had mustered first in Sacramento, California, in 1861 before marching over the Sierra Nevada and the desert to arrive at the Rocky Mountains, where they established Fort Bridger in Wyoming. After the Civil War, the government used its troops to improve communication between East and West. Connor identified a strategic location for a fort in

Fort Douglas.
Photograph by Elizabeth Cotter. Used with permission of photographer.

the foothills of the Wasatch Range, with a view of Salt Lake City below. Ready access to water, abundant land, and visibility made the site ideal for an encampment of the federal government. Ironically, Connor named it after Stephen Douglas, a recently deceased senator from Illinois who was a friend to the Mormons while they were in Nauvoo. To prepare for their first winter, in 1862 the soldiers built thirty-two "Connor's tents" by digging out thirteen-foot-square pits and raising roofs of canvas tarpaulins. Reflecting the grid of Utah villages throughout the region, soldiers laid out log and adobe buildings on a north-south axis, with each of the chief buildings located around a central parade ground. Ordering the wild landscape of the foothills of the Wasatch Range, in this way the government laid claim to this place, certainly marking the presence of the rule of law and the influence of the U.S. government. Fort

Douglas was never walled off but rather was left open to the environment. Still, the order in the manipulated landscape was evident as construction proceeded. The first ordering principle was the placement of buildings in a hierarchy oriented to the parade ground. Second, a strong east-west axis ran through the center, and buildings on either side contributed to an impression of symmetry. Soldiers lived at the fort and organized expeditions throughout the surrounding environs.

Within a decade, a third ordering principle became evident as a greater number of permanent structures appeared near the military field. Reflecting their importance in the military hierarchy itself, officers' quarters were built with higher-quality materials and in more fashionable styles. Between 1872 and 1876 red sandstone buildings replaced the earlier, more temporary structures with stone quarried in Red Butte

Canyon to the east: five new barracks, ten officers' quarters, a commanding officer's quarters, and a hospital. Departing from the rough vernacular structures of the 1860s and utilizing Gothic Revival detailing such as pointed arches, finials, and bargeboards, the charming buildings at Officers' Circle were inspired by books such as A. J. Downing's *Architecture of Country Houses*. The next building phase between 1884 and 1886 continued the theme and resulted in more Gothic Revival–style buildings constructed of wood.

In the early 1900s new buildings at the fort were more institutional than domestic in size and style; much more like schools, hospitals, or other government buildings than their residential counterparts in the fort, they symbolized the federal government's presence in Utah. These buildings resembled those built elsewhere during the period and reflected a certain standardization of form and plan.

The U.S. Army transferred the northern half of the fort to the University of Utah in 1993, including the parade grounds, Officers' Circle, Army Chapel, and other National Historic Landmark properties. New dormitories nearby, built with funds from the federal government, housed athletes during the 2002 Winter Olympic Games in Salt Lake City. The southern half of the base continues as the headquarters of the Ninth Army Reserve Command, serving as the steward of historic resources remaining at the fort such as Officers' Circle and the base theater and PX.

Walter P. Cottam Visitor Center
Red Butte Garden and Arboretum
300 Wakara Way
1996

The Red Butte Garden and Arboretum functions like an ecotone, a rich transitional zone between the built complexity of the city and university campus and the canyon that spreads from the foothills toward the east. As a threshold to the canyon itself, the Cottam Visitor Center is a place where the visitor moves from the stark efficiency of a parking lot to natural paths that wind their way up the mountainside. Red Butte Garden provides a welcoming and enticing backdrop for summer concerts and natural strolls on autumn evenings. The location of the gardens and the reverence they show for the natural world seem to belie the possibility of a visitor center—a built intrusion into this natural refuge seems unlikely at best, but the Cottam Visitor Center does this in a thoughtful, gentle, and unobtrusive way, a highly successful response to the need to create an enclosure for certain activities associated with Red Butte Garden. Located in the foothills southeast of the University of Utah, the visitor center forms one entrance to the gardens and the natural areas surrounding them. This 8,000-square-foot building houses a gift shop, classroom, and visitor orientation and reception lobby.

Because the site slopes to the northwest, the building moves in different levels up the hillside, allowing the visitor to move gradually up the slope through the building to the garden courtyard above. Red Butte reflects the patterns established by the natural world—red sandstone retaining walls divide gardens from terraces. Blooming plants native to the area seem to emerge naturally from the site. The glass walls of the visitor center itself create a space that reads like a big greenhouse, filled with light and views of the mountains to the east. Reflecting the historical character of arboretums, conservatories, and greenhouses, the building uses extensive glass and a simple steel frame. Exterior awnings help manipulate and control light levels and the amount of heat that pours into the room. Pergolas at various points around the building also help smooth the transition from the built to the natural features of the site.

In 1998 the Utah AIA recognized the respectful and interesting way the visitor center resolved the issue of intruding upon the natural and beautiful indigenous environment.

Old Deseret Village
This Is the Place Heritage Park
2601 Sunnyside Avenue, Salt Lake City
Reconstruction of mid-1800s buildings
Expanded significantly under the auspices of the Utah Statehood Centennial Commission and through the generosity of numerous donors, Old Deseret Village is Utah's answer to Sturbridge Village or Colonial Williamsburg. Designated by the commission as a Living Legacy Project, it expanded in preparation for the state centennial. This living history museum provides a glimpse of pioneer Utah from settlement in 1847 to the coming of the railroad. The formula includes wide streets and irrigation canals running on each side, with pioneer-era blacksmith shops and houses. Together they work to re-create the atmosphere and physical reality of the past, focusing on the pioneer experience of community building. The park is not without its critics, who fault living history museums as "fake" environments.

Many of these houses were lifted from the site where they were built and transported to their new home in agricultural fields that stretch north of 900 South in the city. Other buildings such as the Manti ZCMI building were dismantled on-site and reconstructed at Deseret Village. The Pine Valley meetinghouse, on the other hand, is a total reconstruction. Smaller in scale than the original, which still exists in Pine Valley, this version allows a wider audience to see the unique structural system (which resembles an upside-down ship bottom) and simple Classicism so typical of a nineteenth-century meetinghouse. Whether one agrees with the premises behind reconstruction or even a living history museum in general, Deseret Village makes history accessible and available for popular consumption. Volunteers dressed in period costumes act as historical interpreters, responding to visitors in the manner of nineteenth-century farmers, housewives, or children, enlivening the space with activity and conversation and making visitors consider what it might have been like to live in another time and place.

This Is the Place Monument
Old Deseret Village
2601 Sunnyside Avenue, Salt Lake City
1947
Mahonri M. Young
The legislature appointed a special state commission in 1937 to create a monument memorializing the Utah pioneers. The commission chose nationally known Utah sculptor Mahonri M. Young to create a monument that commemorates the entrance of the Mormon pioneers into the Salt Lake Valley on July 24, 1847. The monument, articulating Brigham Young's statement "This is the right place, drive on," was dedicated in 1947. Sixty feet high and eighty-six feet long, this granite monument with panels of bas-relief bronze sculpture tells the story of the pioneers, fur trappers, traders, explorers, and others who paved the way for the permanent settlement of the region. At the top of the central shaft stand Heber C. Kimball, Brigham Young, and Wilford Woodruff, well known Latter-day Saint general authorities and leaders of the

This Is the Place Monument

pioneer companies that descended into the valley.

Although the richest narratives of the nineteenth-century experience exist in the pages of diaries carefully preserved by individual men and women, the panels flesh out a story of sorts. The panel at the center of the column at the base depicts the first men to enter the valley as scouts—Orson Pratt and Erastus Snow. The doomed Donner-Reed Party is portrayed on the other side. On the west side of the base are images of pioneer wagons traveling down the trail into the valley, and on the east are six important historical characters from the period—Étienne Provost, Chief

Washakie, Peter Skene Ogden, Captain Benjamin Bonneville, Father Pierre-Jean De Smet, and John C. Frémont. Domínguez and Escalante, the earliest nonnative men to enter the valley, are found on the south pedestal, and the fur trappers on the north.

This Is the Place Heritage Park Visitor Center
Old Deseret Village
2601 Sunnyside Avenue S.
1996
Cooper/Roberts

The design for a visitor center for this living history museum at the base of Emigration Canyon presented a unique dilemma—how to create a building that would be fully functional as a modern, state-of-the-art visitor center and exhibit hall but also architecturally responsive to the historic character of Deseret Village. Deseret Village creates the ambience and look of an 1847–69 pioneer village, typical of the settlement of the Great Basin by the Mormon pioneers. As such it combines reconstructed buildings and buildings moved to the site from other locations. With streets laid out according to the guidelines of the Plat of the City of Zion, it gives visitors to the park the chance to imagine themselves in a different time, interacting in a physical way with spaces that might have existed in the past.

Architect Allen D. Roberts's keen sense of Utah history enriched the design. His architectural team searched for a historical prototype that that would provide the context for a 12,000-square-foot, multilevel, pioneer-era industrial structure. They chose to use architect Truman O. Angell's original 1853 drawings of the sugar factory built in Sugar House (and torn down in 1928) for a starting point, adapting them to the needs of the new function. From the exterior, the visitor center reflects this connection to the past materially with red sandstone adobe

Harvard-Yale Neighborhood.
Photograph by Elizabeth Cotter. Used with permission of photographer.

walls and rough-sawn timber posts, beams, and trusses. From the interior one can see exposed king-post trusses that support the roof and that are identical to the ones Angell designed 143 years earlier.

The firm received recognition for this design with the Utah AIA's Award for Excellence in Architecture in 1996.

Harvard-Yale Neighborhood
Area surrounded by 800 South, 1300 South, 1300 East, and 2100 East
Early 1900s
Samuel Campbell

Almost anyone who lives in Salt Lake City knows where the Harvard-Yale area is—it is one of the most compelling, architecturally distinctive neighborhoods in town. Driving along 1300 East between 1300 and 900 South and below 1500 East you can

see hints of the warm red brick, Tudor Revival, and Colonial-style houses that sit close to the street and create a charming, intimate residential neighborhood. The historic architectural styles and materiality of the buildings establish a sense of district as much as neighborhood, a community of buildings that share common attitudes toward design and style. Early homes here—bungalows and Prairie-style houses—were built at the turn of the century, but after the 1920s the majority were instead Colonial Revival and English Tudor. Red Butte Creek runs down a ravine behind some lots on the south side of Yale Avenue, creating a canyon backyard for many of the area's homes, a unique natural feature that enhances the neighborhood and is an important defining element. One important builder and contractor in the Harvard-Yale area was Samuel Campbell, who was responsible for many of the most beautiful homes in the neighborhood after 1913. His most ambitious undertaking to date was the Princeton-Laird cottage district. Campbell bought the land for this development from the Marist Fathers of All Hallows College, who had purchased the land to expand the Catholic parochial school system. Campbell built sixty homes on these streets. Other important builders here were J. A. Shaffer, William E. Hubbard, Graham H. Doxey, Howard Layton, Carl Buehner, and Gaskell Romney.

Westmoreland Place
Area of 1300 South and 1500 East
1913

In contrast to the picturesque Revivalism of the Normandie Heights or Harvard-Yale neighborhoods, Westmoreland Place began as a bungalow neighborhood mirroring those typically found in Southern California. In 1913 Earl and Clark Dunshee purchased land east of Westminster Heights (another bungalow subdivision) for the development of an exclusive new neighborhood, which they would call Westmoreland Place after a fashionable bungalow neighborhood in California. They planned for this part of the city at 1500 East and 1300 South to be connected directly with downtown by streetcar lines. Westmoreland Place would offer a respite to white-collar workers from the chaos and traffic of downtown in an accessible and convenient location on Salt Lake City's east side. The neighborhood and its houses were aggressively marketed locally. Newspaper articles mentioned its favorable location on the route to the new country club, highlighting the two shrub- and flower-filled

Westmoreland Place

parks that would be built at its entrance along 1000 South and 1500 East, appealing to the middle class and easily accessible by streetcar lines. Sales were brisk and by the time of World War I, the company had sold twenty houses. Construction slowed during the war years but by 1922 another seven houses were built. The Dunshees designed houses using California pattern books and prototypes from Southern California, with a narrow selection of floor plans and materials. The result was a visually varied and texturally pleasing neighborhood with modest-sized Period Revival cottages inter-mixed with the predominantly Arts and Crafts bungalows. Westmoreland Streets physically manifested the Arts and Crafts philosophy about neighborhood and the total environment.

Crossroads District

Technical High School / West High School
241 North 300 West
1911
Lewis Telle Cannon and John Fetzer
During the decades of the Perpetual Emigration Fund, pioneers poured into Utah Territory, funded in part by the LDS Church. When they first arrived in Salt Lake City they camped at Union Square on 300 North and 300 West. At this way sta-tion and temporary resting spot, newcom-ers oriented themselves to the rest of the valley and made plans to settle elsewhere in the territory.

When the original plat of the city was drawn, this block was designated for educa-tional purposes. West High School is on the west side of the block. Over time a series of educational facilities were located here, including the University of Deseret, the State School for the Deaf, Dumb, and Blind,

a grade school, Union Public School, and finally Salt Lake High School. In 1911–12, the city built the Technical High School on the west edge of the block, and a little more than a decade later, West High School. Utah architects Cannon and Fetzer designed the Technical High School building, easily the finest example of a Prairie-style educational building in Utah.

The Technical High School reflected the community's dedication to preparing students for work in the skilled trades in the spirit of the Arts and Crafts move-ment, popular at the turn of the century and embodied in the Prairie style itself. Eventually West High School absorbed its industrial arts curriculum, which was on par with that of comparable schools in other parts of the country. Wood turning, carpentry, machinery, pattern making, a finishing forge, and a foundry were on the first floor. On the second floor was space for exhibitions and lecture halls, as well as areas for drafting, carving, and study-ing. The school added a wing in 1920 that housed a general shop, an auto repair shop, space for sheet metal work, and welding and electrical shops.

Unlike many turn-of-the-century Utah architects, Lewis Telle Cannon and John Fetzer were professionally trained. Born in Salt Lake City in 1872, Cannon studied architecture at MIT, graduated in 1896 with a bachelor of science in architecture, and practiced architecture between 1905 and 1909 in Salt Lake City. In 1909 he joined John Fetzer, a Bavarian who had completed a five-year course in architecture in 1903. When he first came to Salt Lake City, Fetzer worked for Richard Kletting, another Ger-man immigrant, and for a period for Walter Ware and Alberto Treganza. Cannon and Fetzer worked together until 1937, when both men became partners with their sons.

Technical High School / West High School

Salt Lake Hardware Building
155 North 400 West
1905
William H. Lepper (original); FFKR (renovation)

It is important to consider the size of the Salt Lake Hardware Building relative to others built during the early twentieth century. The *Salt Lake Tribune* boasted in 1909 that it was "the largest building in the United States west of Chicago and there are few others that are larger." The warehouse includes five stories each measuring 280 by 165 feet, for a total of six acres of floor space. According to the *Tribune*, "eight wagons can be driven on the ground floor to load or unload stuff, and at the same time eight cars of freight could be loaded or unloaded and there would be no confusion while the work was going on."[3] Each of the five floors contained an acre of office space and formed the center of operations for a hardware company that distributed products throughout the Intermountain West.

Through an adaptive reuse process, this 1909 five-story warehouse building metamorphosed, resulting in a fully functional office building for the twentieth-first century. Perhaps the most dramatic move was opening the building's central space to allow natural light to pour in and fill the interior. This meant that circulation patterns had to be altered significantly to subdivide the tenant space in new ways. Except for a reception area on the main floor, the interior is filled with exposed heavy-timbered post-and-beam construction with exposed wooden decking on the floor joists, providing a great opportunity to see the way a building works.

Gastronomy Inc. and SLHNet Investments LC bought the building in 1990 when it was in bad shape and poured $15 million into a renovation project directed by FFKR Architects. The original steel chute used to transport orders from the storage rooms to the will-call desk on the first floor is

Salt Lake Hardware Building

now exposed. Modern materials for light
fixtures, atrium railings, and fire doors
were chosen with sensitivity to the historic
integrity of the building. The building was
brought up to code in every aspect, including a complete seismic upgrade.

Although it has changed, you can still
tell that this was once a warehouse, a work-
horse of sorts that required massive timbers
to sustain the weight of its effort. The historic character of the structure was maintained carefully throughout the project; the
rooftop water tower, fire escapes and land-
ings, fire bells, and the south loading dock
were retained and given new uses.

The Utah Heritage Foundation recognized this project in 1997 for its contribution to Salt Lake City's visual environment.

Triad Center
North Temple and 400 West
1980s
Edwards & Daniels Associates
The original plan for the Triad Center development at 400 West and North Temple was
a twenty-six-acre development. Strategically located on Block 84 near the Union

Pacific Depot, Devereaux Mansion, and the
edge of the new Boyer Company's Gateway
Development, it conceptualized an ambitious redesign of an urban neighborhood,
community space, office, restaurant, and
retail complex with a total of 4.5 million
square feet. Part of the original plan for the
Triad Center was a 450-seat live theater,
a 400-seat Omnimax theater, an international bazaar, and a 600-room world-class
hotel. On the south half of the block would
be three residential towers, a film theater
complex, and a retail center. Perhaps the
most ambitious element of all was two forty-
story mixed-use towers that would frame
and visually enhance the termination of west
South Temple to complete the project. The
city restored the Devereaux Mansion on the
site with an urban development grant, and
the northeast corner of the site was built.

Architects Edwards and Daniels
responded formally to the earlier warehouse and industrial complexes that had
been part of the historic environment of the
neighborhood and set a dominant theme
in terms of form, mass, and texture. They
selected masonry and stone to materially

Triad Center

contextualize the new buildings in this historic environment. The scale of openings in the lower levels subtly referred to past forms as well and would be inhabited by small businesses—retail stores, arts and entertainment facilities, and public spaces. The masonry base contrasted with the smooth, taut, glass curtain wall of the main vertical mass of the building. The two were carefully interlocked vertically to express the complex and dynamic relationship between them.

At the beginning of the twentieth-first century, the northeast corner of Triad was converted to the Salt Lake campus of the LDS Business College.

Dancing Clowns Sculpture
North Temple and 300 West (in the median)
1992
Kazuo Matsubayashi
This playful example of public sculpture activates what is traditionally dead space in the center of a busy city street—a traffic median. *Dancing Clowns* is made

of curvilinear stainless-steel pipes that obscure the images of several jolly clown figures. "Spirit of place is everywhere," Kazuo Matsubayashi says of his playful work, and "it is up to us to revive it."[4] Besides clowns, the lines suggest worms, seagulls, and other creatures of the earth. The colors of the striped pattern are those used in the Olympic logo. A longtime beloved professor of architecture at the University of Utah's Graduate School of Architecture, Kazuo Matsubayashi was known for his architectural design and public art as well as his important contribution to the community.

Union Pacific Railroad Station
South Temple and 400 West
1908–1909
Union Pacific Railroad Company
Built within a couple of years of each other, the Rio Grande Depot and Union Pacific Railroad Station are similar in terms of massing. Both buildings are multistory, horizontal, rectangular blocks with a

Union Pacific Railroad Station

dominant central space and flanking wings. The Union Pacific's central room is 100 feet by 136 feet, topped by a domed ceiling with wings that measure 71 by 125 feet, making it look more like a ballroom than a waiting room for travelers, fully in line with the grand chamber of Grand Central Station and other great railroad stations. Employing the most up-to-date building technologies, the walls of the basement are constructed with reinforced concrete with some brickwork. On the exterior, walls on the first level are made of cut gray sandstone over structural walls formed with reinforced concrete.

What most distinguishes the building from those around it is the mansard roof, which is covered with black slate shingles. Fancy metal entablatures and crest work conform to the French Renaissance style, as do small, circular French Second Empire dormers. The cornice is heavily molded, boxed, and bracketed with a molded frieze.

Windows are square, segmented, and Roman arched, some with decorative brick framing in the form of radiating voussoir headers or corbeled square brick frames. The facade includes twin front towers and quoins that define its edges. Although we might identify stone gargoyles with a Gothic cathedral, here they adorn a railroad depot, adding interest and variety. Classical details surrounding the entry canopy, colorful stained-glass windows, and original gas lamps contribute to a building that is lively, original, and elegant.

When it was first built and used as a railroad depot, the interior contained rooms typical of a station—waiting rooms, baggage rooms, ticket offices, clubrooms, and other specialized rooms that provided every service necessary for the modern traveler. French Renaissance details create an elegant interior space including Classical wall pilasters, cartouche motifs at the capitals, round-arched hallways and balcony bays, and Classical treatment of moldings and other decorative elements.

Devereaux Mansion
334 West South Temple
1857
William Paul

The Devereaux Mansion represented affluence at its best in Utah Territory. Built in 1857 by early Utah horticulturist William Staines, just a decade after the pioneers first arrived in the Salt Lake Valley, it was an early center of social life in Utah, complete with two fine garden lots on the sides, each one and a quarter acres. The house deviated from the strict guidelines of the city of Zion in some very basic ways, such

as its orientation and its deeper setback of 130 feet from the street. As such it was the place where visiting dignitaries were often entertained, such as Thomas L. Kane, who visited Salt Lake City in 1858, and Governor Cumming and his "lady friend," who arrived later that year. Brigham Young's son Joseph A. Young bought the house in 1865 for $20,000. Two years later, he sold it to prominent businessman William Jennings. It was Jennings who gave the house the name Devereaux in honor of the family estate in Yardley, near Birmingham, England.

William Jennings lived with his two wives, Jane and Priscilla, and their twenty-five children in the Devereaux Mansion after 1865. Jennings was famous for his fancy parties, where he entertained national figures and local celebrities alike. After the Civil War, William Seward, who was then

Devereaux Mansion

secretary of state, visited the Devereaux Mansion with Brigham Young. General Philip H. Sheridan visited Jennings's home when he came to Utah to "insure federal authority." President Ulysses S. Grant, General William T. Sherman, and President Rutherford B. Hayes also spent time at the house.

One of the original board members of ZCMI, Jennings was involved in stock raising; he built a tannery when he first arrived in Utah and supplied mining camps with meat for decades. After succeeding in each of these businesses, in the 1860s he branched out into merchandising, banking, and brokerage. When Jennings bought Stainses' house and property he purchased land that encompassed more than half the city block, and the entire frontage running along South Temple. Fruit trees were razed from the area in front the house and the grounds were transformed into more ornamental, formal gardens. Iron gates were added to an entrance that included a broad carriageway leading to the front door. The interior was reworked as well. Again, speaking to wealth, albeit relative to the context of pioneer Utah, the fireplace, windows, and other woodwork were engraved with vines, flowers, and various designs,

featuring the artistry of Ralph Ramsey, one of the finest wood carvers in the territory. As was so popular in Utah, the wood was faux painted to resemble oak.

Delta Center / Energy Solutions Center / Vivint Arena
301 West South Temple
1991
FFKR

When it was built, this arena created a new home for the Utah Jazz and replaced the Salt Palace's more outdated space; the Vivint Arena is in the heart of Salt Lake City's historic Gateway district. Named the Delta Center, Energy Solutions Center, or Vivint Arena based on corporate sponsorship, the building commands attention on an entire city block west of downtown Salt Lake City. Historically the site of the rich ethnic neighborhoods of the warehouse district, the Vivint Arena sits kitty-corner from the Union Pacific Railroad Station. Linked spatially as well with the axis that runs toward Abravanel Hall and the Salt Palace, the building is part of an urban network that runs in each direction. Besides being a beautiful glittering box, the building is distinguished by its orientation to the lot. Placed on a diagonal, challenging the strict

Delta Center / Energy Solutions Center / Vivint Arena

Japanese Church of Christ

rectangularity so characteristic of the city, the Vivint Arena demands attention.

The Vivint Arena is experienced like a very large lantern surrounded by heavily landscaped plazas. Rotated to a forty-five-degree angle on the city grid, it is distinguished by style, size, and materiality. The plaza in front now has its own light rail station and addresses the city from an unusual vantage point, providing a view of the mountains to the northeast, the cityscape, and other important landmarks such as Temple Square downtown. It is at the center of a historic thoroughfare and transportation hub, which extends to the east and links the arena to the Salt Palace Convention Center. The Vivint Arena benefits from this proximity to urban areas and the business, public, and social activities that carry on just blocks away.

The building's transparency exposes the activities inside to the street, tempting the city to join in. Principal circulation areas—stairs, elevators, and escalators—are found on the periphery of the arena and permit smooth circulation of crowds at basketball games, hockey matches, and concerts.

Although it's a tough call, the Vivint Arena is best read at night when it seems to fill with light, or in the early evening when the images of nearby buildings move across its surfaces like fleeting images in a mirror. The Utah AIA awarded FFKR a 1993 Award for Excellence in Architecture for its design of the Delta Center.

Japanese Church of Christ
268 West 100 South
1924
E. Chytraus

Utah's Japanese American community has made an important contribution to the state's history. Reflecting significant religious and cultural diversity, the community included a number of Christians as well as Buddhists, many of whom had converted while in Japan or upon their immigration to the United States. San Francisco was home to the first Japanese Christian Church in 1877, initially an independent group without any affiliation to a sect or church organization. During the 1880s when Presbyterians, Methodists, and other Protestant groups were engaged in missionary work in the West, they established missions for the Japanese in San Francisco. It was not, however, until October 1918 that the Japanese Christian Church was founded in Salt Lake City through a collaboration of Congregational churches and Japanese Presbyterian churches along the Pacific Coast. Two men—Reverend M. Kobayashi and Reverend H. Toyatome—organized the church and began missionary activity themselves, spreading throughout the West into Idaho, Nevada, Wyoming, and Colorado to try to recruit new members. They started a Sunday School and a Bible class and in 1953 divided the congregation into Issei, or first generation, and Nisei, second generation Japanese branches, a division they maintained until 1967. Local Japanese and American citizens, the Presbyterian Board, and the American Missionary Association funded the building.

Reflecting Protestant and Christian heritage instead of ethnicity, the Japanese Church of Christ most resembles a Gothic Revival church, with pointed Gothic arches, stone tracery in the windows, and an irregular and asymmetrical facade. This modest red brick building is a single story and includes a main rectangular wing with the gable end facing the street and a cross wing that houses smaller rooms.

Intermountain Buddhist Church
247 West 100 South
1924, demolished 1981
In subtle ways, Asian motifs hinted at the function of the Intermountain Buddhist

Church from the exterior. A projecting portico resembling a Shinto shrine came to a peak from a slightly pitched gable above a doorway framed with heavy timbers. Built in 1924 and dedicated on December 7 of that year, the building serviced Salt Lake City's Japanese Buddhist population until it was demolished in the fall of 1981. It was across the street from the Japanese Church of Christ in the historic Japan Town, the Nihonjin-Machi neighborhood of the west side. When the Japanese government lifted its ban on emigration to the United States, the first Japanese men came to Utah seeking employment on the railroad or in agricultural work. In fact, the census of 1900 listed 417 Japanese—11 women and 406 men—a number that increased to 2,000 by 1910 and 3,000 by 1920. Japanese Americans shared a rich community life that turned inward instead of outward to the rest of Salt Lake City. Raising vegetable gardens on the interior of their city blocks typified the way they created their own world amid the Mormon hegemony of downtown Salt Lake City. Most members of the Japanese community were Buddhist; this Buddhist church was an important community institution and center, the symbol of both faith and religious commitment. Tucked closely between a pair of two-story commercial and apartment buildings, the Buddhist Church was plastered over to create a smooth exterior wall.

N. O. Nelson Manufacturing Company / Salt Lake Stamp Company / Dakota Lofts
380 West 200 South
1923
Scott and Welch
Changes made during an adaptive reuse project are usually relatively hidden beneath the established exterior of a building, but on the Dakota Lofts the change is exposed

on the exterior. Architects Carl W. Scott and George Welch originally designed the building for the N. O. Nelson Manufacturing Company, a 1923 heating and plumbing supply firm that occupied the building until 1958, when it was purchased by Salt Lake Stamp. It proved perfectly adaptable to a variety of different types of business uses.

This five-story structure has a rectangular plan and a structural system based on a steel frame and reinforced concrete, the most modern technologies of its time. During the late twentieth-century renovation, the structure was exposed. The historical concrete system created a grid of vertical and horizontal elements. The facade includes vertical supports that read like Classical pilasters and create three bays. Each bay forms a rectangle and includes twelve windows and horizontal concrete banding. This same type of treatment wraps around and articulates the side elevations as well. Additional decoration was applied to the facade, and rock-faced modern ornamental patterns are found on the vertical concrete pilaster forms.

Saint Vincent de Paul Center / The Road Home
427 West 200 South
Gillies Stransky Brems Smith Architects

Important to the city as a symbol of hope and caring for Salt Lake City's homeless population, the Saint Vincent de Paul Center is found in a transitional neighborhood of warehouse conversions among deteriorating and forgotten buildings on the southern edge of the Gateway development. Designed and constructed with pro bono services, the building is in large measure a gift to the city. It provides shelter and hundreds of hot meals daily to homeless individuals along with clothing and counseling for transients, victims of domestic abuse, and children.

The building itself is quite straightforward in design—a chapel at one corner is the focal point, offering a spirit of hope. A protected courtyard moving off from the space at the street where the homeless line up for their meals creates a sense of entrance into the center. A full-service kitchen, used for a variety of different meals and events, is also key to the center's function. The site provides space for homeless individuals to sit in the sun or rest before they move throughout the city.

Henderson Block
375 West 200 South
1897–1898
Walter E. Ware

Wilber S. Henderson's career typified the self-made man. He began his career in freighting at age seventeen. After coming to Utah from Colorado to purchase cattle for the railroad, in 1889 Henderson joined forces with his uncle Chester S. Henderson in the Henderson Company, a retail grocery business. Most of Utah's earliest grocery owners operated their stores out of small buildings, growing their own produce or buying it directly from local farmers. During the 1870s and 1880s, cooperative stores were formed under the auspices of ZCMI, creating a network of related businesses. Non-Mormon merchants had a difficult time competing.

With Silas W. Eccles, Henderson purchased land along a major rail line at the intersection of 200 South and 400 West. The next year, Henderson secured a business permit for a "brick and stone warehouse, 3 stories, $2000, W. E. Ware, architect." The building, long recognized as one of the most handsome produce warehouses in the district, was completed in 1898.

The Henderson Block's three-part elevation reflects the Palazzo Medici or other

Henderson Block

secular buildings of the Renaissance. Formally, the building presents the basic vocabulary of an early twentieth-century commercial building: a clearly articulated division between the main floor's large rusticated stones, Roman arches, and string course; the second level's more carefully incised stones and paired window groups; and the prominent cornice level with a small pediment over the central entrance. The warm, rich sandstone and other building materials create an attractive and commanding presence.

The Henderson Company didn't occupy the building immediately but instead rented it to another wholesale grocery company, the Cosgriff-Enright Company. After his own business had grown, in 1906 Henderson moved it into his own building. The Utah Liquor Control Commission also occupied the building for a time.

The building first transformed through adaptive reuse in 1977 for the Clark Leaming Furniture store. For a few years, Fuggles brew pub occupied part of the space. In the mid-1990s, Gillies Stransky Brems Smith Architects renovated and reconstructed the one-hundred-year-old Henderson Block from a restaurant into 14,500 square feet of office space for what is described as a "multidisciplinary design firm." Located in the Gateway district of Salt Lake City, this building celebrates the past while acknowledging the demands of the present—the best in sustainable design.

Artspace / California Rubber and Tire Company
353 West 200 South
1910/1996
Celebrating Artspace's mission of creating affordable housing in Salt Lake City's

historic west-side neighborhood, the Utah AIA honored its adaptive reuse of the California Tire and Rubber Company building with an Award for Excellence in Architecture in 1996. The transformation of the historic warehouse space into fifty-three apartment units of affordable housing and commercial space extended the life of this industrial building and converted it into a vibrant community center. Considerable flexibility on the part of the local building officials and lending institutions facilitated this innovative project, which contributed significantly to the revitalization of this urban neighborhood. In combination with two other adaptive reuse projects in the immediate vicinity—Twirl Town Toy to the east and the Salt Lake Stamp Company building to the north—it stimulated the revitalization of the west side.

The ground level of the California Tire and Rubber Company building contains fifteen thousand square feet of commercial and retail space, as well as five residential units. Tenants on this level include two retail spaces. The upper three levels are apartments—one-, two-, and three-bedroom units as well as studio spaces. A skylight-capped atrium extends the full length of the building and houses elevated walkway entrances into each of the units. An exterior walkway moves through the building and creates midblock pedestrian access to Pierpont.

The building utilized modern technologies when built. It features a concrete post-and-beam structure with concrete floors and masonry infill panels on the north and south walls. Windows and balconies were created by large openings cut into the exterior walls. Floors were removed to create the atrium and to bring light into the corridor. Freestanding concrete beams were exposed in the space, as were concrete and

masonry, piping, conduits, and ductwork. What was once a dark and unappealing warehouse space was transformed into an environment filled with interest and light.

Crane Building
307 West 200 South
1910
Ware and Treganza

First well known outside Salt Lake City, the Crane Company manufactured metal pipe fittings based in Chicago and expanded its operations throughout the United States. By the late nineteenth century it had expanded the products it offered to include valves, fittings, steam warming systems, and hydraulic elevators. In addition, Crane engineers performed premier metallurgical research in the company's chemical laboratory.

Crane hired a team of talented Utah architects, Ware and Treganza, to design a building to house its Utah operations in 1910. During the early twentieth century, money from Utah mines poured into local businesses and cities. The Crane Company led the way by providing up-to-date plumbing, heating, and engineering equipment. Although most of the area's building projects would be hidden from view, many projects used Crane supplies.

The Crane Building is a five-story rectangular industrial building with a full basement. When it was built it was described as having fireproof construction; it had a steel frame wall-bearing system and had an elevator shaft made of plaster blocks, like similar buildings in Chicago. The first floor was used for offices and a machine shop, and the upper levels as a warehouse. The name of the company is displayed on the raised parapets of the north and east facades. In the late 1970s the state renovated the building for use as office space for

the Utah State Historical Society for a few
years before these offices were moved to the
Rio Grande Railroad Depot.

Free Farmers' Market / Artspace
325 West Pierpont Avenue
1910
Samuel T. Whitaker

The energy and leadership around Artspace
inspired the movement to save the historic
west side of Salt Lake City. An institution
as well as a place, Artspace began as an
artists' co-op in the late 1970s with sculptor
Stephen Goldsmith at the helm. Artspace
successfully renovated the Free Farmers'
Market, reconfigured the space into artists'
studios and apartments, and reclaimed
the blighted land behind for a community
garden, demonstrating its characteristic
ethic of community revitalization and dedication to urban change. Artspace sponsors
a range of community projects including
an art program for underprivileged kids,
the Bridges project—a multicultural ethnic
center for the neighborhood—and various
other warehouse conversion projects, perhaps the most successful across the center
of the block, the California Rubber and Tire
complex.

In 1910, the home for Artspace was
the Free Farmers' Market, built by the
Eccles-Browning Investment Company for
$100,000. Before that, farmers had typically
sold their wares from wagons parked at various locations throughout town. The Free
Farmers' Market was a permanent location
and allowed wholesale operations of various
firms. The farmers resisted efforts to regu-
late them and built their own facility farther
south, between 400 and 500 South. Most
of the original occupants were wholesale
dealers—S. B. Clark, "wholesale meat, produce, commission agents"; Fallas, Price, and
Richardson, "wholesale meat and produce";

Free Farmers' Market / Artspace

W. I. Frank, "fruit, produce, and commission
agent"; Hancock Brothers Fruit, "wholesale"; Hanes-Vinegar, "produce"; E. L. Price
Commission Company, "produce and commission agents." Today the loading dock that
runs the length of the building is a sidewalk
and porch where colorful metal chairs create a lively community space. The railroad
spur ran along the building to the west.

MSJN Architects received an award of
excellence from the Utah State Historical
Society for the adaptive reuse of the city
center warehouse for Artspace at 230 South
500 West, a renovation of the original 1905
ZCMI warehouse.

Denver and Rio Grande Railroad Depot
300 South Rio Grande
1910
Henry S. Schlachs

The Denver and Rio Grande Railroad Depot was the historic gateway for immigrants coming to settle in the Salt Lake Valley. In the decades after it was constructed, thousands of Greeks, Japanese, Slavs, and other ethnic groups came in on trains, carrying their entire lives in carefully guarded bags to build homes in this desert environment, many taking temporary residence in the neighborhoods nearby. Also the scene of departing soldiers for the two World Wars, the depot is a fitting backdrop for the passage of time, and a poignant reminder of the importance of transportation to the shifting tides of history.

Utah historians point to the coming of the railroad as a landmark moment in the stream of Utah's history. There is no more significant date marking the end of one era and the beginning of a new one in the nineteenth-century history of this place, for the railroad connected Utah to the world outside, causing irreversible changes that went far beyond the worst fears of Brigham Young. The waiting rooms of the grand railroad station feel more like ballrooms than a pragmatic or even usable space, but these were the transition points or thresholds for immigrants who came here to find work in Utah's mines, businessmen who came to impact the economy, and a steady stream of outside forces—new technologies, styles, and tastes that would change the way the state was built.

The Denver and Rio Grande Railroad Depot is at the nexus of 300 South and 500 West, near a cluster of homeless shelters, warehouse renovations, and new small businesses, and it still forms a commanding presence on Salt Lake's west side. Henry S.

Denver and Rio Grande Railroad Depot

Schlachs of Chicago designed the building in 1910, competing with the Union Pacific, but ran out of money during the process.

This Beaux Arts building is exuberant in every way—in its monumental scale, in the spaces it creates, and in its detailing and form: stone quoins at the corners, Roman-arched front window bays, keystones (one has a stone eagle), stone medallions, and stone balustrades across the level of the second floor. Square windows and door bays are found throughout the building with decorative stone lintels and frames, and deeply recessed bays.

Although it might seem like a tremendous amount of wasted space when you first enter it, the waiting room at the center of the building might have been the largest and most grand interior space some immigrants had experienced, a place where tired travelers waited for their trains or anticipated their new home. Measuring 144 feet long by 83 feet wide and rising to a height of 58 feet from floor to ceiling, this huge room is lit by three large arched windows on each side (about 28 by 30 feet) with green opalescent glass. Classical details and a color scheme of a subtle brownish red and gray for the walls with a deep brown for the ceiling result in a quiet, dignified atmosphere that filters through the room.

Originally the side wings provided all the necessary space to support a railroad depot—baggage, express, and parcel rooms, a men's smoking room, a women's retiring room, a restaurant, and so forth. In the center of the large waiting room were the ticket offices, newsstands, and telegraph and telephone offices.

Today, however, the Utah State Historical Society occupies much of the interior space, and displays fill the central room with memories of the state's past. It was used in the 2010s as an art gallery. The

State Historic Preservation Office, Antiquities Office, and administrative offices are located in the building's two wings.

Ford Motor Building
280 South 400 West
1923
Albert Kahn

The Ford Motor Building is one of the best examples in town of the exciting potential of shifting perspective on an old building through adaptive reuse and bringing it new life. From the exterior of this typical industrial structure, you have no suggestion of the excitement that awaits you inside. But as soon as you walk in the door, you know. This is a building that demands that you touch its walls, stop and look up and around corners, peek into intriguing windows that tempt you; it sweeps you through the space with curving walls and a dramatic skylight and truss system. It is a building best experienced. It is also a sort of teacher. Who wouldn't want to work in this building? You suspect that every day you would discover something new, maybe even better than the day before. It teaches us to expect more and better things out of our buildings, designers, and architects.

When the Ford Motor Building was built in 1923, it housed an assembly plant. Since then it has been used for a variety of different enterprises. Designed by a nationally known architect of industrial complexes, Albert Kahn, it was one of many buildings he designed for Ford, part of a group of elegant industrial structures.

Gastronomy Inc. bought the building and hired FFKR to design an adaptive reuse of the building in the early 2000s. Some elements of the original design were preserved to qualify the project for tax credit incentives. The first tenant in the newly configured building was a communications

Holy Trinity Church

was divided according to need. Although earlier generations of warehouses might have been built with heavy timbers and brick, this innovative use of reinforced concrete expanded the possibilities, resulting in a relatively fireproof building complete with brick and glass curtain walls, Classical ornamentation, and huge interior spaces. Reinforced concrete also facilitated wider gaps between load-bearing elements such as columns, opening up more space for windows.

A straightforward rectangular mass, the Ford Building measures 164 by 264 feet and includes 85,000 square feet, a stone and concrete foundation, a reinforced concrete structure, and two-story exterior walls of brick. Capitalizing on the natural features of this warehouse space, designer Louis Ulrich played with the dramatic potential of exposed concrete members, sweeping steel trusses, and large daylight factory windows that fill the interior spaces with light and color. The result has the same effect as a breathtaking cathedral interior—it makes you love architecture and expect seemingly ordinary buildings to be nothing short of wonderful each time you enter.

Holy Trinity Church
279 South 300 West
1924
Hyrum Pope and Harold Burton
Greek immigrants first came to Utah because of opportunities promised by Utah mines and railroad construction at the turn of the twentieth century, and they soon accounted for the largest ethnic

group that owned a group of radio stations and the Union Pacific Railroad. A challenge was presented by the installation of a radio station because of the specialized communications equipment, cableways, and isolated sound rooms required.

Positioned perfectly kitty-corner from Pioneer Park and half a block away from the Denver and Rio Grande Railroad Depot, the Ford Motor Building is emblematic of an era when the terminal district was a vibrant industrial section of the city. Its extravagant plate-glass windows look out from the two public elevations.

Always about greater efficiency, Henry Ford's interest in housing several different functions under a single roof is demonstrated effectively with Kahn's design. This building was conceived as a service building that housed automobiles delivered to nearby rail yards. As a warehouse it provided an expansive interior space that

labor force in the state. Many found work through a patron, usually centered in Salt Lake City, who represented local mines, mills, and smelters, which were all experiencing boom years. When they first arrived, they moved into ethnic enclaves near the railroad station, or to mining towns in Carbon or Emery County. In Salt Lake City, in the historic Gateway neighborhood, Greek coffeehouses offered lively Greek music, restaurants, saloons, candy stores, and pastry shops with native goods such as dried octopi, Turkish tobacco, olive oil, goat cheese, figs, and dates, as well as the opportunity to socialize and acclimate to the new world. There were enough Greek immigrants in the area by 1924 for them to build a community church—Holy Trinity—for $150,000 at 300 West and 300 South, a building that testified to their commitment to the religious rites of life and death but also to their need to share religious activities.

Prominent Utah architects Pope and Burton designed Holy Trinity in the shape of a cross using the Byzantine style of lush and contrasting burnished colored brick and brownish-red brick, alternating vertical and horizontal brick courses to create a rich textural surface. It would be hard to imagine a more sensorially rich historic exterior. But the interior is just as exciting and is also dictated by traditional ideas about iconography, the requirements of ritual, and available resources. As was customary, the altar faces east toward the rising sun, the source of light and the symbol of Christ. A central dome is adorned by a cross, as are the two tower belfries to the sides of the central entrance door. Four heavy doors lead to the interior space lit by candles. The columns supporting the dome symbolize the physical representation of the link between heaven and earth. Icons on each of the columns represent the four Evangelists and their traditional symbols—Saint Matthew, the winged man; Saint Mark, the lion; Saint Luke, the ox; and Saint John, the eagle. Above the altar is the icon representing the Virgin Mary and the Christ child, called the Platyera. Flat icons or pictures rather than sculptures decorate the interior space, and these objects of worship are visual reminders of church doctrine and faith.

Old Pioneer Fort Site / Pioneer Park
300 South to 400 South, 300 West to 400 West
1847 (fort); 1890s (park)

In some ways, Pioneer Park is the historic heart of the city. The first pioneers to arrive in the Salt Lake Valley started to build a fort in August 1847. Capitalizing on the dry, hot weather, they were finished the next month. The seven-foot walls were three feet thick at the bottom and reduced in width toward the top. The settlers constructed them cooperatively with adobe bricks they had made themselves that were eighteen inches long by six inches wide by twelve inches thick. Interior rooms or the equivalent of individual cabins were formed with logs and adobe bricks, and their flat roofs sloped toward the center of the fort.

As many as 160 families could live in the fort at any given time. The rainy months in the fall and the severe winter challenged the structure. The roofs leaked badly, and many pioneer women, such as Zina Diantha Huntington Smith Young, recorded in their journals that they held up umbrellas at night to protect their children from the rain and melted snow that freely entered their flimsy shelter. Various diaries also mention women holding umbrellas while they cooked over fires in their stoves. Mice and other critters plagued the pioneer families as well. Despite the severe difficulties, families felt lucky to have rooms at the fort. Many others lived in

Old Pioneer Fort Site / Pioneer Park

tents, wagons, or other makeshift shelters until more permanent homes could be built, and they had it even worse.

Besides the rain and the rodents, they had no privacy because all openings in the walls faced into the central courtyard. Despite the humble conditions at the fort, on December 9, 1848, the settlers held a meeting in the rooms of Heber C. Kimball to organize the provincial State of Deseret, and they held the first territorial government elections in an adobe school constructed in the fort. Eventually they built a second fort two blocks south of the first, and additional houses to the north. For years after it was no longer used as a fort, new immigrants used the block as a campground.

On July 24, 1898, the city dedicated the block as Pioneer Park. During the Reform Era, public parks became a much desired and valued public amenity. For a while, it had a public swimming pool, among other attractions.

Chapman Library
577 South 900 West
1917
Don Carlos Young

This Classical Revival one-and-a-half-story building sits proudly on the corner at 577 South and 900 West. Two seventy-five-foot wings form an *L* connection at the corner, which is highlighted by a grand staircase and entrance portico. A distinctive stone belt course caps the red brick wall. Windows and the entrance door have sweeping arches above with Gothic tracery. Referencing the Classical style, double Doric columns are found on both sides of the entrance, topped by a plain entablature and parapet that rises above.

Brigham Young and Emily Dow Partridge Young's grandson Don Carlos Young designed the plans while employed by Joseph Don Carlos Young. From the beginning, the library was praised for its contribution to Salt Lake City's west-side neighborhoods. The *Deseret News* on May 28, 1918, identified its significance as "the beginning of the greatest social, intellectual and civic development the west side of the city has yet known." Steel magnate and philanthropist Andrew Carnegie believed that those with wealth should serve those without. He articulated the view that the public library was the key to an informed citizenry and a powerful means of "moral elevation."[5]

Downtown

Salt Palace 2000 Expansion
Between Abravanel Hall and 300 West on South Temple
Edwards & Daniels Associates

Like other convention centers in major American cities, the Salt Palace dominates a city block. Spreading like an organism, the building seized the streetscape on West and South Temple, eventually moving along 300 West across from the Delta Center. Edwards & Daniels Associates designed the 2000 expansion of the Salt Palace between Abravanel Hall and 300 West along South Temple, made possible by a land trade between the Salt Palace and the Holiday Inn. Traveling over 200 West in a sort of sky bridge structure, this 150,000-square-foot addition to the Salt Palace makes it possible for traffic to flow uninterrupted beneath the meeting space. In anticipation of growth from the original design of the building, its linear scheme opened the door to future expansion. The hotel to the west

benefited from the midblock pedestrian access that connected the hotel to the circulation system of the convention center. The expansion created a new front door to the exhibition space—a huge display facility to South Temple. The city also benefited from this facility, as it activated the western part of South Temple.

Abravanel (Symphony) Hall
123 West South Temple
1979
FFKR

Dramatically challenging the strict regularity of the grid, Abravanel Hall forms a sweeping and elegant contrast with the rest of the city, moving on the diagonal toward the center of the block. The Utah Symphony first organized in 1936, but it was after 1947 and under director Maurice Abravanel that the symphony received national acclaim. After Abravanel's 1979 retirement, the symphony moved from its home at the historic Mormon Tabernacle to Abravanel Hall, with Varujan Kojian as the new director and conductor.

The concert hall provides seating for 2,820 people in a rectangular auditorium that has been acclaimed for its acoustical quality. Abravanel Hall is dimensionally similar to the Avery Fisher Hall, the Minnesota Orchestra Hall, and the Kennedy Center in Washington, D.C. Deviating from tradition, the auditorium space eliminates a central aisle and uses continental seating for the orchestra level, which provides more comfortable leg room and seating in the center. Tiered seating in continuous sloping rows provides an unrestricted view of the musicians' platform.

But as important as comfort, what one really notices when one enters the auditorium is the hall's extraordinary beauty. Wood covers most surfaces and was chosen

Bicentennial Commission citation in 1980 and architects FFKR won an Honor Award from the AIA for the Western Mountain Region that same year. The Utah Heritage Foundation gave the project an Award of Merit in 1979.

Abravanel Hall is the centerpiece of the $18 million Bicentennial Arts Complex and the home of the Utah Symphony. Dedicated in September 1979, the complex includes the Salt Lake Art Center and the Capitol Theatre at 24 West 200 South, which houses the Utah Opera Company and Ballet West.

Temple Square
Block defined by South Temple, Main Street, North Temple, and West Temple
1857

Temple Square forms the heart of the city. All roads radiate out from the southeast corner of this block in every direction following Orson Pratt's survey of the city in 1847. Creating a visual separation from other city blocks with daunting fifteen-foot walls, the ecclesiastical buildings of Temple Square are living chronicles of Mormon history—a story of sacrifice, devotion, and belief. Temple Square is a ten-acre block surrounded by an adobe wall sitting on a sandstone base that was built in 1857 through Brigham Young's public works program to put newcomers to work, and it was partially rebuilt in the 1960s.

For the Church of Jesus Christ of Latter-day Saints, Temple Square functions as a sort of Vatican City, or the Mother Church of the Church of Christ, Scientist, in Boston. It is the center of the international church network, from Block 88 to the east and Main Street Plaza in between. Sacred space for the Mormons, for outsiders it is a beautiful space for contemplation apart from the busy city streets. It is rich in history, with

Abravanel (Symphony) Hall

for its optimal reverberation and mixture of tones and overtones. The gold leaf on the banisters and railings creates an extravagant and sensual entrance, and chandeliers with individual crystals light up the center of the space.

Abravanel Hall's lobby allows patrons to move through the vertical space and experience it from a variety of different levels, providing breathtaking views of the cityscape, Temple Square, the rooftop spires of Assembly Hall, and the plaza fountain in front, creating a sparkling, glittering world of culture and art. The hall reads like a massive wedge of glass and granite-like brick, a sweeping angle in the extreme gridded regularity of downtown Salt Lake City. Abravanel Hall received a Utah American

Temple Square

some of the most architecturally unusual and significant buildings in the city, and it holds a special significance for believers.

Temple Square is home to some of Utah's most easily recognizable buildings—the temple, tabernacle, and Assembly Hall are sentimental favorites in the state and appear on countless objects of material Mormonism—quilted into blankets, etched into glass, and inscribed onto jewelry. These buildings represent home and heart, the center of the Mormon world.

Assembly Hall
Southwest Corner of South Temple and West Temple
1877–1882
Obed Taylor
It is virtually impossible for a building to hold its own in the context of the Salt Lake Temple and Tabernacle, but the Assembly

Hall gives it a great try. The design Obed Taylor created for the Assembly Hall is more completely Gothic Revival than the temple and is intended for a different purpose. Rather than the special sacred rituals that play out in the temple, or the General Conferences that were held for more than a century in the tabernacle, this 120-by-68-foot building had more modest intentions. Originally designed in 1880 to accommodate overflow crowds from the tabernacle, it has historically been used for stake conferences and for cultural events throughout the year by different congregations.

Many of the early LDS Church architects like Angell, Folsom, and Ward were familiar with national styles. They had traveled through Europe either to do missionary work or to look at ecclesiastical architecture, and some had worked on Mormon temples in Kirtland and Nauvoo. Obed Taylor had already distinguished himself by helping to design the facade of the ZCMI structure on Main Street, and here he used Gothic Revival vocabulary. Henry Grow, designer of the truss system for the tabernacle, also worked on this building. The Assembly Hall has a square interior with spires on a series of levels running along the periphery of the roof rather than the more traditional rectangular shape of a Gothic church. Eight octagonal buttresses and eight square pilasters support handsome Victorian Gothic pinnacles. The building has a sandstone foundation and rusticated and relatively rough granite for the walls. The tallest spire rises 130 feet into the center of the building.

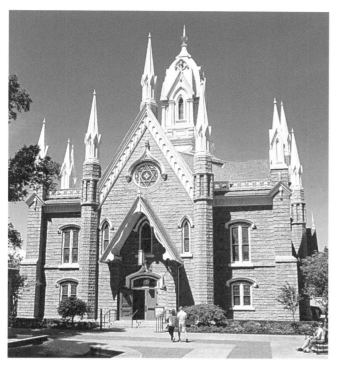

Assembly Hall

dictating design, craftsmanship, and construction technology and poured the best local resources into the project, engaging the most skilled and talented architects, draftsmen, stonemasons, and other craftsmen to work on the project over several years.

The Salt Lake Temple is an unquestionable landmark, a monument to the sacrifice of the Mormon settlers, their industry, and their devotion to God. Brigham Young identified the site for the temple four days after the first band of pioneers entered the valley, placing his cane on the ground and adamantly maintaining, "Here we shall build a temple to our God." The Salt Lake Temple was to be Brigham Young's shining moment, the focal point of the city and the physical representation of the Mormons' ecclesiastical power. Church members laid the cornerstone on April 6, 1853, and dedicated the temple on April 6, 1893.

The LDS Church renovated the building between 1980 and 1983. At that time, builders refashioned the trusses, installed a new hardwood floor, and added elaborate draperies and a ceiling accented by gold leaf designs that brought new life and beauty to the interior of this historic structure.

Salt Lake Temple
50 West North Temple, Temple Square
1853–1893
Truman O. Angell

Church architects Truman O. Angell and Joseph Young oversaw the construction of the Salt Lake Temple during a period that spanned four decades. Just about every major figure in architecture employed in the state during these years contributed in one way or another to the project. Brigham Young himself played an important role in

Like many early general authorities of the LDS Church, Brigham Young was familiar with the Gothic and Romanesque styles because he had gone on missions to England between 1839 and 1841. British landmarks like Westminster Abbey, the Tower of London, and Worcester Cathedral made an impression on Young. The walls of the temple are rich with religious iconography and symbolism from Mormonism as well as other familiar religious and philosophical traditions such as Freemasonry. Carvings of the earth, moon, and stars are carved on the exterior walls, reflecting scriptural descriptions of the heavens—"Celestial bodies . . . one glory of

Salt Lake Temple

the corner emphasize the vertical upward sweep of the building. Deeply recessed windows reveal the thickness of the walls, which range from six to eight feet thick and were constructed with granite from Little Cottonwood Canyon. Crenellations along the roofline emphasize as well the strength and permanency of the building, a living physical metaphor for the Mormon kingdom of God.

The dedication of the Salt Lake Temple was an event many Latter-day Saint diarists noted in the daily accounts of their lives. On April 6, 1893, thousands of Mormons from settlements as far away as Cardston in Alberta, Canada, gathered for the hallelujah shout, waving their white handkerchiefs in the air.

Salt Lake Tabernacle
50 West South Temple, Temple Square
1851 (original); 1863–1867 (second)
Truman O. Angell (original); Henry Grow and William Folsom (second)

Less than five years after they first arrived at Utah, and because religious instruction was so integral to the connection between members of the church, the pioneers turned their attention to building a large-scale shelter for religious activities. The pioneers were generally poor, having used their resources to make it to the Salt Lake Valley. Church leaders launched a subscription campaign to gather funds for the tabernacle construction project during the spring of 1851. Brigham Young asked church architect Truman O. Angell Sr. to help with the design. In anticipation of the October conference just around the corner, construction began on May 21, 1851.

Truman Angell, a builder, carpenter, and architect, designed the first tabernacle, along with many others of the first generation of Utah's early buildings. His design

the sun, and another glory of the moon, and another glory of the stars."[6]

Perhaps the most distinctive feature of the Salt Lake Temple is the golden statue of the angel Moroni, the last ancient prophet to write in the Book of Mormon. Sculpted by the well-respected Paris-trained artist Cyrus E. Dallin, the sculpture is highly symbolic and again refers to scripture from the New Testament—"And I saw another angel fly in the midst of heaven, having the everlasting gospel to preach unto them that dwell on the earth."[7]

The six towers and spires form the distinctive signature of the Salt Lake Temple. Buttresses running along the wall or at

Salt Lake Tabernacle

included a wooden truss system of elliptical arches to support the roof without visible columns or posts and to accommodate space for a large congregation. The walls of this first tabernacle to be built at Temple Square were made with adobe bricks.
As with much of the construction during pioneer-era Utah, donated labor, materials, and tithes provided the resources for the building. Though the tabernacle, built on the southwest corner of Temple Square, was finished by the time of the April General Conference, the church had outgrown it before the fund-raising campaign was completed.

Competing with the Salt Lake Temple for the most unusual silhouette on the Salt Lake skyline, the next Salt Lake tabernacle, built in the center of the west side of the square, was a 150-by-250-foot oval with an elliptical roof. Designed by Henry Grow and William Folsom, this unique Remington lattice-truss roof is supported by great wooden arches. The resulting roof rests like a huge inverted bowl on forty-four red sandstone buttresses. Constructed long before the common use of steel girders or other structural members, the tabernacle features instead the crude wooden nails and buckskin braces of pioneer technology.

During the dedication it became clear that the structure had acoustical problems. President Young asked Angell to come up with an innovative solution. His idea was to construct a thirty-foot gallery around the interior wall, supported by two rows of freestanding wooden columns and attached to the wall every twelve to thirteen feet, which prevented echoing and added three thousand more seats. Countless crowds

Brigham Young Monument

Hotel Utah / Joseph Smith Memorial Building

have been entertained by the demonstration of a pin dropping at the front of the room that can be heard at the back.

Overall, the Salt Lake Tabernacle is one of the most unique structures in the state and possibly the region. It testifies to pioneer resourcefulness and is the oldest remaining structure on Temple Square. In 1971, the American Society of Civil Engineers designated it a National Historic Civil Engineering Landmark, making it the first American building to receive this recognition.

This Is the Place Brigham Young Sculpture
Main Street and South Temple
1892–1900
Mahonri Young

Moved at various times during its hundred-year history, the *This Is the Place* sculpture of Brigham Young perhaps rightfully

establishes Utah's first territorial governor in his position in the nineteenth-century history of this place. Alluding to Young's famous statement upon arrival in the Salt Lake Valley that this valley was the place the Mormon pioneers would stop and plant roots, this landmark is the embodiment of myth—one of the foundational stories of this place. Folk tradition has surrounded the statue during its history as well; some say Young is pointing to the former ZCMI department store, asserting its importance in the Mormon world, with his back to Temple Square. Sculpted by Mahonri Young, a nationally known, turn-of-the-century Utah sculptor and descendent of Young himself, this is a first-class example of public art, a constant visual reminder of the past that activates a particular space with a powerful narrative.

Hotel Utah / Joseph Smith Memorial Building
15 East South Temple
1909–1911 (original)
1990s FFKR (adaptive reuse)

When the Hotel Utah was built at the intersection of South Temple and Main Street, it was amid considerable controversy over the demolition of the Bishop's Storehouse—the center of tithing activity for nineteenth-century Salt Lake City. But the Hotel Utah was such a brilliant and extravagant addition to the downtown landscape that it quickly established itself as a new type of landmark—what was once called the "Grande Dame" of Utah hotels. Because the LDS Church was the principal stockholder, the hotel was a focal point of the Mormon-dominated end of Main Street and hosted distinguished visitors to the state for both commercial and religious purposes. Originally a $2 million project, the Hotel Utah was an elaborate expression of the LDS Church's desire to reach out to the world. Although the style of the building's exterior is a very traditional Neoclassical Revival, it was built with the most up-to-date technology of reinforced concrete and steel. Luminously sheathed in white matte–glazed enameled brick, the hotel had lavish detailing throughout consistent with Classical motifs, topped by a typical folk symbol of the state—a substantial plaster and brick beehive cupola.

The LDS Church closed the hotel in 1987. During an adaptive reuse of the old hotel in the early 1990s, local architects FFKR gutted floors and changed eight levels into a more open-plan office environment. The grand lobby and Empire Room on the ground level were extensively renovated but still have the air of a grand hotel. For the most part the exterior historic architectural character was maintained, except on the top floor where the new construction formally completes the original Beaux Arts design.

When the building was rededicated in 1994, its name was officially changed to the Joseph Smith Memorial Building. The project received several awards and distinctions—the Honor Award from the Utah AIA in 1994, the Utah Heritage Foundation Heritage Award in 1993, and the American Consulting Engineers Council, Utah Council, and Engineering Excellence Grand Conceptor Award in 1994.

LDS Church Administration Building
47 East South Temple
1914–1917
Joseph Don Carlos Young and Don Carlos Young

Unlike the taller buildings surrounding it—the Joseph Smith Memorial Building and the LDS Church Office Building—the LDS Church Administration Building is a modest five-story structure. But in terms of first impressions, there is no doubt this is the center of a serious enterprise. Impressive

LDS Church Administration Building

in every way—from its references to an ancient Greek temple with pilasters running around the perimeter to the podium base or grand staircase, to the granite used for its construction—this notable Neoclassical block was built between 1914 and 1917 and serves as the offices for the senior leadership of the Church of Jesus Christ of Latter-day Saints. Before it was built, the church offices were located in a domestic-scale building between the Lion and Beehive Houses, the historic structures constructed under Brigham Young. One might assume the building is of masonry construction because it gives the impression of great weight, but instead it is steel and concrete with stone facing. Twenty-four Ionic pilasters run continuously around the building, each composed of eight tons of granite. The granite used for this building is the same as that quarried for the Salt Lake Temple and used in other buildings in the sacred precinct, a sort of material design motif. Church architects Joseph Don Carlos Young and Don Carlos Young, the son and the grandson of Brigham Young, respectively, designed the building. Joseph Don Carlos was the church's architect between 1880 and 1935.

Lion House
63 East South Temple
1855–1856
Truman O. Angell Sr.
If there is an architectural language of polygamous living, the Lion House speaks it. In fact, the complex of structures including the Beehive and Lion Houses and the outbuildings toward the back exemplify Young's notions about family kingdom. Here his family raised enough food to ideally be self-sufficient. They attended a family school, swam in a pond at the back of the property, and moved through the

many rooms of the family homes. Located within a block of the Salt Lake Theater, in the shadow of the tabernacle and temple block and the Bishop's Storehouse, and surrounded by a rock wall built as a public works project, the physical structures here spoke in tangible terms of belief and human relations. About thirty-five structures originally occupied twenty acres, or two full city blocks. Brigham Young believed all was possible in the Mormon vision of the good life, and here was living proof that he meant to make it happen.

There were no ground rules on how to best house a polygamous family, certainly no handbooks on plural family relations. But Brigham Young was good at solving unusual problems. Although the exteriors

Lion House

of these two houses rely on fairly traditional massing and decoration, the interior arrangement of space indicates the highly complicated familial relationships that transpired within. Arranged as much for efficiency and harmony as anything, the homes have a unique mixture of private and public space, clearly an accommodation to the unusual demands of plural families. The greatest number of family members that ever lived in the Lion House at the same time was twelve wives, nineteen daughters, and eight sons. Another wife and her children lived in the Beehive House. Besides this immediate family, nonconjugal wives, adopted children, and servants lived in the house from time to time.

Brigham's best efforts to spatially organize his family are evident in the ten gables running along the longitudinal sides of the house. Twenty bedrooms on the upper level of the Lion House provided "equal comforts" for his wives and children. Some wives still in their child-bearing years had bedrooms with adjacent sitting rooms on the main floor, which reflected a sort of hierarchy based on child-bearing roles in the family.

Besides plural wives, the Lion House expressed spatially contemporary ideas about physical fitness and health and included closed-in porches so the children could breathe good clean air during the night, gymnastic equipment for the girls, and space for recreation. Connecting passages allowed convenient movement through and between the buildings, exhibiting a lively, creative attitude toward space and building.

Beehive House / President and Governor's Office

The gabled end of this two-story, 45-by-139-foot building faces the street and has a facade. There is a granite Gothic-style entry vestry with cornerstone buttresses and a crenellated balcony parapet above a stone lion crouching on the edge, which was sculpted by William Ward, a family reference to the "Lion of the Lord," as Young's friends called him. In the same way, the beehive cupola at the top of the Beehive House had local relevance as the symbol of Mormon diligence in communal work.

Beehive House / President and Governor's Office
67 East South Temple
1852–1855
Truman O. Angell Sr.

Young built his public residence, the Beehive House, adjacent to the President and Governor's Office in 1855. He lived there with his first plural wife, Lucy Ann Decker, and her seven children between 1855 and 1856. As governor and church president, Young entertained public visitors and made a home in these three conjoined structures. His private office was on the first story in the southwest corner, a room connected to the President and Governor's Office by a private entry. His private bedroom was located just behind. The north end contained a large kitchen and men's dining room.

Between the Lion House and the Beehive House is a single-story President and Governor's Office, built in 1854, which created easy access to Young's office as territorial governor and president of the LDS Church. This smaller building mirrors the same Classical details favored on the two houses on both sides—a gabled roof, boxed cornice and returns, and most importantly, a sense of formality. As was true of the Beehive House, the office had stuccoed adobe brick walls painted a pale yellow.

The Beehive House was built between 1853 and 1855. This two-story house includes Greek Revival and other Classical details, with two main rooms at the front and two at the back on each level. The impression of formality created on the exterior is due in part to the gabled roof, which has paired chimneys on the east and west ends, a bracketed porch cornice, an ornamental roof deck balustrade, and a cupola with the symbolically carved beehive. A widow's walk at the top is reminiscent of those found in East Coast towns, where many of the early Latter-day Saints might have lived. A two-story porch across the full length of the facade was added in 1986.

At the turn of the century the LDS Church purchased the Beehive House from Young's family and used it for the offices and residence of the church president. In 1918, it converted the building into a home for use by single Mormon women until a major restoration was undertaken in 1959.

Eagle Gate
North corner of South Temple and State Street
1859
Ralph Ramsey

An iconographic landmark in town, the Eagle Gate spanned twenty-two feet across State Street at South Temple when built in 1859. It was attached to the eight-foot rock wall that surrounded Brigham Young's personal family estate and that impoverished newcomers built under the public works program. The gate has an interesting history of its own. Originally, it was believed the gate would keep trespassers out of City Creek Canyon, but over time it became a distinctive landmark more celebratory than foreboding. After 1890 the city removed it for a time to facilitate easier travel of streetcars up State Street. In the early twentieth

Eagle Gate

century, a group of concerned citizens lobbied to enlarge the gate and even raised funds for the project. Ralph Ramsey, a craftsman who built much of Brigham Young's furniture and the woodwork in the temple, hand carved the first eagle and a later iteration electroplated in copper, a version that was damaged in 1960 by a trailer-truck accident. The original eagle was placed in the Daughters of Utah Pioneers Museum and a replica placed back on South Temple.

Bransford Apartments / Eagle Gate Apartments
Northeast corner of South Temple and State Street
1903

Salt Lake City's grandest boulevard, South Temple, was distinguished by wealth accumulated in Utah's mines. The Bransford Apartments represented the transition

from a pioneer outpost to a more secular and stratified city. Susanna Bransford, Utah's Silver Queen, built them in 1903 with her brother, John Samuel Bransford, on the site of the historic schoolhouse Brigham Young had built for his children on his family estate. This was prime real estate in downtown Salt Lake City from the first, and wealthy Salt Lakers lived in the apartments, which were fully equipped with the most up-to-date accoutrements including fully modernized kitchens and bathrooms. This six-story building is basically rectangular but moves back and forth from the street facade in a series of recessed spaces to allow better lighting for interior rooms. Built with stone and Classical detailing, the building wraps around the corner and embraces both South Temple and State Street, in one of the best locations in the city.

The equivalent of a local celebrity, Susanna Bransford was easily Utah's

wealthiest woman at the turn of the twentieth century. Accumulating husbands as well
as wealth, she obtained money from mining
interests that she inherited at the death
of her husband Colonel Edwin F. Holmes,
a lumber magnate. Bransford married twice
after her first husband's death, once to a
Russian prince. When she died in 1942 at
eighty-three years of age, she had lived an
extravagant, exciting life.

Elks Club Building
139 East South Temple
1902
Scott and Welch

Fraternal organizations have been important in the state's history, providing the
backdrop for male relationships, networking, and ritual that helped men focus on
developing character and strength as well
as building alliances for entrepreneurial
activity. Sometimes the built environment
reveals larger social realities, exposed in
spatial patterns or practices. The 1902 four-
story Elks Club Building is half a block east
of Brigham Young's Beehive House, the
Lion House, and the Eagle Gate on State
Street, and it expresses the social division non-Mormons felt in this Mormon-
dominated city. Like the Odd Fellows and
the Masons, the Elks organization provided
an alternative to LDS priesthood organizations. At the height of the Elks' prominence
as an organization, this six-story building
was the largest club structure in the state,
serving 3,400 members.

Emphasizing its importance to the
community and built on an elevated site
on South Temple as a monumental piece
of architecture, the Elks Club Building is
imposing. This reinforced concrete structure with a Classically detailed interior was
built for $300,000. Distinguished Utah
architects Carl W. Scott and George W.

Welch designed the building. They were
both engineers before becoming partners
in an architectural firm, and they designed
other revival buildings, including the
Masonic Temple near 700 East on South
Temple, and South High School.

Alta Club
100 East South Temple
1897–1898
Frederick Albert Hale

For more than one hundred years, the
Alta Club has been at the corner of South
Temple and State Street, an anchor in Salt
Lake society. Several well-known Utah politicians, bankers, and businessmen founded
the club in 1883, and the original club
members were primarily mining entrepreneurs and non-Mormons, all of whom
benefited from the social and networking
opportunities of their association. Membership in the Alta Club was exclusive from
the first and was emblematic of the schism
between Mormons and non-Mormons at
the end of the nineteenth century. Over
time, the club opened membership to
Latter-day Saints in business, law, education, and other prominent industries. Since
1987, the Alta Club has welcomed female
members as well.

Architect Frederick Hale, who designed
many of the mansions along South Temple,
picked the Italian Renaissance style for the
Alta Club, a style favored by similar fraternal orders or men's clubs nationally for its
elegance, formality, and grace. The color of
the stone and the overall weightiness of the
building create a different impression from
the Capitol Theatre, another Italian Renaissance building, although the two share a
similar horizontal emphasis. Other prominent and familiar features include arches
over windows and doors, and balconies that
step back in an arcade.

Salt Lake City Public Library / Hansen
Planetarium / O. C. Tanner Company
15 South State
1905
Heins and LaFarge, New York

Within only a few years after settlers first
arrived in Utah Territory, the legislature
solicited federal funding for a territorial
library, adding the stipulation that the state
would hire William C. Staines as librarian.
The Ladies' Literary Club and the Masonic
Orders of Salt Lake City worked vigorously
to promote lending libraries for the public
throughout the late nineteenth century.
In 1898, the Ladies' Literary Club sponsored
a bill in the territorial legislature that provided a tax levy to support public libraries.
The city stored a collection of books in
the City and County Building until mining
magnate John Q. Packard provided both
land and financing for a new building to
house the collection. A perfect expression
of the progressive belief in the redemptive
power of books for moral education, the
library was a symbol of the commitment
of local philanthropists to the cultural and
intellectual life of the citizenry of the city.

A nationally known New York architectural firm—Heins and LaFarge—designed
the Salt Lake City Public Library building
in the Beaux Arts style, a style much preferred at the turn of the century for large
public and commercial buildings. Beaux
Arts exuberance began with the formal
Classical preference for columns, capitals,
and pediments as well as symmetry with

Salt Lake City Public Library / Hansen Planetarium / O. C. Tanner Company

other decorative elements. An elaborate stone gable projects above the roofline. The entrance is announced with a grand pavilion that rises two stories and has columns with decorative keystones.

Social Hall
35 South State Street
1853
Truman O. Angell Sr.

Rounding out Brigham Young's vision for the good life, just half a block away from his home, Salt Lake City's Social Hall was the backdrop for theatricals, dances, banquets, musicals, and other social activities—the scene of public gatherings. Church architect Truman O. Angell Sr. designed the simple 33-by-73-foot rectangular structure, and William Ward (Angell's assistant on the temple) supervised the stonecutters.

As originally constructed, the main floor adobe walls were left unstuccoed and accented with quoins at the corners. A formal entrance staircase was added later and created a more dignified look. The room's main chamber often held as many as 300 to 350 people. Two elegant chandeliers provided lighting from an elliptical ceiling. A stage along the east end featured a bust of Shakespeare in the center of the proscenium.

A decade after it was built, the Salt Lake Theater replaced the Social Hall for theatricals and formal presentations, but the building continued to be used for community-wide events. It was demolished in 1922, but later generations tried to retrieve its historic footprint and acknowledge the ghost of this important pioneer-era building.

In 1990, Zions Securities Corporation hired Cooper Roberts Simonsen and Associates to create a "memory" of the historic structure. During the excavation of a

Social Hall

subterranean passageway under State Street that connected the site with the mall to the west, the construction crew found some of the original stone foundation of the Social Hall. During construction of the walkway, the foundation was moved, but it was later put back in its historic location. A steel framework and glass enclosure reference the historic size and shape of the Social Hall, holding its place on the northern end of State Street.

Mountain States Telephone and Telegraph Building
98 South State
1939

When the Mountain States Telephone and Telegraph Building was first completed in 1939, it was only two stories tall. Telephone service became much more popular, and in response to the demand, four additional stories were added in 1947. Qwest Corporation acquired the company in 2000 and has occupied the building ever since.

The Mountain States Telephone and Telegraph Building is the only important Art Deco building in downtown Salt Lake City. This style is more common in Ogden, although it is still unusual in Utah. This example of the style features the typical shallow wall surface with subtle bas-relief pilasters dividing the facade into narrow bays that emphasize the vertical lines of the building. Contrasting with the vertical sweep, low-relief decorative ornamentation at the top of the first story travels around the building.

Deseret Building / First Security Bank Building
79 South Main Street
1919
Lewis Telle Cannon and John Fetzer
This site has been the scene of a series of bank buildings. First was the Deseret

National Bank in 1875, led by Brigham Young for two years before his death; then the Deseret Building, which replaced the pioneer-era home of the bank in 1919; and currently it is the First Security Bank Building, which resulted from a merger between Deseret National Bank and Security National Bank in 1932.

Utah architects Lewis Telle Cannon and John Fetzer designed the First Security Bank Building. A fourteen-story skyscraper in the Chicago tradition, it has a clear differentiation between the main floors on the ground level, the office shaft, and the prominent cornice that caps off the building, jutting out from the modulated wall surface and highlighting indigenous images in terra-cotta relief—the heads of Indians or buffalo in medallions run along the third level. A massive roof cornice terminates the line of the shaft at the top of the architectural composition. Some described the building as the finest constructed in the state during World War I.

For years, First Security was the commercial bank of the Latter-day Saints in Utah and was the leading bank in the territory until well into the twentieth century.

Zion's Cooperative Mercantile Institution (facade)
15 South Main Street
1876, 1880, 1901
Obed Taylor and William H. Folsom
ZCMI organized in 1868 as part of Brigham Young's effort to combat the growing threat of outside dominance of Utah Territory's economy. The organization was the result of the collective effort of a group of businessmen who pooled their resources to create what would later be called "America's First Department Store." In 1868, ZCMI's headquarters was in the Eagle Emporium building, with departments located in

Zion's Cooperative Mercantile Institution

small false-front stores along Main Street, where the designation "More Holiness to the Lord" and the all-seeing eye announced that this was the store for the Mormon faithful. As much a sign of devotion and loyalty as of wise shopping, support of ZCMI and its local cooperatives became a line drawn in the sand, certainly a boundary between insiders and outsiders. Within a decade, ZCMI included 146 co-ops in 126 different settlements in the area.

Not quite a decade after a group of church leaders and businessmen organized ZCMI in 1876, the new department store was given its own home, bringing the associated businesses under the same roof. Designed in 1876 by Obed Taylor and William Folsom, the building with its cast-iron front spanned seven bays originally, and after additions in 1880 and 1901,

twenty-three bays. Besides the strength added to the building with masonry and load-bearing walls to the sides and back, the cast-iron facade opened it and created decorative moldings surrounding windows and doors, a triangular pediment at the top, and large open windows for the display of material in the store.

ZCMI was all about Brigham Young's desire to create a self-sufficient empire in the West. Combating the perceived power of non-Mormon businessmen who came into the state with the railroad, ZCMI provided state goods and convenience to local shoppers. Shopping at ZCMI was yet another way Mormons could prove their faithfulness. The all-seeing eye that appeared on the fronts of many cooperatives throughout the territory was a poignant reminder that this was the people's store, the official merchandising institution of the LDS Church.

Cast-iron facades were first used in the United States in the early 1840s. Greatly strengthening the structure of a masonry building, cast-iron walls opened window space significantly and allowed light to freely move into offices and store display rooms. ZCMI's architects, Obed Taylor and William Folsom, traveled widely to become familiar with the technology described by one architectural historian as "street architecture," a facade that was made to resemble stone but with greater sculptural freedom.[8]

City Center Trax Station / Art in Transit
Main Street, between South Temple and
100 South
1999
Bonnie Sucec and Day Christensen
Bonnie Sucec and Day Christensen's City Center Station "Art in Transit" features the vitality of downtown Salt Lake City with bright yellow windscreens and bronze honeybees. Representing a partnership between the Utah Transit Authority, Federal Transit Administration, Salt Lake City Corporation, Redevelopment Agency of Salt Lake City, Salt Lake Art Design Board, and Salt Lake City Arts Council, the Art in Transit program commissioned the two artists, who designed one hundred bronze bees swarming around the station, reflecting the energy, industry, and vitality of the beehive. The bright and vibrant colors and forms evoke the image of the city itself.

McIntyre Building
68 South Main Street
1908–1909
Richard K. A. Kletting
Richard Kletting designed this modest-sized skyscraper in 1908–09. Kletting,

a lifelong member of the Utah Society of Professional Engineers, was well familiar with the latest skyscraper technology. The McIntyre Building became a sort of demonstration piece of that knowledge. It is perhaps the best example of the Sullivanesque style along Main Street. Kletting designed the building for a prominent Utah rancher and mining entrepreneur, William McIntyre.

Although it is not as tall as other skyscrapers nearby, the building emphasizes vertical movement with unbroken piers that terminate under the cornice. The spandrels between the piers are recessed slightly, emphasizing the work done by the different structural elements. Above, ornamental cartouches identify the building as a Kletting design, a sort of indulgence he allowed himself, a signature he developed for his commercial architecture. From a purely technological standpoint, the McIntyre Building became a prototype for later reinforced concrete skyscrapers in Utah.

McCornick Block
74 South Main Street
1891–1893
Medelson and Fisher, Omaha, Nebraska
Within a decade after the McCornick Block building was built in 1891–93, skyscrapers would tower over it on both sides, but it formed an important transition between the tall masonry buildings of the late nineteenth century and the even taller, metal frame skyscrapers of the twentieth. This seven-story building had the city's earliest elevators, which facilitated the movement of workers to offices on all levels. At the top of the office shaft juts a dramatic copper cornice. On the Main Street level, an elaborate portico framed by large columns announces the entrance to the building.

William S. McCornick was an entrepreneur who accumulated wealth through lumber industries related to the construction of mine shafts in Nevada as well as numerous other business ventures in the state. The McCornick & Company Bank was housed in this building, as were his other principal business enterprises.

Salt Lake Art Center / Utah Museum of
Contemporary Art
20 South West Temple
1979
FFKR

When the Salt Lake Art Center first opened, the staff were often asked, "What is it like to work in a triangle?" "Isn't it awkward?" They would answer, "Perhaps, but it is beautiful." Playing off the same theme as Abravanel Hall—slices of dynamic geometric forms—the main gallery space of the Utah Museum of Contemporary Art (UMCA) introduces a dynamic conversation with the world outside. Mirroring the materiality of Abravanel itself and the materials of modern architecture more broadly, the museum feels like a wedge sliding in and out of the earth, providing a view but then obscuring it like a sleight of hand.

Seeming to emerge from Abravanel Hall and expressing the same attitude toward space, form, and mass, the Salt Lake Art Center is also part of the Bicentennial Arts Complex and is adjacent to Abravanel Hall. Unlike any other building in the downtown area, the Salt Lake Art Center is triangular, which relates it to the diagonal orientation of the main building and opens its northeast face toward the street. Because of this site, the main gallery wall of windows faces Abravanel Hall, the cityscape beyond, and the pedestrian lane running along the street.

No other exhibition space in town is as elegant and dramatic as the Salt Lake Art Center's main gallery. Stimulated by this exciting contemporary environment and the Salt Lake Art Center's commitment to art that challenges our sensibilities and makes us question what we know and already understand, the UMCA presents contemporary art in a setting perfectly harmonious with its mission. Because it is so visible and so elegant, the UMCA is often used for public gatherings and events from dance performances to weddings. With outside sculpture near the main gallery exit and framed by a sloping grassy hillside, the building also has a complex of studios, a small auditorium, and classroom and exhibition spaces. A street-level gallery exhibits traveling shows and displays local artists as well.

Windmills / Salt Palace
100 South West Temple
1996
Patrick Zentz, Montana

Salt Lake County hired Montana artist Patrick Zentz to create the twelve large windmills along the east wall of the Salt Palace Convention Center. Wind gusts move the windmills, sending electronically encoded signals that create the sound of twelve tonally distinct percussion instruments in the building's cylindrical entry tower. The patterns of the natural world, the seasons, and the climate are transferred into shifting patterns of sound within the tower atrium.

Many visitors to the convention center are confused by the tones and don't make the connection to the movement of the windmills outside. Others believe they have started the tones by opening the entrance doors.

Salt Palace Convention Center / Media
Center for the Olympics
West Temple between 100 South and
200 South
1969–1994
1995–present
Thompson Ventulett Stainback & Associates,
Atlanta, Georgia
Richard K. A. Kletting, original Salt Palace
architect

Richard Kletting designed the first Salt Palace for a site on 900 South using innovative panels made of salt from the Great Salt Lake. The most recent version of the Salt Palace, constructed in 1994, fills most of an entire city block. The 600-foot-long West Temple elevation features an art installation called *Point of View* that invites viewers to engage with the signs and be "part of the art." The piece uses more than 150 familiar road signs that include words that are opposites. The general manager of the Salt Palace suggested that the signs and the word play "align with the Salt Palace's sense of place. It's a facility in which there is discourse, questioning and learning."[9] Rejecting the notion that a convention center has to be a gigantic box, the Salt Palace attempts to do something different, creating visual complexity more like a city itself as it moves both vertically and horizontally, with curves and straight lines sweeping their way around the block. A whimsical row of windmills creates additional movement and complexity along the West Temple facade.

Integrated into the Abravanel Hall and Arts Complex by continuing the masonry wall material and hinting at the triangular format at some corners, the entrance tower sits at the point where 100 South ends, just about as spectacular a point as is possible in downtown Salt Lake City if you like axial orientations. The lobby and interior concourse are particularly grand in scale and bring the natural light provided

Windmills / Salt Palace

by the round entrance tower into the space, as does a two-story glazed wall that permits a panoramic view of the exhibit hall from the mezzanine level of the concourse.

The city remodeled the Salt Palace Convention Center in 1995 for $80 million, anticipating growth in convention business for Salt Lake City. The Salt Palace is a downtown landmark in all the various guises it has taken in the past hundred years, and it was the media hub of the Olympic Games in 2002.

The 150,000-square-foot expansion of the Salt Palace between Abravanel Hall and 300 West along South Temple was designed by Edwards & Daniels Associates and spans 200 West, allowing traffic to flow uninterrupted beneath the meeting space. This provided midblock pedestrian access tying the hotel into the circulation system.

Patrick Dry Goods Company Building
163 West 200 South
1913–1914
Headlund and Kent

Reflecting a very different idea about commercial block design from the skyscrapers built near Exchange Place, the five-story facade of the Patrick Dry Goods Company Building plays with the contrast between dark brown and red brick walls and white trim. Variations in the patterns of window placement, in groups of five at the center and pairs to each side, also animate the street elevation.

Designed by the national firm Headlund and Kent, the Patrick Dry Goods Building exemplifies later commercial-style

architecture that deviated from the strict formality and regularity of earlier examples inspired by Chicago to create a livelier and more diverse elevation once innovations in skyscraper technology had become more standard. Headlund was well known for his design of the McDonald Chocolate building to the south, and John H. Kent, his partner after 1914, had practiced architecture with Richard C. Watkins and John S. Birch. Perhaps their most significant project was the Second Church of Christ, Scientist, a three-story building at 566 East South Temple, which was demolished in 1977. The building was originally owned by the Syndicate Investment Company, which also built the Smith-Bailey Drug Company building to

Patrick Dry Goods Company Building

the west, and the Decker-Patrick Company has occupied the building since 1914.

Bertolini Block
145 West 200 South
1891–1892
William Carroll

Speaking to the rich ethnic diversity that existed at the turn of the century in Salt Lake City's west side, the Bertolini Block was built in 1891–92 for Ignazio Bertolini, a prominent Italian American real estate developer. Bertolini built this eleven-room building to house his real estate offices and his family's residence upstairs. Bertolini served the ethnic populations of the neighborhood surrounding the railroad

depots—a variety of different ethnic businesses used the space over the years, including Andrew J. Edgar Groceries, 1899; Henry B. Wae, cigars, tobacco, and fruit, 1907; Enrico de Francesco's Italian American Venice Cafe, 1915; and barbers Anthony Brajkovich and Nick Frisco, 1919. At different times it also housed a café, billiards hall, tavern, and confectionary.

The Bertolini Block is a two-story red brick building with white stone trim, iron columns, fancy corbeled brick, and a tin cornice in the front facade parapet. The texture of the wall is interrupted with rough stone at the corners, imitating pilasters, and fancy corbeled stonework over arches on the second level.

Bertolini Block

Oregon Short Line Railroad /
Old Salt Lake High School / Utah
National Guard Armory Building
122–146 Pierpont Avenue
1897–1898
Carl. M. Neuhausen

Well-known Utah architect Carl Neuhausen (architect of the Cathedral of the Madeleine) designed this building for a hybrid use by the Oregon Short Line Railroad Company and the Salt Lake High School between 1897 and 1898. Born and trained in Germany, Neuhausen came to Salt Lake City in 1892 and worked for a time for Richard K. A. Kletting before he branched out on his own in 1895. This was his first major project.

As a whole, this brick complex is two stories, but the height varies as it moves along the street front. The building has a facade on the north and on the west. Three sets of Roman arches become progressively smaller as they move up the building to the north, and a plain parapet caps the building at the top. The west facade is more elaborate and includes tall window bays, a central window with a Classical pediment above, and stylized pilasters to the sides of the entrance. Other decoration includes a copper parapet wall and a corbeled brick belt course.

Rose Wagner Performing Arts Center
138 West Broadway
2000
Prescott Muir

The facade of the Rose Wagner Performing Arts Center seems to shift before our eyes, playing on the idea of transformation, performance, and illusion. Using materials more familiar to industrial complexes than more traditional cultural arts centers, the building has a rich materiality and texture that begs you to drag your hand along the wall surfaces and consider it from multiple vantage points. The projecting sound booth in the lobby is clad in silver leaf, creating an ambiguity about the back and front of "the house." Concrete masonry, a steel frame, and a flat roof system along with an indigenous gray granite facade suspended from the underlying masonry wall create a building that is almost startlingly different, incongruous with others on the same block. It was previously the site of a restaurant supply store, and the sign was salvaged, reclad in aluminum, rotated, and rehung over the entry.

Built in phases, the Rose Wagner Performing Arts Center was first used by performing arts groups in the community as a 150-seat "black box" theater with flexible seating. This same space could be converted into two full rehearsal spaces with spring

Rose Wagner Performing Arts Center

dance floors; there were also two additional stage-sized rehearsal spaces with direct load-in for use as alternative black box performance spaces; dressing rooms; a green room; and administrative office space. An enclosed public walkway connected it to the city's inner block walking system for a time.

Freeing up the Capitol Theatre from extensive use by Repertory Dance Theatre and offering new space for rehearsal by other Capitol Theatre groups, the building is used by the Utah Opera, Ballet West, Gina Bachauer International Piano Competition, and Sundance Film Festival along with a number of other arts organizations.

Peery Hotel
110 West 300 South
1910
Charles B. Onderdonk

Ogden merchant and banker David Harold Peery's two sons built the Peery Hotel in 1910, one of a group of early twentieth-century hotels to welcome businessmen who came to Salt Lake City, mirroring the growth and development of this new state capital. Located three and a half blocks west of the Denver and Rio Grande Railroad Depot, the Peery is a three-story cream-colored brick building, today painted a taupe gray, with Prairie-style elements along with Classical motifs. The hotel's floor plan is shaped like an *E*, which maximizes the number of rooms with natural lighting.

The main level has large picture windows with transoms above, and smaller windows on the upper two levels for each of the hotel rooms. Decoration includes Classical columns, a projecting cornice formed with galvanized tin on the upper level with paired brackets, and an egg-and-dart band and quoins on the edges of the forms moving toward the street. Just below the level of the cornice, a stone belt course underscores the horizontality of the building. Subtle, green and rust-colored tiles are used to create inlaid Latin crosses on the sides of the center upper-level windows.

J. G. McDonald Chocolate Company /
Broadway Lofts
155–159 West 300 South
1901
John A. Headlund
1914 addition, Headlund and Kent

J. G. McDonald started in business by selling saltwater taffy from bags carried by a packhorse he would ride through the territory during the 1850s. One of the state's earliest merchants, he had wholesale grocery stores and a confectionary store in 1863 and built this headquarters for his candy company in 1901. By the turn of the century the company specialized in boxed chocolates, receiving national recognition for its superior-quality candies. The company stayed in the building until 1941, when Dixon and Company, wholesale paper dealers, occupied the space.

Swedish immigrant John A. Headlund designed the building after coming to Utah in 1890. Headlund designed many commercial buildings and houses in the area but was perhaps best known for his design of the Immanuel Baptist Church, the YMCA, and the Salt Lake County Infirmary.

The building is a narrow, four-story rectangle, constructed with brick and stone, with a split-level entrance and raised basement. It has a modest amount of decoration including the letter *M* in brick relief at the top of the outer piers, Classical wooden moldings, and corbeled brickwork.

In the late 1990s, Jim Lewis embarked on a massive adaptive reuse renovation of the building, creating upscale condominiums that range in size from 750 to 3,000 square feet.

Eagle Emporium / Zions Bank
102 South Main Street
1864
William Paul

Before the railroad came to Salt Lake City, Main Street resembled streets in just about any other dusty frontier town, with its combination of frame and brick false-front commercial buildings. Single- or two-story buildings were sometimes built of adobe bricks, an uncommon use of the building material in the West. Perhaps the most unusual feature after the 1860s and the organization of ZCMI was the logo of member stores—the all-seeing eye and the inscription "Holiness to the Lord." Faithful Mormons, as a sign of their loyalty, would shop at designated church businesses instead of spending their limited money at non-Mormon, or Gentile, stores.

Eagle Emporium / Zions Bank

The Eagle Emporium is the oldest remaining commercial building from this period, built between 1863 and 1864. British architect William Paul designed the building for William Jennings, a well-known local businessman.

When ZCMI was organized in 1868, Jennings became a member of the board of trustees, exchanging his entire inventory for capital stock in the company as well as leasing the Eagle Emporium to the company. Zions First National Bank has occupied the building since 1890.

The building began as a single-story stone commercial block. In the mid-1880s, two additional stories were added above, meshing with the original Neoclassical design elements. These include a wide Classical cornice, upper-level pilasters with Corinthian capitals separated by decorative spandrels, and lower-level engaged columns with Corinthian capitals.

The ornamental clock in front of the Eagle Emporium is an artifact of 1873, one of the only remaining decorative features from the late nineteenth century on Main Street.

Daft Block
128 South Main
1889
Harrison & Nichols

One of the architects of this building, E. L. T. Harrison, was part of the dissident group of scientologists during the late nineteenth century to separate from the Mormon Church and form their own group, the Godbeites. The firm Harrison & Nichols designed this building for Sarah Daft after the death of her husband in 1881. Built in 1889, the Daft Building features Harrison's fascination with elaborate decoration, including a wealth of carved stone and wood details.

The four-story building has a basement level. Contrasting in texture, color, and materiality, the principal exterior building materials are red brick, sandstone, and wood. Pinnacles, pilasters, and stone carvings in floral patterns create decorative interest. Overall, the building's surface is richly textured and interesting in its contrasts and movement across the walls.

The Daynes Jewelry Company bought the building in 1908 and painted an advertisement on the north side that is still readable. Daynes was also Brigham Young's watchmaker and an expert jeweler.

Kearns Building
136 South Main Street
1909–1911
Parkinson & Bergstrom, Los Angeles, California
Few figures in the early twentieth century in Utah impacted local politics and economic and social life more than Thomas Kearns. Kearns was a wealthy, politically powerful, philanthropic-minded man. Rich because of wise investments and incredible luck in Park City mines, Kearns was a U.S. senator for a time and part owner with David Keith of the *Salt Lake Tribune.*

Because land at the center of town became increasingly scarce and expensive, vertical construction started to become the norm during the early twentieth century in downtown Salt Lake City. The Kearns Building was also heavily influenced by Louis Sullivan's ideas about tall buildings— emphasis on vertical lines, the use of an elevator, and a subtly modulated wall surface.

In terms of structure, the building features fireproof reinforced-concrete construction. For decor, white terra-cotta tile facing on the front facade and brick veneer on the side and rear elevations create an elegant look along with up-to-date

Kearns Building

technology. Piers emphasize the vertical sweep of the building and are separated horizontally by slightly recessed spandrels, creating a modulated wall surface. The Kearns Building is arguably one of the finest examples of Sullivanesque architecture downtown.

Ezra Thompson / Salt Lake Tribune Building
143 South Main Street
1924
Hyrum Pope and Harold Burton
The Art Deco decoration of the Tribune Building distinguishes it from other Main Street buildings. With a highly unusual style in the state, the Tribune Building has a relatively plain facade with a strong vertical emphasis, and a relatively flat terra-cotta

cornice at the top. Art Deco motifs such as stylized geometric patterns appear at regular points along the path to the top. Although the Art Deco style was popular during World War I and into the 1920s and 1930s, few Art Deco buildings were ever built in Salt Lake City. Nevertheless, Ezra Thompson built this building in 1924 to house his mining and real estate businesses, choosing this unusual decorative style that he most likely saw elsewhere and that connoted a certain modern attitude. The *Salt Lake Tribune* bought the building from Thompson in 1937 but then moved out of it in 2008 and into new offices at the Gateway.

Salt Lake Herald Building
169 South Main Street
1905
John C. Craig, Chicago/Salt Lake City
The Herald Building breaks up the monotony of the streetscape with its U-shaped plan opening to the street, and its deviation from the strict flat wall alignment with the sidewalk more typical of other Main Street buildings. Instead, it moves back to open more office space to sunlight and fresh air. Although this was a popular configuration during the nineteenth and twentieth centuries for both office and apartment buildings because of the way it opened up a central courtyard for light and circulation to interior offices, it was not used elsewhere in the Main Street commercial district.

The *Salt Lake Herald*, like the *Deseret Evening News*, was a news alternative to the *Salt Lake Tribune* and lined up on the side of the Mormons and the Democrats. After 1905, this building served as the newspaper's central office space. It was designed by John C. Craig, an architect who had a practice in both Chicago and Salt Lake City. The *Herald* vacated the building in 1913 to be replaced by the Little Hotel, which had

occupied the building next door. Since 1919, Lamb's Restaurant, a downtown Salt Lake institution, has provided the backdrop for countless business lunches and dinners.

Walker Bank Building
175 South Main Street
1912
Eames & Young, St. Louis, Missouri
The sixteen-story Walker Bank Building was the tallest building west of the Mississippi when it was built in 1912, a fact that was boasted about in numerous publications promoting Salt Lake City. It mimicked the skyscraper style developed in the Midwest and brought a new level of architectural sophistication to Salt Lake City.

The four Walker brothers who founded Walker Bank—Samuel, Joseph, David, and

Walker Bank Building

Matthew—capitalized on potential markets in Salt Lake City as a key way station on the journey toward the Pacific Coast and launched this enterprise in 1859. Their mercantile company quickly prospered, and eventually the brothers began their own bank as well.

The Walker Bank Building typifies turn-of-the-century skyscraper construction. These buildings followed the model set by Louis Sullivan in Chicago, who said that skyscrapers should have a base, shaft, and capital, as the Classical column does. Typically the first two floors are seen as a unit and the next several levels as the shaft, and then a projecting, heavily ornamented cornice juts out into space, identifying the top of the building with great energy. At the top is one of the most distinctive landmarks of the city, a three-story observatory topped by sculpted eagles, with flashing lights signaling changes in local weather.

Salt Lake City's population increased sixfold between 1880 and 1920. As a result, the city underwent a tremendous building boom. The earlier technology of cast-iron-front buildings was left in the dust, and instead steel frame construction ruled the day. Louis Sullivan and his partner Dankmar Adler designed one building for Salt Lake City—the Dooly Block, a steel frame stone-clad structure that was only six stories tall, but the firm's work influenced dozens of other buildings in the downtown commercial district, including this one.

New Orpheum Theatre / Capitol Theatre
46 West 200 South
1912–1913
G. Albert Lansburg, San Francisco, California
One of the most beautiful and colorful facades in Salt Lake City is that of the Capitol Theatre (once called the Orpheum Theatre), which incorporates new building

materials such as tapestry brick (brick of a variety of colors meant to alternate across the surface) and pastel terra-cotta. Combining the decorative elegance of the Italian Renaissance style as well as making the most of modern mechanical technologies, this elegant building challenges the staid formality of the downtown business district. Besides the steel frame popularized in Chicago at the turn of the century as a fireproofing response, the building featured a "water-curtain" and "plenum system" air conditioning. San Francisco architect G. Albert Lansburg designed the building, bringing his experience from the École des Beaux-Arts and his Diplôme d'Architecture de Gouvernement Français. Before the Orpheum Theatre, Salt Lake City did not have a building that featured exquisite terra-cotta figurines, moldings, and brackets of this caliber. This building was a first for the city. The Capitol/Orpheum Theatre is a brick building adorned with polychromatic terra-cotta and tapestry brick. Roman arches form a portico on the main floor level, and Palladian windows, cartouches, foliated bands, cherubs, and classical heads, all composed with terra-cotta, add exuberance, interest, and charm. A band of drama masks sits above the bracketed cornice, referencing cultural activities. The interior space was particularly noteworthy. Between 1,800 and 2,000 people could sit on the main floor without posts interrupting their view. Twenty-six box seats and a central "royal" box offered more exclusive viewing spaces above. The lobby space was a sensorial, luxurious mix of marble, mirrors, bas-relief sculpture, and wall murals, an environment apart from the everyday world.

The Orpheum Theatre was the second in the Orpheum chain built in Salt Lake City between 1912 and 1913, an impressive facility for visiting vaudeville troupes and

New Orpheum Theatre / Capitol Theatre

entertainers. In 1927 the Louis Marcus chain purchased the building and remodeled it into a "Louis XVI style theater," where it showed motion pictures until 1976, when the Salt Lake City Redevelopment Agency bought the building and began restoration work. Since that time, both the Utah Opera Company and Ballet West have called the Capitol Theatre home.

Commercial Street / Regent Street
40 East between 100 and 200 South
1870s

Even the most religious of towns has its share of vice. In Salt Lake City prostitution existed just around the corner from the commercial district that developed along Main Street. From the 1870s until the 1930s Salt Lake City's red-light district was Commercial Street. Several Commercial Street buildings housed brothels and cribs regulated by the city. The city required that prostitutes maintain updated licenses and pay monthly fees of ten dollars. Usually on Regent Street, a variety of businesses were on street level, and a lively, diverse, and exotic atmosphere prevailed. The houses of prostitution were upstairs. Only one of these historically colorful buildings remains—the Leader Cigar Factory Building.

Leader Cigar Factory Building
165 South Regent Street
1893
Gustave S. Holmes

National Bank of the Republic director Gustave Holmes erected the Leader Cigar Factory Building in 1893. During its heyday, the factory employed immigrants who came to Utah hoping to achieve the American dream—on the first level the cigar factory employed primarily immigrants from Italy or Greece. The brothel upstairs offered women for service until the late 1910s, when the prostitutes were relocated to the stockade near 200 South and 500 West.

Plum Alley
65 East, between 100 and 200 South
1880s

Although the Gateway district was the principal location of ethnic neighborhoods until the end of the nineteenth century, Chinese immigrants lived in a world of their own in the block between 100 and 200 South on Plum Alley. Chinese workers were integral to the construction of the railroad, which transformed the American West and connected Utah with the rest of the United States. Afterward many stayed in the territory, sending for picture brides and raising families. By the early

1900s most Chinese lived in cities rather than agricultural areas, where they began new businesses—laundries and groceries, restaurants and stores. They conducted life largely separate from the rest of the city and maintained their unique and colorful culture, segregated by language, prejudice, and cultural misunderstanding.

Orpheum Theatre / Promised Valley Playhouse
132 South State Street
1905
Carl Neuhausen

The first of two Orpheum Theatres built in Salt Lake City, later known as the Promised Valley Playhouse, opened on Christmas Day 1905 with a vaudeville performance, and 1,300 people attended opening night. The first Orpheum was built near the historic location of the Salt Lake Theater, a familiar cultural zone along State Street. When vaudeville became less popular with the

Orpheum Theatre / Promised Valley Playhouse

Salt Lake

advent of motion pictures, the Orpheum was adapted for use as a moving picture theater. Called at different times the Wilkes, the Roxy, the Lake, and the Lyric, it featured a popular "cry" room for babies and a specially furnished ladies' restroom.

All that is left of the Orpheum Theatre is a three-story Second Renaissance Revival facade with contrasting stone trim and brick walls (the result of a "facadectomy"), a larger-than-life-size statue of Venus, two large stone busts of Zeus, and a metal cornice running along the top of the wall with a prominent broken pediment in the center.

Carl M. Neuhausen, an architect and a German immigrant, designed this building as well as the Thomas Kearns Mansion, St. Ann's Orphanage, and the Oregon Short Line Railroad / Salt Lake High School building. When the Orpheum Theatre was built in 1905 it became Salt Lake's premier vaudeville theater.

The *Deseret News* celebrated the opening of the theater, saying, "In point of architecture, appointments, size and all the latest improvements, Salt Lake can now truthfully boast of having one of the finest theaters in America."[10] The Church of Jesus Christ of Latter-day Saints bought the theater in 1972 and restored it, renaming it the Promised Valley Playhouse.

Continental Bank / Hotel Monaco
Main Street and 200 South
1923–1924
Frederick Albert Hale and George W. Kelham
The thirteen-story Continental Bank Building was built for James E. Cosgriff, a sheep rancher turned banker, in 1923–24. Cosgriff bought the National Bank of the Republic and merged it with several other pioneer-era banks to create Continental Bank.

Cosgriff asked Salt Lake architect Frederick A. Hale along with George W. Kelham

of San Francisco to design the building. The lower levels reflect the Second Renaissance Revival style, with carved stone faces in the keystones above large arched windows and simulated balconies, and there are also bas-relief panels below the windows of the third story. The verticality of the building is emphasized by the narrow three-bay facade, which faces Main Street and contrasts with the longer 200 South elevation.

During the summer of 1998, the Kimpton Group of San Francisco, well known for its renovation of historic buildings for upscale hotels and restaurants, bought the building as well as seven smaller buildings along Main Street to the south. The result was Salt Lake City's new fancy lady—the Hotel Monaco.

The transformation of the Continental Bank Building into the new stylish Hotel Monaco represents a preservation success story. A building threatened with demolition received not only a facelift but a new life. The Kimpton Group, the Salt Lake City Corporation, and other government agencies found a way to revitalize a deteriorating landmark and turn it into a lively and interesting new destination space.

Karrick Block
236 South Main Street
1887
Richard K. A. Kletting
The Karrick Block is an excellent example of a Richard Kletting commercial design project, the oldest extant structure in his body of work. The distinctive facade displays Kletting's confidence with a variety of different styles, which together create an extravagant textural wall surface combining ornate carved stone, attenuated cast-iron columns on the third story, and a galvanized iron cornice as particularly interesting elements displaying his virtuoso design skill.

Constrained by the narrow lot, the building becomes attractive through its varying planes, materials, and detailing and its formal and careful composition. As with other tall buildings of the late nineteenth century, the facade reflects the divisions of a Greek temple with a base, columns, and entablature or cap at the top. Rusticated stone banding occurs along the first level in ornately carved stone belt courses, and large pilasters at the sides define the separate parts of the building and create geometric interest. The wall surface is modulated with corbeled stone, brick, and tin decorative elements and recessed spaces, creating a subtle movement of light and shadow.

Lewis Karrick was the original owner of the National Bank of the Republic in 1887. Over time the building was occupied by a drugstore and then a jewelry shop, and, although it might be apocryphal, it is believed the upstairs was the scene of illegal activity—both gambling and prostitution.

Lollin Block
238 South Main Street
1894
Richard K. A. Kletting

Also the work of Richard K. A. Kletting, the Lollin Block at 238 South Main celebrates Classical motifs, giving the surface of a fairly traditionally shaped commercial building new exuberance. Classical details include the ever-present Roman arches, formality, and symmetry as well as details like the dentil moldings that run along the edge of the entablature, Roman arches, and egg-and-dart

window trim. The building was constructed of brick with a stone foundation but was plastered over with gray stucco and then scored to resemble stone. The facade has four sections and a flat parapet at the top. Danish immigrant John Lollin owned this building as well as a saloon on Main Street, and his family lived upstairs after 1894. Various businesses occupied the street-level space—a music company, a fur store, and an art goods store owned by Gabriel Shihadeh.

David Keith Building
242 South Main Street
1902
Frederick Albert Hale

David Keith hired prominent Salt Lake architect Frederick Hale to design his downtown commercial building. Like Thomas Kearns, David Keith earned his wealth in mining ventures in Park City's most lucrative silver mine, the Silver King, and built both a mansion on South Temple and this impressive commercial structure in a strategic location on Main Street. A close

David Keith Building

friend and associate of Kearns, Keith also began the Keith O'Brien department store, which was housed in this building.

Hale preferred the Classical vocabulary for his commercial architecture, and compared to his other designs, this example is far less ornate.

The Keith Building has a brick superstructure and stone cladding on the facade that is organized in three vertical divisions, clearly differentiating between the Main Street level, the office shaft, and the cornice at the top. The facade has a flat, smooth texture and a polychromatic gray color scheme. Classical cartouches and other Frederick Hale signature decorations enliven the surface somewhat, as do Roman arches near the top. Small square finials break up the cornice line along with low-pitched pediments. Under one of these is the letter *K* for Keith.

Gallivan Trax Station
Main Street between 200 South and 300 South
1999
Norie Sato, Seattle, Washington

Norie Sato of Seattle had already designed art for light rail stations and airports in other cities before she came to Utah.
As part of the design, markers in the paving at the Gallivan Station are engraved with facts about Utah, creating visual and narrative reminders of the early settlement of the Mormon pioneers and stories from Native American tradition.

Clift Building
10 West 300 South
1919–1920
James Leslie Chesebro

After the death of her husband, Francis D. Clift, Virtue Clift hired architect James Leslie Chesebro to design this building in 1920 in his honor. A merchant, mining entrepreneur, and real estate developer, Clift left a significant fortune to his widow. The Clift Building housed several important Salt Lake City businesses over time—the United Cigar Stores Company, the Schubach Optical Company, Western Union Telegraph, and the Cinema Theater, which operated until 1968.

Like many of the tall office buildings constructed in the early twentieth century, the Clift Building has a metal frame and three-part organization—a main level, an office shaft, and a projecting cornice. What distinguishes this example is the abundance of terra-cotta facing modulating the wall surface. The building conforms to the Second Renaissance Revival style with its regularity of window patterning, formal detailing, and overall ambience. There is an interesting contrast between the emphasis on the vertical sweep of the office shaft and the horizontal belt courses. Offices throughout this modern building have ample light and window space, convenient elevator transport, and an advantageous location near the commercial center of the city.

American Stores / Wells Fargo Building
Northeast corner of 300 South and Main Street
1998
FFKR

Salt Lake City talked for months about the devastation caused by the 1999 tornado. Pieces of plywood blocked gaps in the Delta Center's window wall, reminding the city of the forces of nature that could so quickly disrupt the illusion of calm. In much the same way, a new dominant figure can change the visual landscape, disrupting the way buildings relate to one another and forcing new relationships and shifts in perception.

American Stores / Wells Fargo Building

buildings. Easily the most dramatic structure in the visual field surrounding the Gallivan Center, this building deviates from the strict rectangularity of buildings nearby and forms a glass and steel wedge on the site. The owners dedicated the building in June 1998, when it was intended to be the headquarters of the American Stores Company, one of the country's largest food and drug retailers. Besides the two thousand jobs the company would provide for Salt Lake City, the building became a sort of miniurban community center itself, with a first-class Italian restaurant, a specialty grocery store and restaurant, a beauty salon and barber shop, and other retail shops. When profits fell along with stock values, Albertsons Inc., which is headquartered in Boise, Idaho, bought the company.

Since 2001 Wasatch Management Company has managed the property and Wells Fargo is the principal tenant.

John W. Gallivan Utah Center
Block 54 surrounded by 200 South, State Street, 300 South, and Main Street
1993

The Gallivan Center is a true community urban center in the best sense. Since it was first built by the city, it has been the scene of countless community-wide activities, annual events, and weekly meetings that have filled it with life and made it a symbol of community unity. The center displays artwork, includes an amphitheater for summer music events, and is home to public art such as murals and a huge outdoor chess board. Performance areas are found in comfortable and spacious areas of the block, and inviting, more intimate spaces are perfect for picnics in the summer. A self-acknowledged people's place, it serves as a backdrop for a wide range of activities as diverse as First Night concerts,

The American Stores / Wells Fargo Building had this effect on downtown Salt Lake City. It is a dominant figure in the urban landscape. Because of its distinctive orientation—a diagonal in a sea of right-angled grids—and because of its looming height and color and the reflective quality of its wall surfaces, it commands attention. The Wells Fargo Building creates dynamic movement in this part of the city and forces new relationships between surrounding

Through the Shelter of Love by Jane Dedecker, one of many sculptures at the John W. Gallivan Utah Center.

fireworks displays, motocross races, and brew fests. Owned by the Redevelopment Agency of Salt Lake City, the Gallivan Center has partnered with Salt Lake City Recreation for management and programming.

The Gallivan Center demonstrates how artwork can enliven a space and create community definition. Created primarily by Utah artists, the Gallivan Center's art is an integral part of the overall design. At the entrance to the center on 200 South, two stone steles or slabs, which would typically be used on a facade, create a grand announcement of the plaza. Designed by Neil Hadlock of Highland, Utah, the slabs have two sides that are highly polished, with the other sides showing the marks of drills, chisels, and breaking. Dennis Smith, also from Utah County, created a bronze sculpture of two kneeling children playing a game of cat's cradle, which is placed on top of the small semicircular presentation area just east of

the Aviara. The Aviara flight cage is a simple steel frame structure that is seasonally enclosed with special aviary netting around native Utah bird habitat. The Tracy Aviary fills the flight cage during the summer months with native Utah birds that are being rehabilitated because they have been injured or for some other reason are not able to survive in the wild. John E. Pace & Associates designed the cage.

Artists Silvia Davis and Jim Jacobs designed ten custom five-by-five-foot bronze tree grates with snowflake patterns that surround trees in strategic locations around the plaza. The plaza's information center is in a kiosk that includes lit, etched glass gables that show the time on a clock facing each of the four directions. The Story Wall, created by artist Day Christensen, includes eighty 24-by-24-inch connected bronze panels that form a border along the plaza's sunken lawn area. The text sculpturing features Native American legends. A pedestrian bridge called "Utah Sandscape" bisects the plaza east to west and is constructed of eight-by-eight-inch glass blocks. The designer carefully selected native Utah sands and soils to fill the blocks, creating a sandscape. Light moves through the blocks and creates a varying bridge of color as the time and seasons change.

Asteroid Landed Softly
Gallivan Center, 200 South between Main Street and State Street
1992
Kazuo Matsubayashi
Kazuo Matsubayashi's *Asteroid Landed Softly* has become a landmark in Salt Lake

Asteroid Landed Softly

City at the Gallivan Center. The design guidelines for this artwork called for an idea that reflected Utah's natural environment.

The resulting piece is a tower-like sundial constructed of a pink sandstone boulder supported on twin columns clad in copper and reflective glass. Matsubayashi "hopes this sundial with its floating rock will trigger the observer's mind to the basic scientific curiosity and artistic imagination in their most innocent beginning and to wonder about the mystery of natural forces, to ponder what is nature and reality, what is time and space. Or perhaps one can simply kill time by standing in front of it. Today many of us are being chased by time."[11]

The forms are reminiscent of the boulders in the red-rock country of southern Utah, or the important spiritual forces of places like Stonehenge. Matsubayashi's piece locates the sundial in both the red

rock of southern Utah and the tradition of clock towers in piazzas throughout history. "The rock, which might be a visitor or an asteroid from outer space, is balanced on a tower clad by reflective glass. Images of downtown buildings, sky and clouds are reflected on the glass and become a part of the sculpture."[12] Children play in the shadows of the tower, trying to catch time in their hands and playing hopscotch on its sundial forms. Adults sit quietly watching its changes as light moves across the copper column and illuminates form.

One Utah Center
Southwest corner of Main Street and
200 South
1991
Valentiner Crane Brunjes Onyon Architects
Today, it is difficult to remember the Salt Lake City skyline without the distinctive pyramidal copper roof of the One Utah Center. The first of the three anchor buildings was constructed on three corners of the Gallivan Center, the historic Block 57. When it was built, it was the first new skyscraper in the city for several years. Award-winning architect Niels Valentiner of Valentiner Crane Brunjes Onyon Architects referenced Salt Lake City's historic fabric with granite cladding and the regular patterning of the window wall, a postmodern play situating it in the particular space of Salt Lake City's commercial downtown. Postmodern in the way it references the past in the use of stone and terra-cotta, clad in granite with punched windows instead of the smooth glass window walls of so many contemporary downtown buildings, the One Utah Center reflects instead on its historic counterparts—the nearby Walker Bank Building just kitty-corner from Block 57 has lines that similarly emphasize the vertical sweep of this early tall building,

One Utah Center

with a modulated wall surface that moves in and out with window openings. The copper sheathing on the roof adds a distinctive touch, again setting it apart from other buildings in the downtown skyline.

This twenty-four-story granite and glass building has four wings that jut out slightly from a central core. Three are equal in size and shape, while the fourth moves to the northwest recesses from the corner to create an intriguing zig-zag pattern that opens up the corner plaza space and sets off an elegant spacious entrance to the building from Main Street. As is typical of contemporary skyscrapers, the wall includes regular and patterned levels of windows but in a new way, with alternating and contrasting colors of stone panels defining divisions and creating a grid that carries through the length of the building shaft.

International Order of Odd Fellows Hall
26 West Market Street
1891–1892
George F. Cistercian, Salt Lake City
Preserving its presence as a tangible, living reminder of the cultural diversity that existed in Salt Lake City at the turn of the century, the International Order of Odd Fellows Hall demonstrates the competing interests that vied for control in the economic, social, and cultural life of Salt Lake City. The city, its streets, and its buildings can be read like the pages of a book. It is a vivid history of shifting spaces and the meanings attached to them by successive generations.

Combating the exclusivity and secret nature of the Mormon priesthood and the inclusive nature of the commercial life conducted at the other end of Main Street, the Independent Order of Odd Fellows built this hall in 1892. The Odd Fellows is a fraternal, benevolent and social group that originated in the early eighteenth century in England. With rites and organization similar to those of Freemasonry, the Independent Order of Odd Fellows organized in Utah on May 4, 1865. Between 1865 and 1872 the Masons and the Odd Fellows shared common meeting space. Their quarters were small and inadequate, described as "anything but inviting."

By the end of the nineteenth century, Salt Lake City was moving from the original vision of its founders to something quite different. City streets became lined with commercial buildings, but also pool halls, third-rate cafés and hotels, and increasingly

International Order of Odd Fellows Hall.
Photograph by Elizabeth Bradley-Wilson. Used with permission of photographer.

by agents of diversity—like the Masonic lodges or this building, the International Order of Odd Fellows Hall. This rectangular commercial building is three stories tall and has larger assembly rooms on each floor at the south end. Designed in the Richardsonian Romanesque style, it has a flat roof and symmetrical facade with three bays on each level.

The surface of the facade is a lively combination of corbeled brickwork, contrasting rusticated stone, and reddish-brown brick, and stone pilasters emphasize the vertical movement of the building. Along with these strong vertical lines are horizontal bands of stone, metal, and corbeled brick. A parapet wall has brick and stone in a checkerboard pattern, as well as the inscription I. O. O. F. and the date of construction, 1891.

In 2009, Layton Construction moved the Odd Fellows Hall to the other side of the street to make way for the new Frank Moss Courthouse. "We're going to pack it up and move it," said Alan Rindlisbacher, director of corporate communications for Layton Construction. "Everything is done in 90-degree movements. If it were a car, we could just swing it around and back it right in there. But this is an old, unreinforced masonry building." This effort to preserve this historic treasure required an original, nontraditional solution to make it happen.[13]

New York Hotel
42 West Post Office Place or 48 West Market Street
1906
Richard K. A. Kletting
The New York Hotel illuminates the narrative around the competition between the Mormon and non-Mormon sectors in downtown Salt Lake City at the turn of the century. Richard K. A. Kletting, designer of the Utah State Capitol and Utah's most

prominent architect of the period, designed the hotel for prominent mining magnate and businessman Orange J. Salisbury in 1906. One of more than a dozen or so commercial structures built by non-Mormons during the first decade and a half of the twentieth century, the New York Hotel had a distinctive facade that faced the Independent Order of Odd Fellows Hall, built a decade earlier on Market Street, until the latter was moved to the other side of the street to make way for the Frank Moss Courthouse addition.

Mirroring the dualistic spatial pattern that marked development along Main Street during these years, this hotel offered a housing alternative to the Hotel Utah at the other end of Main Street. While Mormon businesses tended to be located near ZCMI at the top of Main Street near Temple Square, non-Mormon businesses were more likely to be found south of 200 South. Built in proximity to the Exchange Place district, the New York Hotel was one of a dozen hotels of various sizes built in downtown Salt Lake City during the Progressive Era of the late nineteenth and early twentieth centuries, in response to the construction of both the Union Pacific Railroad Station and the Denver and Rio Grande Railroad Depot.

The facade of the New York Hotel includes a flat-roofed portico supported by Doric columns, and a parapet above provides entrance into the hotel, capped by a cornice lined with modillions, perhaps the most elaborate ornamentation on the front of the building.

Federal Building and Post Office / Frank E. Moss Federal Courthouse

Federal Building and Post Office / Frank E.
Moss Federal Courthouse
Northwest corner of 400 South and Main
Street
1902–1905; 1911–1912
James Knox Taylor, Supervising Architect of
the Treasury, 1931–1932; James A. Wetmore,
Acting Supervising Architect of the Treasury

Whenever a major federal building is constructed in a city, it is a sort of sign that the
city has arrived. When the Federal Building
and Post Office was erected between 1903
and 1906, it made just such a statement. The
federal government established a permanent
and enduring presence with this impressive
Neoclassical building, distinguished above
all else by the colonnade that runs its full
length along Main Street. Monumental in
every way, ponderous in style, and distinctive in materials, presentation, and form, the
courthouse used the Neoclassical Revival
style, a government-promoted style that
found its way into commercial, religious,
and residential Utah architecture to assert
its importance. It is the oldest building in
the district and establishes a visual boundary or border for Exchange Place.

Judge Building
8 East 300 South
1907
David C. Dart

Around the block from the core Exchange
Place buildings is the Judge Building, built
for Mary H. Judge, a well-known Salt Lake
City businesswoman who inherited interest
in several railroad companies and mining
enterprises in Park City upon her husband's death. John Judge was a partner with
Thomas Kearns and David Keith in developing the Silver King Mine in Park City.
Mary Judge put her inheritance to work
and hired architect David C. Dart to design
this building to house railroad industries,

which features a protected steel frame with
a straight front, a flat roof, sparse ornamentation, and a prominent and unusual
projecting copper cornice. Within a couple
of years after it was built, twenty-two companies occupied the building, known as the
Railroad Exchange Building.

Mary was also well known locally as a
generous philanthropist. She endowed the
Judge Miner's Hospital, which later became
Judge Memorial High School, and donated
liberally to the Cathedral of the Madeleine
project. A nine-story commercial-style
building with a solid presence on both Main
Street and 300 South, the Judge Building
stretches horizontally rather than vertically. Trojans projecting at each corner of
the cornice, colorful ceramic tile triangles,
and swags of carved stone fruit above the
seventh-story windows enliven this commercial building and the streetscape.

Exchange Place Historic District
Alley between 300 South and 400 South,
between Main Street and State Street
1903–1917

No place in downtown Salt Lake City is
better at telling the story of the enmity
and competition that existed between the
Mormon and non-Mormon worlds at the
turn of the century than Exchange Place.
The dream child of mining entrepreneur
Samuel Newhouse, this urban commercial
neighborhood is the result of his concept of
building a western Wall Street in downtown
Salt Lake City. Exchange Place is still an
impressive grouping of turn-of-the-century
commercial buildings in terms of style,
technology, and the attitude toward architecture they convey.

Exchange Place was designated as a
historic district because of the integrity
of the buildings and the unique history of
this place. It includes ten closely grouped,

significant buildings that fell within the appropriate time period and therefore contributed to the National Register's designation of Exchange Place as a historic district, and one building that did not contribute to the designation but is located near Exchange Place, a narrow street of one block that runs east and west between 300 and 400 South and Main and State Streets.

Exchange Place originated as the city's second commercial district, the non-Mormon anchor of Main Street, with buildings oriented inward into this commercial neighborhood rather than outward to embrace the rest of the city. The ten buildings were built between 1903 and 1917, and each features a steel frame, masonry-type construction that was considered the most up to date at the time in terms of fireproofing, and other features such as elevators and pneumatic tube systems.

Salt Lake Stock and Mining Exchange Building
39 Exchange Place
1908
John C. Craig, Chicago/Salt Lake City

The first building one sees upon leaving 400 South and driving into the Exchange Place district is the Salt Lake Stock and Mining Exchange Building, a low-riding Neoclassical Revival block. Constructed in 1908 for the Salt Lake Stock Exchange, the building was built with steel frame construction, a facade clad in gray stone, and sidewalls with brick. Only two stories high, rather than falling in line with the skyscraper theme developed farther down the street, the Stock Exchange is nevertheless a monumental and impressive building. The front facade is five bays wide and has a massive Greek-style pediment at the center, framing the three central bays. Four two-story

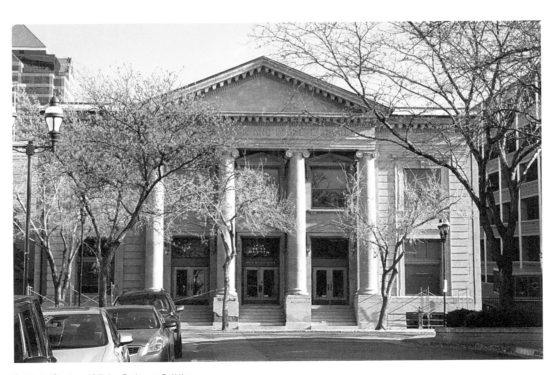

Salt Lake Stock and Mining Exchange Building

freestanding Ionic columns support the pediment and create an even pattern of movement across the front of the building.

The Salt Lake Stock Exchange was the only registered exchange between Chicago and the West Coast states and was one of the last registered exchanges that established market stock prices with the call or auction system. The exchange was especially active during the uranium boom of the 1950s, when it was an important center for the trade of uranium stock. Samuel Newhouse donated the lot for the exchange, which functioned as such until 1979.

Boston and Newhouse Buildings
9 Exchange Place
1908 and 1910
Henry Ives Cobb, Chicago/New York

Samuel Newhouse provided the financing for both the Boston and Newhouse Buildings. These elegant twins were the

Boston and Newhouse Buildings

centerpieces of the Exchange Place area. Newhouse's original intent was to build a second pair of skyscrapers at the other end of the block. The second twins were never built, in part because Newhouse could no longer afford to build them, but several other significant and interesting buildings were.

Newhouse commissioned Henry Ives Cobb, a noted Chicago and New York architect, to design these two vertical shafts. Conveying the look of a larger urban environment and more sophisticated than many other commercial buildings in town, these buildings set the standard for Newhouse's vision of Wall Street.

Both buildings are commercial style, built with steel frame construction and stone cladding on two walls, and brick on the other two. The buildings are organized into three sections—distinct and slightly different Main Street levels curve around the buildings' base, each with its own style of decoration in the entrance. The Boston Building's lobby walls are covered with a beautiful and intricate mosaic design, and the Newhouse lobby is far more dignified and restrained, with Classical details similar to those on the exterior. The first two floors form the base where public spaces were found, the third through the ninth make up the shaft with the main office space, and the upper two floors appear like an elaborately decorated capital—a heavily decorated cornice that juts out into the sky.

The buildings are ornately decorated with stone and terra-cotta relief work. But instead of the more familiar motifs of the Classical styles, here the designs are industrial symbols, cartouches, and buffalo or lion heads. Bundles of wheat weave up the pilasters instead of vines and grapes, mirroring the products of Utah rather than ancient Greece.

Commercial Club Building
32 Exchange Place
1908
Ware and Treganza

The non-Mormons who had offices in the Boston and Newhouse Buildings or other nearby office structures came to the Commercial Club Building to relax. This beautiful Italian Renaissance Revival building is not as tall as the other two main anchors at Exchange Place (the Boston and Newhouse Buildings) but is easily just as elegant. Its distinctive polychromatic cornice decorated with terra-cotta relief is one of the most beautiful in the state. The building is gracious and lovely, like an incredibly elegant host.

Samuel Newhouse donated the land for this building, hoping it would be like the New York Athletic Club. Architects Walter E. Ware and Alberto O. Treganza chose a warm, cream-colored stone for the Commercial Club that contrasted with the gray severity of the commercial structures nearby.

Ware and Treganza's Commercial Club Building is surely one of the loveliest buildings in downtown Salt Lake City. Because of its polychromatic wall surface and lively, joyful decoration, it is a colorful, optimistic addition to the commercial environment of Exchange Place. Reminiscent of the color and exuberance of the Italian palazzo, the Commercial Club is six stories tall and has polychromatic terra-cotta work, fluted columns, ornamental faces, lion heads, inlaid panels of colorful mosaic tile, a bracketed copper cornice, western motifs of plaster cattle skulls, and swags in the ceiling dome. Besides meeting rooms, the Commercial Club Building at one time had a swimming pool and dressing rooms, a lounge and a banquet room, private dining rooms, and a ladies' parlor. Game rooms and private suites for business meetings once made it a popular and comfortable destination for local businessmen.

Commercial Club Building

New Grand Hotel
369 South Main Street
1910
John C. Craig, Chicago/Salt Lake City

Supporting the business district to the north at Exchange Place, this hotel built in 1910 played off the wealth produced in Park City mines. When it was built by John Daly, the New Grand Hotel had 150 rooms and was five stories tall. John C. Craig, an architect who also designed the Salt Lake Stock Exchange, designed this building as well as the Salt Lake Herald Building and the Eagle Gate Apartments. The New Grand Hotel provided convenient lodging near Exchange

New Grand Hotel

Place, the Judge Building, and other commercial buildings on Salt Lake City's Main Street near 400 South.

The polychromatic wall surface includes geometric panels, a projecting cornice, and Chicago-style windows for hotel suites. Red brick walls contrast with the variety of materials used for decoration that enliven the wall surface.

Federation of Labor Hall / Hotel Plandome
69 East 400 South
1903
Richard K. A. Kletting

Richard Kletting designed a number of distinctive commercial buildings and hotels for downtown Salt Lake City, this one for Jewish immigrant Albert Fisher in 1903. The purpose of the building was to provide housing for members of the Utah Federation of Labor and other unions. It included large meeting rooms, lodge rooms, and a variety of office spaces. After 1913, Fisher repurposed part of the building as a hotel. Kitty-corner from the City and County Building, the Hotel Plandome was conveniently located near political, cultural, and commercial activity.

First Security Bank Building
405 South Main Street
1955
W. Sarmiento, St. Louis; Slack Winburn, Salt Lake City

When it was built in 1955, the First Security Bank Building was Salt Lake City's acknowledgment of the influence of modernist architect Mies van der Rohe and the first skyscraper to be built after a gap of thirty years, between the Depression of the late 1920s and the economic recovery after World War II. As a result, after years

First Security Bank Building

and it would not be until the late 1990s with the building of the new Grand American Hotel that the traditional length of Main Street's commercial district would change.

Courthouse Trax Station
Main Street between 400 South and
500 South
1999

Art at the Courthouse Station addresses themes of justice and balance, both duties of the city's legal system, and features metal cutouts of individuals who might be waiting for the light rail train from the city.

Scott Matheson Courthouse
450 South State Street
1998
MHTN Architects, Salt Lake City; HOK
Architects, San Francisco

Pragmatically it made perfect sense to bring the Third District Juvenile and District Courts, the Office of the Court Administrator, and the Utah State Supreme Court into one common facility. Reflecting the conservative nature of the state's judicial system, the concept drew heavily from Classical design elements so popular nationally in public building design. The Division of Facilities Management and Construction completed a Judicial Facilities Master Plan and Architectural Program for the proposed Courts Complex and opened a design-build competition for a $72 million facility.

The winning design team, MHTN and HOK, and Big D Construction created a traditional-style building that responded to the conservative tenor of the state. Relating in terms of height to the building across the street, the City and County Building, the five-story Courthouse building centered around a large central rotunda facing east onto State Street. Public building

of privation and sacrifice, this building seemed to be ample evidence of a new era of prosperity.

The First Security Bank Building exemplified the principles of modernism—a glass window wall and steel frame, porcelain-coated steel panels, a flat roof, and a general lack of ornamentation. Its sleek geometric forms and lines speak to a different design idea—the machine aesthetic. When it was built, local papers compared it to other modern buildings like Le Corbusier's United Nations Building in New York City or Mies van der Rohe's buildings.

With the building's intentional location at the corner of Main Street and 400 South, First Security Bank president George S. Eccles believed this exciting new building would pull commercial development past the turn-of-the century Exchange Place structures. This dream failed to materialize,

Scott Matheson Courthouse

circulation radiated out from this space, and a two-story gallery extended east to west.

The design was completed after the bombing of the Oklahoma City Federal Building, which raised serious questions about security. In response to these new concerns, many significant blast-resistant features were incorporated into the design. The building also benefited from the Utah State 1% Funding for the Arts program. Six major art projects were also incorporated into the design, including an engraving reading "The Scott M. Matheson Courts Complex" on the face of the building in the exterior cornice band of the rotunda. Other decorative artwork included extensive and colorful stenciling of patterns into the oculus and dome of the rotunda. Recognizing it as an important new public building for Utah, the Utah AIA gave it an Award for Excellence in Architecture in 1998.

Salt Lake City and County Building
Between 500 South and 400 South, State Street and 100 East
1891–1894
Monheim, Bird and Proudfoot
A landmark building in downtown Salt Lake City, the City and County Building is a commanding presence that surrounding buildings are forced to address. It has had a rich history, serving at various times as the center of city, county, and even territorial government. Demonstrations, festivals, state and local celebrations, and government activities are staged both in the building itself and on Washington Square as a public space. When it was built, it was intentionally a conjoined city hall and county courthouse. It was built after a decade of rapid growth when the populations of both the city and county had doubled. It was originally planned for a location two blocks

away from Temple Square, but by 1891, after considerable political intrigue, a new location was identified at Washington Square.

After a design competition, the city and county hired the design team of Monheim, Bird and Proudfoot, a Salt Lake City architectural firm, to design the building. They chose the Romanesque Revival style, but the building also conjures images of castles in France. It is unlike any other building in the city. Built with the familiar and popular Utah Kyune sandstone (used for the Cathedral of the Madeleine and other monumental buildings), in terms of materiality it is very much rooted in this culture and environment. The elaborate sculptural ornamentation on virtually all expanses of wall roots the building as well in the history of this place. Not didactic like the bas-relief sculpture of a Gothic cathedral but more like a biographical lineup of important figures from Utah history, the images include busts of Jedediah M. Grant, the first mayor of Salt Lake City; Mayor Robert N. Baskin; and federal judge Jacob Blair, as well as portraits of Chiefs Joseph and Wahkara and various women who played key roles in the suffrage movement and the movement for women's rights. Symbols taken from Freemasonry, the American eagle, and symbols of brotherhood, justice, and sacrifice are found along rooflines, surrounding windows and doors, and perched on the peak of the roof.

The building contains more than one hundred rooms and has beautiful onyx tile lining the floors of the hallways on each level.

Salt Lake City and County Building.
Used by permission, Utah State Historical Society.

Capitol Hill and Marmalade District

Salt Lake Nineteenth Ward Meetinghouse
225 West 500 North
1890–1892; 1908
Robert Bowman (church)

The exuberant exoticism of the Nineteenth Ward Meetinghouse reflects the trend at the end of the nineteenth century toward revivalism and the picturesque. Designed by English-born architect and stonemason Robert Bowman, who was the contractor for the City and County Building, it moves from the strict rectangularity of a simple box to diversity in terms of mass, materiality, and style. The best term to describe this

Salt Lake Nineteenth Ward Meetinghouse

Salt Lake Nineteenth Ward Relief Society Hall
168 West 500 North
1908
Robert Bowman

As in many other wards throughout the LDS Church in the last quarter of the nineteenth century, the Nineteenth Ward's women had their own building, a Relief Society Hall measuring fourteen by twenty-six feet and located west of the older meetinghouse two blocks away (it was later moved to the present site). Used for philanthropic activities, the Relief Society Hall has a gabled vestry with a deep cornice return and a semicircular plaque that reads "19th Ward Relief Society, 1908." The entrance is beneath a Roman arch with a small, bracketed canopy above.

The Nineteenth Ward was one of the first to be organized in the city in 1849. Before the building was built, local members met in private homes or at the Warm Springs Bath House. Meetings were also held in two different adobe buildings—a schoolhouse and an 1866 church—before a revival-style church was built in 1890–92. Since 1982, the building has been home to the Salt Lake Acting Company.

Thomas Quayle House
355 North Quince Street
1884

During the 1970s, the Thomas Quayle House was the home of the Utah Heritage Foundation, the state nonprofit advocacy organization for historic preservation. The building, built in 1884, was originally closer

church is eclectic, a definite deviation from Bowman's earlier work and the churches of earlier generations. Also in 1892 he designed the Dinwoodey Block, the Clark-Eldredge Block, and the Constitution Building, other prominent Salt Lake landmarks.

A combination of styles and details includes an onion dome over a central projecting entrance, an elliptically vaulted ceiling on the chapel space, and round-headed arches over windows and doors. These features distinguish this meetinghouse, which stretches to reflect the world beyond Utah, accommodate the liturgical needs of the Mormon congregation that used it, and create an exotic, lovely backdrop for the religious lives of its people.

Salt Lake Nineteenth Ward Relief Society Hall

brother John followed the gold rush to California, where they bought a small store, began a freighting business, and transported goods from Sacramento to the mines. Eventually they brought their business back to Utah and expanded into Idaho and Montana.

James Watson House
335 North Quince Street
1866
James Watson

The *T* shape of this vernacular house's floor plan maximized available space on a small site in a densely built part of Salt Lake City, the Marmalade. Over time, James Watson added Victorian elements including elaborate woodwork, an Italianate oriel in the front bay, and decorative porch features. A small cornerstone recorded the date of construction as 1866.

English convert James Watson immigrated to Utah in 1863 along with his brother Joseph. The two worked together, founded a company, and specialized in stonework. The pair helped construct many important local buildings including the Hooper-Eldredge Block, the ZCMI Shoe Factory, and part of the main ZCMI building. Joseph Watson was a member of the City Council for a time.

Richard Vaughn Morris House
314 North Quince Street
1861–1866

The Marmalade district features some of the most colorful, lively Victorian and pioneer houses in the city. Hugging the unique geography of this hill dropping to the west of the State Capitol, the district housed working-class people in a convenient

to the city center near the Farmers' Market but was relocated to Quince Street in 1975 when the site was sold to the Hilton Hotel. This difficult, but effective, move to a new site was made possible through the collaboration of city officials, utility companies, and others. Completely restored and also listed on the National Register of Historic Places, the building responds in every way to the historic character of the neighborhood.

The house is unusual in terms of its frame construction, but picturesque in every way. Thomas Quayle built his family's own Carpenter Gothic–style house. Distinctive features include steep gables, corner wooden quoins, decorative bargeboard, and Eastlake-style porch ornamentation.

Thomas Quayle was born on the Isle of Man in 1835, converted to Mormonism with his parents in 1847, and not long afterward immigrated to Utah with his family from Nauvoo with the John Taylor company in 1847. For a short time, Thomas and his

location just north of the city center. The Richard Morris house is one of the oldest intact residences in the city. This vernacular two-story central-passage house is symmetrical in terms of plan and elevation, reflecting the influence of Classical styles familiar to this British immigrant. A porch was later constructed to imitate the Victorian. Constructed with simple adobe brick, it is an excellent example of early domestic Utah architecture, a substantial home for a recognized community leader, Richard Vaughn Morris—a government official, businessman, and lawyer who immigrated to the United States from North Wales in 1855. Morris served in the Nauvoo Legion during the Indian Wars and received the rank of lieutenant. He was secretary of the Deseret Telegraph Company, president of the Utah Soap Factory, auditor of the Utah Central Railroad, and secretary to congressional delegate William H. Hooper in 1870. His plural wife Harriet lived in this house with her eight children.

This one-and-a-half-story adobe building has walls covered with stucco for extra weatherproofing and a hipped roof. Windows frame a centrally located door on the symmetrical facade. The entrance door has a transom and sidelights, and chimneys on both ends. Typical of vernacular practicality, the interior of the home has plain molded woodwork, which is nevertheless carefully worked. Coved ceilings in the hall and parlor with relatively plain moldings, and a beautiful staircase with a turned balustrade in the central hall, are significant interior details. Original floors were hand grained, a treatment also evident in the doors and moldings.

Daughters of Utah Pioneers Museum
300 North Main Street
1950

The Daughters of Utah Pioneers Museum is west of the capitol on a triangular piece of ground at the top of Main Street. The building references the historical style of

Daughters of Utah Pioneers Museum

the old Salt Lake Theater, a Neoclassical design complete with engaged pilasters running rhythmically around the building's exterior and an elaborate entablature and hipped roof at the top. Instead of a grand auditorium space, the museum is filled with artifacts from the pioneer period of nineteenth-century Utah. Floral arrangements made with women's hair are displayed here along with quilts, clothing, china, and other precious items brought to the valley by the pioneers (including a stuffed two-headed goat). On the site, poignant sculptures remind one of the suffering of pioneer women who lost children on the wagon train traveling to Utah or who contributed to community building in the Salt Lake Valley.

Utah State Capitol
State Street and 300 North
1912–1916
Richard K. A. Kletting

The Classical vocabulary was most popular for public buildings in the United States, reinforcing a link with the democracy of the ancient world. Utah architect Richard Kletting was inspired in his design for the Utah State Capitol by the essence of Classical architecture, here relying on details from the Corinthian style. Formality, order, harmony of proportion and line, and rationality are embodied here. The building is 404 feet long by 240 feet wide, and the distance from the top of the dome to the center of the ground floor level is 165 feet. Despite the prominent vertical movement of the dome, the building is overwhelmingly horizontal in its massing. The symmetrical facade is organized around a central pedimented entrance with a colonnade moving around the building—thirty-two Corinthian columns sit on a podium foundation level and are topped by an entablature.

Artwork from primarily local artists enlivens the interior. Particularly significant are murals (4,500 square feet each) in spandrels at the base of the central dome, completed under the Federal Art Project of the New Deal program and the WPA, each depicting one hundred figures that are ten feet high. Utah artist Lee Greene Richards prepared the sketches for the four murals, which depict important scenes from Utah's history—Father Escalante first entering Utah Valley in 1776; Peter Skene Ogden at the Ogden River, 1828; John C. Frémont's visit to the Great Salt Lake in 1843; and Brigham Young and the pioneers entering the valley in 1847. Also designed by Lee Greene Richards, the friezes of the dome feature historical scenes, each measuring fifteen by twenty-five feet—*The Pony Express and Stage Coach*; *Peace with the Native Americans*; *Advent of Irrigation*; *Driving the Golden Spike*; *The Seagulls and Crickets*; *A Party in the Old Bowery*; *Naming Ensign Peak on 26 July 1847*; and *General Connor Inaugurates Mining*.

Plans for the capitol grounds were sketched out by John Olmsted, Frederick Law Olmsted's son, and were conceptualized as an elegant, natural setting for this impressive building. In some ways, the capitol grounds form the largest park in the state. Surrounded by forty acres of lawns, paths, and rows of trees and flowers, the capitol grounds include monumental sculpture as well as the Vietnam War Memorial, sculpted by Clyde Ross Morgan, dedicated to the soldiers from Utah who lost their lives in the war, 388 men and women who died or are missing in action.

By midcentury the state had outgrown the office space in the capitol and built a new state office building to the north. Mirroring the east-west horizontal organization of the capitol itself, the new building

Utah State Capitol

has steel frame construction, aluminum sun louvers overhanging windows on the south, recessed lights, spandrels of porcelainized steel around certain windows, and other more up-to-date technologies.

The award-winning restoration of the building in 2008 brought numerous accolades to MSJN Architects, the state Historic Preservation Office, and the Capitol Restoration Committee, resulting in a systemic upgrade, refurbished and restored materials, and landscaping according to the Olmsted plan.

Council Hall
300 North State Street
1866
William Folsom

One of the earliest public buildings built in Utah and the backdrop to key events in territorial government history, the

Council Hall was first located on the corner of South Temple and Main Street, kitty-corner from Temple Square, and constructed in 1866 for $70,000. Listed as a National Historic Landmark, this Federal/Greek Revival–style building was dismantled in 1960 and its sandstone slabs carefully numbered, transported, and reconstructed at its present location south of the capitol at the top of State Street. During the thirty years after it was first built, the Council Hall was an important seat of government. The Utah territorial legislature met in its upstairs meeting room, and the organizational meeting of ZCMI was held there as well. The building combined offices for the police department, the Board of Health, the mayor, and in 2000 the Utah Travel Council. LDS rituals were briefly performed in the building besides commercial

Council Hall

and territorial government meetings. The interior includes a dogleg staircase with turned balustrades leading to the upper story. The second-floor open space was called the Rose Room and served as both a general courtroom and meeting place. During the late nineteenth century, it had a grand piano that crossed the plains in a pioneer oxcart. The Rose Room measures thirty-five by forty-five feet and features an elaborate plaster cornice.

When plans were made in 1948 to relocate the Council Hall to a prominent new place on Capitol Hill, the city provided the land and the LDS Church funded the moving and reconstruction costs, which totaled $300,000.

White Memorial Chapel / Eighteenth Ward Meetinghouse
150 East 300 North
1883
Obed Taylor
This Gothic Revival church, the Eighteenth Ward Meetinghouse, featured a single steeple tower, pointed-arched windows, and a steeply pitched roof and influenced the design of other late nineteenth-century churches throughout the area. It was originally built on Second Avenue in 1883 but

White Memorial Chapel / Eighteenth Ward Meetinghouse.
Photograph by Elizabeth Bradley-Wilson. Used with permission of the photographer.

was dismantled and reconstructed across from the capitol in 1980. It has been completely renovated, and the state uses it for nondenominational meetings and public gatherings.

Architect Obed Taylor was originally from San Francisco, and he also designed the original ZCMI building. Several early church leaders—President Brigham Young, Heber C. Kimball, and Newell K. Whitney—attended church at this building.

After the building was threatened with demolition, Kenneth and Ada Marie White joined the Community Memorial Chapel

Group, determined to save the building. They donated $240,000 toward a $300,000 restoration project to rebuild the church at a different location on Capitol Hill. Stephen T. Baird, a Salt Lake architect well known for his preservation efforts, was the architect for the project, which became known as the White Memorial Chapel. They dismantled the building brick by brick, carefully coding and numbering each along with the tower, pews, doors, large Gothic stained-glass window, and carved wooden pulpit in 1973.

Meditation Chapel and Memorial House
Memory Grove Park, 370 North Canyon Road and 485 North Canyon Road
1948

The Meditation Chapel at Memory Grove memorializes Ross Beason Jr., son of Mr. and Mrs. Ross Beason, and all the other soldiers from Utah who died during World War II. A diminutive Greek temple, the building is constructed with Georgia marble, has four columns with Doric capitals running across the front, and sits on a podium with stairs leading to the entrance porch. The doors to the small chapel it contains are formed with bronze and the roof is made of Utah copper. Mayor Earl J. Glade and Governor Herbert B. Maw dedicated the building in July 1948 and accepted the gift of the chapel from the Beasons on behalf of the state. It is estimated that twenty thousand visitors from the city came to the park that day. Four stained-glass windows representing the four branches of the armed forces—the army, navy, air force, and marines—are on the two sides of the building. Granite markers memorializing more than three hundred soldiers who lost their lives in World War II are found on a small plaza in front of the chapel. On any given day, you might spot brides posing in front of the Meditation Chapel or people sitting quietly nearby.

Meditation Chapel and Memorial House

The offices of the Utah Heritage Foundation are upstairs in the Memorial House, which forms the backdrop for countless weddings and other social events throughout the year. Historically the building housed a stable and a storage shed owned by the P. J. Moran Company. It was built in 1890, and Pope and Burton designed a new facade in 1926 for the new owner—Salt Lake City.

Ottinger Hall
233 North Canyon Road
1900

This public building, tightly sandwiched into the space between the bank of the canyon and the sidewalk of Canyon Road, goes far beyond function to create a building distinctive for its unusual corbeled brick, stepped parapet, and square tower above, which create a handsome facade and sophisticated appearance. Ottinger

Hall was important as a meeting place for firemen who came together for social and other types of meetings. Three years after first settlement, Salt Lake City's volunteer fire department was organized, although its first fire chief wasn't appointed until 1853. Deseret Engine Company Number One was established in 1860, as well as Deseret Hook and Ladder Company Number One. Successive chiefs included John D. T. McAllister, Charles M. Donaldson, and Utah artist George M. Ottinger in 1876. Ottinger was a well-known photographer and set painter for the Salt Lake Theater. The fire department evolved from a volunteer to a paid organization the year of a devastating fire in 1883 that proved the city needed a professional force.

In 1890 Ottinger organized the Veteran Volunteer Firemen's Association and became its first chief. Ten years later, they built this hall.

Ottinger Hall

Miller-Geoghegan House
204 North State Street
1890

This vintage Queen Anne house was a showcase in its peak, with its sweeping wraparound front porch, three-story tower topped by a steeply pitched conical roof, and brick and red stone exterior. The house has the characteristic abundance so typical of the Queen Anne, combining several different building materials—red sandstone, gingerbread, brick, shingles, columns, wood, and decorative woodwork. As is common in this style, the house has an asymmetrically arranged mass. An intricate cast-iron fence surrounded the property.

Charles C. and Millicent Godbe Brooks built this sixteen-room house in 1890.

Successful as a mining engineer, Brooks was also the U.S. deputy mineral surveyor for Utah, as well as county surveyor and a member of the Salt Lake County Board of Public Works. His wife's father was William Godbe, one of the founders of the Godbeite movement, an oppositional group of liberal businessmen who left the Mormon Church because they objected to its economic policies.

Ashby Snow House
158 North State Street
1909

The Ashby Snow House demonstrates the growing cosmopolitan nature of Salt Lake City during the first decade of the twentieth century. Rivaling the best examples of

Frank Lloyd Wright architecture nationally, this two-story Prairie-style house conveys a sense of spaciousness and is constructed with brick and stucco, emphasizing the horizontal lines of the prairie. Contrasting with the verticality of many of the Victorian houses in the district, this house has broad overhanging eaves, and bands of casement windows that contrast with the dramatic vertical swell of the geography itself as it rises toward the State Capitol. Windows feature beautiful leaded-glass border decorations, and the projecting front porch creates the illusion that it is hanging without any visible means of support.

Salt Lake lawyer Ashby Snow was a member of Utah's blue-blooded elite. The son of prominent Mormon St. George leader Erastus Snow, Ashby was a successful entrepreneur and worked with several successful local businesses, including the Utah Portland Cement Company, ZCMI, Hotel Utah, Utah-Idaho Sugar, Saltair Beach, the Salt Lake, Garfield and Western Railway, and Utah Savings and Trust. His son Erastus P. Snow assumed ownership of the house in 1931 and built an underground swimming pool with dressing rooms on the south end of the lot.

Alfred W. McCune Mansion and Carriage
House
Northeast corner of Main Street and
200 North
1901
Samuel C. Dallas

The Alfred W. McCune Mansion and Carriage House forms a stunning contrast to the political buildings to the north and the religious buildings to the south. Possibly the most colorful and richly detailed building in the city, it holds one of the most superb locations on Salt Lake City's Main Street where it starts to rise dramatically to the north.

Built for Alfred W. McCune and his wife, Elizabeth, according to the design of Samuel C. Dallas, the house has a rare style for this area—the Shingle style popular in New England at the turn of the century. McCune was a convert to the Mormon Church who came to Utah from England and made his money both as a railroad contractor and through various mining investments.

The mansion's three stories include twenty-one rooms with a carriage house to the rear. Built with a variety of materials in colors ranging from red to dark brownish red, it includes red sandstone, dark red brick, red-brown roof tiles, and shingles stained to match. The interior is equally rich in color and texture and features superb craftsmanship in woodwork, stonework, wall coverings, and ceiling paintings. A ballroom on the upper level has mirrors on the walls surrounding the dance floor.

When the McCunes moved to Los Angeles in 1920, they donated the house to the Church of Jesus Christ of Latter-day Saints, which changed the use to a music school. The McCune School of Art and Music operated until 1958, when Brigham Young University's Salt Lake Center moved into the space. In 1973, the house transferred into private hands and has been used for office space ever since.

The interior space is lavishly decorated with the finest wood, marble, glass, and other materials, creating a sensual and luxurious experience—English oak is used on the walls of the main hall; a great fireplace built of reddish-brown Nubian marble with lovely natural discolorations runs from ceiling to floor; and hand-finished carvings appear at every point, whether the vestibule, the beamed ceiling, or the mantle. A balcony overlooks the stairs halfway up. Walls covered with rose satin brocade, panels of Watteau paintings over the doorways,

Alfred W. McCune Mansion and Carriage House

white satin–grained mahogany, broad mirrors on the side walls, and chandeliers with cut-glass fittings together create an exotic environment of wealth and opulence.

Gibbs-Thomas House
137 North West Temple
1896
Richard K. A. Kletting

Prominent Utah architect Richard Kletting designed this house for Gideon A. and Margaret Taylor Gibbs in 1896. Kletting was well known for his designs of Saltair, the Salt Palace, and the Deseret News Building. The Gibbs-Thomas House is one of the most elegant houses in the fashionable neighborhood just one block north of Temple Square. Gibbs, a pioneer Utah civil

engineer and surveyor, married a daughter of John Taylor, the third president of the LDS Church. After the Gibbses, Elbert D. Thomas bought the house in 1909. Thomas, a U.S. senator for Utah between 1935 and 1950, held several diplomatic and military positions during his lifetime.

Lush landscaping and a wrought-iron fence frame this house. Like many Victorian houses from the era, this house has multiple colors and textures, with dark green trim contrasting with orange brick and red sandstone sills and lintels. Reflecting Kletting's skill, the house is balanced asymmetrically and has a mixture of roof pitches and planes, projecting bays, and a wraparound porch. Shingles are found on the gable at the top of the projecting bay on the upper level, in contrast with the brick and stone below.

On the interior, the same diversity characterizes the division of space. Inside the entrance is a staircase and a parlor with a curved wall to the side, and a second parlor beyond that. The Dinwoodey Furniture Company of Salt Lake City produced all the fireplace surrounds, mantels, and original furnishings.

Introduction to South Temple

Distinguished originally for its proximity to Temple Square, South Temple was sometimes called Brigham Street for the LDS Church's prophet and president Brigham Young. Young's family complex of houses, outbuildings, schoolhouse, and two-story outhouse is situated on the block just east of Temple Square on South Temple, a site that modeled the physical components of a Mormon "family kingdom." Prominent LDS church leaders and businessmen such as William Jennings, the owner of the Eagle Emporium; and Daniel H. Wells, the attorney general of the State of Deseret, owned the first houses of significance along the street, besides those owned by Brigham Young. The street stretched from the Devereaux Mansion at 300 West to the entrance to Popperton Place or what would become known as Federal Heights at 1300 East and was a boulevard of high-style homes of wealthy mining entrepreneurs, railroad or business owners, politicians, and religious leaders.

After the coming of the railroad to Salt Lake City in 1870, mining wealth came to Utah when troops staying at Fort Douglas prospected on the west bench of the Salt Lake Valley and other miners traveled through the territory and discovered mineral wealth near Park City, Silver Ridge in southern Utah, and other locations along the mountain ranges. Newcomers to Utah included merchants, land speculators, and miners who interpreted the landscape as holding the promise of wealth and prestige, rather than religious refuge. They displayed this wealth with new homes that lined South Temple like a line of elaborately costumed ingenues at a ball. Many were Victorian mansions that were bedecked with the finest building materials available. By 1903, South Temple had paved sidewalks, and the next year the roadbed itself was paved. Several large-scale institutional buildings were intermixed with the homes of the rich and famous, including the Cathedral of the Madeleine, the First Presbyterian Church, Holy Cross Hospital, and the Masonic Temple. Regardless, as a group, these buildings are architectural landmarks, self-consciously located in styles made popular elsewhere and representing a diversity of people, ideas, lifestyles, and practices that contrast with the pioneer origins of the city.

Rowland Hall–St. Mark's School / Madeleine Choir School
Block between A and B Streets and First and Second Avenues
1862

Before it moved to Guardsman Way near the University of Utah campus in 2002, the lower-division campus of Rowland Hall–St. Mark's School (which originated as an Episcopalian mission school) occupied the block between A and B Streets and First and Second Avenues for more than a century. This complex of domestically scaled structures originally all faced south to maximize a view that spread over grassy open spaces and tennis courts and looked out toward the city itself, resembling the campus of a small college in New England.

In wasn't until 1970 that the view moved inward instead, when a classroom building was erected on First Avenue and created an interior quad or courtyard space, perhaps more in line with the educational mission of the school. The first building Rowland Hall occupied was the Watt-Haskins House. This impressive, two-story adobe structure built in 1862 was inhabited by the school in 1880. A gracious front porch runs the length of the facade of the house. As it grew, the school built or bought other houses on the block. In 1906, the school constructed a large brick classroom building. Set back from the street in a way that created a three-sided courtyard, a 1910 chapel has a bracketed cornice and a roof topped by a cross, signaling its function and mirroring the design motif of the other structures.

Eventually Rowland Hall purchased three large houses nearby for faculty offices, classrooms, and housing, including the Joseph Rawlins House, which was built in 1887. This two-and-a-half-story Italianate-style brick home has a gabled roof and dormer windows, an irregular plan, and a two-story rectangular tower at the southeast front entrance. In 1956, the school acquired the 1888 Joseph E. Caine House, distinguished by its unusual brick and stone decoration and mass. Today, the site is the location of the Cathedral Choir School.

Cathedral of the Madeleine
331 East South Temple
1900–1907
Carl Neuhausen and Bernard Mecklenburg

When you walk through the doors of the Cathedral of the Madeleine, shake the snow off your coat and hair, and walk through the narthex and into the nave, you know you have arrived someplace special—a world of color and ritual, with towering spaces and diffuse colored light.

For the Catholic population that settled in the Great Basin, the cathedral was their spiritual and social home, the symbol of years of successful missionary efforts by a series of Catholic priests. The first Catholics to enter the territory were Fathers Francisco Atanasio Domínguez and Silvestre Vélez de Escalante, who are remembered primarily for their exploration of the region. Many of the earliest Catholic immigrants to Utah came to exploit mining opportunities—men like Thomas Kearns, David Keith, and others were important sponsors of the cathedral and built mansions along South Temple. Bishop Lawrence Scanlan was the most important Catholic leader between 1873 and 1915, a much beloved religious leader and colorful character. His dedication led to the expansion of the Catholic Church in the region and the institutionalization of many of its special programs. Under Scanlan's direction most mining towns built churches and schools. He organized and supervised the construction of St. Mary's Academy, St. Ann's Orphanage, and Holy Cross Hospital.

Father Scanlan was described as a darkly handsome, vibrant and athletic man who served for a time in Pioche, Nevada, working with Irish miners before he arrived in Salt Lake City in 1873, ready to take on the challenge of converting Mormons. His responsibilities included parishes in Frisco, Silver Reef, Eureka, and Park City as well as the railroad town of Ogden.

Perhaps his greatest accomplishment was the construction of the Cathedral of the Madeleine, which was dedicated in 1909. Architect Carl M. Neuhausen chose the Romanesque Revival style for this gray Kyune sandstone structure, which has an interior brick lining and sits on a granite foundation. The building measures 190 by 103 feet at the transepts. The floor apex is

Cathedral of the Madeleine

represent the twelve apostles, and the transept windows, which represent the Mysteries of the Rosary. A clear focal point of the cathedral is the lovely rose window representing Saint Cecilia and reflecting the influence of the rose window in the Toledo Cathedral in Spain. Distinguished by its bright, colorful interior paintings and the painting of virtually all decorative detailing, the cathedral reflects the Spanish Gothic but is overall the work of singular and highly creative individuals, including the fresco mural paintings by Felix Lieftuchter and wood carvings by the William Ross Company.

The cathedral has gone through a series of restorations—the first in 1970 when a copper roof was added and the stone was cleaned. The building was seismically retrofitted, as were the towers and roof, and several elements of the interior were updated.

The cathedral was put on the National Register of Historic Places in 1971. The National Trust for Historic Preservation awarded the Cathedral of the Madeleine a National Trust Honor Award in 1994 for its second outstanding restoration, recognizing the way the entire community mobilized to save a landmark building. The 1993 restoration of the Cathedral of the Madeleine represented ecumenical cooperation in bringing a community monument back to its original beauty. Today a virtual showcase for the arts, the cathedral stages an annual series of art events including concerts, organ recitals, other performances, and community events. The treasure of murals, stained-glass windows, mosaic, and sculpture that are part of the building's inherent decoration were restored to their historic character. The restoration began in 1988 with research into the extent of the deterioration and a feasibility study. They

65 feet high, and the ridge of the main roof is approximately 100 feet high.

Neuhausen oversaw construction until his death, and then Bernard O. Mecklenburg led the construction of the towers and roof, making some alterations in the plans. He eliminated the clerestory windows and covered all three aisles instead with a single roof plane. The configuration of the cathedral exterior aligns it comfortably with a traditional Catholic Church design, and heavy rusticated stone and Roman arches are typical elements of Romanesque Revival, but the interior is a distinctive and original design.

George Sotter of Pittsburgh created the beautiful sanctuary windows, which

studied each historic feature—wood carvings, marble, decorative paint and murals, and stained-glass windows. The Utah AIA gave an Award for Excellence in Architecture to the cathedral in 1966.

William Culmer House
33 North C Street
1881

A Second Empire mansard roof, prominent tower, and beautiful ironwork draw attention to the exterior of the two-story red-brick William Culmer House, but the interior is one of the most remarkable and unusual in town. The house was built in 1881 at a time when luxury homes were beginning to be built in Salt Lake's Avenues area, representing a changed economy and growing diversification of people and institutions in town. Located on the same street as both the Beehive House and Lion House, it was part of the lineup of houses built by ecclesiastical and economic leaders of the Mormon community as well as mining magnates at the turn of the century.

Culmer and his brother, nationally known painter Henry Culmer, were both colorful local figures. William, Henry, and their brother George became successful businessmen in the wholesale and retail distribution of paints, oils, varnishes, and window and art glass, as well as the manufacture of mirrors. They lavished the fruits of their trade on this beautiful house on South Temple. One enters the house through double mahogany doors with hand-etched panes of glass. A hand-painted faux marble entrance hall and gray-blue granite walls create a colorful and welcoming entrance to the home. In the sitting and drawing rooms are hand-painted wood-burning fireplaces made of green slate, as well as hand-painted ceilings signed by Culmer himself.

Henry Culmer painted the wall murals when he was done with his "real" job. His principal medium was secco or fresco painting, which required that he apply a plaster coating to the wall surface and paint while the plaster was still moist. The subjects of the paintings include scenes reflecting the natural diversity of Utah or Utah history, including Black Rock at the Great Salt Lake (1884); Mount Olympus (1887); the Utah War (1857–58) in Echo Canyon (1884); waterfalls in Emigration Canyon (n.d.) ; and various forest scenes that are not signed or dated.

When the family sold the house, the next owners painted over the murals, and it wasn't until the Lamar Merrel family bought the house in 1972 that the restoration of the paintings began. When Donald and Jane Stromquist purchased the home in 1976, they continued the restoration and hired a conservationist to restore the artwork and clean it at the same time.

First Presbyterian Church
12 North C Street
Late 1800s
Walter E. Ware

Presbyterian missionary work was complex and included setting up congregations, schools, and social services. The first Presbyterian congregation was established in Corinne, Utah, in 1869, and Reverend Josiah Welch organized the First Presbyterian Church in Salt Lake City in 1871, opening a school in the church in April 1875 with sixty-three students, called the Salt Lake Collegiate Institute. By 1884, the Presbyterian Church was managing thirty-three day schools and two academies—Wasatch Academy and the Salt Lake Collegiate Institute. Plans were in place for others, including All Hallows College. Within a few

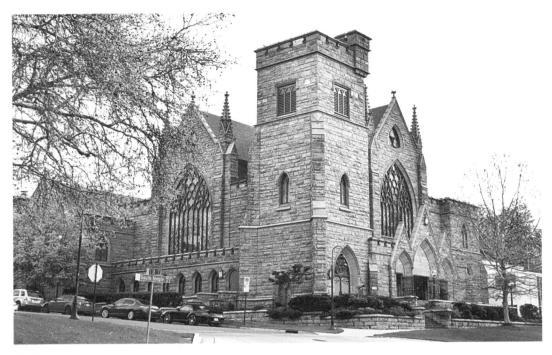

First Presbyterian Church

decades there was a sufficient population of Presbyterians and enough financial support to build an impressive and monumental church on South Temple.

Prominent Utah architect Walter E. Ware designed the First Presbyterian Church in the English-Scottish Gothic Revival style. It was based on Carlisle Cathedral in England, where Ware traveled to expand what he understood visually about revival styles. This red sandstone building used stone quarried at Red Butte and transported to the site on narrow gauge rail lines. The tripartite entrance on South Temple includes three bays with pointed arches. Stained-glass windows face east, south, and west and are similar to Tiffany windows of the period, with color fused into the glass. The pipe organ was first played at its dedication on April 10, 1911, to an audience of nine hundred.

The church underwent a significant renovation in 1957, when the modern Christian education wing was added to the north and the choir loft and altar area were modernized.

Enos A. Wall Mansion
411 East South Temple
1904
Richard K. A. Kletting
Besides sophistication and elegance, Richard K. A. Kletting displayed his familiarity with the most advanced structural technology in the Enos A. Wall Mansion, including steel frame construction and reinforced concrete. Purchased by Wall in 1904, the house was an enlargement and remodel of an earlier house owned by James Sharp, former member of the House of Representatives, prominent LDS businessman, and mayor of Salt Lake City. The

house expansion cost about $300,000 and included gilded frescoes, a new electric elevator, a built-in vacuum system, fireplaces in every bedroom, a ballroom on the third floor, game rooms, and guest quarters.

Wall was locally known as "Colonel," a title of respect and dignity that reflected great affection for the man. The entrepreneur was one of the originators of the Utah Copper Company and partly responsible for the method of refining low-grade copper ore at Bingham Canyon. He was chair of public works for a short period, a post that included supervising the grading and improving of Salt Lake City streets during the years of the City Beautiful movement in the early twentieth century.

The LDS Church purchased the Enos A. Wall Mansion in 1962 to house the LDS Business College. It donated the property in 2014 to the University of Utah. Today it is the Kem C. Gardner Policy Institute.

Keith-Brown House
529 East South Temple
1900
Frederick A. Hale

South Temple was home to LDS Church leaders, government officials, and wealthy mining entrepreneurs who made their wealth in Park City mines and lived in Salt Lake City. Perhaps none were more wealthy and powerful than Thomas Kearns and David Keith. This 1900 mansion was designed by Frederick A. Hale for David Keith in the Renaissance Revival style. Extravagant features include the second-floor skylight by the Tiffany Glass Company in New York City as well as numerous chandeliers throughout the house. A wine cellar, a ballroom, an octagonal rotunda, a bowling alley, and a shooting gallery suggest a life of leisure and elaborate entertainment.

Servants' quarters were found in the carriage house to the east.

Scottish immigrant David Keith moved from Nova Scotia to Utah because of the promise of great wealth hidden in the mountains surrounding Park City. He met Kearns in 1883, struck up a partnership, and within years was enormously wealthy. The two bought the *Salt Lake Tribune* in 1901 and were involved in civic causes through the Reform Era.

The house has a strong central mass with wings that jut out slightly in each direction, the epitome of monumentality. A two-story portico supported by freestanding columns, an entablature, and a triangular pediment enhance the sense of importance and wealth. Built with native limestone, the building creates a formal, elegant presence on South Temple, vying in monumentality with the Kearns Mansion.

This was the first of the impressive entrepreneurial mansions to undergo restoration during the late 1960s and 1970s. Bought by Terracor in 1969, it was a model for other such efforts on this street, demonstrating the viability of the idea of restoration instead of demolition.

Governor's Plaza
550 East South Temple
1983
Edwards & Daniels Associates

Governor's Plaza includes approximately 150,000 square feet of office space, seventy-six condominium units, a health club, an atrium, a ballroom, and 550 parking spaces in an underground parking garage. A stellar example of contemporary architecture that sensitively responds to its neighbors and the streetscape, Governor's Plaza is a successful mixed-use complex. The stepped-back nature of the South

Temple elevation helps the building relate to the street and its historical architectural context and creates tiered garden and patio space. The high-rise condominium in juxtaposition against the lower level creates an interesting and dynamic contrast. Governor's Plaza was built with poured-in-place, post-tensioned concrete with a sandblasted finish and was designed by Edwards & Daniels Associates.

Thomas Kearns Mansion
603 East South Temple
1902
Carl Neuhausen

Architect Carl Neuhausen designed this house for mining magnate Thomas Kearns in the French Renaissance style, with native Utah Kyune limestone and exotic imported woods for the interior, using both indigenous materials and construction products imported from abroad. Extravagant details include French moiré silk wall coverings and a floor of hand-cut marble in a mosaic design. In the library, African red marble frames the fireplace, and the black Flemish oak floor proves the perfect backdrop to lush Persian rugs, all demonstrating the immense wealth pouring out of Park City's mines.

Thomas Kearns was a poor immigrant when he arrived in Utah in 1883 at the age of twenty-one, but within a few years he was a partner with David Keith in the Silver King Mining Company, a venture that paid out dividends of $10 million between 1892 and 1907. It was an extremely lucrative enterprise. Besides his mining activities, he was a partner in the *Salt Lake Tribune* and was elected to the U.S. Senate.

When Jennie Kearns's husband died, she donated the mansion to the state in 1937, and the state's governors lived in the stately mansion on South Temple until 1957.

Thomas Kearns Mansion / Governor's Mansion

Governor J. Bracken Lee chose instead to live in a mansion in Federal Heights, and the Kearns Mansion became home to the Utah State Historical Society. When Scott Matheson was governor, he proposed restoring the Kearns Mansion and reinstating its use as the governor's residence in 1980.

In the 1980s, Utah's governors and their families resumed the tradition of residing in the home. But a fire in 1993 caused by an electrical short in a strand of Christmas lights led to serious smoke damage in the central grand hall and staircase, perhaps the most elegantly decorated parts of the house. The restoration of the Kearns Mansion attempted to preserve the past but also accommodate present needs. Original materials were cleaned and restored where possible. Those too badly destroyed were duplicated as authentically as possible. Colors from the bright Victorian palette were used for the walls and furnishings.

The building also underwent systematic seismic upgrading in 1926, and all mechanical, electrical, and communication systems were upgraded. The Utah Heritage Foundation gave the project an award of merit for its successful restoration effort in 1997.

Masonic Temple
650 East South Temple
Scott and Welch
1926

Salt Lake architects Carl W. Scott and George W. Welch designed the Masonic Temple according to the liturgical requirements of Masonic ritual and maximized the advantages of modern technologies. Scott and Welch were well known locally for their design of several area schools, as well as the development of housing types and the town plan for Copperton. Masonic ritual and belief dictated the design of the temple, which is a literal and physical embodiment of content.

Masonic Temple

Masonic ritual in large measure reflects the ancient work of the builders of King Solomon's Temple depicted in biblical scripture. Rhetorically, the rituals contain building terms, methods, tools, and practices throughout. The ancient descriptions of King Solomon's Temple contain considerable details about measurements of various parts and more particularly their specific relationships to each other. For instance, the numbers three, five, and seven have a particular significance in Masonry. Therefore, these numbers appear prominently throughout the design of the Masonic Temple and were the basic units repeated in the design, determining the placement of structural and ornamental columns.

The temple is three stories high, equivalent to the three degrees of Masonry, each of which contains a ritual room. The staircase leading to the South Temple entrance includes clusters of three, five, seven, and nine steps, number combinations related to the number of steps on Jacob's ladder of ancient myth that reached to heaven. The temple sits on seven courses of carefully cut granite, locating the building materially in the context of this particular place.

Although many Masonic temples adopt the Neoclassical style, this one was designed in the Egyptian Revival style. Scott and Welch considered this appropriate because of the amount of surface area devoted to Masonic symbolism. Consistent with the Egyptian style, many surfaces have inscriptions or bas-relief sculpture. Flanking the entrance are two sphinxes, which seem to guard the public facade. With a lion's body and man's head, these sculptures signify great strength and "master intelligence," according to Masonic tradition. Lodged between each lion's paws is a polished granite sphere; one is inscribed

to represent the Celestial Sphere and the other the Terrestrial Sphere, symbolizing the intersection between heaven and earth. The sphinxes are made of Utah granite, and the spheres of granite from the eastern United States. On the interior several ritual rooms are thematically decorated, such as the Colonial room, the Moorish room, and the Gothic room, although they have similar key elements. The auditorium, which includes seating for 1,400, includes a grand stage at the front with more than 180 stage sets that can be raised or lowered to accommodate specific rituals, and a ceiling painted like the nighttime sky.

Emmanuel Kahn House
678 East South Temple
1890
Henry Manheim

A quintessential Victorian house, the Emmanuel Kahn House displays all the exuberance and enthusiastic celebration so typical of the style. A blatant display of wealth and prosperity, the Kahn House was designed by out-of-state architect Henry Manheim in 1890 in the Queen Anne style. Lavishly conceived on both the exterior and interior, the house features extensive exterior gingerbread woodwork, stone trim, a corner turret, and porches with detailed fan carvings in the arches. An original hand-cast wrought-iron fence still surrounds the property.

The story of the illustrious owners of the house demonstrates the importance of immigrants to the history of Utah. Emmanuel and Samuel Kahn were Prussian immigrants who came to Utah in 1867 to open what would become a major wholesale grocery business. Successful and well respected locally, Kahn was a trustee of the B'nai Israel Synagogue, an active member of the Masonic Order, and a key organizer and fund-raiser for the Masonic Library, which was the first non-Mormon library in town that was open to the public.

Ladies' Literary Club
850 East South Temple
1913
Ware and Treganza

The impulse to join in female association for intellectual or philanthropic activity runs through the nineteenth-century history of American women. The Ladies' Literary Club is the oldest women's club west of the Mississippi, beginning in 1877 and incorporating in 1882. In 1875, Mrs. B. A. M. Froiseth began a club called "The Blue Tea" for cultured women who met in her home periodically for group discussion. A small group of broad-minded, forward-looking women met at the home of Tina R. Jones in February 1877 to design the Ladies' Literary Club, one of the twelve clubs modeled after Sorosis, a club founded in New York and generally regarded as the pioneer of women's clubs. The Ladies' Literary Club impacted the shape of the city in more ways than the enlightenment of its members. In 1896, for instance, it helped usher the Library Bill through the Utah legislature, which led to the creation of the first free public library in 1898.

Eliza Kirtley Royle was the first president of the Ladies' Literary Club when it met in the homes of members, and then at times in the Odd Fellows Hall, the Continental Hotel on West Temple, or the Deseret Bank Building, wherever they could find space. In 1913 the group hired the firm of Ware and Treganza, recognized for their fine Prairie-style designs and buildings reflecting the Arts and Crafts aesthetic, to design this spectacular Prairie-style building on the city's principal residential street, South Temple. The horizontal planes and bands of contrasting materials of natural hues are familiar Prairie components expressed in elements such as the overhanging eaves. Beveled and stained glass, an ample porch, a porte cochere, and elaborate woodwork combine to create a clubhouse that is richly textural and modulated, contemporary in terms of style, and a substantial backdrop to the club members' activities.

Haxton Place
940 East South Temple
1909
Thomas G. Griffin

Haxton Place reads like a place apart, mirroring the architectural scale and impressive character of houses that line South Temple, Salt Lake City's grand boulevard of wealth, but moving back from the street in an early twentieth-century version of a gated community in a small cul-de-sac. Haxton Place creates a domestic space of elegance and charm, with natural and architectural distinction, including architecturally significant homes like the Keith and Griffin Houses designed by Frederick A. Hale.

Imitating the look of a similar neighborhood in Great Britain, Haxton Place, Salt Lake City's quaint neighborhood off South Temple, was the work of James T. Keith, a local dentist who purchased the property in 1909 and commissioned Thomas G. Griffin, an English immigrant to Utah who was familiar with the British prototype, to design the space. Each house is conceived as a separate entity, although the group shares common Colonial Revival detailing and forms. The entrance is marked by four stone pillars with ornamental ironwork that stand at the street. When first built, the pillars held bronze plaques that identified the name of the subdivision, but those were stolen at some point.

George Badger House
16 South Haxton Place (940 East)
1915
Paliser & Hills

Designed only eight years after Frank Lloyd Wright's Robie House in Chicago, Illinois, this impressive Prairie-style house reflects a growing sophistication and cosmopolitanism in Salt Lake's most prestigious neighborhoods. Although it was designed by a relatively unknown team of architects, this house is an excellent example of the Prairie school. The original owner, George Badger, was a wealthy stock and commodities broker. During the economic downturn of the Depression years, he sold the house in 1929 to Julian Bamburger, the son of Governor Bamburger. The house's use of natural earth tones and materials and the sweeping horizontality typical of the style are emphasized with the low-pitched roof with wide-open eaves, rows of continuous windows, and earth tones and natural textures of the walls, overall creating a handsome house of considerable warmth and appeal. The interior includes extensive built-ins and woodwork of gum and oak. The design is much like those of Oak Park, Illinois, created by John Van Bergen.

J. T. Keith and T. G. Griffin Houses
34–35 Haxton Place
1910
Frederick Albert Hale

All the houses at Haxton Place deviate slightly from the way buildings were sited, set back, and oriented to each other along South Temple. The first house to be built in the area is actually two buildings that share a common facade and are built a little more than a foot apart. Unlike the Prairie-style building nearby, this house reflects instead the English Arts and Crafts style like that of buildings designed by C. F. A. Voysey and M. H. Baillie Scott, with steeply pitched roofs and asymmetrical facades. Frederick Albert Hale was the architect of numerous dwellings for wealthy businessmen along South Temple and had a strong sense of high style and elegant design.

The Keith and Griffin families shared this lot and a tennis court built behind the two homes. Many prominent Utah families have lived at Haxton Place over time, including the Bambergers, the Pearsalls, and the Schubachs.

Holy Cross Hospital / Salt Lake Regional Medical Center
1050 East South Temple
1883
Carl Neuhausen

The Holy Cross Hospital / Salt Lake Regional Medical Center occupies the entire block between South Temple and 100 South and between 1000 and 1100 East. The original Gothic Revival buildings wrap around the block, today separated from the street by parking terraces, historic landscaping, and the well-known rose garden. The hospital was the result of the organizational efforts of the Sisters of the Holy Cross and the direction of Lawrence Scanlan, a Roman Catholic bishop in Utah in 1875. Scanlan was both a great social entrepreneur and spiritual leader. When the first hospital opened, it was on 500 East just south of South Temple and had thirteen patient beds. A larger facility was needed immediately, and in 1883 it moved to a new 125-bed hospital at 1000 East. Over the years, the hospital has expanded to include 343 beds. Well sited because of easily obtainable water from Red Butte Canyon, and easily accessible to downtown Salt Lake, the hospital had two wings constructed of brick, with decorative work on the spires that rose from the corners. A chapel, designed by Carl Neuhausen, was built on the site in 1904 and offered a sacred space for those whose loved ones were staying in the hospital. It was renovated in 1965 with beautiful arched stained-glass windows, a bell tower, and a rounded altar. The landscaping surrounding the hospital reflects the Sisters' great love of beauty and nature. They planted groves of trees and landscaped various lush gardens and walkways around the hospital. Before it made way for a parking garage, the north-side rose garden was a popular city landmark.

Henry Dinwoodey House
411 East 100 South
1890
Richard K. A. Kletting

Prominent Utah architect Richard Kletting designed this house for Mormon polygamist and British convert Henry Dinwoodey two decades before his work on the State Capitol in 1890. Trained and apprenticed as a carpenter in England, Dinwoodey constructed a frame building for his production facility and began manufacturing furniture upon his arrival in Utah. His incredibly successful furniture business, Dinwoodey Furniture, served Utah, Wyoming, Idaho, Nevada, and Arizona and was significant to the local economy. As a result, Dinwoodey became a wealthy and influential man. Regardless of his influence, he was imprisoned for a time during the polygamy raids of the 1880s for unlawful cohabitation.

Besides its association with a well-known and wealthy polygamist, the home is a beautiful three-story Victorian structure with the excess so typical of the style. It is built with a special burned-red brick that Kletting had transported to Utah from

Denver, and much of the exterior decoration is formed with native cut sandstone from Red Butte Canyon east of the city.

Besides the beautiful textural and material richness of the exterior, the interior features a range of luxurious materials as well—hardwood parquet floors on the main level, maple trim in the living room, oak in the dining room, and mahogany trim in the parlor differentiate the rooms with a particular function and public presentation from the more private upstairs bedrooms. Inlaid wood is also part of the dining room fireplace, enriching the interior with a great love of natural materials.

Golden Braid Bookstore / Oasis Cafe
151 South 500 East
1996

Befitting the names "Oasis" and "Golden Braid," this welcoming bookstore and restaurant building wraps around a central open-air courtyard and includes ten thousand square feet of space. Located within a central city district, the building has perimeter walls of ten-inch-thick concrete forms made of recycled Styrofoam bound by Portland cement. The use of these materials in combination with reinforced steel and concrete creates a structural matrix as well as a high insulation value. Old-growth timbers used as structural columns and beams were reclaimed from a disassembled railroad trestle that had been left to weather, bringing together the old and the new. The building includes interesting and compelling spaces for art displays or for sitting, reading, and dining. Cupolas with light openings on all sides bring natural light into the interior spaces. The Utah AIA recognized the Golden Braid Bookstore / Oasis Cafe with a 1996 Award for Excellence in Architecture.

Jonathan C. and Eliza K. Royle House
635 East 100 South
1875

The Italianate is a relatively rare style in Utah, so when you see a fine example like the Jonathan C. and Eliza K. Royle House, it is worth noticing. When it was constructed in 1875 it was one of the earliest "high-style" houses built on 100 South, a neighborhood that became a prestigious residential area close to South Temple at the turn of the century. The Royle House is one of two frame Italianate houses in Salt Lake City; most other examples are built with adobe, brick, or stone. Here the Italianate is given full expression with the two-story main mass and truncated hipped roofs, wide overhanging eaves with brackets, a wide frieze, and tall, narrow windows. Overall the effect is formal, elegant, and impressive. The Royles lived here for more than thirty years, and both were prominent social leaders in legal, cultural, and religious affairs of the city. Jonathan was a mining attorney and served as a member of the legal counsel team in the famous Emma mine litigation, which had international ramifications affecting British and American stockholders and entrepreneurs. He was also instrumental in organizing the First Presbyterian Church in Salt Lake City. Eliza was important in the city's cultural life, helping organize the Ladies' Literary Club and serving as its first president.

B'Nai Israel Synagogue
249 South 400 East
1890
Philip Meyer and Henry Monheim

Possibly the first Jewish man to come to Utah was Alexander Neibaur, who arrived in 1848 and converted to Mormonism soon after. He was joined by Julius Gerson Brooks and his wife, Fanny, in the summer of 1854. When Colonel Sidney Johnston came to Utah in the 1850s and Colonel Patrick Connor in the 1860s, their troops produced new demand and the opportunity for new businesses. Many Jewish merchants saw the potential for economic benefit. They came to Utah willing to compete in the predominantly Mormon commercial scene and develop a counterpoint to LDS hegemony. Familiar with discrimination, Jewish immigrants understood some of what the Latter-day Saints had experienced in the Midwest and were willing to peacefully coexist. At the same time, the West seemed to provide relief from the persecution

B'Nai Israel Synagogue

they had experienced in so many other places.

In 1866 Salt Lake City's Jewish population gathered for the Jewish Family Service, an auxiliary that offered a range of services. Brigham Young donated land for the B'nai Israel Cemetery. The B'Nai Israel congregation incorporated in 1881 and built a synagogue in 1883 on Main Street. Not long afterward, the building proved too small, and they built a new building at 249 South 400 East in 1890. The name B'Nai Israel literally means "children or sons of Israel." The design for the synagogue was produced by a partnership between a native of Germany, Philip Meyer, and Henry Monheim, a local architect. The *Salt Lake Tribune* described it as having an "air of quiet elegance,"[14] with stained-glass windows, an airy interior space, and beautiful decorations. The exterior walls were built with Kyune sandstone, and the cornerstone was laid, as was Jewish custom, on the northwest corner of the lot.

St. Mark's Episcopal Church
231 East 100 South, Salt Lake City
Late 1800s
Richard Upjohn

After working in Montana in 1866, the Right Reverend Daniel S. Tuttle came to Utah at the urging of Episcopalians who wished to establish a religious alternative to Mormonism. In response, Tuttle sent two missionaries to Salt Lake and established Utah as part of the jurisdiction of the bishop of Montana. George W. Foote and Thomas W. Haskings held the first Episcopalian services the next year on May 5, 1867. Tuttle came two months later and

stayed for the next two decades, serving as the bishop of Utah, Idaho, and Montana.

The most frequently told story about Tuttle was his grand entrance into Salt Lake City on top of a stagecoach, allegedly covered with road dust and carrying a rifle across his legs. A man of considerable charisma and charm, he was enormously effective and energetic as an Episcopalian leader, establishing the parishes of St. Mark's, St. Paul's, and the Church of the Good Shepherd as well as numerous private schools, including Rowland Hall–St. Mark's, and the territory's first hospital, St. Mark's Hospital.

St. Mark's Episcopal Church is best remembered as a design by nationally renowned architect Richard Upjohn. Upjohn donated the blueprints for the church, which were similar to those of other churches he had built throughout

St. Mark's Episcopal Church

the East Coast. Founder of the American Institute of Architects, Upjohn designed a church that was highly symbolic, traditional in form and detail, and beautiful for the congregation to use for worship. It was built of red sandstone—a combination of carefully cut stone and rubble—both of which located this traditional design in this particular place. It is a one-story building with a basement and gabled roof. A distinctive belfry and chimney extend from the facade, the nave windows have Gothic arches, and the gables have rose windows. The altar area or chancel was added to the original structure in 1910, and a front vestibule was added in 1958, funded by a gift from the James Hogle family.

Introduction to University of Utah

Illuminating the American emphasis on public education and the LDS pioneer desire for a well-rounded society, the University of Utah was the first land-grant school west of the Mississippi River. When the legislature created Utah Territory, it allocated $5,000 for the University of Deseret, following the model it had completed in Nauvoo.

Regardless of the impressive name, the University's start was modest. In fact, the first classes were held for only twenty-five young men on November 11, 1850. Since that humble beginning the University has grown. In 2014 upward of twenty-seven thousand undergraduate and five thousand graduate students attended the University of Utah, the flagship of the Utah state educational system. Classes were held in the Council Hall, in the Union Academy Building at Union Square, and in other temporary situations before moving to their current location. Two years after the first classes

were held in 1850, classes were held in private homes, with Chancellor Orson Spencer teaching and W. W. Phelps assisting. That same quarter, young women were enrolled as students, but because finances were tight in 1852 the legislature rescinded the appropriation for the university, which closed until 1867.

The Board of Regents reopened the University of Deseret in November 1867. Classes were held at the Council Hall and John R. Park was hired as principal. Park divided the school into two branches of study: the Normal or Teachers Course, which included English, mathematics, commercial business, and natural sciences; and the Collegiate Course, which included all of the above plus German, French, higher mathematics, and Latin and Greek. With this, the school became a true university, with 223 students.

Like many nineteenth-century institutions in Utah, the university felt the political pressures of the 1870s and 1880s—the fight against polygamy and the hegemony of the LDS Church—and experienced growing pains. Park and Brigham Young had different ideas about what curriculum was appropriate. Park refused to allow classes about Mormon doctrine to be taught, perhaps conscious of the different missions of Brigham Young Academy and the university, and Brigham Young ordered that Greek and Latin no longer be taught because he considered them useless. Young sent Park back East to study national trends in education, and when he returned with a number of new ideas, the faculty was increased to four, including Joseph Kingsbury, who later became president. By 1880, the University of Deseret had moved to a two-story building called the Union Academy Building at Union Square. A decade later, President Park introduced a bill to the legislature asking the U.S. Congress for a grant of a strip of land from Fort Douglas. Governor Arthur L. Thomas approved an act that changed the name of the school to the University of Utah in 1892, the same year Park resigned.

From the 1880s until the present, the University of Utah has benefited from land annexations from Fort Douglas. In 1894 Congress granted sixty acres from the Fort Douglas military reservation to the University of Utah, which included land between 100 and 400 South, with a western boundary running east of 1300 East and an eastern boundary running 1,200 feet to the east of that. In 1899, the state legislature approved a bill removing the university from its old location and constructing new buildings for the school at its new site. President Joseph Kingsbury and architect Richard Kletting visited schools back East to come up with good ideas for the layout of the new campus, creating what they hoped would resemble an East Coast college.

Only three educational buildings were initially built—the Library, the Normal Building, and the Physical Science Building—along with a modern heating plant. By 1902, Kletting was no longer associated with the university, and Samuel C. Dallas, another prominent architect from Salt Lake City, designed the museum building in 1902. This building was named the James E. Talmage Biology Building in 1976.

The keystone in the arch formed by these impressive buildings, which was later known as Presidents Circle, was the Park Building. Architects Samuel C. Dallas and William S. Hedges were given the commission to design a main building between 1912 and 1914—intentionally grand and imposing, it announced the seriousness of the endeavor. The building was named the John R. Park Building after the school's first

president, and the regents hired Mahonri Young to sculpt a portrait of Park for the front of the building.

The other buildings completing the horseshoe design around a central quad were Kingsbury Hall, Gardner Hall, and the George Thomas Library, built with WPA funds provided under the National Industrial Recovery Act. Raymond Ashton and Raymond Evans were the architects for this project. In the 1960s the library was remodeled for use as the Utah Museum of Natural History, and in 2016 as the Crocker Science Center.

In 1904 the university acquired an additional thirty-two acres, as well as sixty-one more acres from Fort Douglas in 1934. Three hundred additional acres extended the campus to the east in 1948. By the end of the century it had grown to over 1,500 acres.

David P. Gardner Hall
1375 Presidents Circle
University of Utah
1931
Raymond J. Ashton and Raymond L. Evans
Although Gardner Hall has housed the Music Department and its various activities since 1957, when it was first built in 1931 it was the Student Union and included facilities for student meetings, dances, and other social activities. The university staged a competition to select the architects, stipulating only that the resulting building be harmonious with the style of the Park Building, like all the buildings at the historic center of campus. Raymond J. Ashton and Raymond L. Evans won the commission for their proposed Neoclassical Revival building. Students organized a fund-raising campaign with alumni between 1922 and 1928 and raised $180,000. When it was built it was the twenty-seventh student union to be built in the United States.

David P. Gardner Hall
Photograph by Elizabeth Bradley-Wilson. Used with permission of the photographer.

Gardner Hall had been deteriorating for several years before the university decided to remodel and upgrade it in the 1990s. The university hired FFKR to design a new concert hall to bring the facility up to the latest technology and industry standards as well as manage the renovation of the existing Gardner Hall building. The new building provides a competitive and comprehensive platform for administration, faculty, and students. Gardner Hall houses the Music Department, its studios and offices, classrooms, and a library. The largest single space in the structure is Room 200, which was renovated and returned to its original grandeur during the renovation project.

The new concert hall provides space for performances, performance education, and rehearsals. The range of performances given at Gardner Hall includes solo programs, lectures, and performances by full symphony orchestras. Acoustical properties and conditions were a primary consideration in the restoration and renovation of Gardner Hall. In terms of materials, form, and style the addition harmonized with the original structure and the surrounding buildings in Presidents Circle.

Joseph T. Kingsbury Hall
1395 Presidents Circle
University of Utah
1930
Edward O. Anderson and Lorenzo S. Young

Throughout its history, Kingsbury Hall has reflected the commitment of the University of Utah to excellence in the performing arts. For years home to Ballet West and other performing arts groups as well as the backdrop to countless university student productions, Kingsbury Hall was built in 1930 according to a design by architects Edward O. Anderson and Lorenzo S. Young. Both architects were well known and respected locally. As would be true for Gardner Hall, the one design stipulation was that the building correspond gracefully with the Park Building, the centerpiece of Presidents Circle. Unlike other buildings in Presidents Circle, Kingsbury Hall reflects the Egyptian Revival style, including four fluted portico columns and adjacent porch elements. Most impressively, the building is built up on a podium that enhances its monumentality and formality, and the exterior is covered with terra-cotta tiles. The building also includes Neoclassical elements such as pilasters, a plain entablature, and an overall symmetry. Two murals painted in 1946 by Utah artist Florence E. Ware were funded by the WPA's Federal Art Project. Depicting the "Evolution of Drama through the Ages," the paintings were evidence of the federal government's commitment to equal employment under the auspices of the WPA. Ten percent of the funding from the Federal Art Project had to be distributed to women. Florence Ware was one Utah woman to benefit from the program. Above each of the entrances is an inscription—above the west door, "Praised be the fathomless universe, for life and joy, and for objects and knowledge

Joseph T. Kingsbury Hall

curious," Walt Whitman; above the center door, "Learning is ever in the freshness of its youth, even for the old," Aeschylus; and above the east door, "There is only one good, namely knowledge; and only one evil, namely, ignorance," Socrates.

The building is named for university president Joseph T. Kingsbury, who served during 1892–1894 and 1897–1916. Kingsbury directed the construction of most of the buildings in Presidents Circle during the early 1900s.

Leroy E. Cowles Building
155 South 1400 East (Presidents Circle)
University of Utah
1901
Richard K. A. Kletting

Richard K. A. Kletting designed the Cowles Building and was hired initially to design all the buildings on Presidents Circle, but he had a disagreement with the board of trustees and withdrew from the project. Kletting was Utah's premier architect of the day, having designed the original Salt Palace, the State Capitol, and many distinguished homes throughout the Avenues and along South Temple. Kletting chose the Second Renaissance Revival style for the buildings on Presidents Circle; this one was constructed with brick and sandstone. A straightforward and relatively undistinguished classroom building, the Cowles Building was built in 1901 and housed the original library of the university until 1913, when the collection was moved to the Park Building and the Liberal Arts Department moved into the space vacated by the library. After 1957, the Cowles Building became home to the Math Department and in 1976 to Communications.

The entrance to the building is on the west end of the facade, which runs broadside to the curving street and is marked by two columns, with a modest portico double-arched doorway. The hipped roof sits above lacy brickwork that enlivens the surface somewhat and is the principal decoration added to the building. Anna Campbell Bliss's art installation examines the connection between mathematics and the arts and runs through hallways and stairways, creating an intriguing, challenging, and engaging link between the building as a whole and as an intellectual environment.

John R. Park Building
201 Presidents Circle
University of Utah
1914
Samuel C. Dallas and William S. Hedges
The Park Building creates a grander sense of entrance than any other spot on campus, emphasized by the staircase that leads to the pathway moving in both directions around Presidents Circle. Designed in 1914 by Samuel C. Dallas and William S. Hedges in the Neoclassical style, the Park Building is the central administration building for the University of Utah, and for a time it housed the library as well. After a new library building was constructed in 1935, the Psychology, Anthropology, and Law Departments moved into the Park Building until 1949. An art collection was on display on the fourth floor until 1971. In 2016, the President's Art Gallery opened in the same space.

The building was named for John Rockey Park, the first president of the University of Utah, who served between 1869 and 1892. Called at various times the "Father of the University," Park ushered the school through a period of considerable growth.

The building is distinguished by granite steps that lead up to the main entrance

John R. Park Building

and facade, and there are Classical details throughout. Pilasters with Doric capitals are on each side of the central entrance, and egg-and-dart detailing can be seen around the brass doors. In a niche on the north side of the entrance is a statue of John Park sculpted by Mahonri Young. The interior space creates a lush and extravagant entrance to the building, along with a marble-trimmed foyer and staircase, and five murals, painted by Lee Greene Richards, depicting the "Great Men of Knowledge."

George Thomas Building / Crocker Science Center
Utah Museum of Natural History
Presidents Circle
University of Utah
1935
Raymond J. Ashton and Raymond L. Evans

Raymond Ashton and Raymond Evans designed the George Thomas Building in 1935 in a Neoclassical style perfectly in harmony with the other buildings of Presidents Circle. However, this building includes details that also suggest an Art Deco influence. Using reinforced concrete, stone, and decorative metalwork, the building represents the technological advancements that occurred after the first buildings were built in the circle until 1935. At the same time, in terms of style and form, it is in line with its predecessors. It housed the University Library from 1935 until the Marriott Library was completed in 1968, when it was remodeled to become the Utah Museum of Natural History.

Named for university president George Thomas (1921–41), the building was partially funded by the WPA. Instead of the PWA Moderne style often used for such buildings, this building reflects its academic environment and the surrounding

Classical Revival buildings. For instance, the entrance reflects the earlier portico-style entrances found in Presidents Circle, and the facade is symmetrically organized. Lion heads similar to those on the Park Building appear along the parapet. A balcony resting on the portico projects out from the entrance and focuses attention on this area of the facade. Art Deco details are found on the metalwork at the window lintels and around the entrance. The foyer is also decorated with birdseye marble with Art Deco detailing.

Alfred C. Emery Building
Presidents Circle
University of Utah
1901
Richard K. A. Kletting

The Department of Family and Consumer Studies is the current inhabitant of the Emery Building, a current use that reflects the past. When it was built it was used for home economics classes and called the Normal Building. Named for President Alfred C. Emery, who served at the university between 1971 and 1973, the building was designed by Richard K. A. Kletting in the Second Renaissance Revival style, harmonizing with the other important and monumental buildings on Presidents Circle.

The Emery Building features sandstone details around the entrance to the north, including a large keystone over the central arch and other carved details. Three levels tall, the building has regular rows of windows running along each side that reflect the placement of classrooms on the interior. It was renovated and restored in 1990, and an award-winning concrete and glass addition was added to the east side, designed by Utah architects Brixen and Christopher. The mirrored glass adjacent to the main building allows the roofline of the structure to be visually continued. The new addition also references the stringcourse and window bays of the main building, overall creating an interesting mix of old and new elements.

Rice-Eccles Stadium
University Street and 500 South
University of Utah
1997
FFKR

The Rice-Eccles Stadium is a dominant, dramatic figure in the eastside landscape. The contrasting tensions between the strength of the steel structure's details and the transparency of the upper levels demand attention and exude a sense of power. The stadium features incredible views of downtown Salt Lake City. The setting for the opening and closing ceremonies of the 2002 Olympic Games as well as the home of the University of Utah football team, the stadium was expanded from 32,000 seats to 45,807.

At the beginning of the project, the design team at FFKR focused on several issues, including the concepts that the stadium be replaced instead of expanded, and the seating configuration be formed as a bowl with seats running in continuous rows from the field to the top. The dramatic sweep of the window wall and exposed truss systems on the stadium's west side created an elegant, dramatic curve energizing this end of campus. The space is exciting, establishing a new corridor from the library and central campus to the lower campus, with a sweeping walking space in between. The reconstruction of Rice-Eccles Stadium was completed in August 1998, four years before it would be used for the Olympics.

Marriott Center for Dance
330 South 1500 East
University of Utah
1980s
FFKR

For decades the university's dance departments were housed in odd locations around campus. On September 25, 1989, the Alice

Rice-Eccles Stadium

Sheets Marriott Center for Dance opened for ballet and modern dance students, a one-of-a-kind resource with studios, performance space, and training facilities. The most formal performance space, named for longtime ballet faculty Elizabeth R. Hayes and William Christensen, has a proscenium stage and seats for an audience of 333. The program for the Marriott Center for Dance was a complicated mixture of offices for faculty and administration, classrooms, dressing rooms and locker areas, an audio/visual resource room, and a 333-seat theater with adjacent support rooms (a costume shop, quick change room, electric room, and prop storage). The materiality of the lobby is enriched with maple-paneled walls, an exterior roof deck, and a student lounge, creating an elegant, functional backdrop to the movement of the dancers through their university activities.

As is appropriate, the heart of the building is the studio space. To bring uniform natural light into the space, all teaching studios are on the north side of the building. Each department has two studios that measure forty by sixty feet and one larger studio measuring forty by seventy feet, which doubles as a lab theater. A special theater for dance performances has steeply ranked continental seating to maintain clear sight lines to the stage.

The exterior of the building corresponds to the historic materials of the buildings surrounding it. Materials here range from elegant bronze to wood panels to concrete and brick. Overall the general impression is of an exciting sensuality playing through the materials, enhanced by the lines and shapes of the building. Recognized with both the Utah AIA Merit Award in 1990 and the Western Mountain Region AIA Merit Award in 1990, the building's

architects, FFKR Architecture/Planning/Interior Design, wedded the arts here in a beautiful expression of form and celebration of movement.

Art and Architecture Complex
375 South 1530 East
University of Utah
1970
Edwards & Daniels Associates

The Art and Architecture Complex connects a pair of buildings by a covered passageway on the first level and a hallway on the second. They are twin sisters in a sense, each providing a neutral backdrop to the creative endeavor. To the east architectural students meet in studio spaces, and faculty offices on the second floor radiate around a central lounge. The Bailey exhibition space is a two-story expanse with a window that at one time looked out at the Wasatch Range, but today views the business building next door. To the west, the art wing does much the same. The Gittins Gallery southeast of the main office area provides display space for student work and visiting shows. Studios are found on each of the upper levels, with an open courtyard at the top. The Utah Museum of Fine Arts was housed in the west wing, which moves out from the art side of the building, until it moved into its new home to the east in the Marcia and John Price Museum of Fine Arts. With a style termed Brutalism for its exposed structural materials—in this case reinforced concrete and cedar paneling—and its heavy, raw forms, the AAC uses dark spaces and an intriguing system of paths and staircases to create a challenging and, for some, creative space apart from the rest of campus for the exploration of space, light, color, and form by future architects and designers.

Sugar House
Granite Stake Tabernacle
2005 South 900 East
1929–1930
Edward O. Anderson and Lorenzo
Snow Young

Originally, the Granite Stake Tabernacle was built at 3300 South and State Street (torn down in 1956) but was relocated to 2005 South 900 East in 1929. Edward O. Anderson and Lorenzo Snow Young designed the building in the Byzantine style, or what is sometimes called Late Roman or Eastern Roman Empire. Here the style is articulated with rich, textural wall surfaces combined with red brick, native stone, and distinctive warm ornamentation of cream-colored stone. An octagonal tower engages with the facade at the southwest corner and rises in a tiered and highly decorated series of stages to the top. The church's plan is a Greek cross with an addition to the north. The lush interior chapel is more square

than is typical of LDS church design, and ornamented with colorful murals that run across the front and part of the sides.

St. Ann's Orphanage
430 East 2100 South
1890
Carl Neuhausen

Carl Neuhausen was best known for his designs of the Cathedral of the Madeleine and the Capitol Theatre. Although St. Ann's Orphanage is less elaborate than either of these two buildings, it is wildly eclectic and colorful, an optimistic combination of Renaissance and Mannerist details. The building lies on a basement level that sits halfway out of the ground, and it rises two stories. Thomas Kearns's wife, Jennie Judge, funded the project with $55,000 to both purchase the land and build the building. The building appears to be symmetrical, with two prominent wings on both sides and a central octagonal tower

Granite Stake Tabernacle

over the entrance. At the top of the tower is a domed roof and cupola, and at the bottom a covered porch with Doric columns. The curvilinear parapets at the top of the wings are the most distinctive character-defining element

The Sisters of the Holy Cross lived in the attic story, with the dormitories and classrooms on the second level—girls to the west and boys to the east.

Copperton

Copperton Historic District
500 East, Hillcrest Street, 200 West, State Highway
1926–1955
Scott and Welch

Located on the west bench of the Salt Lake Valley, Copperton's historic district originated as a company town—a collection of houses, apartments and duplexes, recreation facilities, a high school, sidewalks and curbs, and a town park—for the employees of the Utah Copper Company. When the company was founded in 1903, it combined smaller mining operations nearby into a single organization. In total, Copperton provided more than two hundred modest-sized homes complete with

the most modern conveniences, a range of distinctive styles—and, in four model homes, the creative use of copper. Most of the homes were either bungalows or Period Revival cottages with English Tudor or Spanish Colonial styles. Between 1936 and 1938, Scott and Welch designed four prefabricated copper-clad houses. One of these "experimental houses" was introduced to the public in 1936 at a weeklong open house. The *Bingham Bulletin* gave the project an enthusiastic review in its April 30, 1937, edition: "Visitors were particularly impressed with the economy of the arrangement of rooms in the house and characterized it as 'the biggest little house' ever planned. Another feature that will help to see copper houses is that a house like the one on display at Copperton is everlasting. Roof, gutters, downspouts, window frames and screens, radiators and piping are all of copper and the framework of steel make the house termite proof." The Utah Copper Company stopped providing housing for its workers in 1955. Although Copperton still exists (according to the 2010 Census it had a population of 826), it has been subsumed by subdivisions around it. Nevertheless, it is a historical rarity, a treasure worth seeking out and discovering.

Region A

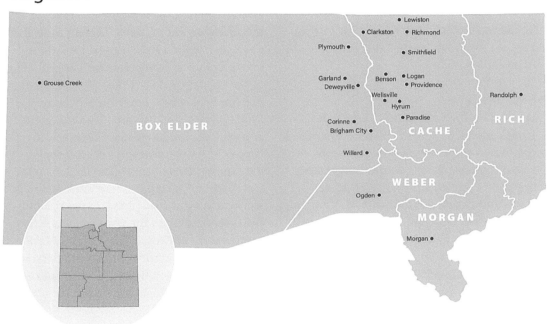

Box Elder, Cache, Rich, Weber, and Morgan Counties

Introduction

Between 1847 and 1860 more than forty thousand immigrants had come to Utah Territory, where Brigham Young organized colonization in every direction from church headquarters in Salt Lake City. A steady stream of white settlement identified the most fertile valleys and the sources of water that flowed down from the foothills of nearby mountains. Church leaders systematically distributed both land and water rights, and Brigham Young handpicked the first round of town members and "called" them to the work of settling the region. Towns to the north visually mimicked those along the Wasatch Front and in central and southern Utah. Organized around a strong visual core—a town center with a meetinghouse, tabernacle, or temple—family lots spread out in each direction. A Zion's Cooperative Mercantile Institution (ZCMI) store, Relief Society hall, tithing office, or granary might be part of the formula as well. But regardless of where you go throughout the state, you have a sense of visual connection to the whole, a series of variations on a theme with no town being exactly like another.

The second major connector between towns to the north and the rest of the state was the railroad. On May 10, 1869, at Promontory, Utah, the Central and Union Pacific Railroads drove the final spike in a transcontinental railroad system that connected the East and West Coasts. Within a week, Brigham Young had instructed workers to commence construction on the Utah Central Railroad line, which would connect Salt Lake City to the transcontinental line and markets beyond the scope of the Great Basin. After 113 days, workers completed the line on January 10, 1870. In August 1871, construction began on the Utah Northern Railroad line, which would connect Ogden and Logan to national markets and facilitate the transportation of people, state goods, and ideas. Utah would never be the same.[1]

Besides the narrative about native people and another about Mormon settlement of the region, the history of Weber County and Ogden City includes three prominent themes: (1) the activity of the fur trappers; (2) the importance of transportation; and (3) the influence of the federal government. Ogden City was named for Peter Skene Ogden, a fur trapper for Hudson's Bay Company who came into the region in 1825 from the Northwest in an attempt to dominate the market in beaver pelts and prevent American trappers from moving into Oregon, Washington, and British Columbia. The railroad traveled through Weber Canyon once it came to Utah in 1869, making Ogden the only Utah city on the transcontinental railroad route. Ogden is located between two canyons in the mountains to the east that provide easy access to three ski resorts and recreational opportunities at Pineview Reservoir. The federal government positively impacted the local economy with the establishment of the Ogden Defense Depot, Clearfield Naval Supply Depot, and Hill Air Force Base, which provided jobs, produced a ready market for supplies and services, and tied the county to federal activities. Weber State University was founded in 1889 and today offers a range of associate, bachelor's, and master's degrees in the liberal arts and technical fields. When it was founded, Weber State was a church school—the Weber Stake Academy—but the school was sold to the state in 1931.

Cache County includes an extensive valley, approximately forty miles long by twenty miles wide, encompassed by mountain ranges and traversed by both the Bear River and Highway 89, which connects Logan to southern Idaho, the Bear Lake region, and Brigham City and Ogden to the south. Shoshones traveled through Cache Valley from the north, hunting and gathering food. Fur trappers searching for beaver, led by Peter Skene Ogden, entered the valley while employed by the British Hudson's Bay Company in the 1820s but trapped primarily in Weber County.[2] Jim Bridger, Jedediah Smith, and other trappers came through Cache Valley regularly. In the words of one, "Numerous streams fall in through this valley, which, like the others, is surrounded by stupendous mountains, which are unrivaled for beauty and serenity of scenery."[3] Logan would become a regional governmental, educational, and religious center complete with an LDS temple and a major public land-grant university, Utah State.

Brigham Young established a herd of cattle in Cache Valley before he sent settlers in 1855, capitalizing on a ready supply of water, grasslands for grazing, and cottonwood trees for construction. After 1856, a series of Mormon villages spread across the valley, extending Young's influence to the north. Wellsville, Mendon, Providence, Logan, Smithfield, and Richmond were settled in the next few years. Ezra Taft Benson and Orson Hyde reported to Young on their progress: "For beauty of landscape and richness of soil, Cache Valley can hardly be equaled."[4]

The Utah Northern Railroad line came through Cache Valley to Logan in 1871–72, connecting local businesses and farms with national markets and making state goods more readily available. Sixteen local branches of ZCMI were established in the valley, linking local cooperatives with both the merchandising and manufacturing arms of ZCMI in Salt Lake City.

The Morrill Act of 1862 had a provision creating the land-grant system, which gave each state or territory the chance to establish one land-grant college and an appropriation of up to thirty thousand acres to do so. Since its founding in 1888, Utah's land-grant institution, Utah State University (USU), has had different names, including the Agricultural College of Utah and the Utah Agricultural College. In 1957 it became Utah State University, with a focus on agriculture, engineering, and liberal arts. Besides its main campus in Logan, USU has extension regional campuses in Brigham City, Tooele, and the Uintah Basin. In 2010, the College of Eastern Utah in Price became Utah State University Eastern. At the mouth of Logan Canyon on a site overlooking the rest of the valley, the main campus includes five hundred acres northeast of Logan's Main Street. More than half of its students live on campus, and many others in apartments nearby. USU is one of the most prominent assets of Cache Valley.

Box Elder County

Grouse Creek
Grouse Creek Tithing Office
1890

Communicating the cooperative nature of nineteenth-century Utah towns, the Grouse Creek Tithing Office transferred donations from Latter-day Saints to impoverished newcomers who needed help building a new life in a new home. In the nineteenth century, the tithing office was an important community center, gathering donations and distributing goods to newcomers who had little when they first came to settle the area. Because this was an agricultural community, the tithing office was filled with in-kind donations—farm products like eggs or wheat. Scarce cash made livestock or hand-fashioned goods much more likely donations. Besides the building itself, it is likely some sort of outbuilding was also located on the lot, although there is no physical evidence of auxiliary structures.

Quarried locally, long, irregular, rectangular slabs of light-colored stone formed the walls of the tithing office, a building oriented like a residence with the broad side running parallel to the street, unlike most public buildings. The two-story Albert F. Richens House, located east of the tithing office, was most likely constructed by the same stonemason. Customers entered the building through a central doorway in the facade, although much later, in the 1960s, wooden garage doors at the south gabled end opened the building for more efficient deliveries.

Plymouth
Plymouth School
135 South Main Street
1934–1935
Public Works Administration

Unlike this example, most public buildings constructed during the New Deal years adhered to the PWA Moderne style. Built between 1934 and 1935, this single-story, red-brick Tudor Revival–style building includes a steeply pitched hipped roof that sweeps over its basic rectangular plan. Small gabled extensions give the building an asymmetrical appearance and include artificial half-timbering. A parapeted gabled porch with stepped shoulders and heavy concrete quoins emphasizes the front entrance door, which is topped by an ogee arch and a panel with the Plymouth School name.

Garland
Bear River High School Science Building
1450 South Main Street
1934–1935
Public Works Administration

Utah was one of the states that benefited the most financially from the programs of the New Deal. The Bear River High School Science Building brought funds to the state under the auspices of the Public Works Administration, one of seven PWA buildings constructed during the period. It was built between 1935 and 1936 in Box Elder County, where construction boosted morale in a community reeling from the effects of the Depression. A sort of textbook example of the PWA Moderne, the Science Building is a two-story rectangular box with a pronounced central bay on the main facade, a recessed entrance with an ogee arch over the door, and a plaque framed by hard-edged low-relief geometric ornamentation, all typical elements of the style. The horizontality of the Science Building's brick walls is emphasized by a decorative belt course above both rows of windows, a low parapet, and a contrasting concrete cap. The county added a large addition to the back of the building in the 1960s.

Garland Carnegie Library
86 West Factory Street
1914
Watkins & Birch

For late nineteenth-century Americans, Andrew Carnegie was evidence of the rags-to-riches ideal. A generous and broad-minded philanthropist, Carnegie funded the construction of over 1,650 library buildings in the United States because of his belief in the redemptive power of literacy. Twenty-three Carnegie libraries were built in Utah alone. After communities met the basic criteria—that they would donate the building site and provide an annual maintenance budget of at least 10 percent of the original grant amount—the Carnegie Foundation entertained proposals from virtually any small town in America. In 1908, a group of civic leaders who formed the Garland Library Board discussed the idea of approaching Carnegie. As secretary of the board, R. L. Bush applied to the Andrew Carnegie Foundation in January 1912 for a grant of $8,000 for library construction. The *Salt Lake Tribune* noted that Garland was the first town in Box Elder County to receive a donation from Carnegie, an important benefit to local culture.

Although the architect is unknown, the building closely resembles the Carnegie

Garland Carnegie Library.
Photograph by Tricia Simpson, CC BY-SA 3.0.

Library in Richmond, designed by Watkins & Birch, who did five Carnegie libraries for Utah towns. The town dedicated this building and the Bear River Stake Tabernacle across the street on the same day.

The Garland Carnegie Library is a one-story brick rectangular building with a raised basement and a flat roof. Simple Classical Revival detailing distinguishes the exterior. Symmetry reinforced by a central pavilion seemed most appropriate for an institution that fostered civility, literacy, and good citizenship. The raised basement brought sunlight into rooms below and doubled the square footage. Classical details played out in the regularity of pilasters running around the building, with capitals that resemble a modified Ionic style, and a pronounced cornice with dentils on the frieze topped by a parapet.

Garland Tithing Office / Bishop's Storehouse
151 North 100 West
1907

Some of the first standard-plan buildings erected in Utah were tithing offices. On May 17, 1907, Bishop Walter L. Grover of the Garland LDS Ward received a letter from the presiding bishopric of the LDS Church, which read as follows: "Pursuant to your request of May 15th, you will find enclosed a plan of our tithing office No. 2 to be located in Garland." This plan was one of three used by the church around 1905, called Type No. 2. As was true of so many early Mormon buildings, the structure served a variety of purposes. In addition to being used as a tithing office, it was the bishop's office and might have been the scene of functions staged by other auxiliary organizations as well.

All about business, this tightly built brick building is a single story high, square in plan, and topped by a hipped roof. Despite its overall regularity, the facade is asymmetrical. An arched porch sits at the northwest corner, balanced by three windows on the other side. The building's name, the Garland Tithing Office, is inscribed in a large sandstone block centered over the arch. Sandstone was also used for windowsills and triangular vents over the front roof sections.

Deweyville
Fryer Hotel
3274 West 11300 North
1903

Deweyville experienced an economic boom when the railroad came through Box Elder County in 1872. The Utah Northern Railroad, later known as the Oregon Short Line Railroad, provided transportation and shipping services for the agricultural Bear River Valley. Even though Deweyville, conveniently located on the eastern edge of the valley, would become the rail center for the region, the town's population was modest—only two hundred people lived there by 1900. Capitalizing on the business driven by the railroad, the Fryer Hotel provided accommodations and livery services for travelers who debarked from the train at the railroad station in town. This two-story brick hotel is a residential hotel type, distinct to the nineteenth and early twentieth centuries, a variation of the central-passage type house seen throughout the region.

Businessman Robert C. Fryer capitalized on the opportunity he saw in Deweyville during this period of great change. He opened both Planter's Restaurant in 1902 and the Fryer Hotel the next year. Contributing to the town's cultural life, he built a library barn nearby. By the time Deweyville's brief period of prosperity had peaked, the Fryers had run the hotel for a decade and were ready to retire and move to Salt Lake City.

Region A

Corinne
Methodist Episcopal Church
Corner of Colorado and South
Sixth Streets
1870

Known in nineteenth-century
Utah as a predominantly non-
Mormon or "Gentile" town
(the local term), Corinne was
an important strategic spot as
the headquarters of northwest
freighting after construction of
the Utah Northern and Oregon
Short Line Railroads. Rather
than the homogeneity more
typical of the rest of the state,
it had great ethnic, social, and
religious diversity because of
railroad workers and those who
came into town on related business. The superintendent of the
Methodist Mission in Utah, the
Reverend G. M. Pierce, gave
his first sermon in Corinne on

Methodist Episcopal Church.
Photograph by Bobshaw25, CC BY-SA 3.0.

June 15, 1870, to an audience eager for religious instruction. Bishop Aimes, Chaplain
C. C. McCabe, and Reverend Pierce held
services on July 17, 1870, in the opera house
at Corinne and on that alone day raised
$1,100 for the construction of a new church,
and the next day another $450, toward a
total cost of $4,000. Two months later,
on September 20, 1870, Chaplain McCabe
and Reverend Pierce dedicated the building.

The simple Methodist Episcopal Church
includes a Gothic arch over the double door
entrance, the only reference to familiar
religious architecture elsewhere. A modest-
sized, one-story rectangle measuring
twenty-six feet by fifty feet, the building has
salmon, buff-colored brick walls that sit on
foundations formed with battered concrete.
Eventually a small louvered belfry was
placed over the vestibule.

Brigham City
Brigham City Fire Station / City Hall
6 North Main Street
1907
Andrew Funk

Unlike other buildings in town, the city
hall was most distinguished by the Spanish
Colonial Revival style, unusual for a public
building in a state that seemed to prefer the
Classical Revival. In 1910 architect Andrew
Funk designed this rectangular, two-story
brick building with a hipped roof and originally a garage door at the center of the
facade. When the city purchased the Glover
property to store the fire department's
equipment in 1935, it remodeled the building to house the city offices, redesigning the
facade to include a central projecting pavilion topped by a Spanish Revival, curvilinear
gabled parapet.

Originally the walls were formed with buff-colored brick. During the remodel, new red brick cladding covered the earlier wall in front, and to the side and rear the walls were painted red to match. Continuing the theme to the rear, a later addition has a flat roof with a stepped parapet and round-arched windows and doors that match the ones on the original building.

Although it is not a perfect example of the Spanish Colonial style, the building does include arched doors and windows and a curvilinear gabled parapet. The city operated out of this building just north of the county courthouse with consolidated offices between 1935 and 1973, and then it moved to a new facility and leased the building to the chamber of commerce.

Oregon Short Line Depot
800 West Forest Street
1907
Union Pacific Company
Distinctive in terms of both style and function, the Oregon Short Line Depot is one of the few Craftsman-style buildings in Brigham City and the town's only railroad passenger depot since it was built in 1907.

The Union Pacific purchased the Utah Northern in 1876, consolidated it with the Oregon Short Line in 1889, and renamed the line the Utah and Northern. The Oregon Short Line was established first in 1878 through the combination of existing railroads that provided Union Pacific access to the Pacific Northwest. The company announced in 1906 that it would soon construct a new depot with modern conveniences—water, electricity, steam heat, and lavatories—at 800 West Forest Street in Brigham City. The depot, measuring thirty-eight by ninety-eight feet, also had waiting rooms, an agent's office, and telegraph and ticket offices as well as express and baggage areas.

Even before it was completed, rail service to Brigham City was already important. In fact, the average number of passengers leaving town by train each month averaged about six hundred according to one account. By 1916, the Oregon Short Line was scheduling thirteen daily departures from Brigham City. The rail line was critical to local agricultural commerce. Farmers shipped their produce—peaches, tomatoes, cherries, watermelons, and

Oregon Short Line Depot

cantaloupes—from the depot to markets in Salt Lake City and beyond. Farmers sent Deweyville celery and fresh trout from the Mantua Hatchery by rail from Brigham City as well. In 1910, the Brigham City Fruit Growers' Association sent 140 straight car-loads of fruit to markets across the country. Mail came through the depot as well.

The building has a long projecting bay on the west side. The principal east-side pas-senger entrance has a tall wooden double door under a round-arched window. Sev-eral Craftsman details distinguish the build-ing and add to its charm, including large overhanging eaves with wooden brackets.

Brigham City Co-op Planing Mill
547 East Forest Street
1876

Yet another building associated with one of Utah's most successful nineteenth-century cooperative ventures, the Brigham City Mercantile and Manufacturing Association, is the Planing Mill. When it was built in 1876, the Co-op had several departments providing virtually all the goods and sup-plies needed for life in this pioneer com-munity. The mill helped produce cabinetry, furniture, and square nails that enhanced the organization's already flourishing con-struction enterprises. After the period of cooperative endeavors, former employee John Finley Merrell purchased the mill on November 30, 1892. For years he managed the business with his sons and sons-in-law, after 1905 calling it John F. Merrell & Co. and Merrell's Lumber Company. Family members ran the company until 1983, when it ceased full-time operations.

The Planing Mill is a rectangular adobe building two and a half stories high, with a gabled roof and stone foundation. One-story frame additions have been added to the side and rear elevations, but the overall

form and appearance are still evident. The mill measures forty-four feet wide by fifty feet long. The wall material changes from quartzite on the first level to adobe bricks on the second. Some of the original wood-working machinery—a mortise machine, a drum sander, a molder, and huge leather belts and pulleys—are still operable.

Brigham City Co-op Mercantile Store
5 North Main Street
1891

When constructed in 1891, the Brigham City Co-op Mercantile Store was connected to the Brigham City Mercantile and Man-ufacturing Association (the Co-op). One of the most successful cooperative endeav-ors in Utah Territory, in a town where the United Order most fully materialized, the Co-op operated between 1864 and 1895. Although most other cooperative attempts failed, Brigham City's flourished. The store is one of five remaining buildings associated with the Co-op. The store's demise in 1895 marked the transition from a cooperative economic system to one based on private enterprise. The period of private economic growth extended until the Depression years of the 1930s, when this building was con-verted to a bank.

Lorenzo Snow, a member of the Quorum of the Twelve Apostles of the LDS Church and founder of the town, helped found the Co-op in 1864. Local businessmen united private mercantile businesses already oper-ating locally, and everyone in town had the chance to buy stock and share privileges and benefits. By 1869, the store had two hundred shareholders and a capital stock of $20,000. The Co-op had many different divisions, including commerce, industry, agriculture, horticulture, and construction and employed most available workers in town for three decades.

The store was the last building constructed by the Brigham City Mercantile and Manufacturing Association, completed January 20, 1891, for $30,000. This three-story Victorian Eclectic commercial building with a basement has brick exterior walls on the primary facades and stone on the secondary facades.

Overall the eclectic design includes elements from the Victorian, Romanesque, and Classical Revival styles and measures 54 by 106 feet. The building is a typical two-part commercial block—the first street-level section includes large plate-glass windows set between light-colored concrete-plastered walls. The second section on the upper level includes pairs of smaller windows between engaged columns of red brick. Granite ornaments include double-arched windows on the third floor

and hood-molded window heads on the second floor.

Box Elder County Courthouse
1 North Main Street
1857

The Box Elder County Courthouse was the first public building in the area, begun as early as 1855 and enlarged in 1910. Like many early pioneer buildings, this was a multipurpose facility that was used at various times as a church, school, dance hall, and theater. For years it was the largest hall in town, with a gallery built into the west end and a choir loft under the gallery. A stage at the east end of the room used a table as a pulpit during church meetings. Teachers taught school in the east room on the first floor as late as 1880, and actors performed theatricals in the basement, with

Box Elder County Courthouse

scenery sometimes painted on the walls. The clock tower, built by the early 1870s, signaled the public function of the building, which housed most departments of county government, the court and judge's chambers, commission chambers, and offices of the clerk, recorder, assessor, and other county officials. No other courthouse has ever been built in the county. The courthouse is the best example of the Neoclassical Revival style in both Brigham City and Box Elder County.

Hotel Brigham
13 and 17 West Forest Street
1914 and 1924
Wood & Smith, Ogden

At the turn of the century, Brigham City had a population of three thousand, was the principal city of Box Elder County, and had a central business district with 175 businesses that stretched a few blocks. There were twice as many businesses by the 1920s—grocery stores, banks, restaurants, saloons, clothing shops, hotels, theaters, and specialty shops created a lively commercial core for Brigham City.

Architects Wood & Smith of Ogden designed the first section of Hotel Brigham in 1914 for James Knudson, a prominent figure in town. James's Danish father, LDS convert William Knudson, settled in Brigham City in 1854 and became a successful farmer and fruit grower, running the Knudson Brothers business. Besides running this hotel, James and his wife, Amelia, ran an ice cream and confectionary store in town.

The building's basement measured forty by seventy-three feet and had a steam heating plant at the west end, lavatories, and facilities for billiards at the east end. The ground floor space was shared by four businesses: Security Savings Bank, a jewelry store, the hotel, and the Rex Barber Shop. The building's upper two stories featured twenty hotel rooms with their own hot and cold running water and steam heat, many with their own bathrooms. Spacious lobbies were located on each floor as well. Additions built in 1924 brought the number of hotel rooms to fifty-four. The Hotel Brigham is a two-part commercial-block brick building with wide overhanging eaves.

Brigham City Carnegie Library
26 East Forest Street
1915
Shreeve & Madsen

Brigham City received a $12,500 grant from Andrew Carnegie for the Brigham City Carnegie Library. Architects from around the state competed for the design of this 1915 building. Watkins & Birch of Provo submitted two plans, as did Monson & Price of Salt Lake City. C. F. Wells of Brigham City and Shreeve & Madsen of Ogden prepared the winning plans. The building design conformed to the Prairie style, which was used for only two other Utah Carnegie libraries. Its basic form, rectangular boxlike shape, flat roof, one-story elevation, and raised basement are typical of Carnegie libraries across the state.

The building includes several rather common features of the Prairie style, including geometric designs in the stained-glass panels; geometric patterns on the piers; terra-cotta decorative squares that top the piers; mullions in the window panels; and most important, an overwhelming emphasis on the horizontal. By contrast, vertical elements include the brick piers framing the entrance and at the corners of the building, rectangular windows, contrasting white bands that frame parts of the entrance area, and decorative cross patterns on the brick piers.

Box Elder Flouring Mill
327 East 200 North
1854–1855
Frederick Kesler

The Box Elder Flouring Mill was the first important industrial building erected in town, established in 1854–55 by Mormon pioneers and the only remaining building from the initial period of industrial and commercial growth. The mill operated in the mid-1860s in conjunction with the Brigham City Mercantile and Manufacturing Association. Lorenzo Snow, the leader of the Co-op, hired Frederick Kesler to build the mill. Snow owned it for at least thirty years. When the town shifted from a cooperative economy to private enterprise, the mill was sold and converted into a monument factory in the late 1890s.

A master mill builder and pioneer industrialist, Kesler brought the most up-to-date mill technologies to the territory. He directed construction of the two-story stuccoed adobe mill between 1855 and 1856. Frame additions were attached to the rear and side elevations between 1892 and 1933. The original mill measured thirty by thirty-nine feet, sitting on a stone foundation at the corner of 200 North and 400 East.

The distinctive trademark Kesler feature of the building is the clerestory monitor roof, now shingled with corrugated metal. Portholes in some of the first-story walls provided visibility in case of Indian attack. Although the building changed use from a flouring mill to a monument factory with living quarters, the interior space still gives evidence of Kesler's original design. The heavy-timber frame and most of the columns, beams, and floorboards were still in existence until the mill was destroyed by arson in 2008.

Box Elder Flouring Mill

Brigham City Relief Society Granary
100 North 400 East
1877

The Brigham City Co-op built this small stone Relief Society granary in 1877 on the northwest corner of the block known by Co-op workers as Co-op Square. Relief Society Women conducted business and organized various projects from the granary building, including the grain storage program, from the late 1870s until 1913. Almost two hundred different Mormon communities had Relief Society granaries during the late 1800s. Besides storing grain, the Relief Society was involved in a wide range of auxiliary LDS programs such as the retrenchment movement, the sale of home-produced goods, the promotion of home industry and sericulture, nursing, midwifery, and hospital maintenance. Tradition has it that Brigham City's children gathered old glass that was crushed and mixed with mortar to stick into holes in the building's walls to prevent mice from getting the grain.

Typical of many such granaries, the Brigham City Relief Society Granary is a single-cell (single-room), one-story stone building measuring forty-four feet by twenty-two feet with no windows. The foundation and walls are both formed with roughly dressed fieldstone and mortared with a mixture of lime, sand, and crushed glass.

Box Elder Stake Tabernacle
Main Street between 200 and 300 South
1890
Truman O. Angell Sr.

Brigham Young chose the site for the tabernacle on Sagebrush Hill, on the crest of an alluvial fan typical of those in rural Utah towns across the Wasatch Front. Water ran from that spot to the north, south, and west.

Over the next eleven years, rocks for the tabernacle walls were hauled to the site, and construction began in 1876. Mormon church architect Truman O. Angell Sr. designed the Box Elder Stake Tabernacle

Brigham City Relief Society Granary

A major fire damaged the building in 1896, but the community landmark was rebuilt with additional elaboration. The construction crew added sixteen brick buttresses to the exterior with steeples topping each one; a more significant central tower to the front; and on the interior a vestibule that increased the seating capacity by 400, for a total of 1,600. Simple hand-carved designs embellished the new balcony, which was wood grained and painted to look like more extravagant materials. Beautiful glass windows and other detailing attested to the care and attention the pioneer builders gave to this important religious monument.

Willard
Willard Historic District
200 West 200 North / 100 East 200 South
1860s

The twelve-acre Willard Historic District provides an unusual glimpse into nineteenth-century pioneer farm fields with animals grazing nearby. Barns, granaries, corrals, sheds, and fences remain, as do forty-six houses, commercial structures, and churches, with a stuccoed brick town hall at the center. Combined with open spaces defined by small orchards and pastureland, it is the quintessential bucolic rural landscape.

Like so many towns in rural Utah, Willard spread along the general guidelines of the Plat of the City of Zion on a north-south and east-west grid, with a large central block at the town center. Houses throughout town were set back twenty-five feet or more, and there were usually about four to eight houses per block. The warm earth tones of the buildings give a feeling of harmony and uninterrupted space. Willard Creek is lined with trees and forms a natural link between the mountains to the east and Willard Bay to the west.

Box Elder Stake Tabernacle

in 1890. When first constructed, the tabernacle measured fifty feet by ninety-five feet, with a tower rising above each of the four corners, and was made of fieldstone from the surrounding fields. When finally completed in 1890, the interior featured a gallery on the north and south walls and an elevated speaker's stand on the east end. Workers hauled lumber for the building from nearby mountains, sawed it in the mill, and delivered it to the site.

When Willard was settled in 1851 it was called Willow Creek because of the willows lining the creeks descending from the nearby mountains. The settlers built one of the largest forts in any Utah town, measuring a half mile in length and a quarter mile in width, with walls twelve feet high and two feet thick at the top. After their initial fear of Indian attack abated, the settlers dismantled their fort and used many of the stones for their homes.

In Willard the pioneers built primarily in the Gothic or Greek Revival style, with rectangles of one and a half or two stories, and they used high gabled roofs. The simplest homes have two rooms on the main floor and one large room above. These hall-parlor houses have a centralized main entrance leading directly into the parlor. The other room, the hall, is slightly smaller. Exterior walls are eighteen to twenty-four inches thick and are sometimes lined with adobe. Interior walls are usually formed with rock. On the houses with Gothic elements, finials, bargeboards, dormers, and pendants are frequent decorative elements. But it is the harmonious use of stone that most distinguishes these buildings as a group. The town had its own master builder, Shadrach Jones. Shadrach was a Welshman who converted to Mormonism in 1850. His stonemasonry reflects his Welsh heritage. He and his workers demonstrated tremendous skill with the use of modest hand tools to create some of the most beautiful buildings in the state. In 1883, he served a mission in his homeland, where he died on June 24, 1883, after contracting pneumonia.

Willard's stone buildings tell a narrative—the influence of European house styles on the Mormon frontier; the group's philosophy of building as permanently and beautifully as their resources would permit;

and their amazing resiliency in adapting to this environment. Abundant rock marked this landscape, in some ways creating an obstacle to plowing fields and building streets. The pioneers embraced the land and used this indigenous natural resource to build sturdy and beautiful homes to last. Most often only one side of the rock was cut for the facade. The gaps between stones were filled with a mortar mixed with lime and mud, with straw or even randomly shaped rocks added as a binder. On facades facing the road, the mortar was sometimes pointed to give a more elaborate appearance. The result resembled quarried rock rather than rock just transported down from the mountain.

Cache County

Clarkston
Clarkston Tithing Granary
10212 North 8700 West
1905

Tithing granaries were typically built in one of two ways. Some were built with a balloon frame with an interior wall that kept the grain tightly contained. The second type used two-by-fours laid on top of each other to create a thick, tightly constructed, heavy wall, as in the 1905 Clarkston Tithing Granary where the walls are spiked at the corners. Called false timbering, this second type of construction was popular between 1890 and 1920. A central door on the broad side of the building on the south is covered by a shed-roofed porch. On the gable ends there are doors on the top level, and a pulley above that was used to haul grain up to be poured into the granary. The site included a tithing office that was demolished in the late 1950s and an extant Relief Society granary.

Lewiston
Lewiston Community Building
29 South Main Street
1935
Public Works Administration

For many rural communities, the PWA Moderne structures built during the 1930s were the most modern buildings to be constructed to date in town. Flat roofs and simple, unadorned surfaces might have seemed foreign, even austere to towns used to more traditional styles. Moreover, structures like the Lewiston Community Building were often the first large-scale public buildings built locally, making this innovative architecture more palatable. Built in 1935, the Lewiston Community Building was fairly characteristic of the PWA Moderne style—the building is a large rectangular box with an overhanging cap of contrasting cast concrete. Three large bays marked by narrow, vertical panels break up the wall surface of the side wings, with a series of concrete-capped pilasters. Mullions on the central bay extend upward beyond the roof edge, appearing like small crenellations. The stylized pediment of the entrance has a frieze that contains the name and date of the building on the cast-concrete entrance.

Lewiston Tithing Office and Granary
87 East 800 South
1898
Johnson & Worley

The Lewiston Tithing Office is one of the best examples of Italianate architecture in Utah. Unlike most nineteenth-century tithing offices, which are simple vernacular structures, this is a two-story brick Italianate box. Though this style was typically used more for residential architecture, this Italianate building housed the office of Lewiston's tithing operation. During the nineteenth century and early decades of the twentieth century, tithing offices were key institutions in Latter-day Saint towns. Church members were asked to donate one-tenth of their surplus to the church for distribution to the poor or for other economic activities. The tithing office and lot became important storage centers for the collection, storage, and distribution of in-kind donations given as tithing by church members. In these cash-poor towns, tithing was almost always in the form of products—cattle, cloth, eggs and butter, home-fashioned brooms or hats—all were fair and welcome donations.

The building is basically a rectangular mass that emphasizes the vertical movement upward, topped by a low hipped roof with overhanging eaves, with the main entrance on one side and a projecting bay

Lewiston Tithing Office

Lewiston Granary

on the other. A brick stringcourse defines the line between the two floors. A small hood over the front door repeats the low pitch and overhang of the roof and has a decorative spindle band supported by functional brackets. The hood-shaped stone headers are accented with keystones.

The building was built on a five-acre plot of land donated to the LDS Church by Harvey M. Rawlins. Johnson & Worley, a Logan construction firm, built the building as well as the Lewiston First Ward Meetinghouse (since demolished). Brick for the building and for most brick buildings in town came from a local brickyard southeast of town. A barn, large granary, and root cellar were also located on the lot. The office and outbuildings were sold in 1914 to Fred Taggart, a local farmer.

Richmond
Richmond Carnegie Library
6 West Main Street
1913–1914
Watkins & Birch

The Richmond Library is a one-story yellow brick building with a raised basement. Like other libraries built between 1913 and 1920, it is a straightforward rectangle with a flat roof and symmetrical facade. While detailing varies from Prairie-style horizontality to Classical Revival elements, the general configuration is much the same. Classical details include a symmetrical facade; pilasters with geometric capitals that run across the front, dividing the facade into five bays; and a parapet above a molded cornice. At the center a projecting pavilion forms the entrance to the building and is framed

Richmond Carnegie Library

by brick piers with geometric capitals slightly different from those on the building itself.

The Richmond Carnegie Library was built in 1913–14 with $8,000 from Andrew Carnegie. The town held a special election on July 1, 1912, to gauge public support for a city library tax. The response was overwhelmingly positive and a Board of Directors was created, which three months later passed a resolution accepting the Carnegie grant and committing to the $800 annual maintenance fee.

Watkins & Birch was a Provo-based architectural firm that designed several Carnegie libraries during the second decade of the twentieth century, each a rectangular single-story structure with a raised basement, a configuration determined to be particularly well suited to the needs of a small-town library. The building was completed in 1914.

Richmond Relief Society Hall
15 East Main Street
1880–1882

After Relief Societies were organized in 1867, local Relief Society units owned property, organized local relief projects, and managed small businesses. The Richmond Relief Society Hall, built between 1880 and 1882, is a one-and-a-half-story wooden frame structure that measures twenty-one feet by forty-one feet and is one of the oldest known extant Relief Society halls in the state. The matter-of-fact building has no exterior decoration or pretense to style. Walls feature simple novelty siding with corner boards and sit on a stone foundation. The porch on the gabled front end of the building facing north was an early addition to the original building. Three of the four historic simple paneled wooden doors have transoms. The interior includes one large room downstairs and a slightly smaller room upstairs, with walls made of lath and plaster and wooden floors.

Richmond women used the Relief Society Hall as a school, for food storage, for care of the sick, and for raising money for missionaries and the Logan Temple construction, until the 1904 construction of the Richmond Meetinghouse and the consolidation of ward auxiliary activities under one roof. The Daughters of Utah Pioneers purchased it in 1919 for a relic hall and meeting place.

Richmond Tithing Office and Bishop's Storehouse
31 South State Street
1907

In nineteenth-century Utah, tithing offices played a critical role in distributing donated farm products among newcomers and those struggling to establish themselves in agricultural communities. In cash-poor environments the tithing office was a center of trade, welfare assistance, and economic activity. Built for the most part from standard plans, these buildings express the centralized building approach that would come to typify Mormon building efforts in the twentieth century. The Richmond Tithing Office was built in 1907 and is a one-story, square, red brick building with a pyramidal roof, a coursed ashlar foundation, and a projecting gabled pavilion, a style described as Type No. 3. The symmetrical facade includes the central pavilion with a flat arched opening and an inset rectangular panel above. Decorative elements include a wide frieze wrapping around the building below the cornice line and formed with stringcourses of brick projecting at different levels. Rock-faced brickwork highlights the arches over the windows. A small domed cupola crowns the building.

Richmond Tithing Office and Bishop's Storehouse

Richmond Community Building
6 West Main Street
1936–1937
Public Works Administration

This excellent example of an eclectic PWA Moderne architectural style was built between 1936 and 1937. Here the basic elements of PWA Moderne are added to Colonial Revival design for a rural Utah public building. The main mass of the building is a one-story rectangle with projecting identical wings and a flat roof. The building is symmetrical in terms of mass, decoration, and placement of windows and doors, and a cast-concrete architrave moves around a centrally placed entrance. Gray concrete coping caps the walls, and the corners are rounded in the Moderne pattern. Three brick belt courses below the eaves accentuate the smooth curves of the corners, all distinctive elements of the PWA Moderne.

To the north or rear of the building are several large additions. The west half is a large rectangular gymnasium with a parapeted gabled roof capped in contrasting concrete. A finial of applied stylized sculpture is on the roof apex facing the street. Concrete-capped piers are placed at wide intervals along the sides, breaking up the walls into vertical sections.

The Richmond Community Building was built as part of the New Deal's effort to pump life back into towns struggling from the force of the Depression, putting local men to work and giving a boost to infrastructure. In fact, during the 1930s almost every public building in Utah was constructed with aid from the federal government. County courthouses, city halls, fire stations, national guard armories, public school buildings, and many others were built under several different federal agencies—the Civil Works Administration, the Federal Emergency Relief Administration, the National Youth Administration, the Works Progress Administration, and the Public Works Administration. Most of these buildings would never have been built without this help.

Architects Scott and Welch from Salt Lake City designed the building using local brick and local builders for the work. As a community center, the building was the scene of motion picture shows, speeches, and theatricals, and its auditorium was well used.

Smithfield
Smithfield Public Library
25 North Main Street
1912
Fred W. Hodgson

Perhaps no figure represents the rags-to-riches story of success more than Andrew Carnegie. Carnegie, an Irish immigrant, made his fortune in the steel industry and felt an obligation to use his wealth to improve the human condition. Believing that reading was key to what he called "moral elevation," he funded construction of libraries for small rural American towns unlikely to be able to afford them on their own. Hoping to stimulate local commitment to such projects, he required that towns match the funds he donated, creating a partnership and an ongoing commitment. Carnegie gave a grant of $12,000, or slightly more than half the total cost, for the Smithfield Public Library. In addition, the town issued a one-mill tax levy in 1917 and another in 1921 for the remainder.

Fred W. Hodgson was the architect of the project. He was Cache Valley's most prominent architect of the era and brother of well-known Ogden architect Leslie S. Hodgson, who designed Ogden High School. Hodgson studied architecture in San Diego and with his brother in Ogden, most likely becoming familiar with the

Smithfield Public Library

elements of the Prairie style under his tutelage. Hodgson designed several other public buildings in Cache Valley, including the Cache Valley Bank, the Utah State Agricultural College Library, and the Smithfield Junior High School.

The 1912 Smithfield Public Library is a fine example of the Prairie style used for a small public building. Like most other Carnegie libraries, it is a one-story brick building with a raised basement and a flat roof with a strong emphasis on horizontal details—coping at the roof edge, projecting windowsills embodying the overhang so common to the style, and leaded-glass windows arranged to resemble horizontal bands.

The city acquired thirty-two paintings by Utah artist Mary Teasdel in 1929 for the paltry sum of $120. About eighteen to twenty of these paintings are on display at any given time to this day in the library. Although a few are large scale,

these paintings are for the most part small, usually between eighteen and twenty-four inches wide. Many of the paintings were done during Teasdel's summers in the French countryside at the turn of the century when she was a student.

Douglass Dry Goods and Mercantile
100 South Main Street
1883

The Douglass Dry Goods and Mercantile is the oldest commercial building left in Smithfield, a town first platted in 1864. The building has a surface richness because of the use of stone, brick, and coursed ashlars. Rubble ashlar masonry was used for the back and two side walls, brick for the upper half of the facade, and coursed sandstone for the lower half.

Scottish convert William M. Douglass built this store in 1883. Four years after his arrival in Utah in 1854, Douglass started his first store in Salt Lake City with partner

Thomas Richardson. After he married Cyntheann Merrill eight years later, they went to Smithfield. When the settlers vacated the original fort and moved onto city lots, Douglass opened a store in his home to make goods available that were shipped north from Salt Lake City. Douglass built a building for the store in 1883 and operated it until 1897, when he sold it to James Cantwell, a former employee. The building functioned as a store until 1964, when the Smithfield American Legion Post established its headquarters there.

Smithfield Tithing Office
101 West Center Street
1910s

The Smithfield Tithing Office first shows up on a Sanborn Fire Insurance map in 1917. After the Smithfield Second Ward built the building for tithing exchanges, in the 1900s the Relief Society also used it for offices. It was likely used as a public library until the Smithfield Carnegie Library was built in 1922. Unlike other tithing offices in the area, the Smithfield Tithing Office looks more like a bungalow than a religious building. It is a one-story brick building with a hipped roof and concrete foundation. The roof's low pitch and wide overhang are typical of Prairie-style bungalows, as is the porch that runs along the facade, but unlike a home, this building has a smaller rectangular form that moves back about half as far as in a traditional bungalow. The facade itself is symmetrically organized, with a door and window on both sides of a slightly projecting central bay.

The ward sold the building in 1951 to the Board of Education of Cache County School District.

Smithfield Tabernacle
Center Street and Main Street, Smithfield
1881–1902
James Quayle

The Smithfield Tabernacle's yellow brick is characteristic of the region and is the same brick used for the construction of Old Main on the Utah State University campus. It can be identified as an LDS building by the "Holiness to the Lord" in the center of a Gothic pointed arch in a central engaged tower on the facade. The interior space originally included beautiful wooden pews and a balcony that flowed around the second level from one side to the other. When it was reconfigured into a recreation center in the 1950s, all this was lost. The caps

Smithfield Tabernacle

for the tower and corner pinnacles were removed in 1946.

The term "tabernacle" means dwelling place in Hebrew, and in the Mormon landscape, a tabernacle holds special significance for church members. Rather than being the site of weekly services held by a local congregation such as Sunday School or Sacrament meeting, a tabernacle was a larger scene for regional instructional meetings that helped unify the church and perpetuate church doctrines.

Gothic Revival detailing is found throughout the exterior—steeply pitched Gothic arches, historically over windows and doors (although some have been filled in with brick), are organized in five main bays. The building is subtly presented by a raised platform, and the principal entrance is to the side of the central tower, which juts forward slightly and has two fake buttresses on each side.

Benson
Benson Elementary School
3440 North 3000 West
1935
Public Works Administration

Barely an expansion of the old one-room schoolhouse type, Benson Elementary School was built in 1935 and had three classrooms where three teachers taught six grades. Besides classrooms there were also a lunchroom, an office, and "clean, modern restrooms." In 1969, the building deviated from its original use and instead served as the Cache Instructional Workshop, a vocational training school for developmentally and physically disabled people older than sixteen, funded by the Americans with Disabilities Act. Typically, the workshop taught sixty students and had a staff of ten.

The most modern building in town when it was built, the Benson Elementary School was a PWA Moderne design. This one-story, yellow brick building has a raised basement, and on the west wing is a parapeted gabled roof—a stylized, geometric pediment. At the side are pairs of narrow windows with semicircular heads. Between them is a large rectangular plaque stating the name and date of the building.

Logan
Logan Union Pacific Depot
600 West Center Street
1890s
Union Pacific Company

The style of the Logan Union Pacific Depot is called "Railroad Queen Anne." The excessive ornament so characteristic of the Queen Anne might include wraparound porches, bays, and elaborate gingerbread on a residential example. On a railroad depot the Queen Anne is expressed through extravagant massing, elaborate woodwork, and general opulence.

The Logan Depot Foundation partnered with public entities to restore the station in an adaptive reuse project, modeling creative preservation collaboration. The foundation received funds from the George S. and Dolores Doré Eccles Foundation and a Community Development Block Grant as well as from a federal Intermodal Surface Transportation Efficiency Act grant. Currently, the building houses the Café Sabor restaurant, and in the future, the depot will serve as a new type of intermodal hub, providing connections for bus service and bike and pedestrian paths.

Logan Temple Barn
368 East 200 North
1884

After the Logan Temple was finished in 1884, it was immediately evident that the hitching posts in the temple yard were insufficient for the number of horses and buggies of those attending the temple. As a result, on February 2, 1887, the Temple Association applied to the city for three acres of land east of the temple to serve as a stable and wagon yard. Six years after it began negotiations, the church bought it from J. Z. Stewart for $4,000.

In February 1893 the Temple Association issued a call for rock to be hauled to the site to build a barn for temple use, which was completed and ready for use by January 1897. Construction workers built corrals, sheds, and outbuildings on the lot by that summer. The barn is a two-story, thirty-six-foot-square stone building with a pyramidal roof topped by a cupola added in 1925. On the main level, the barn included space for carriages and horses, with a hay loft above. Stone segmental arches over openings are the only decorative elements.

Logan Temple Barn

David Eccles Mansion
250 West Center Street
1907
Joseph Monson and Karl C. Schaub

Bursting with the exuberance of the Victorian style, the David Eccles Mansion parades financial prosperity and opulence. David Eccles was Utah's version of the rags-to-riches tale—a poor immigrant from Scotland when he first came to Utah, Eccles became one of the most successful businessmen in the West.

David Eccles was born in Glasgow, Scotland, in 1849, two years after the Mormon pioneers first came to Utah. In 1863 David and his family benefited from the LDS Church's Perpetual Emigration Fund and came to Utah. Here he worked in sawmills in Utah and Oregon and eventually invested in railroads, sugar beet industries, food processing enterprises, construction, coal, land, livestock, banking, and insurance companies and started fifty-four different businesses. By the time of his death in 1912 his estate was valued at $6 million.

The David Eccles Mansion is one of several fine eclectic Victorian residences designed by Logan architects Joseph Monson and Karl C. Schaub. They worked together for eight years, during which they designed several prominent buildings for the Agricultural College of Utah (now Utah State University) and most of the schools in Cache County. Joseph Monson worked at age sixteen on the Logan Temple and became the supervising architect for state schools after 1885. He was a member of the territorial legislature and the state house and senate.

Logan Center Street Historic District

Karl C. Schaub was born in Zurich, Switzerland, in 1869 and came to Utah with his family in 1888. He began his architectural career in 1891 and worked as a draftsman for the U.S. government in Washington, D.C. Schaub helped design Old Main, Logan High School, and Budge Hospital and codesigned the Eccles Hotel.

This house combines elements from the Queen Anne, Chateauesque, Victorian Eclectic, and Neoclassical Revival styles. Despite this eclecticism, the asymmetry and varied context come together in a coherent, balanced, and appealing design. When built in 1907, this three-story house contained twenty-four rooms and some eleven thousand square feet of floor space. It was easily the largest home in Cache County. When the family vacated the home in 1943, it became a dormitory for the college. The third-floor ballroom became eight bedrooms and bathrooms, with six bedrooms filling the second floor and one on the first floor.

Logan Center Street Historic District
200 North, 200 South, 200 East, 600 West,
Center Street
1870s

Explorers sent by Brigham Young in 1847 to identify favorable locations for settlement determined that Cache Valley was lush and rich with natural resources. It would be little more than a decade before Peter Maughan received permission from Young to lead a group of families into the valley to start a small community. During the next two years ten different communities started in a line through the valley, including Providence, Logan, Hyde Park, Smithfield, Richmond, and Mendon. Because of its favorable location along the Logan River and its equal distance from outlying towns, Logan became the most important town—the religious, economic, and cultural center of the county.

Logan's first building effort was a fort. Two groups of settlers built log homes with contiguous walls, forming a fort along what is now known as Center Street. Just about every type of early pioneer building is still standing on the blocks of the Logan Center Street Historic District. As a group they provide a glimpse into nineteenth-century life. Commercial, government, religious, and social life are all represented. The district is unique in that it includes a Mormon temple, tabernacle, and meetinghouse—the three principal structures in the LDS hierarchy of ecclesiastical buildings—as well as the Cache County Courthouse and the Union Pacific Railroad Depot. In short, Logan had the main types of structures a Utah town would aspire to build as it developed, following the model of Salt Lake City. Also important to the district are residential neighborhoods that have some of the earliest extant homes in the area.

The oldest homes in the district are simple vernacular structures built with native materials and a very straightforward, practical approach to design and plan. All are built of wood or adobe except for four rock structures. Homes built after the railroad came to Logan include materials shipped in from distant markets and exhibit national trends in style and form. Brick became a popular building material, and Victorian, Stick, Queen Anne, Shingle, Prairie, Classical Revival, and Romanesque buildings proliferated in the district.

The commercial district, built between 1870 and 1915, is for the most part constructed in Neoclassical and Victorian styles and is three blocks long and two blocks wide. The blend of commercial and religious, public and private helps us interpret Logan's unique character. As was true throughout Mormon territory, it was also the manifestation of the American dream and depended on trade and capitalism, opportunity and inspiration.

Logan High School Gymnasium
162 West 100 South
1935–1936
Public Works Administration

Yet another PWA project for Logan was the Art Deco–style Logan High School Gymnasium. Built between 1935 and 1936 for $125,000, it was first used in January 1937. A total of twenty gymnasiums were built in Utah with PWA funds. The report of the Utah State Building Board highlighted the building's "tiled pool, tiled showers" and noted that it housed "an R.O.T.C. unit, together with a firing range." Construction of the new facility ensured, according to the report, "an adequate high school plant both for classroom instruction and for extracurricular programs."[5]

Like many other buildings built under the PWA program, the Logan High School gym is a large, rectangular building with a flat roof and projecting flat-roofed square towers at the front corners. A flat-roofed, central entrance porch is located beneath a low parapet. A series of square piers separate vertical window bays and emphasize the vertical orientation of key decorative elements.

Capitol Theatre / Ellen Eccles Theatre
43 South Main Street
1923
B. Marcus Priteca

Logan's original Thatcher Opera House burned down twenty-two years after it was built in 1890. G. W. Thatcher was an amateur actor and entrepreneur of some renown connected to New York and the world of theater, and he performed in a continuing series of Broadway and traveling Lyceum shows that came to Logan, facilitated by the railroad that came through town. Although he rebuilt in 1923, he continued to dream of a more magnificent

Capitol Theatre / Ellen Eccles Theatre

setting for theater in northern Utah. Designed by B. Marcus Priteca, the new Capitol Theatre was perfect for both live productions and movies. Certainly, the ornate Neoclassical auditorium mirrored the most significant opera houses in the western United States.

As was true of many other theaters, and reflecting the change in tastes in cultural entertainment, the Capitol converted to motion pictures in the 1950s. But after it was donated to Logan City in 1988, the building fell into disrepair. Believing it was worth saving, community leaders and non-profit groups launched a $7.5 million restoration campaign to restore the building near the heart of Logan's downtown. As a result, the theater reopened in 1993 as the Ellen Eccles Theatre, and the renovation won a Utah Heritage Foundation Heritage Award in 1993 for excellence.

Logan LDS Sixth Ward Church
395 South Main Street
1883
Joseph Monson and Karl C. Schaub

The Logan Sixth Ward building is the only Gothic-style Mormon church in Logan. Located in a commanding place on Main Street, it helps create nostalgia for the history of this place. Anthon L. Skanchy was the first bishop of the Logan Sixth Ward, an offshoot of the Logan First Ward. Before the twenty-by-thirty-foot building was built, members met in private homes and planned for the construction of their new meetinghouse. In 1884–85, an addition to the building doubled its size. By the turn of the century the Logan Sixth Ward had 672 members, or 131 families. By 1907 the congregation had outgrown its home and was making plans for a new meetinghouse. The architects of the new building were Joseph Monson and Karl C. Schaub.

Though basically a symmetrical rectangle measuring 45 by 114 feet, with a lateral wing toward the west end, the Logan Sixth Ward Church is distinguished by Gothic detailing. The gabled end of the facade had a central engaged tower that culminated at the top in a way that looked like a model of the Salt Lake Temple but actually resembled Ithiel Town's Trinity Church in New Haven, Connecticut, and other elaborate towers in Gothic Revival churches from this era.

Perhaps the most unusual decoration on a Mormon building in the state, this was removed in the 1980s when another congregation purchased the building.

Other Gothic features include large pointed-arched windows between stepped buttresses, with pinnacles on top of the front corner that meet the wall at a forty-five-degree angle. The chapel's sloped auditorium and gallery seat about sixty people. A podium with a spherical cavern improves the acoustics. The ceiling vault has exposed trusses and braces.

Logan Tabernacle
Entire block between Main Street and 100 East, Center Street and 100 North
1865–1891
Mormon pioneers first came to Cache Valley in the late 1850s, and not long after they arrived, they surveyed and reserved

Logan Tabernacle

a block in the center of town for public buildings, as was customary with the Plat of the City of Zion. President Moses Thatcher petitioned the mayor and city council of Logan to sell the square to the LDS Church for $40.50, or $5.00 per acre. A group of local Mormons met with Brigham Young, Apostle Ezra T. Benson, and Thatcher to plan construction of a tabernacle on December 7, 1864.

Up until about the turn of the century, Mormons built tabernacles as regional centers in areas with significant populations of members. Usually high styled rather than vernacular, tabernacles served as settings primarily for large-scale ecclesiastical meetings and represented the best in terms of materials, design, and technology that could be built locally. Rather than the multipurpose meetinghouses built during this period, tabernacles were more singularly focused in terms of function and use, which was one reason they became obsolete in the early twentieth century when all church auxiliary functions were pulled under one roof and Mormon meetinghouses became religious and cultural centers for geographic wards.

Tabernacles had special meaning in nineteenth-century Utah. Important as gathering places for quarterly conferences, they were also a physical reminder of the importance religion played in the lives of these people and the connections between people dispersed geographically.

To raise money for the project, Elder Benson organized a subscription drive, and eventually 175 different individuals subscribed a total of $26,450. During spring 1865 the project began in earnest and excavation commenced. Because most labor was voluntary and other projects in town pulled men away from work on the tabernacle, progress was slow. Population grew quickly in Cache Valley and numerous

meetinghouse projects ran parallel with the tabernacle and competed for labor, cash, and materials. The death of local leaders Ezra T. Benson and Peter Maughan and the absence of Bishop William B. Preston on a mission had a significant impact as well. Brigham Young visited the building site on June 28, 1873, and asked that it be redrawn, suggesting both a larger footprint and an accelerated construction schedule.

The first conference was held in the lower tabernacle on January 26, 1877, when Apostle Franklin D. Richards dedicated the basement. President Wilford Woodruff dedicated the building, which had been built for a total cost of $98,000, on November 4, 1891.

Although the architectural style of the Logan Tabernacle is somewhat eclectic, the overall impression is one of enthusiasm. The building is a lively celebration of materials, shapes, details, and textures. A beautiful building in large measure because of the hope and energy poured into it by its builders, it has footings and walls formed of Swan Peak quartzite quarried in Green Canyon, about eight miles northeast of the building site. The contrasting stone of the corners and trim is argillaceous limestone, quarried from a formation east of Franklin, twenty miles to the north. All timber in the building is either red or white pine, sometimes called Douglas fir or Engelmann spruce.

The plan is 126 feet by 66 feet and has a main assembly room that is 120 feet by 60 feet, with a gallery on both sides and toward one end with elevated seats on both sides of the choir. The main assembly room seats 1,500 people. In the basement story there is a baptismal font and smaller meeting rooms. The walls rise 44 feet, and the tower's spire is 133 feet high. The building is a showcase of pioneer craftsmanship and design. The interior includes columns, seats, and moldings specially grained to resemble fancier grades of wood.

The building has elements from the Gothic, Greek, Roman, Byzantine, and other revival styles. The general rectangular form of the building was typical of early Mormon churches—a simple gabled box with an engaged central tower in the front facade. Relief and interest are created through detailing, however, including buttresses built of multicolored stone, a molded cornice with a full return across the front wall and moving into the tower, and a vestry extending outward from the tower, capped with small stone pinnacles. The center of the tower is a curious round window with a Star of David and a wooden lantern or steeple that is ornately milled and topped with a golden dome and several finials.

Logan Temple
Between 200 and 300 East and 100 and 200 North
1877–1884
Truman O. Angell Sr. and Truman O. Angell Jr.

In the hierarchy of Mormon buildings, the temple commands an imposing position. Lavished with the best available materials and design, the Logan Temple was the third to be built in Utah Territory, started in 1877 and completed in 1884. Situated on a hill overlooking the city, the temple grounds include a full city block of eight acres with a beautifully landscaped elliptical garden planted with trees, shrubs, lawns, and carefully tended flower beds.

Church architect Truman O. Angell designed the building, but because he was so preoccupied with the Salt Lake Temple and the St. George Temple as well as the Territorial Capitol at Fillmore, the brunt of responsibility fell on his son Truman Angell Jr., who is credited for his innovative interpretation of interior space.

Logan Temple

The temple project required supporting industries to provide materials. Sawmills up Logan Canyon supplied wood for the construction, firewood for the lime kiln, and scaffolding for workers. Rock was quarried at Green Canyon, east of North Logan; at Hyde Park Canyon; and north of Franklin, Idaho. Because workers used materials from these industries to build their own homes, the project greatly enriched the local economy. A total of $607,000 was donated to the temple construction—$30,000 in merchandise; $30,000 in livestock; $71,000 in produce; $93,000 in cash; $380,000 in labor; and $3,000 in wagons and teams. More than 150 men and fifty teams worked on the temple for more than seven years.

The temple is 171 feet long and 95 feet wide, with an octagonal tower at each corner that is 100 feet high, and a large square tower at each end in the center. The tower on the west end is 165 feet high and the one on the east is 170 feet. Crenellated battlements at the tops of the towers and massive buttresses strengthen the walls. Deep window bays are Roman arched, with mullions arranged in Gothic patterns. Groupings of three towers symbolize the LDS concept of the trinity.

The temple expresses the Latter-day Saint belief that life is eternal and has significance beyond the daily physical struggle.

Old Main
Utah State University
1888
Sommer, Peterson and Company

The Utah territorial legislature created the Agricultural College of Utah in 1888. The newly formed Board of Trustees met on March 26, 1889, to accept an offer for a proposed campus site and to instruct the secretary to "advertise for plans for a $20,000 building, plans to be delivered to the secretary before the 15th of April."

The board next met on April 15 to accept the plans of architect C. L. Thompson, who had proposed a three-section structure of buff-colored brick and stone that measured 270 feet by 100 feet for Old Main. Each section could be built in phases—the south wing was built first and the north wing and the east portion were authorized by the board in 1892. The Agricultural College was dedicated on September 4, 1890, and officially opened the next day. In 1901 eighty additional feet were added in front, including the tower. Old Main is the oldest remaining educational building under continual use in the state.

The school's 1892 catalog described the building's many uses: "It contains recitation rooms, workshops, cooking, sewing, householding, dairying, laundering, engineering, agricultural and business departments ... laboratory, museum, library and gymnasium rooms and a military drill hall of ample size. Its audience room or chapel will hold 1,600. Three large rooms have been set aside for halls for the literary societies. Its rooms are light and pleasant to a rare degree and its halls wide and roomy, extending on each floor the entire length of the building. In the near future, large bath rooms will be put in for the accommodation of both sexes, where baths can be taken at pleasure."[6]

Old Main

Home Economics / Commons Building
1935
Leslie S. Hodgson and Myrl A. McClenahan
Contrasting with the traditional symmetry and configuration of Old Main and other early buildings on the Utah State University campus, the Home Economics / Commons Building is an excellent example of the Art Deco style. Designed by Leslie Hodgson and Myrl McClenahan of Ogden, the same architects who designed the Ogden High School and the Ogden Municipal Building, this large two-story flat-roofed building has a rectangular plan and an off-center main entrance. The verticality and the rhythmic interaction of narrow, recessed window panels and crenellated parapet distinguish the style. Details like brick mullions with corbeled corners are capped by stylized geometric capitals; stainless-steel doors at the entrance have decorative geometric window panels; and tall transoms with zigzag tracery continue through spandrels linking the two flanking columns.

In 1935 the building was constructed for $325,226 and was described by R. A. Hart, the Utah PWA director, as "the second most important item" in the state's building program after the George Thomas Library at the University of Utah.[7] The university dedicated the building on September 27, 1935. The Home Economics Building housed offices, classrooms, and laboratories for the department, as well as a cafeteria, dining rooms, lounges, kitchens, student offices, and a bookstore. When completed, it was three stories high, 165 feet wide at the east end, and 122 feet wide at the west.

Cache County Courthouse
181 North Main Street
1880s, additions 1915, 1917
Truman O. Angell Jr.
This two-story Beaux Arts building was designed by LDS church architect

Cache County Courthouse

Truman O. Angell Jr., the architect of the Logan Temple and son of the architect of the Salt Lake Temple, Truman O. Angell Sr. From above, the plan of this distinguished building would look like an *H*, with modest-sized wooden porticos to the east and west. A round cupola sits at the center and is topped by a gold domed roof.

The 2003–05 renovation of the historic property included adding a wooden frame to seismically retrofit the building from the inside. Existing wooden details like trim around doors and windows were preserved. The renovation architect was Lanny Herron of Architectural Nexus.

Providence
Providence LDS Chapel and Meetinghouse
20 South Main Street (Main and Center Street)
1869–1873

The Providence Meetinghouse, built in 1869–73, is evidence of the determination of Utah's nineteenth-century settlers to build sturdy buildings that would last. Permanence, durability, and attention to craftsmanship mark this simple structure. A one-story stone building with a gabled roof, this building type is common enough, vernacular in the context of this environment. But it is also beautiful and typical of the early meetinghouses in Utah that are variations on the Greek Revival temple form. It is one of twenty-one such buildings still standing in the state. The building is four bays long and has the main entrance on the gabled end facing the street, as was customary among this generation of public buildings.

The walls are thick and consist of twenty-two inches of random rubble stone with beaded mortar joints and quoins of cut rusticated stone. Stone was located nearby in Dry Pole Canyon, and lime for the mortar burned in the kilns was found in Providence Canyon. The simple boxed concrete cornice has a full return on the west end and a partial return on the east, creating a temple-form silhouette. Windows as on the north wall have round arches and an ornamental keystone. There is also a round arch over the original entrance, including a cast ram's head instead of a keystone.

This round-arch motif is continued on the interior, with deep sills formed by the thick walls. A stage originally ran across the east wall, with a broad arch flanked on either side by arched doorways set in wooden paneling, again repeating the arch motif. Later the stage was torn out and a rostrum built in its place. In 1925 a two-story brick hipped-roof classroom wing was added to the southeast corner and a front vestibule in 1935.

Wellsville
Wellsville Tabernacle
75 South 100 East
1902–1908
C. T. Barrett

The spires of the Wellsville Tabernacle tower above the more modest buildings of this agricultural town in Cache County. Located on the southeast corner of the Wellsville town square, the tabernacle is of central importance to the town's history and built environment. Built between 1902 and 1908, this Gothic Revival building reflects the influence of late nineteenth-century revival religious architecture like that of Richard Upjohn and others working with the picturesque Gothic nationally. Utah architect C. T. Barrett prepared the plans under the direction of Bishop Evan R. Owen. Bishop William H. Maughan broke ground in 1902, and local dignitaries Apostle Owen Woodruff and President Seymour B. Young laid the cornerstones the next year. Anton H. Lund of the Mormon

Wellsville Tabernacle

in semicircular rows toward the pulpit. A semicircular apse for the choir is behind the pulpit.

Local men quarried rock for construction in nearby Sardine Canyon and prepared lime and brick in facilities established for the work. William S. Poppleton directed stonework and Job Miller Sr. made the red brick. Lumber came from Alex Hill's sawmill in Blacksmith Fork Canyon. The total cost of the building was $65,000.

George Bradshaw and Joshua Salisbury House / George Bradshaw Barn
73 Center Street
1872–1880
Joshua Salisbury

It is surprising when the unusual mansard roof of the Second Empire style appears in a place as remote as Wellsville, Utah. Most examples in the state are in cities—such as the Beaver County Courthouse, and the Devereaux Mansion in Salt Lake City—but regardless of location, this distinctive roof type speaks of the lively eclecticism of the Victorian style in rural Utah.

Local tradition says that when Brigham Young visited Cache County in 1864 he said, "Why not quarry rock and build stone houses and make rock fences?" Wellsville stonemasons Joshua Salisbury and the Glenn brothers—Israel, Joe, and John—apparently followed his advice and built a number of vernacular stone buildings during the next three decades. Joshua built the Bradshaw house and barn sometime between 1872 and 1880. He learned stonemasonry as an apprentice in North Wales before he immigrated to Utah in 1855, where he worked on the Logan Temple for two and a half years. The stonemason also helped develop dry farming techniques and spoke before the Dry Farming Congress in Salt Lake City in 1908. He sold the property

Church's First Presidency dedicated the tabernacle on June 28, 1908.

The building is 65 by 115 feet, with a projecting cross gable on the north side. The main facade tower is a particular focal point with pinnacles at the corners, and an arcade without a passageway behind. The gabled roof planes, corner buttresses, and tall, thin windows emphasize the building's verticality, the "scaffolding of heaven," in the words of French sculptor Rodin. After a fire partially destroyed it in 1959, the new tower was built lower and the central spire reduced in size.

The interior space is highly unusual for a Mormon tabernacle—the main vaulted space has a pulpit in the northwest corner, and the main aisle extends in a diagonal from the entrance under the corner tower. The slatted wood pews move

to George Bradshaw, a farmer, in 1901. It was Bradshaw who built the Second Empire house.

The 1875 vernacular stone barn was built with a quartzite variety from a nearby quarry in Sardine Canyon, and the timber was cut in Blacksmith Fork. The walls are irregular coursed ashlars, with more carefully cut stones on the front. The dimensions of this two-story building are twenty feet by twenty-six feet, which was unusual for Cache County, which favored a proportion of two to one. Bradshaw used the barn as a carriage house, country store, and home for the family of his brother-in-law Robert A. Leishman.

Also on the site, the two-story brick Bradshaw house, built in 1903, faces the tabernacle block and is topped by a bell-cast, shingled mansard roof. Contrasting

yellow brick is used for decoration at the water table level, for the segmental arches over window and door openings, and for a diamond-shaped window on one side opening into the interior hallway. A one-story addition with a hipped roof was later added to the back of the house.

Wellsville Relief Society Hall
67 South Center Street
1875–1877

The familiar form of the Wellsville Relief Society Hall—a simple one-story cross-wing house—is appropriate, for these women were doing what one historian calls "social housekeeping." No different from the domestic architecture that appears in virtually every small town in the state, the style of this building was appropriate to the needs of the Relief Society. The *Deseret*

Wellsville Relief Society Hall

News announced the building project in its November 10, 1875, issue. "The Relief Society has commenced operations on a house which they will call their own, a very handsome building, according to the design, and one of which they might well be proud. It is to be in the form of a cross, having three rooms, the center one being 30' × 15' for meetings, quilting, and such like, with a room on either side 12' × 14' for shop and store room." Typical of the house type, the house has a cruciform plan with a central gabled roof section facing the street, flanked by cross wings on either side. The Relief Society first occupied the building on October 24, 1877, and used the house for the next twenty-five years. In 1903 the Relief Society moved into the newly completed tabernacle on the other side of the street and the building was used as a residence.

Hyrum
Hyrum Stake Tithing Office
26 West Main Street
1910
Jeff Brothers

A Logan firm, Jeff Brothers, built the Hyrum Stake Tithing Office in 1910, and it was used to house the Hyrum Stake president's offices, a meeting room for the stake high council, a supply room complete with a steel vault for storing cash tithing donations, and a large room upstairs used for various functions.
It was built according to one of the three standard plans used by the LDS Church during the first two decades of the twentieth century for tithing office design, and similar buildings in Manti, Sandy, Panguitch, and Richmond had the same configuration.

The Hyrum Stake Tithing Office is a one-story, square, yellow brick building topped by a pyramidal roof. A projecting gabled pavilion on the symmetrical facade wall has a central round-arched opening and pilasters at the corners, and a single door flanked by sidelights provides entrance into the building.

Hyrum First Ward Meetinghouse
290 South Center Street
1903–1905
Karl C. Schaub

By the end of the nineteenth century, Mormon meetinghouses deviated from the strict geometry of the Classical Revival to the asymmetry more typical of other revival styles, with a square tower on the southeast corner of the building. The Hyrum First Ward Meetinghouse was designed by Logan architect Karl C. Schaub and overlooks the town from the crest of a hill. Built on four-foot-high stone foundations covered with a layer of cement inscribed to look like stone, the main walls are built of red brick hauled to the site from

Hyrum First Ward Meetinghouse.
Photograph by Ntsimp Own work, public domain.

Wellsville, five miles to the east. James L. Jenson and his son William laid the stone foundation and the brick. As was true for many religious buildings built during this era, the ward paid $8,000 for construction but much of the labor was donated by the members themselves. Entries on both sides of the tower are arched and originally featured double wooden doors. High-arched windows appear on each side of the building, with stone accents separated by pilasters that imitate the upward movement of buttresses. Above the windows on each side of the tower is a circular design formed with brickwork.

On the interior, carved pew ends continue the theme of arches and curves from the outside. Beautiful curved oak pews move in a quarter circle around the chapel. A balcony from the north side to the west repeats the same curve and is supported by posts and carved wooden scrolls underneath each end. The ceiling is a barrel vault with a large carved rosette at the highest point.

Holley/Globe Grain and Milling Company Elevator
100 North Center Street
1918
Alfred J. Peterson

There are only two examples in the state of grain elevators built using the false timbering construction technique. False timbering, or what is also called crib construction, uses two-by-four planks placed one on top of the other to create a tight, strong wall to store large quantities of loose grain; these are connected with simple butt joints at the corners rather than the notches used in log construction.

This snug fit also has the incidental benefit of making the structure virtually rodent proof. Although the false timbering technique was often used for small granaries during the early twentieth century in the state, it is found on only a couple of other grain elevators, the Barton granary near Verdure in southeastern Utah and the granary behind the Ephraim Granary.

The Holley/Globe Grain elevator processed grain between August 1918 and the 1960s. Construction coincided with the extension of the railroad to Hyrum in 1905, although it wasn't finished until 1918. The Ogden, Logan and Idaho Railway Company opened in 1914 one block north of Main Street in Hyrum. A spur ran north of the grain elevator, facilitating the loading of grain.

The grain elevator is sixty-eight feet tall, with a body twenty-five by twenty-eight feet. On the inside, it is organized into nine chambers—eight are grain elevators. The chamber at the center housed a dipper and belt mechanism for loading and unloading grain. The arrangement of chambers on the interior is hinted at on the exterior—butt joints exist at the corners of the overall structure and at the corners of each of the nine interior chambers. Concave chamber floors bring the weight of the grain downward and reduce pressure on the walls. A drive-through delivery area facilitated loading of trucks directly from the elevators.

Paradise
Paradise Tithing Office
8970 South 200 West
1876

The Paradise Tithing Office was built in 1876, long before the LDS Church began using standard plans during the first decade of the twentieth century. It is a one-story Greek temple form, common to the era. Mirroring the distinctive pitch and triangular form of the Parthenon or other Greek temples, the gabled end of these rectangular buildings faced the street and featured cornice returns. The brick for the building came from the Hyrum brickyard, one of the first brickyards in Cache Valley. Above the door on the facade a large, inset, semicircular decorative arch was most likely designed to post the name of the building and the date of construction. A chimney slightly off center on the ridgeline suggests that there were two rooms on the interior.

Rich County

Randolph
Randolph Tabernacle
State Highway 16 and Main Street
1898
John C. Gray

In the hierarchy of Mormon architecture, the tabernacle is somewhere between the ward meetinghouse and the temple. The Latter-day Saints built tabernacles during the late nineteenth and early twentieth centuries for large-scale regional instructional meetings of members. The Randolph Tabernacle is easily the most significant piece of architecture in Rich County and was built shortly after the organization of the Woodruff Stake of the LDS Church in 1898. Local leaders believed that a "good, large meetinghouse" should be built for the Randolph Ward, a "house that should be modern and large enough to accommodate people from far and near." This was essentially the purpose of a tabernacle, to provide a meeting space for regional conferences of the church. Later replaced by stake centers,

tabernacles were usually high styled, built with the finest available materials, and used for one principal purpose—large-scale religious meetings.

As was true of many early LDS buildings, the Randolph Tabernacle was built with local labor and donated materials. It was designed by John C. Gray, a local contractor and builder. Ward members contributed 82 percent of the $23,884 required for construction, and less than 10 percent came from church headquarters. Construction began in 1898.

The Randolph Tabernacle stands out as an interesting example of a single-story Victorian Eclectic building with a two-story tower and sandstone foundation. A sensitive addition was later added to the back of the building that matches the scale and massing of the earlier section.

False buttresses separate the bays, and a round-arched opening is included in each

Randolph Tabernacle.
Photograph by Tricia Simpson, GNU Free Documentation License 1.2, CC SA 3.0, Wiki Commons.

of three bays on the side. The irregular roof planes are typical of the Victorian style, as is the gabled roof, which is higher than the broadside gable at the last of the three side bays. Fish-scale shingles in the gabled ends of the gabled roof add interest and texture, as does stickwork in each of the roof gables.

Weber County

Ogden

Ogden U.S. Post Office and Federal Courthouse
298 West Twenty-Fourth Street
1905–1909
Federal government

Built during the same decade as Salt Lake City's Post Office and Federal Courthouse on Main Street, the Ogden Post Office and Federal Courthouse is also a Classical Revival building. Both cities prospered because of extensive federal installations in the area. The Ogden Post Office and Federal Courthouse was evidence of a new federal supervision over aspects of life that had either not been regulated or had been loosely attended to by a distant authority.

After the railroad came to Ogden in 1869, it brought with it a predominantly non-LDS population. Before the 1890 Manifesto, which officially ended polygamy in the LDS Church, federal authority was centered in this cosmopolitan city rather than Salt Lake City. This long history of identification with the federal government was acknowledged when Ogden became the site of a federal building and post office. This building attested to the new connection between Utah and the federal government and the power of the government with an architectural style that made reference to republicanism and democracy inherited from Classical cultures.

Built between 1905 and 1909, this square, symmetrical, five-bay building was built for $320,000 and was expanded in 1930. At the center of each facade is a central pedimented three-bay projection divided by engaged Corinthian columns, and on the east facade, pilasters. Two-story wood-paneled courtrooms and the marble interior of the main floor lobby are particularly beautiful extant interior details.

Ogden Union Railway and Depot
198 West Twenty-Eighth Street
1889
John and Donald B. Parkinson, Los Angeles, California

When the transcontinental railroad was finally completed on May 10, 1869, at Promontory Summit, four different towns competed to become the principal transportation hub for the Intermountain West. Promontory and Uintah never attracted enough settlers to compete for this distinction. But Corinne, a town founded by non-Mormons in 1869, and Ogden could. Despite its early promise, by the late 1870s, Corinne had declined in population. It was not, however, until the 1880s that Charles Francis Adams, who was president of the Union Pacific Railroad Company, announced plans for the construction of a depot.

By the time the company dedicated the depot on July 31, 1889, Ogden was the hub of an extensive network of railroad lines—the western terminus for the Union Pacific and the Denver and Rio Grande Railroads; the eastern terminus of the Central Pacific; the southern terminus of the Utah Northern, which extended through Idaho to Montana, at which point it connected with the Oregon Short Line and the Northern Pacific; and the northern terminus of the Utah Central, running to the mining town

Ogden Union Railway and Depot.
Photograph by Tricia Simpson, CC BY-SA 3.0.

of Frisco in southern Utah. In addition, the Echo and the Park City railroads terminated at Ogden, connecting Ogden to Park City.

John and Donald B. Parkinson out of Los Angeles designed the depot, which is at the west end of Twenty-Fifth Street on Wall Avenue. This Spanish Revival–style brick building has a red tile roof and rounded windows on the end gables. Inlaid designs of varicolored bricks in diamond shapes appear at regular intervals. Under the arches of the two front entrances that jut out from the main building are bright blue decorative mosaic tile designs and heavy wrought-iron chandeliers. The passenger waiting room at the core of the interior is a large two-story space with exposed wooden trusses with hand-hewn edges at the ceiling, from which huge chandeliers are suspended. Some of the original wooden benches are still in the waiting room. Wings at the lower level house office and baggage areas.

Royal Hotel
2522 Wall Avenue
1914

Located near the Twenty-Fifth Street Historic District, the Royal Hotel and attached building contribute to the architectural and spatial integrity of the area. This unassuming three-story masonry building owned by John H. Maitia and John Etcheverry attracted workers associated with the railroad during the early twentieth century. During the 1930s, under the ownership of Sam Maruri, it was frequented by Basque immigrants employed in sheep ranching, and during the 1940s, Leager V. Davis owned it and catered primarily to African American porters and waiters.

The building to the east of the hotel was built to play jai alai, a Basque court game. It is a tall, single-story, unreinforced masonry building with a pitched roof and a rectangular plan, measuring twenty-nine

Royal Hotel.
Photograph by Ntsimp Own work, CC0.1.0, public domain.

by ninety-five feet. The main room has a twenty-foot ceiling. The exterior walls match the Royal Hotel and are also constructed with red brick; they are completely smooth without any brick relief, and the west end has been plastered. The two sidewalls are divided into nine bays by brick pilasters that support the roof trusses.

Twenty-Fifth Street
Twenty-Fifth Street between Harrison and Monroe Boulevards
1870s

Twenty-Fifth Street was the center of major social activity at the turn of the century, ranging over time from aboveboard business deals to prostitution, gambling, and the sale of alcohol during Prohibition. Close to the Union Depot, people from around the world debarked at Ogden and visited businesses and service agencies on Twenty-Fifth Street. Families lived in apartments upstairs from their businesses, and the street had a family and neighborhood

character. Street life here included sounds from William Fife's blacksmith shop and the smell of freshly baked apple pie from the Saddlerock Restaurant near Franklin Street. Grand parades would move raucously up the street. Business activity, the railroad, and this colorful diverse street became interchangeable in a way that seemed impossible to separate.

Today Twenty-Fifth Street is but a faint reminder of the past, but it exhibits significant interest in historic preservation, and many business owners are capitalizing on the picturesque and charming nature of these historic properties, hoping to pump new life and interest into this section of the city.

Lower Twenty-Fifth Street Historic District
Twenty-Fifth Street between Wall Avenue and G Street
1870s

One of the rich narratives just beneath the surface in our cities and towns is the way social relationships play out spatially. In Ogden the tension between Mormons and non-Mormons can be tracked through city blocks and sections of town where shifting populations and uses of buildings mirror larger social dynamics. This is particularly true of the Lower Twenty-Fifth Street Historic District between Wall Avenue and G Street in Ogden.

When the railroad came to Ogden in 1869, what had been a predominantly Mormon town changed. Ogden became an important transportation center with a far more diverse population, and forces from the outside changed the social fabric of this city to the north of Salt Lake City, causing

Twenty-Fifth Street

to a manageable part of the city, Lower Twenty-Fifth Street. Rather than allow these powerful forces to pollute the entire city, they restricted them to one of its major commercial streets.

The earliest group of settlers on Twenty-Fifth Street were Mormon converts from England, Canada, the eastern United States, and Scandinavia. They were easily assimilated into the mainstream society. But after 1869 people of all religions and ethnic groups came to Ogden— Chinese and Japanese railroad workers and workers from Italy, Germany, Ireland, Scotland, and other European countries. Jews, Hispanics, blacks, and other ethnic groups made Twenty-Fifth Street their permanent home. Perhaps more than any other single street in the state, Twenty-Fifth Street was known as an ethnic melting pot.

friction between newcomers and the original Mormon inhabitants of Twenty-Fifth Street. To that point, non-Mormons were more likely to locate in Corinne, the town known locally as the "City of the Ungodly," the "Jumping-Off Place," and the "Hell Hole of the Earth." When the same forces that marked Corinne started to appear in Ogden, the Mormon population became alarmed. Mayor Lorin Farr's advice typified the feared change. He said, "Use kindness, be ready for emergencies, and see that guns and pistols are always loaded and powder dry."

The Mormons in control, perhaps unsure of how to deal with "gamblers, robbers, men and women of ill-repute," chose to ignore them and attempted to confine them

The buildings that remain on Twenty-Fifth Street represent commercial design and craftsmanship from 1875 to 1915. Forty-two structures on two blocks were constructed during this period. Only the Ogden Depot was built after 1915. As such, Twenty-Fifth Street offers a view into a typical commercial streetscape at the turn of the century. Evolving from a residential neighborhood to a unique commercial district, Twenty-Fifth Street catered to the needs of travelers on the railroad with hotels, saloons and gambling parlors, restaurants, and specialty retail shops on both sides of the street. All were built of masonry or brick along with a wide variety of other building materials and used load-bearing, post-and-beam structural systems of cast iron or heavy timber. Wall surfaces are rich and composed of brick, stone, painted metal, and wood. Carved, rusticated, or smooth stone; patterned or corbeled brickwork; and plain, stamped, or extruded metalwork make surfaces dance with action and life. Other defining elements include awnings, leaded glass, signs, and other graphic material. The buildings range from one to three stories high and are for the most part rectangular boxes arranged in rows, built right up against each other or in some cases sharing walls. They exhibit varied architectural styles including Greek Revival, commercial vernacular, commercial Victorian, Classical and Renaissance Revival, and Prairie style.

Variety and interest on facades is created in various ways—depth, relief, and light and shadow play off splayed entries and recessed doors, projecting metal cornices, corbeled brickwork, and other modulations of the wall surface. Windows and doors also vary and are either square or segmentally or round arched and usually appear symmetrically on upper levels and sometimes asymmetrically on lower levels. The windows are for the most part tall and have double-hung wooden sashes; they are placed in masonry bays with decorative stone or metal sills and lintels. Many have fancy mullions or raised-panel wooden or glass doors.

As a group the facades are picturesque and quite different, the very picture of late nineteenth-century America. The O. L. Luson Saloon, Grand Hotel, Alpine Hotel, R. D. Lockwood Restaurant, and Colorado Coffee House located at 134–136 Twenty-Fifth Street are examples of the commercial vernacular built in 1898. This two-story brick building features a fancy corbeled cornice and entablatures, square window bays, and a metal first-story facade covered with a newer brick veneer. The

Van Ness Hotel, Charles Iverson Saloon, and Joseph Brody Clothing Store at 148–150 Twenty-Fifth Street is a Prairie-style three-story brick building. On the building's facade two-story piers are placed between square window bays. A metal cornice is located below the parapet wall. The facade also has Wrightian inlaid mosaic details and was built in 1910. The Joseph Rogerson Restaurant and J. E. Davenport and Co. Saloon at 246–250 Twenty-Fifth Street is an example of the Classical Revival style built in 1901. This two-story brick building has metal trim, a raised Greek pediment with a 1901 inscription, three metal cornices, and swags in pressed tin friezes. The entire facade is intact. The London Ice Cream Parlor, Chicago Shoe Store, Bon Ton Restaurant, and T. Ashby Shoe Store at 252–254 Twenty-Fifth Street is a Greek Revival two-story brick building constructed in 1885. Here a molded wooden cornice with paired brackets, a triangular pediment with the inscription "London Ice Cream Parlor," and molded trim and bracketed pediments over round-arched second-floor windows combine to create a very picturesque facade. The Bamberger Depot and Allen Hotel, built in 1875, is a Commercial Victorian with Richardsonian Romanesque influence. This three-story brick and stone building has Roman-arched bays on the third-floor facade and otherwise square bays. A large central arch contains basket-weave patterns in polychrome stone. Other prominent details include first-floor piers and pilasters, and carved stone faces with their tongues sticking out, mocking the viewer. The Windsor Hotel, George W. Murphy Grocery and Saloon, and St. James Hotel was built between 1887 and 1888 at 101–109 Twenty-Fifth Street. This two-story Commercial Victorian brick building was built in three similar sections and had a corbeled brick cornice. The facade includes a metal first-story cornice, cast-iron columns, transoms, upper windows, and Roman-arched windows on the bottom floor. All the windows are square bayed.

Peery's Egyptian Theater
2415 Washington Boulevard
1924

Unquestionably one of the state's architectural monuments, Peery's Egyptian Theater is an exuberant celebration of this exotic revival style. The theater ran movies until 1984, when the doors were closed because of code violations along with slowed business. The facade of this two-and-a-half-story building is covered with polychromatic terra-cotta tile arranged in places to resemble smooth ashlar masonry. Four tapered columns topped by lotus floral capitals run across the facade, and shouldered arches with decorative vultures, sun disk symbols, volutes, and Egyptian ornamentation enliven the colorful, textured, exotic exterior. Constructed with reinforced concrete, the building evokes memories of an ancient time and place.

The Egyptian Theater's restoration was the result of a twelve-year grassroots campaign. The Weber County Heritage Foundation bought the Egyptian Theater in 1988 to avoid demolition, transferring title to the nonprofit Egyptian Theater Foundation, an outgrowth of Friends of the Egyptian. Between 1989 and 1991 the foundation wasted no time in developing a strategy for survival—a step-by-step plan for stabilizing and restoring the building and for fundraising. It was clear that the key was selling the idea as an economic benefit for the community. A public/private partnership was formed between the Egyptian Theater Foundation, Ogden City, Weber County, and Weber State University.

The Peery Egyptian Theater received a National Trust for Historic Preservation Award in 1997—a National Honor Award, one of sixteen chosen that year. The Trust noted that the commitment of local preservationists, the superb nature of the

Peery's Egyptian Theater

restoration, and the way this project communicated Ogden's commitment to preservation were particularly noteworthy.

Reed Hotel / Radisson Hotel
Washington Boulevard and Twenty-Fifth
Street
1891
Leslie S. Hodgson and Myrl A. McClenahan
Known by a series of names in its one-hundred-year history—the Reed, the Bigelow, and the Ben Lomond—this hotel was added in 1995 to the list of Historic Hotels of America by the National Trust for Historic Preservation, the only one in Utah. During the 1880s, wealthy real estate developer A. E. Reed took a $10,000 enticement from Ogden to build a hotel on the corner of Washington Boulevard and Twenty-Fifth Street. Completed in 1891, the Reed Hotel was built for a total cost of $100,000 and was at the time one of the most elaborately decorated and built hotels in the western United States. H. C. Bigelow and his son, A. P., bought the hotel not long after it opened. During the 1920s it went through its first remodel. Backed with the support of civic-minded citizens of Ogden convinced that a world-class hotel would boost Ogden's image, a new corporation of three hundred stockholders formed to commence work on the structure. It reopened in 1927.

They called on the Salt Lake City architectural firm of Hodgson and McClenahan to design aspects of the building, which they did in the Italian Renaissance Revival style. Features such as round arches, balustrades, and rich Classical ornamentation created a new look for the old lady. The upper stories of the hotel meet at a right angle; the Ogden State Bank was in the lower portion of the building projecting from the two wings. During the Depression the bank failed and the hotel was sold to the Eccles family, who renamed it the Ben Lomond. In 1965 the Eccles family sold it to the Woodbury Corporation. The DCA Development Corporation bought it in 1983 and began yet another rehabilitation project, returning it to its historic look.

Ogden/Weber Municipal Building
2541 Washington Boulevard
1930s
Leslie S. Hodgson and Myrl A. McClenahan
Ogden City and Weber County leaders were discussing consolidating their offices as early as March 1934. The Public Works

Ogden/Weber Municipal Building

Administration had made federal aid for public buildings available to the states, giving depressed communities an economic boost and putting the unemployed to work. U.S. senator Elbert D. Thomas helped secure funding for Ogden's building. But this building in no way expresses the privation of the day; instead it conveys a contemporary desire for a more modern or progressive building. During the first half of the twentieth century, Ogden led in avant-garde architecture.

Art Deco design was used almost exclusively in Utah for public and commercial buildings. These buildings have a sweeping verticality, symmetrical elevations, shallow but undulating spatial planes, gradual setbacks at the upper levels, and low-relief ornamentation. All three Ogden Art Deco buildings are consistent with these stylistic elements and demonstrate Hodgson and McClenahan's familiarity with the style.

The most important Art Deco buildings were built in Ogden during the 1930s under the auspices of the PWA. Hodgson and McClenahan designed all three of these significant Art Deco buildings.

The twelve-story mass of the Ogden Municipal Building is symmetrically arranged and sits on a rectangular base with side wings that step down gradually from the taller central mass. Brick pilasters accentuate the strong vertical thrust of the central part of the building, which separates metal-frame casement windows and gently modulates the building surface. As is typical of modern buildings, the walls terminate in a flat roof capped with contrasting glazed terra-cotta trim moving across the walls and pilasters. This has the effect of activating the roofline and terminating the vertical movement of the pilasters with crisp geo-curvilinear shapes. Windowsills and the water table

are also glazed with terra-cotta forms. The entrance to the building is located on the east facade and is accentuated with a flat-roofed pavilion capped with terra-cotta trim. Leading to the four steel-frame doors is a flight of stairs. The doors feature typical Art Deco decor—a tall transom displaying a metal grille with a pierced geometric design. The transom and doors have terra-cotta surrounds, and period lamps flank the entrance. The marble dados, metal and wooden trim, plasterwork, light fixtures, and patterned floors add to the integrity of the building's style on the interior. This important historic landmark was restored during the 1990s.

Jefferson Avenue Historic District
Jefferson Avenue between Twenty-Fifth and Twenty-Seventh Streets
1880s–1920s

The Jefferson Avenue Historic District is the quintessential Victorian celebration of the wealth and prosperity of the turn of the century in Ogden. These impressive, substantial brick and stone buildings were built from the early 1880s through the 1920s for affluent families. With all the variety and enthusiasm of the Victorian style, their asymmetrical facades, multiple roof pitches and planes, and heights reaching two and a half stories, these buildings parade the wealth of their owners. The list of owners reads like a who's who of Ogden's social elite—David C. Eccles (607 Twenty-Fifth Street) was the president of Utah National Bank of Ogden; Patrick Healy (2529 Jefferson Avenue) was a vice president of Commercial National Bank; and Abbott R. Heywood (2540 Jefferson Avenue) was also a vice president of Commercial National Bank. Others owned railroad-related businesses on Twenty-Fifth Street and lived nearby on Jefferson Avenue—Hiram H.

Region A

Jefferson Avenue Historic District

Spencer was the mayor of Ogden, manager of the Eccles Lumber Company, president of Ogden Rapid Transit, and vice president of Amalgamated Sugar. Thomas H. Carr (2520 Jefferson Avenue) was a founder of Rexall Drugstores and owned and operated a prosperous drugstore on Twenty-Fifth Street. The combination of the railroad and good old-fashioned entrepreneurial activity promised success. The diversity that accompanied the railroad changed Ogden's power center, so much so that by 1889 the anti-Mormon Liberal Party assumed control of Ogden's municipal government and won every city office. Several Ogden streets carry the names of U.S. presidents. Many Liberal Party politicians chose Jefferson Avenue for their homes. The perception of prosperity, wealth, and heterogeneity was evident through the neighborhood's distinctive Victorian architecture.

David Eccles Subdivision
Twenty-Sixth Street and Eccles Avenue
1909–1920

From an entirely different era and using another architectural idiom, the David Eccles Subdivision is located several blocks east of Jefferson Avenue. Several of the children of the original property owners on Jefferson Avenue built homes between 1909 and 1920, for the most part in the Prairie style, exemplifying how much architectural taste had changed. Patrick Healy Jr. and his wife, Mary Sodwick Healy, built a Prairie-style home on the corner of Twenty-Sixth Street and Eccles Avenue in 1920.

The Prairie style spread quickly throughout the United States, much like a prairie fire. As evidence of the growing sophistication of the local cultural scene, there was virtually no lag time between when the style surfaced in Chicago and when

David Eccles Subdivision

Utah's architects began designing Prairie-style homes. Architects who had direct connections with Chicago as well as other designers familiar with the work of Frank Lloyd Wright adopted his progressive house forms. Utah architects such as Taylor Wooley, Clifford Evans, Pope and Burton, and Ware and Treganza brought Prairie-style buildings to Utah as early as 1909. Besides houses, several LDS ward meeting-houses mirrored the influence of Wright's Unity Temple.

Although Prairie-style houses were built in Salt Lake City, particularly in affluent neighborhoods like Federal Heights, the style significantly impacted Ogden's architecture, best exemplified in the David Eccles Subdivision. Architects Eber Piers

and Leslie Hodgson designed Prairie-style buildings in an innovative regional way and designed the homes in the David Eccles Subdivision in variations on this common theme. As a group, the neighborhood's structures are similar in color, massing, and detail, distinguishing this subdivision from its immediate neighbors.

As in the Jefferson Avenue neighborhood, prominent Ogden families gravitated in 1909 to the new subdivision organized by David Eccles. Each house deserves serious attention, but two examples capture the eclecticism typical of Piers and Hodgson's interpretation of the Prairie style here. One of the first to be built, the Leroy Eccles home mixes Neoclassical Revival, Southern Colonial, and Prairie-style elements, resulting in a unique combination. By contrast, the last house in the neighborhood, Patrick Healey's house, has more of an Old English Cottage style, detailed with a high-pitched roof and dormer windows, stuccoed lower walls, and rounded arches.

Ogden High School
2828 Harrison Avenue
1937
Leslie S. Hodgson and Myrl A. McClenahan
One of Utah's most distinctive buildings, Ogden High School is considered architect Leslie S. Hodgson's masterpiece, in fact the culmination of four decades of work as an architect. It was designed under the confines of federal funding from the PWA, and the cornerstone announces it as Public Works Project No. 1423.

Besides putting unemployed Americans to work, the New Deal poured money into infrastructure projects in the nation's cities. Capitalizing on this unique opportunity, Ogden City first approached the PWA director, R. A. Hart, for a grant of $1,745,000, and the Ogden City Board of Education asked for $600,000 for a new high school (the high school was built for $1,150,000). At the dedication, Hart articulated the agency's goals of putting men to work and constructing worthwhile buildings and congratulated Ogden City and Weber County on their investment in economic recovery by funding more construction projects than there than in any other part of the state. The city hired the architectural firm of Hodgson and McClenahan to design the Art Deco structure. In the best spirit of community collaboration, the

Ogden High School

Board of Education, PWA, and local voters all provided funding for what became known as Ogden's "million dollar high school."

The Ogden High School makes a powerful horizontal gesture on the landscape. Even so, it is the vertical ornamentation that creates the greatest interest on the wall surface, with a tension that is continued through a group of rectangular sections, each with a flat roof. Bands of metal-frame windows, brick pilasters, and decorative masonry with geometric and floral motifs on the spandrels in between emphasize the prominent vertical movement. The nature of the interior space is hinted at by the group of rectangular sections exposed on the exterior, each with its own flat roof—administrative offices, classrooms, a gymnasium, and an auditorium. Unlike most Art Deco buildings, this one has an asymmetrical mass, conforming to the site and functional demands of the space. But the geometric patterns on the metal grille transoms and the exterior Art Deco lamps are consistent with the style. Auxiliary buildings on the site also reflect the Art Deco style in terms of scale, massing, materials, and trim. Ogden High School subsequently went through a multimillion-dollar rehabilitation.

Ice Sheet
3850 University Circle
Weber State University
1990s
FFKR
In anticipation of the 2002 Winter Olympics, the state built several new facilities. The Ice Sheet represented a creative collaboration between the state and university that would benefit both. The Ice Sheet was Ogden's premier location for ice skating, with seating for two thousand spectators

for ice hockey, figure skating, and short track speed skating. Built on a sloping hillside of Weber State University, the Ice Sheet held the eyes of the world during the Olympics, but its long-term impact on Ogden City would be generations of ice skaters trained at this tremendous facility.

Besides a regulation world championship ice sheet, the Ice Sheet includes team rooms, an instructors' area, an officials' suite, star dressing rooms, skate rental and concessions, a classroom, a lounge, an administration area, a ticket sales area, ice maintenance and equipment work areas, and other spaces for spectators and users of the ice alike.

At such a prominent location, particular attention was paid to the way the building would relate to the natural environment. Special care was taken to provide an unobstructed view of the mountains as well as the valley from the other side, and importantly, to prevent direct sunlight from hitting the ice, as well as to accommodate TV broadcasting and the special lighting and sound requirements of Olympic events. The Utah AIA awarded the 1996 Award for Excellence in Architecture to Weber State University for its Ice Sheet facility.

Morgan County

Weber Power Plant, Weber Station
Interstate 84
1909–1910
The powerhouse, reinforced dam, and related structures of the Weber Power Plant reflect larger trends in the urbanization of the Wasatch Front and the growing demand for electrical power. Built between 1909 and 1910, the modest structures of this hydroelectric power plant cling to the edges of a narrow canyon and capitalize on

the movement of water in the Weber River. Running parallel to Interstate 84 and the Union Pacific rail lines, the site includes a rectangular powerhouse on a concrete foundation and gable, a poured concrete roof, and concrete caps at the top of an irregularly stepped parapet wall. Decorative brickwork interrupts the wall surface and defines five bays on the east and west elevations. Signage announced "Weber Station Utah Power & Light Co., 'Efficient Public Service,'" describing both the company name and intent. Two buildings remain in what was the operators' camp.

Located 1¾ miles upriver is the Weber dam, a 130-foot reinforced concrete structure, along with a fishway, spillway, and other elements designed to direct water toward the powerhouse.

The Weber River Hydroelectric Power Plant was built after E. H. Harriman bought the Utah Light and Railway Company and worked to expand operations. Even though the site and its structures seem simple and relatively forgotten, they collectively represent a key moment in the state's growth, particularly the development of the hydroelectric power industry.

Utah's growth and expansion in the decades after statehood created new demand for modern conveniences, including electric lighting and electrically powered transportation. In 1915, two years after Harriman's death, Utah Power and Light leased Utah Light and Traction Company power facilities.

Morgan
Morgan High School Mechanical Arts Building
230 East Young Street
1936
Likely Scott and Welch, who designed the Morgan Elementary School

Under the auspices of the Works Progress Administration, 232 buildings were built in Utah, including 104 public schools. The state was ninth of the forty-eight states in terms of federal expenditures in the 1930s through programs such as the Civil Works

Morgan High School Mechanical Arts Building.
Photograph by Ntsimp, public domain.

Administration, the Federal Emergency Relief Administration, the National Youth Administration, and the Public Works Administration. The Morgan High School Mechanical Arts Building was part of a $150,000 Morgan County building program in 1936 that included this building along with a new elementary school that served students from throughout the county.

Contrasting with the two-story elementary school, this is a single-story brick Art Deco building. Rectangular in form, the building has a gabled roof bordered by a parapet wall, with a projecting entrance on the short end of the mass. As is typical of the style, verticality is emphasized by pilasters topped by concrete capitals and concrete coping along the roof.

Daniel Heiner House
543 North 700 East
1888

Sometimes the most extraordinary element of a building is the perfection of its site. The Daniel Heiner House is situated with a long view of an expanse of valley, rural Utah at its best, and mountains beyond. Reflecting the prosperity of its owner, the house is an example of the central passageway type, complete with five rooms on the first and second floors, as well as two windows on the sides of central doors on each floor. An ample front porch that opens up to both floors is perhaps the most eye-catching and distinguishing characteristic. Porch details include turned balustrades, railings, and beautiful scrollwork brackets. This beautiful

Daniel Heiner House.
Photograph by Tricia Simpson, CC BY-SA 3.0.

house hints at Heiner's success in business, in his community, and as a representative of the state legislature.

Daniel Heiner converted to Mormonism with his German immigrant parents in the 1850s. Throughout his life he proved to be entrepreneurial, working on the Union Pacific Railroad for a time, managing the Echo Land and Livestock Company, and despite a lack of formal training, teaching at Morgan's school. It would be in mining and banking that Heiner would meet his greatest financial success.

Heiner married two women in 1873 in the Salt Lake Endowment House and between them had nineteen children.

Huntsville
David O. McKay House
155 South 7600 East
1872

One national trend that found its way to Utah and that is exemplified in the David O. McKay house in Huntsville is a love of the picturesque. Architect Alexander Jackson Davis and landscape designer Andrew Jackson Downing popularized the style and approach primarily with plan books such as their *Cottage Residences* and Downing's *The Architecture of Country Houses*. This pattern book showed up in libraries across the country and spread a love of the English countryside's pastoral picturesque, a landscape that sharply contrasted with the industrial city. Huntsville's bucolic, rural landscape was the perfect backdrop for a charming house like this one.

Mormon church president David O. McKay's parents, David and Jeannette McKay, first built a two-room home in 1872, a year before their son David was born. The home grew in complexity and size over time. The symmetrical facade of this central-passage house includes a central door on both the first and second floors flanked by two windows on both sides. A second-story porch spreads across the facade and sits on box columns below. The home features some Classical Revival features such as the balustrade and fanlight, as well as overall symmetry and formality. A steeply pitched gable at the center of the broadside of the roof is more typical of Gothic Revival. This comfortable home's ample interior includes a wide staircase leading to the bedrooms on the second floor, and a Chickering piano that David Sr. purchased back East.

Valley House Inn
7318 East 200 South
1872

Like David O. McKay, Huntsville's first mayor, Lars Magnus Nelson, built what is known today as the Valley House, in 1872. Besides leading his hometown, Nelson was a tinsmith and made a good living for his family—his wife, Mary, and children, Anna Emelia, Lars Emil, Hilma Mary Ann, David Anton, and Emma Divita. A substantial brick home like this speaks to a certain level of economic prosperity but also to the proximity of a brickyard that produced uniform pioneer-era bricks and to the availability of skilled brick masons in the county. Matilda Sprague bought the house in 1916 with plans to convert it into a hotel with a dining room where she would serve trout, chicken, and steak dinners. A succession of owners after her continued to expand the business, eventually converting it to a bed-and-breakfast.

If you looked at the building from above, it would be shaped in the form of an *H*—two, two-story rectangular wings connected by a two-story rectangular structure between, with the main entrance in the center of the first floor. Gabled roofs on both wings mirror the pitch of a triangular pediment on a Greek temple. On the facade, segmented arches top windows formed with contrasting colors of brick and stone. Pilasters line both sides of the wings to the front and stretch from the first to the second floors. A stringcourse suggests where the first floor ends and the second begins.

Region B

DAVIS

Layton
Kaysville
Farmington
Antelope Island
Centerville
Bountiful

TOOELE

Iosepa
Grantsville
Tooele
Stockton
Ophir

Alpine
Lehi
American Fork
Cedar Fort
Pleasant Grove
Lindon
Fairfield
Orem
Lakeview
Provo

UTAH

Springville
Spanish Fork
Payson
Goshen
Santaquin

Davis, Tooele, and Utah Counties

Introduction

The winter after the pioneers arrived in the Salt Lake Valley, they began grazing cattle on land that would eventually be designated as Davis County. Settlers followed, and between 1848 and 1850 they began laying out towns and building houses. They saw the potential for more than cattle raising and started to plant fields and orchards along the base of the foothills, which had ready access to springs that cascaded down the hillside—sixteen canyon streams in total.[1] Davis County seemed to promise success, with plentiful water, rich soil, and proximity to Salt Lake City. First Bountiful and then a succession of towns, including Centerville and Farmington, among others, grew naturally to the north.

The rich history of native peoples in the Utah Valley is revealed in a number of ancient sites, including those along the area's rivers, at the base of American Fork Canyon, and in burial mounds near Provo. One expedition led by George Montague Wheeler (1872–73) reported a sighting of an ancient artifact: "West of the town [Provo], on its outskirts and within three or four miles of the lake, are many mounds." To the north and toward the lake "is a field containing a number of mounds more or less perfectly preserved; some are entirely untouched, except on the outer edges, where Mormons' grain patches encroach upon them."[2] Perhaps the most telling part of this quotation is the mention of encroachment. The nineteenth-century story of native peoples in Utah Valley is one of steady encroachment. The Domínguez-Escalante expedition of 1776 brought Catholic priests close to Utes living near Utah Lake, whom they tried to "Christianize" and teach farming and stock raising. John C. Frémont and members of his expedition traveled through Utah Valley in 1843–44 and interacted with local Utes as well. Frémont identified accessible water and rich soil and formed a generally favorable impression of the opportunities the valley provided. Between the time the county was first settled by Mormon pioneers and 1867, "the Timpanogots of Utah Valley eventually bowed to American hegemony in the region but not without armed resistance," according to historian Richard Holzapfel.[3]

Parley P. Pratt explored Utah Valley in 1847 as part of his larger exploration of the area that would eventually become the State of Deseret. He found Utah's second largest lake—Utah Lake, connected to the Great Salt Lake by the Jordan River—and two mountain peaks higher than twelve thousand feet—Mount Timpanogos to the north and Mount Nebo to the south. Two years after the settlement of the Salt Lake Valley, Brigham Young sent a colonization team of thirty men to Utah Valley. Their efforts to establish permanent settlements there were compounded by tension with the original inhabitants. But by 1850 they had sketched out towns in Alpine, American Fork, Lehi, Payson, Pleasant Grove (Battle Creek), and Springville. Within a few years, others followed. These towns were agricultural communities organized along the guidelines of the Plat of the City of Zion, a template for the settlement of Mormon towns first given to his people by the prophet Joseph Smith. With an emphasis on cardinality—an east-west, north-south orientation—and ten-acre blocks with family plots big enough for a house, a barn, outbuildings, a small orchard, and a vegetable garden, the template emphasized community, an orientation toward God represented by the centrality of the church at the town center, and the importance of order. Utah County was connected to Salt Lake City and national markets when the Utah Southern Railroad came through the area in 1874.

Brigham Young called groups of individuals to join forces for the settlement of a town. Ensuring that there would be a balance of skills and knowledge among the settlers of the town, a calling lent a religious framework and community orientation from the first. Utah County exhibited substantial growth for decades after it was first settled; by 1890 it had 23,768 residents, and Provo was one of the three largest cities in the territory (with Salt Lake City and Ogden). Orem and Provo are the county's largest cities and are centers of commerce, education, and population.

From the 1870s onward, Brigham Young Academy, eventually Brigham Young University, has been an important institution in Utah County. Organized by Brigham Young with principal and educator Karl Maeser, BYA began classes in 1875 classes in a variety of smaller buildings until the 1892 construction of the Brigham Young Academy Building on University Avenue in Provo. After 1903 known as Brigham Young University, the institution today is the largest religious university in the United States, with approximately thirty thousand students, eleven colleges or schools, and branch campuses in Salt Lake City and Jerusalem.

Also important to Utah County's economy are tech industries. Companies from Word Perfect to Adobe to Novell have major offices there along what is called "Silicon Slopes," and a significant concentration of employees in this new sector, primarily software companies, live in the county. Also important to the county's growth have been the freeway system and mass transit, both of which have helped stimulate the local economy.

Davis County

Bountiful
Crystalwood
1289 East Canyon Creek Road
1957
Frank Lloyd Wright
Utah's claim to a Frank Lloyd Wright–designed house is found in the heavily wooded area east of Bountiful. Crystalwood is sheltered by a hillside and overlooks the Great Salt Lake in the distance. Wright designed Crystalwood in 1957 for Don and Jane Stromquist. It was constructed in 1961 (two years after Wright died) with his typical vocabulary of the day—concrete, steel, wood, and glass. The house is designed on

Crystalwood.
Photograph by Peter Goss. Used with permission of photographer.

a parallelogram grid of 60- and 120-degree angles and reflects Wright's ideas about the "usonian" house.

The kitchen and bathroom are in the central concrete core of the building, with living space around the perimeter. Abundant windows create the impression of a merging of the natural and built worlds. The triangular cantilevered deck moves from the master bedroom over the canyon that drops below.

Although the house is modest in size, 2,700 square feet including the decks, it is distinctive in the context of its physical and natural environment. Wright commented on the diminutive size. "Regard it just as desirable to build a chicken-house as to build a cathedral. The size of a project means little in art. . . . It is the quality of the character that really counts. Character may be large in the little or little in the large."[4]

The house was restored in 1991 with the assistance of architects from the Frank Lloyd Wright Foundation as well as the owners, George Frandsen and David Carlquist, who received a Heritage Award from the Utah Heritage Foundation for the sensitive restoration.

Bountiful Tabernacle
55 South Main
1851–1862
Augustus Franham

The Bountiful Tabernacle is the state's oldest religious building, the one most continuously used, and the earliest Greek Revival structure. Located in Bountiful's historic central square, it eloquently speaks to the pioneers' desire to build architecture that was practical but aesthetically pleasing.

The building's designer, Augustus Franham, converted to Mormonism in Andover, Massachusetts, surrounded by Greek Revival–style buildings. A log building was the first to be erected on the site in 1852; then an adobe structure that was twice the size was built entirely with local materials and labor. The Bountiful Tabernacle is a showcase of pioneer-era craftsmanship—the plaster casting, hand carvings, winding stairways, and wood gallery represent the finest artistry of the day. The finish carpentry, for instance, was the work of Thomas Fisher, who brought two chests full of woodworking tools with him from England, where he had done carpentry for Queen Victoria.

For at least half the lifetime of the building, the walls have been covered with plaster or stucco and painted a startling white. A portrait of Joseph Smith by pioneer artist Daniel Weggeland hangs on the wall. Over the choir is a mural painted in green, gray, and white featuring a bust of Joseph Smith in an alcove, with two chubby angels holding a banner with the words "Holiness to the Lord."

LDS Church apostle and future president Lorenzo Snow broke ground for the building with an elaborate ceremony befitting

Bountiful Tabernacle

the event on February 11, 1851, and laid the cornerstone the next day. When it was finished in 1862 it was heralded as one of the finest buildings in the state.

Johnston's Army disrupted construction temporarily before the building dedication in March 1863. Heber C. Kimball offered the dedicatory prayer and Brigham Young presided over the ceremony. At a centennial celebration one hundred years later, Apostle Hugh B. Brown said the tabernacle was holy ground where every prophet after Joseph Smith had spoken from the pulpit.

Farmington
Farmington Tithing Office
130 North Main Street
1907
LDS Church Architect's Office
The Farmington Tithing Office was standard plan Type No. 3, one of three types

of building forms created for LDS tithing offices built around 1905. This tightly designed one-story red brick block has a pyramidal roof and scored concrete foundation. The tithing office served as a clearinghouse for donations from the Saints to be used to help the needy. The design is almost identical to that of tithing offices in Manti, Sandy, Richmond, and Panguitch.

The tithing office's symmetrical facade has a gabled pavilion with a round-arched opening at the center between pairs of windows, and pilasters at the corners. A small domed cupola tops the building, and brick dentils are found under the cornice.

The bishop of the Farmington Ward, James H. Robinson, received a letter from the presiding bishopric in Salt Lake City on May 9, 1907, approving the construction of the Farmington Tithing Office, where "accommodations will be provided for the Stake Presidency, High Council, and so forth" and estimating that the building would cost $3,000 to build.[5] Standard plans like the one used here were created by the LDS Church Architect's Office, part of a trend that would develop with time and become the standard approach to building by the Mormon Church. Rather than asking each local ward to rethink the programmatic needs of a building that was the same for every ward, the church designed three appropriate plans for tithing offices and distributed them throughout the state upon request.

When LDS auxiliary services began to be included and consolidated in the ward meetinghouse in the early twentieth century, the tithing office became obsolete. The city of Farmington bought the building in 1948 to use as a city hall and public library and later doubled its size to become the town fire station.

Farmington Tithing Office

Hector C. Haight House / Union Hotel
208 North Main Street
1852

This is a very rare double-cell, two-story building and the home of one of the first men to settle in Farmington, Hector C. Haight, at forty-two years old. Well respected in political circles, he served as probate judge for nine years as well as assessor, collector, and sheriff. Haight was a polygamist, and while it is unknown whether the different wives cohabited in this house, the double entrances, one for each of the separate cells, would have been a perfect arrangement and are evocative of an era when houses had to accommodate a complicated lifestyle.

The adobe walls are covered with stucco and are eighteen inches thick—good insulators guaranteeing cool summer days and warmth in the winter. Haight built a two-story rear wing in 1870 that greatly expanded the space in the house. A charming two-story porch complete with distinctive turned wooden balustrades spans the facade and has a shed roof that extends from the roofline, offering the house up to the street beyond.

The house's interior gives us a glimpse of a typical nineteenth-century home complete with small rooms and low ceilings. The pine floors are still intact, as are the wooden trim, doors, and windows, and the elaborate hand-carved curving staircase.

Lagoon
375 North Lagoon Drive
1896

A traditional entertainment destination for many Salt Lake Valley families, Lagoon, eighteen miles north of Salt Lake City in Farmington, is one of the area's most successful amusement parks. Prominent businessman Simon Bamberger bought the original buildings that became Lagoon from an earlier resort called Lake Park. The Denver and Rio Grande Western Railroad built this recreational facility, located two and a half miles west of the Great Salt Lake, in 1886. As vice president, Bamberger owned 25 percent interest in the resort, which closed in 1895 when the lake receded. The architect of the State Capitol, Richard K. A. Kletting, designed the cupola for the dancing pavilion at Lake Park, the only remnant of the original buildings to be used at Lagoon. When Lagoon first opened, it advertised: "Bowling, Elegant Dancing Pavilion, Fine Music, A Shady Bowery and Good Restaurants." Over the decades, Lagoon tried the fashionable entertainments found at resorts throughout the country, such as wrestling matches, horse racing, baseball, and bicycle races, besides the traditional range of fireworks and mechanized rides like merry-go-rounds and Ferris wheels, keeping pace with national trends. The historic roller coaster, airplanes, and carousel are all listed on the National Register of Historic Places.

In 1976 Pioneer Village moved from its original location on Connor Street in Holladay, Utah, to Lagoon along with other historic structures, rides, and artifacts from other locations. Not quite a living history museum, it is nevertheless a localized feature of the resort that references Utah's unique pioneer history.

Stayner/Steed House
79 South 100 East
1870
From its appearance alone, the simple rectangular saltbox/hall-parlor Stayner/Steed

House could have been built next to a New England town green instead of on a street in Farmington, Utah. Built in 1870 out of fieldstone, the building emerges from the earth, capitalizing on the abundant native stone. The symmetrical front facade exhibits a simple vernacular Classicism, as does the low pitch of the roof, the unassuming wooden cornice, and the frieze trim. Although the house is not quite two stories, as is customary for a saltbox house, it is one and a half, tall enough to accommodate the lean-to at the back, which adds four rooms to the house.

In terms of plan, the building has two rooms on the first floor, one room larger than the other. The first is a square and the other roughly two-thirds of a square, as is typical of the hall-parlor plan. The owners in the 1950s added a small gabled porch cover supported on metal posts to the central entrance.

The walls of the house are formed with random rubble stone, fieldstone in a variety of colors—gray, dark violet, brown, tan, and rust. The resulting walls are thirty inches thick, with adobe bricks on the interior that have been plastered over. Fieldstone is abundant in the riverbeds and alluvial foothills of the Wasatch Range near Farmington and is gathered rather than quarried, typically in random and varied shapes and sizes. The resulting walls of area houses were typically laid in uncoursed rubble patterns with interesting and varied surface textures.

The owner of the house, Arthur Stayner, was known for his role in establishing the sugar-refining industry in Utah Territory. He was the son of a captain in the British Navy who had attended a prestigious boarding school where he was trained to become a minister for the Church of England. Stayner joined the LDS Church when he was just fifteen; when he came to Utah he settled first in Ogden, and then in Farmington in 1863. A polygamist, Stayner had four wives and twenty-four children.

Centerville
Osmyn and Emily Duel House
271 South 200 East
1878
Charles Duncan

Charles Duncan, a Scottish stonemason in Centerville and Farmington, built this 1878 two-story stone house. With random ashlar masonry and contrasting brick ornamentation at the corners imitating the look of quoins, it is a simple vernacular structure built by a common builder with little pretense for style.

For the house's family, Osmyn Merritt Duel and his fourth wife, Emily Hannah Bowers, this home promised a great future. Osmyn first lived in Salt Lake City with his first wife, Mary Whiting, in a log cabin that is now located between the LDS Church Museum and the LDS Family History Library on West Temple. They were among the first to settle in Centerville, then known as Duel Creek, where he was deeded six hundred acres in 1867.

Thomas and Elizabeth Whitaker House
168 North Main Street
1862–1866
Charles Duncan

Scottish stonemason Charles Duncan built the original one-and-a-half-story section of this house with stone found in the fields of Centerville at the base of the Wasatch Range. The house has random ashlar masonry walls with pseudo quoins at the corners, simple stone lintels, and sills around the doors. Duncan worked with Thomas Whitaker, a British immigrant. Thomas lived in this house with his first

wife, Elizabeth Mills, and their twelve children as well as with his plural wife, Hannah Waddups, and their eight children before he built her a home two blocks east.

Local traditions suggest that the Whitakers were the first to raise silkworms in the area during the local sericulture movement sponsored by the LDS Church. Like many other sisters of the Relief Society, Elizabeth was well known for her silk production and the scarves, neckties, vests, and socks she made from the fabric.

Antelope Island
Fielding Garr Ranch
1849–1850

Antelope Island is one of the most beautiful places in Utah. If you climb to the top of the rocky outcroppings that stretch to the west, on a good day you can hear the wind move across the top of the water and see Stansbury, Gunnison, and Egg Islands in the distance. Creating a sensorial drama different from the red rock of southern Utah, this unlikely stretch of water adds paradox to this desert environment.

It is well worth making the effort to get to the Fielding Garr Ranch on Antelope Island. This pioneer-era cattle ranch tells an intriguing part of the settlement story of Utah Territory. In total, the ranch complex includes a variety of buildings, requisite components in a pioneer enterprise.

Key to the story of the Fielding Garr Ranch is the Church of Jesus Christ of Latter-day Saints' Perpetual Emigration Fund, first established in 1849 and designed to support the immigration of converts to the Great Basin. In 1850, 2,500 British immigrants came to Utah and were reimbursed for the cost of their passage to the United States. After five more years, 56,000 immigrants had come to Utah from the British Isles or Scandinavia. Donations to

Fielding Garr Ranch

the fund came in a variety of forms—farm produce, manufactured goods, or livestock. The LDS Church kept cattle donated for the Perpetual Emigrating Fund Company at the Fielding Garr Ranch, a major portion of the company's revenue. When the federal government dissolved the institution after thirty-eight years in 1887 with the Edmunds-Tucker Act, the Perpetual Emigration Company had helped 100,000 people immigrate—87,000 of whom were from England and northern Europe.

The complex of buildings forming the Fielding Garr Ranch reveals a microcosm of pioneer life. A group of vernacular buildings was constructed of adobe brick produced at the site, including a milk house, rubble-stone springhouse, barn and stable, and blacksmith shop. The main house is a one-story adobe rectangle with a gently sloping gabled roof covering two rooms on both sides. Manager Fielding Garr came to Utah from Nauvoo, Illinois, in 1847, driving his own herd of cattle along with his wagon

train and identifying Antelope Island as a good location for stock raising and a suitable place for his family of seven children, until he died in 1855. Besides a tithing herd, stallions and brood mares that the LDS Church had invested in grazed on the island as well.

The Island Improvement Company took over the property in 1884 and raised stock on the island until 1972. After the 1920s, other ranch structures included a sheep-shearing barn, grain silo, corrals, pump house, and reservoir. Antelope Island became a state park in 1981 and opened to the public for the first time in 1993.

Layton
Farmer's Union Building
State Street and West Gentile Street
1890
William Allen

Layton's first important commercial enterprise was the Farmer's Union Mercantile Institution, which also became the scene of community social life, recreation, and a range of different meetings. Layton was settled in 1850 and farms tended to stretch in virtually every direction instead of concentrating in a bustling city core. It was not until the 1890s that Layton became independent of Kaysville.

This all changed when local businessmen joined forces to establish a commercial district in town and challenge Kaysville's right to tax it. Another group of businessmen combined their capital to house the Farmer's Union Mercantile Institution in 1890.

Davis County architect William Allen designed the Farmer's Union Building and its first addition. Trained through correspondence courses, Allen was well known locally for his design of other important public buildings in Davis County, including the Davis County Courthouse, Barnes Bank, West Layton Ward Church, Presbyterian Church, and Governor Henry Blood's residence.

Building was accomplished in three phases: the first section in 1890, the second a couple of years later, and the third in 1930. This two-story commercial block on the southwest corner of Gentile Street and the old State Road in Layton's primary downtown area featured typical Victorian decoration such as decorative stone, brickwork, and woodwork, and a scrolled pediment with the inscription "Farmer's Union, established A.D. 1882."

Kaysville
LeConte Stewart House
172 West 100 South
1920s
Hyrum Pope and Harold Burton
Besides the sentimental value associated with its owner, one of Utah's most beloved artists, this Tudor Revival cottage is an excellent example of the type of picturesque architecture built by the middle class during the 1920s. Nestled in a typical historic landscape, the home has natural features that add greatly to its charm. The English look is created with an asymmetrical facade, a steeply pitched roof, round-arched openings, and casement windows. Brick walls are covered with pebble stucco and a there is a concrete foundation. Behind the house is LeConte Stewart's painting studio, a one-story stucco-over-frame building built in 1922.

Prominent Utah architects Harold Burton and Hyrum Pope designed the house and the studio for Stewart. The three men had collaborated on the construction and decoration of the LDS Hawaiian temple. Stewart was commissioned by the LDS Church to paint murals in many of the rooms in the temple.

Born in Glenwood in Sevier County, Utah, in 1898, LeConte Stewart was Utah's premier landscape painter, preserving the image of the mountains of Davis County for future generations with his tonalist vision. Important as both a teacher and painter, Stewart focused his paintings on scenes of everyday life typical of the Social Realist movement, and on landscapes around the region.

Tooele County

Iosepa
Iosepa Settlement / Polynesian Cemetery
Skull Valley
1889
One of the most unusual colonizing efforts by members of the LDS Church played out in the West Desert of Skull Valley. The Iosepa settlement was home to Polynesian converts to the Church of Jesus Christ of Latter-day Saints whom the church asked

Iosepa Settlement / Polynesian Cemetery.
Photograph by Ikeosaurus, public domain.

to "gather to Zion." LDS missionaries first went to the Pacific Islands as early as the 1850s. Apostle Joseph F. Smith served a mission in the Sandwich Islands when he was fifteen years old. When these immigrants first came to Utah Territory they grouped near Wasatch Springs (300 West and 800 North) in North Salt Lake City but struggled to assimilate with mainstream culture. Misunderstandings and rumors of leprosy created problems between the dominant white population and these newcomers. As a result, the LDS Church chose to settle members of the group in Skull Valley, starting the Iosepa Agriculture and Stock Company in August 1889, which employed laborers and ranch workers. There Polynesian culture flourished despite the challenging natural environment, and

soon there were 228 members. In 1915, when the LDS Church began construction of a temple in Hawaii, many of the immigrants chose to return to the islands. The church presidency did not directly instruct residents to return to Hawaii but did offer financial support for travel to their historic homes. Within two years, Iosepa was mostly deserted.

Iosepa included 1,920 acres and a community organized on the grid plan familiar to Mormon settlements, with a central block reserved for public buildings—a church, schoolhouse, and other group structures. Irrigation ditches ran parallel to the streets. Although most graves remain unmarked in the cemetery on the northern edge of town, some have simple wooden markers, and stones with folk art remind us of the unique ethnic diversity of this place so far from the inhabitants' island homes.

Grantsville
Grantsville First Ward Meetinghouse
297 Clark Street
1865–1866
This simple adobe brick church attests to the conviction that Greek Revival details would give even the most modest structure a certain air of dignity. Mirroring the rectangular form and height of domestic architecture that would have been built in the area nearby, this meetinghouse was one of the first generation of multipurpose church buildings. It held the hope that the pioneers would be able to endure their challenges, dig in roots, worship God, and socialize and gather until they could build something grander.

This beautiful adobe meetinghouse was built by Scottish immigrant Hugh Alexander Ross Gillespie in 1865–66 with adobe bricks fashioned in Grantsville.

Grantsville First Ward Meetinghouse

The Mormons' use of adobe demonstrated their resourcefulness and willingness to use the materials of the earth in creative ways to build respectable houses that resembled those they had left behind. Rather than the larger adobe blocks used in the Southwest to form pueblos, the Mormons made adobe bricks that were similar in size and form to bricks that might have been made in a brickyard. But in this first generation of settlement of Utah Territory, they made do with what was available. Wood was scarce, and brickyards would come later, but adobe yards made it possible for men, women, and children to come together to stomp the mud and straw mixture into an appropriate consistency, pour it into molds, and then wait two weeks for the adobe bricks to dry in the desert sun. Adobe buildings like this one stayed warm in the winter and cool in the summer thanks to dense walls three bricks thick, and deep windowsills.

The building reflects simple references to the Greek Revival style including a simple temple front, overall symmetry, and quiet formality. A round modillion over the entrance door identified the building as Grantsville's First Ward.

John T. Rich House
275 West Clark Street
1880

Italianate houses are unusual in Utah regardless of where you look for them, but it is particularly surprising to find one in a small town like Grantsville. The John T. Rich House, built in 1880, is also unusual because it is the only Italianate building in the state made of adobe bricks.

This two-story side-passage house has a truncated hipped roof and a stone foundation. In plan, the house is a long rectangle, two rooms wide and two rooms deep, with a rear kitchen extension. A flat roof and overhanging eaves supported by decorative brackets are found over both bays. All the windows have pronounced moldings and articulated hood-shaped headers, emphasizing the verticality of the building.

John T. Rich came to Utah from Illinois with the Mormons in the 1840s. He was a Mormon blue blood in a way; his mother was the sister of Mormon president John Taylor. Rich made his living in livestock and was briefly mayor of Grantsville. In August 1889, Rich sold his Skull Valley Ranch, the 1,280 acres that became the Polynesian immigrant community of Iosepa, to the LDS Church.

Alex and Mary Alice Johnson House
5 West Main Street
1900
Charles Zephaniah Shaffer

This picturesque Queen Anne house is one and a half stories tall and built with two kinds of brick, one a fired red brick and the other lined with adobe laid in a running bond pattern projecting four inches at the corners of the octagonal bays. The house's plan is similar to the familiar cross wing but includes a square tower at the intersection of the wings and is ampler in terms of space and decoration. Distinctive decoration includes trim on the gable made of octagonal shingling with lozenge pattern work at the peak, bracket capitals at the top of engaged pilasters flanking the windows, and a main cornice that moves around the entire house with dentil decorations. The porches on the north and east are also elaborately decorated with lathe-turned columns and console brackets supporting

a spool and spindle frieze, dentils, fan-shaped brackets, pendants, and paterae; scroll-cut woodwork on the balustrades and base enclosure continue the decoration on the varied wall surfaces. Round-arched windows, brick voussoirs, and decorative brickwork help complete the lively exterior, and a metal finial caps the tower's pyramidal roof.

Grantsville School and Meetinghouse
90 North Cooley Lane
1861

Regardless of size, the temple form lends a simple rectangular building a certain dignity and formality, through its distinctively moderate roof pitch, boxed cornice and returns, and gable end facing the street. This 1861 example, the Grantsville School and Meetinghouse, is constructed of adobe with walls three bricks deep; it measures twenty feet by thirty-eight feet and sits on a stone foundation.

In 1950, the adobe bricks were stuccoed to protect them from the weather, and the

Grantsville School and Meetinghouse

Tooele Carnegie Library

the gabled end to the street, this long, rectangular building resembles a temple-front building with a central door between two windows, a portico that spans the length of the facade, and cornice returns typical of the style. Fish-scale shingles on the gabled facade were more commonly used on bungalows or Victorian houses during the same era.

A large brick wing added to the building in 1973 provided significant space for expansion. Designed in line with the original style, it adds to rather than distracts from the integrity of the building.

Tooele built its Carnegie library with a $5,000 grant from millionaire and philanthropist Andrew Carnegie in 1911. Tooele City contributed the site as well as the books and committed to provide at least $500 per year for maintenance of the library. The city organized the Tooele City Library Association in February 1864 under a territorial legislative charter, although the book collection was taken over by the Tooele Ward Ecclesiastical Board in 1878. The Carnegie grant was important to Tooele because it helped replace privately funded and operated small libraries with a public library system that has continued to the present.

original shape of the doorway was altered. When the Daughters of Utah Pioneers started to use the building as a relic hall, they brought three structures to the site— the Clark/Rowberry house, a blacksmith shop, and an iron cage that was used temporarily as a jail.

After it was built in 1865, the Grantsville Meetinghouse served a range of purposes— civic meetings, social gatherings, and religious services—an excellent example of the multipurpose meetinghouse buildings erected by the Mormon pioneers in Utah. Commonly built during the first phase of settlement, they were later replaced by larger, more styled and complex buildings. Between 1894 and 1917 the town used it for a city hall.

Tooele
Tooele Carnegie Library
47 East Vine Street
1911
Adapting to a sloping site, the Tooele Carnegie Library appears to be a single-story building but actually has a second story that drops off to the rear. Oriented with

Tooele County Courthouse and City Hall
71 East Vine Street
1867
This Greek Revival temple-form stone building served as the Tooele County Courthouse and City Hall from its construction in 1867 until 1899. Built with uncoursed rubble masonry containing some red sandstone, the building has a rectangular plan measuring twenty-seven feet by sixty-six feet, with

Region B

Tooele County Courthouse and City Hall

decided to erect a jail. Town President E. J. Raddatz appointed James H. Spaulding to be marshal and street supervisor at a salary of fifteen dollars per month. They planned to locate the jail in the northwest part of town at the base of Tabernacle Hill.

This sturdy concrete structure measures twelve by fourteen by eight feet and has three interior rooms, a metal door, and one small window with iron bars. It housed transients traveling the rails, or drunks who needed to detoxify. This small, single-story building is set up against the hillside to capitalize on the natural slope for greater strength and protection and has a low-pitched, gabled roof. A false-front gabled parapet includes a doorway on one side and a small barred window on the other.

the gabled end facing the street. The gable-roofed building is one story at the front and two stories at the rear. The 1874 belfry is a picturesque rather than a Classical element, with lathe-turned posts accented by scrolled brackets and a distinctive spindle band, and a slightly bell-cast pyramidal roof.

Stockton

Stockton Jail
Utah Highway 36
1902
James H. Spaulding

After Stockton incorporated in 1901, the town began a program of civic improvements including construction of a large railroad depot in 1904–05 for the Oregon Short Line Railroad, which had first come to town in 1901. On September 3, 1902, the town

Soldier Creek Kilns / Waterman Coking Ovens
4½ miles east of Stockton
Mid-1860s to 1870s

The Soldier Creek Kilns / Waterman Coking Ovens are intriguing physical remnants of the mining industry that once flourished near the Ophir and Rush Valley Mining Districts, evoking the high point of the early mining era in Utah. Dating from the 1870s, they are the earliest kilns in Utah. Key to the smelting of ores, charcoal helped make mining low-grade ores economically feasible. Four different smelters—Jacobs Smelting Company Works, Carson and Buzzo Smelting Works, Chicago Smelter, and Waterman Smelting Works—were nearby.

After Colonel Patrick E. Connor's Third California Volunteers came to Utah in

1862, commercial mining began west of Salt Lake City in the mountains on the far end of the valley in Tooele County, in what would be named the Rush Valley District in June 1864. Activity was sporadic in the district until the end of the 1870s. Reflecting an unusual mix of entrepreneurial and civic activity, Stockton was first a military post but eventually became important as a smelting point for mines in the surrounding hills.

The Waterman company built these kilns between the mid-1860s and 1870s. Stockton smelters processed ores that came from Ophir as well as Rush Valley. The local mining journal described the process in 1874: "In the rear of the furnaces are the fuel sheds, in which a supply is maintained of 20,000 bushels of charcoal, and forty tons of coke. The charcoal is obtained under contract, from the adjacent mountains, and produced chiefly from nut pine, delivered at the works at twenty-one to twenty-two and a half cents per bushel. The coke used is obtained from Pennsylvania at a cost of $36 to $42 per ton."[6] About fifteen to twenty families made their living off the Soldier Creek Kilns.

The distinctive beehive shape of the kilns, familiar to mining towns, was built of stone in the shape of a parabolic dome with a base fifteen, twenty, or twenty-four feet in diameter and a height of nineteen to twenty-two feet. The thickness of the walls tapered toward the top, and two openings where miners loaded the kiln with wood were closed with iron doors. The kilns depended on a ready supply of wood transported from the slopes of Bald Mountain about two miles east. The largest kiln held forty-five cords of wood.

The process was quite simple: Fire began at the bottom of the structure and a space left in the upper door drew it upward. When sealed, the door regulated fire through vent holes in the base of the kilns, with a material like stucco used to seal off the hole. Typically, the fire burned for three to seven days and then cooled for three to six days.

Ophir
Ophir Town Hall
43 South Main Street
1870

On the west bench of the Salt Lake Valley is an actual ghost town. Ophir's Town Hall is a two-story rectangular structure that measures twenty-six feet five inches by twenty-four feet. Historically, the building served as a town office, fire station, and jail.

Ophir Town Hall.
Photograph by P. Kent Fairbanks, HABS UTAH,23-OPHIR,1-2, public domain.

A simple false-front frame building constructed of six-inch-wide horizontal clapboard siding, it has a belfry on the gabled ridge of the roof near the front. Interior space included three rooms on the main level—a meeting hall, fire department, and storage room for the firefighting equipment—and a concrete basement jail with two cells, each with its own window.

The Ophir Town Hall is one of only three extant mining-era buildings of this sort in the state, important to the state's transition from total dependence on agriculture to a more diversified economy during the last decades of the nineteenth century. Soldiers from the California Volunteers stationed at Fort Douglas in Salt Lake City first traveled forty miles southwest to the Rush Valley Mining District in June 1864 and organized the Ophir District in 1870. That summer, A. N. Moore platted the town site of Ophir, nestled into a canyon of the Oquirrh Mountains in Tooele County. This little town experienced a significant mining boom until 1874.

Frame construction was typical of the mining town building philosophy: build it fast and cheap. Rather than high-style design, this building was all about business, providing essential services and a location for local government. Just when Ophir

seemed to be moving toward development into a real town, mining activity declined. This building is evocative of a future that never materialized.

Utah County

Fairfield
Stage Coach Inn
1858

The Stage Coach Inn was a temporary stopping place for visitors traveling to Camp Floyd or the greater distance to California, and, for a brief time, a point on the Overland Stage Line until the railroad came to Utah in 1869. It was also used as a stop for the Pony Express between 1860 and 1861. John Carson and his four brothers first settled Cedar Valley in 1855 and built a stone fort measuring four rods square, where they built their living quarters.

When Colonel Albert Sidney Johnston's troops arrived in Utah, complete with 3,500 men, 586 horses, 3,000 mules, and 500 wagons, they camped near Fairfield in Cedar Valley and established Camp Floyd. Largely as a result, the population of Cedar Valley boomed in 1858 to more than 7,000. John Carson capitalized on the phenomenal growth and built this two-story adobe and frame hotel and inn. As a Mormon, Carson didn't allow liquor in his inn, nor would he permit what he called "round dancing." Instead, the inn was known as a decent, clean, well-ordered place to stay while on the trail. When Camp Floyd was vacated in 1861, only eighteen families stayed behind in Fairfield. The inn closed in 1947.

When first built, the Stage Coach Inn was intended to be a large family home with fourteen rooms, including seven bedrooms and large dining spaces. A two-story L-shaped plan structure, it was built with

Stage Coach Inn.
Photograph by Sterling Brinkerhoff Own work, CC A-SA 4.0.

brick and plaster except for a two-story addition to the west, where the frame walls were covered with shiplap cove siding.

Fairfield District School
Approximately 59 North Church Street
1898
Andrew Fjeld

Lehi builder Andrew Fjeld constructed the Fairfield District School in 1898, with Hans R. Petersen doing the brick and mortar work. Fairfield built the school during a period of consolidation when new districts were created near the end of the nineteenth century as state-funded public education replaced the LDS school system. Before this time the state's educational system was irregular—Mormon schools were held in multipurpose ward/school buildings or in private homes, and non-Mormon schools such as the Presbyterian mission schools provided a superior alternative in many cases. At the end of the nineteenth century, education received a needed boost—the state legislature made public education compulsory, with more consolidation and organization statewide.

This school also responded to a period of significant growth in Fairfield because of agriculture and sheep ranching in the area's open spaces. It is a one-story rectangular building sitting solidly on a stone foundation, with a hipped roof and a distinctive entrance tower topped by a bell. Arched openings as well as bricks of contrasting colors and textures are used for the principal decoration, which includes wood brackets supporting the eaves.

Camp Floyd
Half mile south of Fairfield
1858

Although the Utah War was as much hype as substance, Colonel Sidney Johnston's Army, after passing through Echo Canyon and descending into the Salt Lake Valley, stayed for a while in the West Desert at Camp Floyd. At its peak, Camp Floyd consisted of between three hundred and four hundred buildings, constructed mostly with locally produced adobe, wood, or stone from the nearby Oquirrh Mountains, including the camp administration structure, the officers' quarters, theater, storehouses, stables, corrals, and workshops.

The men stayed in simple dirt-floored barracks constructed with four-inch adobe bricks. LDS farmers in the area sold adobe to the army for one cent per brick.

Captain Albert Tracy wrote a contemporary description of the camp in his journal:

> For full a half a mile, the principal street extended, lined at either side with buildings pertaining to minor officers, habitable to look at, and even comfortable, but of the same eternal gray with the soil out of which they were constructed, and with the sign of no green thing—not a little grass, or a shrub—to relieve the gaze. At the head of the camp, just above the Tenth, ran a transverse street, with buildings occupied by the department commander, with his personal and general staff. At the rear and parallel to the first ran a second street, with tenements peopled by officers of the higher grades and staff of regiments. Then, quarters for bands, stores for the soldiers, and behind the whole, huts of wagon masters, and other camp-followers. Great ranges of cedar wood also piled up for fuel, and finally, far down at the right, and rear, acres on acres of wagons, clustered in masses, and with their tongues in the air like bristling, mighty lances of the olden times.[7]

After the camp was vacated, the adobe walls washed away for the most part, and builders searching for stone for the foundations of their homes dismantled the stone walls. Pretty much all that remains is the cemetery for what was at the time the largest troop concentration in the United States.

Cedar Fort
Cedar Fort School
40 East Center Street
1896
Matthew Gibbs & Sons

Alfred Bell came to the west edge of Utah County in 1852 searching for abundant pastureland and water for his farm animals. Other settlers followed at the encouragement of Brigham Young to settle in the area. At one time Cedar Fort was the county seat of Cedar County, which was eventually absorbed into Utah County in 1862. Town residents there made their living from farming and stock raising and by traveling to other towns for work.

The Cedar Fort School was the fifth schoolhouse built in the town. The first was an adobe structure that caved in during a wet season, to be replaced by a log cabin, and then a brick building in 1896. Matthew Gibbs & Sons built this building between 1909 and 1910 with brick walls and sandstone found in Pole Canyon nearby; limestone for the foundation was taken from the original Cedar Fort walls.

The Cedar Fort School is a single-story, two-room brick building with Victorian Eclectic detailing along with some references to the Prairie style. The large entrance bay includes Romanesque arches and at one time had a large bell tower. The wall surface is enlivened by a narrow belt course and wide frieze, transoms over all of the large double-hung windows, and windows with segmental arches.

Lehi
Utah Southern Railroad Depot
813 North 150 East
1873

The first railroad to come through Lehi, the Utah Southern, reached the north edge of town in 1872. In 1881, the Denver and Rio Grande Western Railroad built a line across the southern and western part of town, creating a boon to town development. The Salt Lake and Western Railroad built a line through Lehi the same year to transport freight from the Tintic Mining District to market. The lines intersected at Lehi Junction. Related industries, brickyards, stores, factories, and numerous homes sprang up nearby. The coming of the railroad directly impacted Lehi's appearance; there were two town centers, one to the south along Main Street and the other along State Street at the intersection of the rail lines. The railroad had a positive effect on the local economy and social life and provided readily available transportation, goods for trade, and an influx of newcomers and new ideas from the rest of the state as well as the nation.

The first depot was a simple, temporary log building at the corner of State Street and 200 East. A larger, more permanent railroad depot affirmed the importance of the railroad to Lehi and the belief that it had come to stay. The railroad made this small town south of the Salt Lake Valley a commercial center, important to northern Utah County. The depot was used until March 1973, when the railroad offices were moved to the old hospital building across the street. The depot relocated about four hundred feet to the northwest.

The two-story wood-frame depot building is twice as long as wide, with walls covered with vertical board and batten. This asymmetrical vernacular building has no pretense to style or monumentality. Of the four rooms on the upper level, two were used historically as "Employee's Quarters" or dwellings.

Lehi Historic District
Downtown Lehi
1890

It is true that Lehi was one of the first settlements in Utah County, but it was not until the 1890s that its downtown core developed significantly. Lehi's original survey and plat included sixteen blocks laid out with streets that were ninety-nine feet wide—the intersection of Main and Center Streets marked the center of town. Stores on Main Street such as Trane & Evans Mercantile at 400 West, the Lehi Hotel at 394 West, the Lehi Opera House at 154 West, and Harwood & Sons Harness Shop at 126–130 West, among others, clustered at the core.

Lehi's commercial district emerged in the wake of the organization of the Utah Sugar Company factory in 1890, a time of great growth and development for the small agricultural community. The company provided a strong economic base for the local economy, attracting new workers. In response, new service businesses—saloons, physician's offices, butcher shops, and other specialty shops—soon appeared along Main Street. As in many towns in the American West, most of these buildings were one- or two-part commercial Victorian Eclectic blocks with corbeled brickwork running along the cornices and parapet walls along the top of the main facades; they were built between 1890 and 1945. Many of the buildings downtown have blue-gray limestone in the sidewalks or foundations.

At least eight new buildings appeared along Main Street in the decade after the sugar factory came to town. Both the old Senate Saloon at 169 West Main and the Corner Saloon at 116 West Main entertained men from the factory—in fact, a local antidrinking ordinance was repealed because of the sugar factory workers. A butcher shop at 101 West Main sold meat from animals raised on a feedlot south of the sugar factory. Between 1920 and 1945, new businesses filled in the spaces between older ones, increasing the density of the commercial zone.

One of the most unusual buildings along Main Street is the Art Deco building at 40 West. This small, single-story concrete block building is covered with stucco, at one time painted pale green with Art Deco details along the parapet walls. When first built, the structure was used as a dental office, but it was converted into a house in 1940 and then later back into a business.

People's Co-op Building
151 East State Street
1900

Even before the organization of Zion's Cooperative Mercantile Institution, Lehi had its own cooperative mercantile store. Israel Evans, son of LDS bishop David Evans, saw a working cooperative while he was serving a mission in England in 1853–57. When he returned, he brought the idea home and helped organize the Lehi Union Exchange at 189 West Main Street in 1868. When ZCMI organized in Salt Lake City, the Lehi Exchange became a branch. The railroad impacted the cooperative network, offering readily available state goods and a great variety of manufactured goods for greatly reduced prices, and the historic co-ops couldn't compete. Still, at the end

People's Co-op Building

sandstone foundation and brick walls. The front facade consists of a three-bay street-level section with large display windows and a middle clerestory section with translucent glazing. At the top is a pressed metal Classical cornice with a row of modillions stretching the length of the building.

Harry B. Merrihew Drugstore / State Bank of Lehi
100 West and Main Street
1890s

Maximizing the advantages of a corner lot, the Harry B. Merrihew Drugstore and State Bank of Lehi building has facades on both the south and west elevations, with wraparound display windows and the main entrance at the corner. Typical of late nineteenth-century commercial-style buildings, this example makes the most of limited space and modest means—decoration has to do with function, the sensible division of space, and materials.

Harry B. Merrihew settled in Provo after receiving his pharmacy degree in Des Moines. He moved to Lehi in the late 1890s and opened his drugstore first in the old Garff Building. Within two years he had built this new building and advertised in the *Lehi Banner*: "H. B. Merrihew, Drugs and Medicines, Toilet and Fancy Articles, Perfumes, Cigars, and Stationary. Prescriptions Filled Day or Night." In 1917 he sold the building to the State Bank of Lehi, the second bank in town operating as a branch of the Bank of American Fork.

Lehi Roller Mills
700 East Main Street
1905
Wolf Company (milling machinery)

Lehi Roller Mills is an iconic landmark on Lehi's historic landscape. The first mill to be built in Utah County was in Springville in

of the century, the People's Co-op was the most successful store in town, with two branches—one uptown and one downtown—with clothing, furniture, farming implements, lumber, coal, shoes, and harness departments.

The co-op constructed a new two-story brick building for the store in the spring of 1900 at the downtown location. The company tried to keep pace with the latest in technologies to make the building efficient and convenient, installing electricity, a telephone system, and a pneumatic tube. It sold the downtown branch in 1904 and the following year sold its livery business. Marking changing times, in 1916, it installed a gasoline pump, and two six-hundred-gallon tanks in front of the store accommodated the new automobile driver.

The co-op building was part of a complex that included a lumberyard, coal yard, feed store, livery stable, harness shop, hotel, drugstore, and blacksmith shop. Like many other buildings that lined the main streets of small rural towns, the main building is a two-part commercial block with an ashlar

Lehi Roller Mills

1851, complete with two sets of burrs and a mill wheel. The mill was upgraded by 1885 with more up-to-date roller technology, a method called the "new process" when it was first introduced to Utah.

Rather than massive, historic stone burrs, the roller mill used metal rollers to grind wheat, gradually breaking it up in a series of steps. Wheat moved along the surface of the steel rollers, which were incised with parallel, equally spaced, sharp-edged grooves to cut the grain. As wheat passed from each pair of rollers to the next it was ground more finely. The roller mill produced a type of flour called "Patent," one of the highest grades of refined flour. Roller milling became standard after 1880 and dictated the shape of mill design.

Lehi's boosters promoted the new mill and the Lehi Commercial Club sold the idea among the town's businessmen. They purchased a site on east Main Street near the spur of the Union Pacific Railroad that also ran by the sugar factory, contracting

with the Wolf Company of Chambersburg, Pennsylvania, for the mill machinery, including four sets of double rollers, one washer, two purifiers, two reels, one cleaner, one dust roller, one gyrator, one separator, and one bran duster. A fifty-horsepower motor powered the machinery in the original three-story building.

By 1907, the Lehi Roller Mills dominated milling in the area. The Turkey Red and Peacock brand logos painted on the east sides of the silos have distinguished the structure for decades. A familiar community landmark, it is a testament to community enterprise and of the county's most successful historic businesses.

Lehi City Hall
51 North Center Street
1918–1921
Ware and Treganza

The Lehi City Hall building is interesting and important for several reasons. The Mission style is rarely used in Utah, and this is also reputedly the first memorial building built in the wake of World War I—construction began two weeks after the armistice was signed. But the building is also significant because it was one of the last projects of the prestigious Salt Lake architectural firm of Ware and Treganza, and the only public building it designed in the Mission style. Fluent in a number of different Revival styles—Prairie, Renaissance Revival, Craftsman, and here, the Mission style— the firm responded to national trends and interpreted them for local audiences.

Built between 1918 and 1921, the building was dedicated before the end of 1921 with a program featuring University of Utah history professor Levi Edgar Young. The dedication ceremony focused on the sacrifice of the men who had fought in World War I. According to speaker Governor George Dern, those who served were "heroes all, in the cause of humanity."[8]

Until the 1910s, the town had not had a public library. In 1914, the city appointed a Library Commission to make a grant application to the Carnegie Foundation for funding to help support construction of a new building to house the library and city hall. It received $10,000 from Carnegie with the stipulation that the city council pledge to maintain the building at an annual cost of not less than $1,000 per year.

In terms of architecture, the Lehi City Hall is formed by a complex of buildings, each with elements of the Mission style, including low-pitched roofs with red tiles, smooth stucco walls, round-arched openings, and arched corbeling on the central building. The main double doors, framed by pilasters, brackets, heavy consoles, and a projecting round arch with a semicircular transom, blend with some Prairie-style elements such as the horizontal groups of casement windows on the walls.

Lehi North Branch Meetinghouse
1190 North 500 West
1894
Andrew Fjeld and Charles Ohran

This building is the only historic Mormon meetinghouse in Lehi. Typical of the simplicity of early settlement buildings, it is a simple one-story rectangle with a cross wing. The LDS Church organized Lehi's North Branch on October 1, 1893, with Thomas R. Jones as the first branch president. Jones led a building committee that met to plan and raise funds for the construction of a new meetinghouse.

The congregation chose a building site on the corner of 500 West and 1200 North and asked Andrew Fjeld and Charles Ohran, local contractors, to design and build the building, sometimes called Zion's Hill Meetinghouse. Brick walls lined with adobe bricks for strength and insulation helped create an impressive interior. Creating the look of a Gothic church, projecting brick false buttresses were placed at even intervals around the walls of the building, and Gothic arched windows ran along the sidewalls. A stepped brick cornice accents the steeply pitched gabled roof.

Lehi Ward Tithing Barn / Centennial Hall
651 North 200 East
1872

The Lehi Ward Tithing Barn was first built in 1872 but moved to the ward tithing office yard on west Main Street in 1873. Used as a feed and livery stable for donations to the LDS Church and conveniently located near the Utah Southern Railroad Depot, it provided easy access for passengers and goods coming into town at the end of the line.

The tithing yard was often the scene of community-wide activities, such as Fourth of July celebrations, dances, and musicals. The barn is a simple two-story structure with post-and-beam construction, and rock footings are sheathed with vertical plank siding. The interior space is separated into two bays by a large summer beam, and above, the king post truss supports the roof. Although the barn has been moved twice, it remains intact.

American Fork
American Fork Presbyterian Church
75 North 100 East
1878
Peter Van Houghton

Toward the end of the nineteenth century, revival styles replaced the popular temple form for territorial churches. Salt Lake City architect Peter Van Houghton designed the American Fork Presbyterian Church. The Gothic Revival situated this building in a

American Fork Presbyterian Church

long tradition of ecclesiastical design and distinguished it as a church. Constructed with orange-buff brick and a stone foundation, it is modest in size, measuring only thirty by sixty feet. Gothic details include the distinctive pointed-arched windows, an asymmetrical exterior with a belfry tower, and a tapered bell-cast cap on the side over a ten-foot-square entrance at the lower level.

Hoping to convert Latter-day Saints, Presbyterian reverend George R. Bird first came to American Fork in Utah County in September 1877 and rented space in the "Social Hall" to set up Sunday School as well as a regular school during the week, taught by Miss Ada Kingsbury. The Presbyterians already in the area organized a diverse congregation made up of Scottish, English, and a few Scandinavian immigrants as well as American worshippers. The group formed a Church Erection Board with the principal objective of building a new church building and purchased a shop on a street near the center of town. In 1880 Reverend Thomas F. Day replaced Bird and married Kingsbury.

Alpine Stake Tabernacle
110 East Main Street
1910
Liljenberg and Maeser

This grand yellow brick building on American Fork's Main Street commands a dominant presence on a platform base in the Classical Revival style and is a unique form for an LDS tabernacle. Tabernacles were regional centers key to creating instructional and doctrinal unity throughout the LDS Church in its distant locations. The main assembly room is on the second floor rather than the first. The distinctive hipped roof features a Dutch gable on each end, with entrances framed by semicircular

Alpine Stake Tabernacle

pediments over the cornice, which wraps around the entire building and is flanked by columns to each side. When built, the tabernacle featured an impressive pipe organ, pressed metal ceilings that sloped gently to each side, and a U-shaped gallery that moved around three walls of the assembly room. A baptismal font is in the lower level.

Harrington School
50 North Center Street
1903
Richard C. Watkins

Much of the first wave of construction in a new town like American Fork was accomplished cooperatively—the town's men and women built log cabins, forts, and irrigation canals. In American Fork the earliest school classes were staged in family homes or in tiny log outbuildings and other temporary accommodations, but by the time Utah became a state, it made a commitment to

public education as compulsory and a right of every citizen, coupled with the effort to consolidate all smaller schools into single large buildings for greater efficiency, consistency, and uniformity in curriculum. Between 1862 and 1893 the number of school districts in Utah increased from 76 to 342, and these were organized by county lines, resulting in a more progressive curriculum and efficient school administration. A local man, Leonard Harrington, sponsored a bill in the territorial legislature to give communities the right to maintain public schools supported by taxation.

Consolidation, compulsory education, and the localization of tax support led to the design of new schools between 1890 and 1910 that were larger and more uniformly designed, with a unified vision expressed architecturally. The state and counties hired professional architects who specialized in design, including the state

Harrington School

architect for schools, Richard C. Watkins, who designed some 240 schools in his career, often using the Victorian Romanesque style. Although the architect of the Harrington School is not known, the floor plan is the same as that of Watkins's Peteetneet School in Payson and was clearly influenced by his thinking about the organization of space for consolidated schools.

First built in 1903, the Harrington School was expanded in 1934 by school board architect Walter E. Ware, who prepared the plans for a two-story addition that blended naturally with the original building, ending up with a symmetrical Greek cross building that was consistent in terms of materials, elevation, and detailing. A single large classroom is located at each corner and level. The exterior walls are constructed with multicolored pressed brick with painted wooden trim, and a sandstone foundation with deep eaves is trimmed with

large brackets. Variety marks the building in terms of windows, materials, and texture. Rusticated brick arches contrast with the smooth bricks in the large Roman- and round-arched entryways. The town used the building as a school until the 1960s, when new elementary schools were built.

Bank of American Fork
5 East Main Street
1909–1911

The historic landscape of small-town America's Main Street is composed of simple commercial block buildings and a range of institutions that completed community life in American Fork. Dominant in its corner location on Main Street, the Bank of American Fork is easily the most architecturally significant historic commercial building in the center of American Fork's commercial district, and it was key to local growth and diversification. It represented the economic vitality in town at the turn of the century, and its eclectic and impressive Neoclassical styling speaks to the prosperity of the local business community. Although dozens of other historic buildings remain on Main Street, this is by far the most monumental and impressive structure from the historic period. Built between 1909 and 1911 and proudly asserting its prime importance, this two-story, two-part commercial block sat on the northeast corner of Main Street with two facades, one facing Center Street and one facing Main Street. This elaborately decorated building includes extensive ornamental trim, Ionic and Composite capitals, columns, entablature, sills, brackets, and keystones formed with limestone. The two cornices and ornamented ventilation grilles are made with pressed metal.

The Utah Southern Railroad came to American Fork in 1873, solidifying its position as an important center of trade and commerce. The railroad line running up American Fork Canyon facilitated mining activities and helped diversify the local economy.

American Fork Second Ward Meetinghouse
130 West 100 South
1909
James H. Pulley

By 1901, the American Fork ward had grown to the point that it was divided into four new congregations. During the next few years, the newly organized wards built their own buildings. The Second Ward building was dedicated on February 17, 1909. In 1929, church architect Don Carlos Young designed a remodel of the earlier wing and a new addition.

At first glance, the four buildings look very similar: they are constructed with the

Bank of American Fork

American Fork Second Ward Meetinghouse

same brick, they each have eclectic Gothic Revival styling, and they reflect the design of Protestant churches along the East Coast or in Europe. This example has a rectangular plan with the narrow end facing the street and a square entrance tower topped by a thirty-five-foot spire at the southwest corner. The chapel space beyond the entrance vestibule at the base of the tower projects slightly toward the rear section beyond the sidewalls, making the footprint look like a *T*. Gothic detailing includes Roman-arched windows and doors, Gothic transoms, and lancet bays in the tower. Brick corbeling enriches the wall surface and enhances the textural richness of the building.

Joseph F. Smith dedicated the building in 1915.

Alpine

Alpine LDS Meetinghouse
50 North Main Street
1863
James R. Moyle and Thomas J. McCullough

The hands-down favorite building type constructed by the Latter-day Saints in the first generation of settlement was the gable-roofed, Classically detailed, rectangular box. In public buildings such as schools, churches, or city halls, the gabled end faced the street, and in houses, the broadside faced the street. The Alpine LDS Meetinghouse fits this description perfectly; it measures twenty-one by thirty-two feet and has a single story and a gabled roof. Undistinguished by a steeple or any other tangible allusion to the religious activity that took place inside, the building is constructed of

Alpine LDS Meetinghouse

stone covered with plaster instead of log or adobe and is symmetrical in design. In 1867, raised plaster quoins were added at the corners, defining the edge of the facade. Those along with a pediment over the front door and wooden flat-arched heads at the side windows add to the Classical character of the building.

Local men transported limestone for the church from quarries in Box Elder and Wordsworth Canyons, led by James R. Moyle and Thomas J. McCullough, both local builders. They built a small sawmill on the site to produce the requisite lumber and shingles. The walls were wide and sturdy—twenty-eight inches at the basement level and eighteen inches above ground level. Insulating in both the cold winter months and the dry hot summer months, the walls told volumes about this local environment. Brigham Young dedicated the building in 1863. It served the community well, functioning as a multipurpose community center for social events, dances and plays, and school and worship services.

Alpine City Hall
20 North Main Street
1936
Public Works Administration
Unlike so many of the forty other PWA buildings constructed during the 1930s that exhibit the PWA Moderne or other modern styles, this 1936 building reflects historic architectural trends in the state and the first generation of buildings built by the Mormon pioneer settlers of this town, constructed with modern materials and technologies such as reinforced concrete.

As is true for most public buildings, the gabled end of the rectangle faces the street. Symmetrically arranged, the facade includes a recessed arched entrance with pilasters to the sides, and ornamental winged urns to both the north and south, topped by a central bell tower on the apex.

Although the federal government provided a good part of the funds required for construction, the town held a bond election in November 1935 to raise $6,137.50 for the building, to supplement the $11,923 given to the city by the PWA. Alpine bought the old Alpine Co-op Mercantile Store and land for $500. In spite of the good intentions of the earlier group of city leaders, and because of the delays, the city ran out of money and the work dragged out over the next couple of years, using donated labor and supplies until it was finally completed in the early 1950s.

Moyle House and Indian Tower
606 East 770 North
1858–1860
John Rowe Moyle

The first Mormons entered the Alpine area in 1849 at the direction of Brigham Young. Before then, the Utes had moved freely through the area, which had been their ancient hunting ground, and along an old trail leading from Utah Valley over the low hills to Salt Lake Valley. White settlers interrupted their time-honored traditional life practices and they resisted the newcomers' efforts to claim their land. The settlers

thought this would be a perfect place for stock raising, with two large streams flowing from the nearby hills and a generally favorable climate. Ten families struggled through the winter of 1850, living in hastily constructed dugout homes or covered wagons. By the spring of 1851, six of the families were gone—overwhelmed by the constant threat of conflict with the Indians and what had proved to be difficult rocky terrain.

During the years of the Walker War, 1853–54, Brigham Young told the residents of "Mountainville" to build a fort for the community. British convert and stonemason John Rowe Moyle resisted the idea of moving his family into the fort and instead began constructing a stone watch and defense tower to protect his own family in 1858. It took Moyle two weeks to build a dugout home three or four feet deep with walls above and a roof covered with logs, brush, and earth. Eventually Moyle built a much more respectable hall-parlor house over the

Moyle House and Indian Tower

dugout, using granite from the nearby creek and canyon in a random rubble masonry pattern, as well as a 1917 bungalow Arts and Crafts addition with matching stone. The slow evolution of the family's wealth was mirrored as the small vernacular house took on a more distinctive, nationally recognized architectural style. Besides the typical Classical details of the hall-parlor section, the house had exposed purlins and rafter ends and windows divided into threes.

Perhaps the most interesting structure on the site is the Indian tower that Moyle built between 1860 and 1866 in two stages—the first at the end of the Walker War and the second before the end of the Black Hawk War. Measuring twelve feet in diameter at the base and about sixteen feet tall at the point of the conical roof, the tower has walls two feet thick, built of cobblestone or river rock set in a random rubble pattern—the same stone as in the Moyle house. At the bottom the wall uses mostly granite, but at the top there is a variety of stones. In the lower walls are eight equally spaced, splayed, horizontal gun ports with cut stone lintels. About five feet above the floor level, the tower is entered through a single opening in the west wall, marked by a cut stone lintel and cast-iron barred door resembling a prison door. The conical roof of the tower has a medium pitch. Made of logs, thatching, and mud and sod roofing material, it partially collapsed in 1917 and was reconstructed in 1951.

Pleasant Grove
Pleasant Grove Historic District
Main Street and Center Street
1890s

Pleasant Grove's Historic District includes a sixteen-block area centered in downtown, forming a core of historic single-story Victorian Eclectic commercial buildings surrounded by historic neighborhoods. The single-story David N. Adamson Commercial Building at 15 East Center was built in 1895 and is distinguished by a stepped parapet wall, brick dentils, a flat, sloping roof, and other Victorian Eclectic details. The two-part commercial block of Clark Brothers Store at 43 South Main is constructed with soft rock sidewalls and a brick masonry facade. Decorative features include Victorian brickwork in six arched windows and decorative brickwork on the walls. Modern twentieth-century buildings include the Bank of Pleasant Grove, a Prairie-style building at 2 South Main, built in 1917. The wall surface is enlivened by dark brown brick contrasting with cream-colored vertical and horizontal stucco panels that emphasize the lines of the prairie. Other features of the style include rows of vertical casement windows ordained with corbeled brickwork above and panels with diamond-patterned leaded glass. The city built Pleasant Grove City Hall at 35 South Main in 1938 in the PWA Moderne style using salvaged rock from Clark Hall. As is typical of this streamlined style, its aesthetic appeal comes from its sleek and simple forms and lines rather than elaborate decoration. Contrasting with both the Victorian and Moderne buildings is the Spanish Revival–style Alhambra Theater, built in 1927 at 20 South Main. As a group, these commercial structures of the period between 1895 and 1940 produce a virtual newsreel of architectural styles and tastes.

This is also true of the public and institutional buildings that surround this central block. The vernacular stuccoed adobe school first built in 1861, the Pleasant Grove School / Old Bell School at 61 South 100 East, exhibits pioneer-era building techniques and aesthetics. At 107 South 100 East is a native soft-rock structure with

Federal style, Victorian details, and more pretention to style, the Pleasant Grove Town Hall, built in 1887. A 1940 Art Deco building, the Pleasant Grove LDS Meetinghouse, is found at 494 South 300 East. These buildings contrast sharply with each other but reflect the sweeping changes in buildings in tangible form and coordinate them in terms of scale, setback, and orientation. They include virtually every type of building—hall parlor, temple form, cross wing, and bungalow—as well as architectural styles—Gothic Revival, Federal, Italianate, Victorian, and International.

The residences in Pleasant Grove's Historic District were built during the same decades as the historic commercial structures, between 1860 and 1945. Therefore, they include a similar range of styles, building techniques, and materials, from the log and rock buildings of the first wave of white settlement to Art Nouveau and International-style buildings from the mid-twentieth century. The vernacular-style Cyrus Benjamin Hawley House at 55 East Center Street is a one-and-a-half-story soft-rock house with a Gothic Revival, steeply pitched, cross gable roof. The one-and-a-half-story Elijah Mayhew House at 214 South Main was built in the 1870s in the popular temple form, but in this rectangular clapboard house the gabled end faces the street, an orientation unusual for a residence. The William Black / Reuben Weeks House at 151 East Center is a hall-parlor plan built of soft rock, with a single story and a symmetrical facade divided into three bays.

Pleasant Grove Town Hall
107 South 100 East
1887
Andrew F. Sundberg
Pleasant Grove built this two-room stone building in 1887 for a town hall in place of an earlier log structure that had a jail in its cellar. Carpenter and contractor Andrew F. Sundberg drafted the plans for the building's walls, which included a small room at the back for city council meetings and a main room for the municipal court where the city staged dances, political rallies, socials, and elections. Local stonemason N. P. Poulson Sr. laid the soft-stone walls and other local men donated labor for the finishing work. A separate red brick jail was at the back of the lot.

The Pleasant Grove Town Hall is a simple vernacular structure with subtle references to the Greek Revival style, typical of early nineteenth-century Utah buildings. Classical features include pedimented window heads and a symmetrical temple-form facade. Instead of the more typical gabled roof, this building has a hipped roof. At the west end is a raised entrance porch with a gabled roof supported by Tuscan columns, the grandest feature of the simple building.

Pleasant Grove School
73 South 100 East
1861
Henry Greenhalgh (arched ceiling); William H. Adams (stonemason)
The "Old Bell School" is the oldest remaining building in Pleasant Grove and is one of the state's earliest adobe pioneer school buildings, used over time for virtually every type of community activity including dances, socials, civic meetings, banquets, and other gatherings. It was built cooperatively during a time when wood was scarce and the town didn't have a brickyard.

An even older building predated this one. The first adobe schoolhouse was torn down when the community gathered into a fort during the Walker War. The town saved the adobe bricks and the lumber used in this first building to use in the second. This next schoolhouse burned down in 1860. The third try, the Old Bell School, was built the next year in part with adobe bricks saved from the first two. Henry Greenhalgh, an English convert to the LDS Church, designed the arched ceiling, known for its good acoustics, and William H. Adams cut and laid the stones.

The one-story rectangular building accommodated a simple classroom with two wings, one to the east and one to the west. Wood trim is found at the roof eaves, and a plain boxed cornice has a return at the gabled ends and a simple frieze. A bell tower sits at the intersection of the wings.

Thomas A. Richins House
405 North 500 East
1897

With our twentieth-first century sensibilities it is hard to imagine how a family could have lived in a modest house like this, but many did. The hall-parlor house was as familiar a part of the Utah landscape as the meetinghouse, relatively easy to conceptualize and design, and the common farmer would most likely have had the requisite skills to build this type of home for his family. Based on the same logic as the golden mean, the dimensions of the house would have been familiar and generally understood. The hall-parlor house has two main rooms, one slightly larger than the other, a rectangle formed by swinging the diagonal between the two points of a square to the side. Any farmer who could draw a square could come up with the proportions of this house.

Thomas A. Richins built this one-story house in 1897 with a gabled roof and soft-rock exterior walls. If you use your imagination, the facade hints at the configuration of the interior rooms—a three-bay arrangement includes a central transomed door

flanked by two windows. Brick chimneys at both ends also suggest two interior rooms.

Thomas Richins was raised in Pleasant Grove, and his father, also named Thomas, was familiar with soft-rock quarrying in Painswick, Gloucestershire, England, the place of his birth. Brigham Young sent him and his brother John to Pleasant Grove to use their expertise in utilizing rock from the Pleasant Grove quarries.

Christen Larsen House
990 North 400 East
1876
Christen Larsen

Unlike most of their neighbors who constructed hall-parlor homes, Christen Larsen, his wife, Anne, and their four children built their home in the traditional style of their homeland, the *parstuga* house, which featured three rooms in the main body of the house. When Christen first purchased the lot he built a one-room dugout for his family and scavenged for building materials for a "decent dwelling" over the next few months. Before they emigrated to America, Christen worked as a sailor and fisherman and his children sold fish door to door to help the family save to travel to the United States. When he settled in Pleasant Grove, he did what he had known and worked as a fisherman on Utah Lake. He was also a cabinetmaker and built violins. Christen Larsen used the local tufa, or soft rock of the area, for the walls of his family home, which has a gabled roof and three bays across the facade, with a welcoming hip-roofed porch.

Fugal Blacksmith Shop
Approximately 680 North 400 East
1903

Just outside the central business district in Pleasant Grove, the Christian A. Fugal

Blacksmith Shop is a one-part commercial block built in 1903; the narrow end of this rectangular Victorian structure faces the street. Soft-fired salmon-colored brick walls sit on a granite rubble foundation, with brick laid in a common bond with a header every eighth course, and a corbeled brick pattern along the front of the parapet wall. Such exemplary brickwork speaks to the stratification of Pleasant Grove's craftsman class. Clearly a skilled brick mason lived in town at the turn of the century. At both the front and sides of the building, double-leaf, heavy wooden doors made with two thicknesses of wood open to the interior. The interior batten board is faced with a horizontal pattern on the exterior, as you might find in Europe. Also on the interior, the brick walls are exposed and the rafters can be seen.

Blacksmith shops were key to local development. Transportation was difficult even on the best roads, and travelers depended on blacksmiths to shoe their horses and build or repair their wagons. Nails for construction were also fashioned in blacksmith shops, and farmers counted on blacksmiths to make and repair farm implements. A man like Christian was critical to an area's survival.

Christian, Jens, and Niels Fugal were born in Pleasant Grove in their family's dugout home. Christian was a blacksmith by the age of fifteen. He built a shop with his brother Jens where they did blacksmithing and sold bolts, nuts, nails, rivets, bales of binder twine, rope, horseshoes, and plow and shovel handles.

Beers House/Hotel
65 North 100 East
1885

Although the Beers House functioned as a hotel, it was built as a family home. The form of this 1885 adobe building is a cross wing with Italianate massing and detailing,

Beers House/Hotel

and a hipped roof unusual for Utah County. When the owners remodeled the house in 1930, they stuccoed the walls to protect the adobe brick from deterioration, as was common, and quoins were added to the corners, along with tall, narrow paired windows with pedimented lintels and rosettes in the corners, an asymmetrical facade, bracketed eaves, and cornices. It is a sturdy formal-style house, ready to impress. The adobe bricks used for the walls are twelve by five by four inches and were laid two thick. A stonemason from Lehi, Thomas Featherstone, laid the adobe bricks in 1885 and also plastered the interior walls. As a result, the house is well insulated—warm in the winter and cool in the long summer months.

The Beers House/Hotel is in Pleasant Grove's central core, conveniently located near the railroad depot, the Mormon tabernacle, and the Presbyterian church. It was one of three hotels in town during the late nineteenth and early twentieth centuries. It was also known as the Pleasant Grove Hotel and Beers Hall. The proprietor, Franklin Beers, also owned a mercantile store nearby with a butcher shop, tin shop, tailor shop, and shoe store as well as a livery stable. The Beerses operated their businesses until 1895.

Neils Peter Larsen House
1150 North 100 East
1870

Under the Homestead Act of 1862, Neils Peter Larsen claimed a quarter section in the north fields of Pleasant Grove. The first house he built there was a simple dugout, carved into the earth and covered with a roof of mud and willows. In a complicated plural family arrangement, they lived there until he finished his soft-rock house in

1870. Then he located one of his wives and her children in this house and the other two in a home a mile south. During the underground period when federal marshals pursued polygamists, Larsen would periodically hide out in the attic of his soft-rock home to avoid arrest.

The attic space was also used by Larsen's wife for raising silkworms during the Relief Society's sericulture movement. At one time as many as a thousand silkworms were busy eating mulberry leaves in trays carefully laid out on the attic floor. Larsen's oldest daughter, Annie, taught school in the home to local children who paid her a small fee.

This one-story hall-parlor house has a gabled roof and soft-rock exterior walls. The facade has a three-bay arrangement with a central door flanked by two windows. A chimney at each end provided warmth to the two unequally sized rooms. At one time there were as many as 130 soft-rock houses in Pleasant Grove, but only 13 are still standing.

Peter Axel Johnson House
1075 North 100 East
1876
Peter Axel

Swedish immigrant and LDS Church convert Peter Axel built this house in 1876. An excellent example of the Scandinavian pair house, or parstuga house, it is evidence of a subtle ethnic interpretation of the typical rectangular house form. This house is one and a half stories and built with the indigenous soft rock found in the area. The house has three rooms, a larger one in the middle and two equal-sized smaller rooms on the sides. During the late nineteenth century, a one-and-a-half-story addition extended to the back.

Peter Axel Johnson worked in Salt Lake City for two years after he first came to Utah in 1871. In 1873 he moved to Pleasant Grove and built this house in 1876. Mostly a farmer, Johnson also worked on the construction of the railroad lines through the county and on the lines that ran to the mines in Cottonwood Canyon.

Fugal Dugout House
630 North 400 East
1869
Andreas C. Fugal and Christian
Christensen Fugal

Because they were always considered temporary dwellings, we have no idea how popular dugouts were during the first years of settlement. Lack of resources, workers, or building experience might have forced settlers to choose this more temporary shelter until something better could be built, and there is evidence that dugouts were constructed well into the twentieth century. We know that one man in Orangeville, in Emery County, lived in a dugout during the Depression, and another dugout there served as a store and post office.

A dugout is a subterranean dwelling dug into the earth, not all that different from the pit houses built by the Anasazi. Usually up to six feet deep or carved into a hillside, they were traditionally about twelve feet square. A short stone wall was built aboveground to provide room for adults to walk about the room, and roofs were usually flat or slightly sloped. Evenly spaced, heavy wooden poles held up roofs formed with willow or other branches covered with straw, bundles of sticks, or sometimes sod. The front wall also varied according to what was locally available and might have been vertical logs, willow and mud, or what was called wattle and daub, or even more

finished lumber. With restricted space, interiors had beds that might fold up against the walls, tables made of large pieces of wood for use during the day, and boxes for storage.

Andreas C. Fugal and his father, Christian Christensen Fugal, built this dugout a year after they immigrated to Utah from Denmark. Andreas was thirty-six years old and unmarried when he lived in this one-room dugout with his parents, until his mother died in 1873. One month later, Andreas married a young Swedish immigrant, Hannah Carlson, and brought her to the dugout home, where they had three children.

In 1869 they built a stone hall-parlor house above it and removed the dugout's gabled roof. Now the cellar of the house, the dugout is fourteen by fifteen feet and is a single room. The stone walls are twenty-four inches thick, made of uncoursed rubble masonry with a rough plaster finish. Small windows are on the west and south walls and an entrance is on the east. From the inside it is possible to see the round log ceiling beams and rough slab lumber ceiling that now serve as floor joists and subflooring for the house. The hall-parlor house is a single story, with a gabled roof and a lean-to extension at the back.

Pleasant Grove Tithing Office
7 South 300 East
1905–1910

Although the exact date of the construction of the Pleasant Grove Tithing Office is not known, it is consistent with tithing offices built with the same plan between 1905 and 1910 in Manti, Panguitch, Richmond, Sandy, and Hyrum—it is a one-story, rectangular brick building. At the center of the symmetrical facade, a pavilion announces the

Pleasant Grove Tithing Office

added six more rooms and two porches in 1888–89 after Harper had spent three years on a mission for the LDS Church in New Zealand. Alfred did most of the work by himself, including hauling stone to the site—soft rock quarried nearby and some "pot rock" from Midway, which he traded for a wagonload of fruit. Because the rock was soft and porous, this house, like other rock houses in the area, was covered with stucco in the 1930s or 1940s.

entrance. This example has a flat roof and distinctive Neoclassical elements such as the decorative parapet that extends from the roof, varying slightly from the standard plan. Other Classical elements include columns with Ionic capitals supporting the pavilion, simple pilasters framing the pairs of windows on the facade, and an entrance set behind the rounded arch. Although Pleasant Grove had three different LDS wards by 1908, only one built a tithing office.

Lindon
Alfred William Harper House
125 West 400 North
1877
Alfred William Harper

Alfred William Harper was only fifteen years old when he arrived in America with his family of immigrant converts to the LDS Church from England. After he married Melissa Walker in 1875, the couple bought five acres of land outside Pleasant Grove, in an area known as Lindon Hill where they planned to make their home. The family lived in a tent on the site while the first section of the two-story hall-parlor house with five rooms was built in 1877. They

Orem
Sims McBride Garage
600 North State Street
1917

The Sims McBride Garage reminds us of the era when the automobile became an important element in the American landscape. This one-story, one-part brick commercial building was a familiar landmark on Orem's State Street. During the early 1900s, State Street had few commercial buildings, particularly ones built with brick. So this example was novel for a couple of reasons. Most buildings were temporary structures—fruit stands or other frame construction structures that came with the harvest or different seasons. This garage illustrated the change that began in the 1920s—development in commercial activity, transportation, and construction. Orem's policy of strip zoning rather than developing a central downtown business core also exemplified this pattern of growth.

The Provo Bench became Orem Town in 1919 largely because of the prosperity in agricultural markets. Today a scooter shop, the Sims McBride Garage was built about 1917. As is typical in such buildings, large sections of plate glass with a space above for signs made merchandise visible. Fired red-brown brick divided the building horizontally into three bays and vertically into two sections that have large square openings; there were decorative brick pilasters on both levels and a corbeled brick cornice at the top.

Utah Valley University Campus
800 West University Parkway (University Street Exit, off Interstate 15)
Mid-1970s, 1980s, 1990s
FFKR

The Utah State Board of Education established a two-year technical college beginning in the mid-1940s for vocational training in Provo, which moved to its current location in the 1970s. From that modest beginning it has become a university, in the twentieth century enrolling over thirty thousand and offering both four-year undergraduate and master's degree programs. FFKR Architecture/Planning/Interior Design was involved from the beginning in the development of the master plan for this campus, which would have an integrated design that would deal with present needs as well as anticipate the future. Beautiful outdoor spaces, functional buildings, and a strong design commitment created a distinctive, community-based campus for Utah Valley. FFKR's ambition was that the master plan should reflect a balance of academic functional requirements, aesthetic considerations, environmental factors, and funding restraints.

FFKR received a Utah AIA Award of Distinction for the master plan creation and implementation of Utah Valley University's campus. Its role was the conceptualization of a logical architectural system for the campus. Essential to the plan was a central core around which architectural masses and exterior spaces were grouped. Academic programs were found in a contiguous multilevel structure that was linked to others by a continuous two-level course. Motifs such as transparency, accessibility, and open spaces were followed throughout and created a broadened learning experience for students and ample opportunities to interact with faculty. Also central to the design concept was a spatial cube measuring thirty by thirty by fifteen feet that was repeated and varied according to the terrain. Materials such as concrete, brick, and wood were chosen for ease of construction, durability, availability, and low cost.

David O. McKay Special Events Center and Physical Education Complex
800 West University Parkway
Utah Valley State College
1996
FFKR

Utah Valley State College (now Utah Valley University) built the David O. McKay Special Events Center because of significant enrollment increases and inadequate existing facilities. The new complex provides a place for local sporting events, educational seminars, concerts, large and small business meetings, trade shows, and other college, community, and county events and includes two linked buildings—a smaller-scale physical education, dance, and activities building and a much larger special events arena. Both buildings continue the theme of the campus-wide circulation systems, with strong horizontal lines and planes, contrasting use of concrete and red brick wall surfaces, flat roofs, and open courtyard and public plazas for common spaces. The arena provides seating for seventy-four thousand for basketball games and five thousand for hockey. Major seating groups are retractable, and when the upper seating bowl is retracted four additional basketball courts become available for use by the Physical Education program. The Intermountain Chapter of the American Concrete Institute awarded the building an Award for Excellence in Concrete, and the Utah AIA gave the David O. McKay Special Events Center and Physical Education Complex a 1996 Award for Excellence in Architecture.

Major building elements are exposed throughout, and materials include architectural concrete columns and beams, glass with aluminum frame infill, face brick infill, a steel roof, and a concrete floor. Transparency and views help create a coherent and comprehensible campus landscape.

Stratton House / Orem City Hall
870 West Center Street
1924

George Stratton, the wealthy owner of Stratton Fruit Growers, owned eighty acres of land near the intersection of State and Center Streets. The family sold the house for $14,000 to the town of Orem for a new town hall in 1938. Besides the town offices, the building housed the post office and library until 1969.

The Stratton House is a two-story Prairie-style house with a modified four-square plan that sits on a raised concrete foundation with reddish-brown brick walls and a slight glazed finish. Enlivening the wall surface, the bricks are variegated and range from light orange to dark brown and are laid in rowlock courses. A concrete stringcourse runs around the house just below the upper-story windows, emphasizing the horizontality of the design and the division between spaces. The low-pitched hipped roof has asphalt shingles but was originally covered with Spanish roof tiles.

Like many other historic properties, this structure was extremely modified after

2010, including an addition that is out of proportion with the original building, and alterations throughout the exterior.

Lakeview
Lakeview Tithing Office / Bunnell Creamery
Utah Highway 114
1899
Leslie L. Bunnell

When Leslie L. Bunnell constructed this building in 1899, he thought it would be a creamery. He and his father, Stephen I. Bunnell, were successful dairymen, and this would be the headquarters of their operation for a number of years. As the first creamery in Lakeview, it provided milk, cheese, and butter for an unincorporated farming community between Provo and Utah Lake. Bunnell's family of five children lived in the rooms on the west side of the creamery. He eventually he sold the building to the LDS Church for use as a tithing office, when it served to store grain and other tithing commodities.

The one-story Lakeview Tithing Office is a brick building topped by a hipped roof. At the facade is an impressive frame and a false front with decoration typical of small-town commercial buildings of the era—corbeling along its upper edge, jigsaw-cut decorative elements in the wooden arches, rock-faced shoulder arches over the opening's shed roof, and a rear entrance under the eaves of the main roof.

Provo
Brigham Young University
Campus Drive and 1230 North
1875

Brigham Young founded Brigham Young Academy to combine religious with secular education for Mormon youth in 1875. Sponsored by Provo leaders Abraham O. Smoot and Jesse Knight as well as Young himself until his death in 1877, the school was headed by German LDS convert Karl G. Maeser between 1876 and 1892. By the end of the century, Brigham Young Academy had seven hundred students. From the first, the academy offered teaching degrees, expanding over time to offer both bachelor of science and bachelor of arts degrees after 1902. A women's division was headed by Young's daughter Susa Young Gates, and one of his other daughters, Zina Presendia Young Williams, taught home economics classes there as well.

Lewis Hall was the first Brigham Young Academy site in downtown Provo, occupying first a rehabilitated commercial space and then a variety of other places throughout the downtown area; at one point the school was temporarily located in a ZCMI warehouse. In 1892, the school dedicated a new academy building on University Avenue in 1892. The first new building located away from this site was the Maeser Building, constructed in 1911 on Temple Hill. The rest of the campus expanded nearby. Brigham Young High School remained at Academy Square until the 1960s.

Today, Brigham Young University is the largest church-sponsored school in the entire United States, with 31,441 undergraduate students in 2020. Under Ernest L. Wilkinson's administration between 1951 and 1971, the campus underwent significant physical expansion. Wilkinson managed a multimillion-dollar expansion—almost 350 academic, administrative, residential, and related buildings—and BYU was a changed world when his administration ended. Since that time, a series of university presidents have maintained a close relationship with the LDS Church leadership and have expanded the mission of the university to include a law school and other nationally respected graduate programs.

Harold B. Lee Library
Marriott Library Expansion
Campus Drive and 1230 North
1961 (original), 1999 (expansion)
FFKR

The Harold B. Lee Library was first built in 1961 and was designed by Bob Fowler at FFKR to house Brigham Young University's library collection for the growing student body until the late 1990s, when BYU hired FFKR to design a three-story, 235,000-square-foot underground addition and an 85,000-square-foot remodel of the main campus library, doubling the original size. Landscaping and walkways disguise the expansion and render it invisible from the site.

Although it is largely underground, the library space feels surprisingly light and airy. Preserving open space was a primary consideration in the library expansion design. The resolution was unique in a variety of ways. Burtch Beall and Associates from Salt Lake City worked with BSHA Design Group Inc. out of San Diego and Gunnar Birkerts from Birmingham, Michigan. The design team wished to preserve daylight in the building and bring it into the underground floors. The design includes five skylights, which have two incisions with window walls, and three light courts to add day lighting, an important move in making the subterranean library space psychologically attractive. These also provide transitional zones or separations between the new and old buildings. Interestingly, the addition includes 210,000 square feet on two floors, the equivalent of the 210,000 square feet covering the five floors of the original building. The addition includes classrooms, study areas, a two-hundred-seat auditorium, and a beautiful special collections area with exhibit, work, and archive areas.

Region B

Silver Row
621–645 West 100 North
1890

Although row houses were common on the East Coast in late nineteenth-century cities, they were far less common in Utah. The brick Silver Row, built in 1890 and owned by David P. Felt, a publisher and printer born in Salt Lake City, is an example of a multifamily housing unit in Provo. Consisting of five separate residential units, the apartments are arranged in a line under a common gabled roof. In total, the structure measures about 120 square feet and is a single story tall. In terms of details, the Silver Row combines Greek Revival and Eastlake characteristics and is basically symmetrical.

Although they share conjoined walls, each apartment is an individual home and is roughly twenty-four feet long, similar to the rectangular cabin-form house type. Apartments are entered by separate doors that are centered between two double-hung windows. Segmental relieving arches with applied decorative infill are found over the doors, and a small wall gable contains Victorian details—decorative carved wooden panels along the eaves of each gable with round-arched cutouts.

Thomas N. Taylor House
342 North 500 West
1908

Evidence of the commercial growth and prosperity of Provo at the turn of the century is seen in a group of impressive, high-styled homes of wealthy entrepreneurs near downtown. Both architecturally and historically significant, these buildings established Provo as an important urban center fully in line with the aesthetic and cultural aspirations of the Gilded Age. Like houses on South Temple in Salt Lake City in the same era, these houses reflect the growing wealth that resulted from the mining industries of the period and range in style from the Victorian Eclecticism of the Knight-Allen House to the Craftsman materiality of the W. Lester Mangum House. Here, rather than deriving their wealth from Park City mines, many of the homeowners were investors or players in mining or related activities in the Tintic Mining District some thirty miles southwest of Provo.

Provo was an important commercial and trade center because of both the mining industry and Brigham Young University. By the end of the century, Provo was the state's third largest city, with a diversified economy and significant communication and transportation systems. Many prominent LDS Church leaders lived in Provo, including Thomas N. Taylor.

Taylor managed his father's furniture store, which was eventually called Taylor Brothers, and he was president of the 1904 Provo Building and Loan Society and the 1906 Farmers and Merchants Bank. Taylor was Provo's mayor between 1900 and 1903 and conducted an unsuccessful bid for governor of Utah as a Democrat in 1920.

This Classical Box–style building is two and a half stories tall with Classical detailing, irregular massing, and a basically unaltered condition and makes a proud statement about the family's prestige and contribution to Provo.

Provo Third Ward Chapel and Amusement Hall
105 North 500 West
1903
Richard Watkins

When the LDS Provo Ward divided in 1901 into three new wards, the new Third Ward in the Utah Stake included the oldest section of Provo. Moving away from the more common Classicism of early Utah churches, the Provo Third Ward meetinghouse uses the vocabulary of English Parish Gothic architecture. Designed by architect Richard Watkins, the building has a tall, finely detailed vestry tower with a large Roman-arched bay; thick, tall rectangular windows; and red sandstone lintels above. Corbeled brickwork delineates the next level, and a brick panel with the building inscription engraved in stone is found on the east side. Four pairs of tall brick Roman-arched, open-air bays create the belfry, with more corbeled courses above, and finally, the tower is topped by decorative wooden molding at the base of a two-tiered, segmented, conical steeple, topped by a metal weathervane.

An impressive gable is found at the front of the facade along with a beautiful Roman window with five delicate Gothic-arched mullions and ornate lead-framed and stained-glass panes. At the south of the building the illusion of an apse is created where an interior staircase juts out, built of red stone and extending three stories above grade.

Provo West Co-op
450 West Center Street
1866

Brigham Young's strategic colonization of the Great Basin included the location of settlements along the foothills of the Wasatch Range about a day's carriage ride away from each other. Just two years after the Mormon pioneers arrived in Salt Lake Valley, they settled Provo, a day's buggy ride or forty miles to the south. Provo merchants functioned primarily as middlemen who brought goods to Provo from Salt Lake City to trade for farm products. Even though Young emphasized the value of home manufacturing, state goods were highly desired and valued. Andrew J. Stewart managed the

first store in town out of his home and built the building that would eventually become the Provo West Co-op in 1866. In the 1870s, the Church of Jesus Christ of Latter-day Saints began the cooperative merchandising movement because of the fear of competition from non-Mormons who were coming into the territory in larger numbers along with the railroad. Cooperatives were established in most Mormon towns, receiving state goods from the wholesale center at ZCMI in Salt Lake City.

Besides the Provo West and East Co-ops, a number of other cooperatives sprang up in Provo during the 1870s—the co-op boot and shoe store, grist mill, pottery shop, woolen mills, brickyard, stock yard, meat market, and clothing, tailoring, and drug stores. Most Mormon merchants in Provo became stockholders by putting their stores and goods into the pool, and they also became directors, superintendents, clerks, and investors in the Provo Co-op institutions.

The original section of the Provo West Co-op building has an adobe and wooden core built in 1866, speaking volumes about the scarcity of building materials for the first generation. Not long before it closed, in 1890, a brick facade was added to make it look like other commercial institutions with a three-bay facade. A heavy cornice with scrolls at the corners separates the first from the second levels, and arches with typical Victorian Eclectic ornamentation along with segmented brick arches are above each set of windows.

Russell Spencer Hines Mansion
383 West 100 South
1895
Richard K. A. Kletting

Premier Utah architect Richard K. A. Kletting, the architect of the Utah State Capitol,

Russell Spencer Hines Mansion

designed this Victorian house in 1895. It was built with pressed brown and orange brick produced by the Provo Pressed Brick Company, and the lintels, sills, and trim add to the textural richness of the wall surface, as does the cobblestone foundation. Overall the mass is square, with four extended gabled wings at each corner. The two-and-a-half-story building has the equivalent of four facades. Each is elaborately decorated with tall, square window bays with stained-glass transoms, and corbeled brick belt courses mark the line between the upper and lower floors. A corbeled band of dentils runs around the building under the cornice.

Local entrepreneur R. Spencer Hines made his fortune in mining, business, and real estate. Always considered a showcase, the house advertised economic success in a time of economic instability in Provo and established the position of Hines and his wife, Kitty Ann Leetham Hines, in Provo society.

Brigham Young Academy
Between 500 and 600 North and between University Avenue and 100 East
1884–1891
Joseph Don Carlos Young

The Brigham Young Academy buildings form the sentimental core of Provo. Created on October 16, 1875, by church president Brigham Young, the Brigham Young Academy was the pinnacle of a system of schools throughout Utah Territory. Its first principal, Warren N. Dusenberry, resigned after just one year to practice law, and Karl Maeser, a German immigrant and teacher, ushered the school through its first decades to a position of prominence.

Local church leaders Abraham O. Smoot and Jesse Knight sponsored the school until 1897, when the first presidency of the Church of Jesus Christ of Latter-day Saints assumed primary financial responsibility. The name changed to Brigham Young University in 1903, when it moved from being a normal school to a university dedicated to church theology and the trust that "nothing shall be taught in any way conflicting with the principles of the Gospel."[9]

The school occupied the block between 500 and 600 North facing University Avenue and included a complex of buildings— the Academy, College, Training School, and Arts Buildings—and across 500 North were the Women's Gymnasium and Blacksmith Shop. The earliest Brigham Young Academy building burned down in 1884 and was replaced by a building designed by Joseph Don Carlos Young, the son of Brigham Young, part of the Young dynasty of architects and designers.

The Academy Building constructed between 1884 and 1891 is an exuberant, flamboyant Victorian Eclectic structure with a wealth of decorative detail and variation. The principal feature is a Queen Anne steeple tower rising above the main entry vestibule, adorned by louvers, decorative brackets, pilasters, and a spiked roof. To both sides are Chateauesque gabled facades, corbeled brickwork at the cornice, gables, and arched and rounded bays. The College Hall joined the Academy Building in the middle of the block.

Richard C. Watkins, well-known designer of schools during the era, designed the Missionary and Preparatory Arts Building in 1904. This three-story brick structure's hipped roof, roughly square plan, and Renaissance Revival detailing combined segmental-, square-, and Roman-arched bays, double entrance doors, and sidelight panels for a handsome effect.

Watkins also designed the Training School in 1902 using a vocabulary similar to that of the Arts Building but rectangular in plan, oriented toward the corner of the block on a forty-five-degree angle, with three stories and a hipped roof. The Women's Gymnasium was built across the

Brigham Young Academy

street in 1912 and was Neoclassical in style. In total, the six major buildings of the lower campus have different architectural styles but are similar in materiality and height.

Provo East Central Historic District
100 East to 600 East, 500 North to 500 South
1860s

Provo features beautiful examples of commercial, residential, and institutional architecture from virtually every architectural style and building material of the historic period. The area of the city designated as the Provo East Central Historic District by the National Register of Historic Places includes a fifty-square-block residential area with buildings constructed between the 1860s and 1940s between 100 East and 600 East and between 500 North and 500 South. The district is bordered on the north by apartment neighborhoods of BYU students, on the east by newer residential subdivisions, on the south by industrial neighborhoods, and on the west by the city's central business district.

Different architectural eras are expressed through style, material, and placement on the block. Pioneer residences were typically I-shaped houses or simple rectangles built near one corner of the block, and barns, gardens, and small outbuildings like chicken coops, granaries, and root cellars filled the remaining space. In terms of type, they are hall-parlor, central-passage, or cross-wing houses, which illustrates the arrangement of interior spaces as much as exterior form. Eventually the lot was subdivided and new houses built in a series of waves. Victorian cottages, bungalows, Period Revival cottages, and a few modern buildings were built as the lots were divided into increasingly smaller units.

In the wake of the pioneer generation of buildings were the Victorian and Picturesque era houses, with distinctions that are about mass and detail. The most popular Victorian style in this Provo neighborhood was Victorian Eclectic. Another popular house is the bungalow. As a group, these houses are rectangular and have the short end facing the street, unlike the earlier I-shaped houses, with wide porches and modest Arts and Crafts detailing. Other early twentieth-century housing types are Period Revival cottages, and modest residences with English Tudor or English

Provo East Central Historic District

Knight Block

Cottage detailing and massing. The most elaborate and monumental dwellings in this part of Provo are along Center Street, east of University Avenue.

Adobe was a common building material among the earliest generation of homes, although few remain. A one-story, hall-parlor adobe house was located at 105 East 400 South. Adobe bricks were usually covered with stucco in an attempt to dress up the appearance of the house and to protect the bricks from deterioration. Frame structures or rock buildings were rare in this neighborhood.

A fired-brick business began in Provo in the mid-1860s, lending new variety in building materials. Red and yellow brick structures replaced their plainer gray adobe predecessors. Most of the nearby commercial buildings on University Avenue and Center Street were constructed with a combination of brick and stone.

Knight Block
1–13 East Center Street; 20–24 North University Avenue
1900
Richard Watkins

Commanding a dominant position at the intersection of University Avenue and Center Street, one of the best-known landmarks in downtown Provo is the Knight Block, a three-story rectangular building that measures about 55 feet by 118 feet and has two facades that face both University and Center. A flat-roofed clock tower with large stone arches at the base extends over the roofline of the rest of the building.

A range of window sizes and shapes adorns the wall surface, and there are hexagonal ceramic tiles on the floors of the first level. Much of the original woodwork—banisters, balustrades, doors, hardware, and other decorative work—remains throughout the building.

The Knight Block was the financial head-quarters of prominent Provo businessman Jesse Knight, marking the movement of the city from a farming town to an important regional business center. Knight achieved his wealth in mining, ranching, finance, and industry but was also recognized locally as a community leader. The Utah Democratic Convention offered him unanimous support to run for governor of Utah, but he turned the opportunity down.

Utah County Courthouse
100 East Center Street
1920–1926
Joseph Nelson
Utah County's Neoclassical courthouse is a dominant feature on University Avenue between Center Street and 100 South.

Striking with its bright oolite limestone exterior, its projecting pavilion and sculptural pediment, and its impressive central entrance staircase, the building speaks of a public governmental building with its choice of the Classical style, placing it alongside similar buildings in the state and the nation. But in Utah, this is one of the best. Lavish materials were used throughout—steps formed with granite from Little Cottonwood Canyon, white oolite limestone from quarries in both Manti and Ephraim, pink marble interior staircases and balustrades, and gray Alaskan marble for some of the interior floors. Architect Joseph Nelson designed the sculpture for the pediment, which was created by Joseph Conradi, a Salt Lake City artist.

Utah County Courthouse.
Photograph by Ben PL, CC A-SA 2.0.

Entrepreneurial Residences of Turn-of-the-Century Provo
Harvey H. Cluff House
174 North 100 East
1877

The 1877 one-and-a-half-story Harvey H. Cluff House blends a highly original combination of vernacular temple-form elements and the Gothic Revival style. It is a brick building with a central, symmetrical, rectangular mass and two smaller side wings that meet the main section at right angles, making a rare cross-axial plan more likely to have Greek Revival rather than Gothic Revival detailing as was traditional. Both were popular in Utah between 1870 and 1890, but not on the same building.

The most distinctive feature is that half of an octagonal-framed bay window projects from the ground floor of the central axis with a balcony, setting the home apart from its neighbors. Curvilinear bargeboards on the gables and eaves are headed by Greek Revival pediments.

Harvey H. Cluff was a well-known Provo businessman and church leader who joined the LDS Church in Kirtland, Ohio, before he moved west with his family in the late 1840s and to Provo in 1850. Best known for his role as the superintendent of the Provo Lumber and Manufacturing Company and the construction manager of the Provo Tabernacle and the Academy Building of Brigham Young Academy, Cluff was also a bishop, a counselor in the Utah Stake Presidency, a mission president of the Sandwich Islands in 1879, and a polygamist with three wives.

Samuel H. Allen House and Carriage House
135 East 200 North
1896

Dr. Samuel H. Allen moved to Provo in 1896 to set up a medical practice and built

Samuel H. Allen House and Carriage House

this home with local craftsmen and native materials. He owned the home for only six years before he sold it in 1902 to attorney Samuel R. Thurman, who was chair of the committee that drafted the first platform of the Provo People's Party in 1882. When the Mormons joined national parties, Thurman became a Democrat and eventually a judge on the Utah Supreme Court.

The next owner of the house was John W. Taylor, the son of Mormon Church president John Taylor. An apostle of the LDS Church, John W. Taylor was best known for his refusal to conform to the Manifesto of 1890, which ended official plural marriage. After marrying his sixth wife in 1915, he was excommunicated from the Mormon Church.

The Allen house straddles two styles— the irregular asymmetry of the Queen Anne and the symmetry and Classical detailing of turn-of-the-century Greek Revival styles. Basically, the house is a square mass with a

pyramidal roof. On each side of the classically detailed entrance porch are bays with prominent gabled roofs—one flat and one half octagonal, projecting about three feet from the wall. The entrance porch projects about six feet between the two bays.

A large carriage house built with matching brick and a clerestory roof that runs the entire length of the building sits behind the house. The owners of the house in 1963, Shirley and Monroe Paxman, received a grand prize for their tasteful and practical renovation of the house from *Better Homes and Gardens*.

Jesse Knight House
185 East Center Street
1905
Ware and Treganza

During his lifetime, Jesse Knight was the wealthiest and best-known entrepreneur in Provo. As a mining entrepreneur who was also successful in other businesses,

Jesse Knight House

he helped Provo's economy grow, and his home mirrors his wealth. Ware and Treganza, well-known architects of the Commercial Club building in Salt Lake City as well as numerous other significant properties, designed this 1905 Colonial Revival Box, the only one in town. Unique in terms of style, size, and Knight himself, the home is distinguished by many carefully crafted characteristics of the style including swan's-neck pedimented dormers, corner quoins capped by Ionic capitals resembling pilasters, and rounded bay windows.

Key to Knight's wealth was the Tintic mining area, where he amassed substantial property and established his own mining towns, what some called the "cleanest mining camps in the West" because of his strict rules of morality for his workers.[10] Knight's wealth included Provo real estate, extensive holdings in farming and cattle properties in Canada, a bank, and the Provo Woolen Mills, later known as the Knight Woolen Mills.

practice—plural marriage—although Smoot was not himself a polygamist. Smoot was elected to the Senate five times before he was defeated by Elbert D. Thomas in 1932 in a Democratic landslide. During his years in Congress, Smoot was a prominent national figure, well known for his distinctive economic policies, particularly his approach to the tariff.

Similar in every way to the Spencer Hines Mansion, the Smoot House, designed by Richard K. A. Kletting, is also Victorian, with an asymmetrical plan, multiple roof planes, and decorative excess. Overall it projects a feeling of stateliness, dignity, and wealth. It is roughly square, with four corners accented by extended gabled wings, and it is well suited to a corner lot because each side reads like a facade. Brick walls rise above a stone foundation, and much of the decoration is rusticated stone or corbeled brick. Carefully molded exterior cornices return across the base of the gables.

Reed Smoot House
183 East 100 South
1892
Richard K. A. Kletting

This National Historic Landmark was the home of Reed Smoot, the son of Abraham O. Smoot, the first mayor of Provo City and a prominent LDS leader. LDS Church apostle Reed Smoot was elected to the U.S. Senate in 1902, and his appointment became the focal point of a three-year investigation of the Senate Committee on Privileges and Elections considering the legality of a senator belonging to a church that advocated a felonious

Reed Smoot House

John R. Twelves House
287 East 100 North
1902

This charming Queen Anne Victorian cottage is built of painted brick with sandstone foundations, abundant gingerbread, and overall a richly detailed and textured wall surface. An abundant first-story porch wraps around the home to the side, with a rounded dome at the corner, a common Queen Anne feature. The roof stretches toward the center in a series of levels—the roof covering the porch, a broad expanse of roof with edges that move in and out with the mass of the house itself, and a gabled roof that stretches toward the back, coming to a peak above the pitch of the broadside of the main roof moving toward the front. A parapet sits on top of the bay on the opposite side of the facade from the porch's cornice and culminates in an interesting combination of forms.

Hannah Maria Libby Smith House
315 East Center Street
1878

The list of former residents of Provo's Center Street reads like an inventory of the town's rich and famous. Hannah Maria Libby Smith is a good example of both. As a plural wife of Mormon apostle George A. Smith, Hannah left Nauvoo in the winter of 1846 and lived in Winter Quarters with her fellow plural wives before coming to Utah. Their son John Henry Smith became first counselor in the First Presidency of the Mormon Church, and his son George Albert Smith became the eighth president of the LDS Church. They were the equivalent of Mormon blue bloods.

This single-story L-shaped orange brick building is a modest variation on the simple pioneer *I* house with two wings on each side of the *L* and a porch at the center. Woodwork was grained to simulate oak in several rooms, a favorite decorative practice in pioneer Utah along with twelve-foot ceilings, and cellulose wainscoting in one room. A brick granary was originally located about twelve feet north of the home but is now attached to the house by a shed-roofed kitchen addition with walls sheathed by novelty siding.

Knight-Mangum House
381 East Center Street
1908
Walter E. Ware

The size and scale of many of the houses along Provo's Center Street are striking reminders of the wealth in Utah County at the turn of the century. W. Lester Mangum was a son-in-law of Jesse Knight, one of Provo's best-known local businessmen.

Knight-Mangum House

Mangum and his wife commissioned Walter E. Ware and Alberto O. Treganza to design the house in 1908 and Alexandis Brothers from Provo to build it.

W. Lester Mangum was born in Nephi, met Jennie Knight while attending Brigham Young Academy, and became a leader in many of the family's businesses. He was vice president and manager of the American Colombian Corporation, a company that owned large tracts of land in South America. Like so many of Provo's successful entrepreneurs, he was also an ecclesiastical leader and a member of his LDS stake's high council.

This house is an impressively sized Craftsman bungalow, one of the best examples in the state. As is typical of the Craftsman style, natural materials and textures are celebrated, and exposed and important stylistic elements of the house include purlins, decorative brackets along the roofline, a flat-roofed single-story porch with exposed rafters that wraps around the southeast corner, and unusual clinker brick for the first-story walls. The ample broadside of the roof faces the street, but breaking up the line, a gabled roof tops the open porch that runs across the front.

Knight-Allen House
390 East Center Street
1899
Richard C. Watkins

Richard C. Watkins was best known for his school architecture, but throughout central Utah he was also known for his residential designs. Watkins most likely designed this house for J. William Knight, a well-known Provo businessman and son of Jesse Knight, in 1899, the year of J. William's marriage. This house displays a fascination with exotic forms—a two-story turret with a Moorish domed roof, Classical Revival

details, and a combination of Romanesque Revival, Italianate, and Victorian pattern book designs that come together in this unique Victorian Eclectic design.

Gabled roofs project out toward the east, west, and north, proudly announcing the various elevations. The walls feature a range of textures, materials, and shapes: brackets under the eaves, bricks set at angles at the top of the turrets, coping at the top of the parapet, and stained-glass windows. A variety of window shapes are found around the house, including round-arched windows, a keyhole window, a circular window, and rectangular windows with transoms.

Charles E. Loose House
383 East 200 South
1893

Provo magnate Charles Loose built his family home next to the Maeser School building, making it easy for his children to use the school's playground. Fully in line with the Progressive Era's belief in the connection between physical and moral health, playgrounds promised a generation of strong citizens, morally and physically fit from the time they were young. As a result, on November 11, 1893, Loose decided to buy the quarter lot to the north of the Maeser School and gave it to the Board of Education as the start of a playground project, to the delight of the faculty and student body alike.

The Central Mining Company made Loose rich, and he was one of the most prominent non-Mormon businessmen in town. As befitted his wealth and sophistication, his house combines the Shingle and Eastlake styles, both known for their distinctive woodwork. An ample veranda provided comfortable sitting space for the family, facing the street on warm summer nights.

Maeser School
150 South 500 East
1898
Richard C. Watkins

Maeser School

Without question Karl Gottfried Maeser was the premier educator in nineteenth-century Utah, best known as the principal of Brigham Young Academy. After immigrating to Utah from Germany, Maeser operated a series of schools before Brigham Young asked him in 1876 to establish an academy in Provo for the LDS Church. Brigham Young Academy reflected Maeser's philosophy of education. Recognizing Maeser's important contribution, Heber J. Grant said of him, "Some of our outstanding men . . . attribute largely to the force of character of Brother Maeser and the impression made upon them while under his influence their successes in life."[11]

Distinguished Utah architect Richard Watkins designed Maeser School with the Romanesque Revival vocabulary popular between 1880 and 1900 in Utah. Here the Romanesque lends an air of solemnity and seriousness in a symmetrically massed building with a hipped roof, boxed cornice, brackets supporting wide eaves, and a corbeled brick frieze with an architrave at the top.

Perhaps the most distinctive features of the house, and common to the Romanesque, are a large masonry arch, a fanlight transom over double doors, engaged columns of rusticated brick, and masonry bands with beehive caps accenting the entry. On the east facade is a central engaged tower with a gable that is similar to the Mission style of a 1912 addition. After 1898, four classrooms on each floor were filled with students.

Startup Candy Factory
534 South 100 West
1900

Opening for business in 1900, the two-and-a-half-story brick Startup Candy Factory building mixes Victorian styles into an eclectic and unique combination. The original part of the building has a hipped roof, and later additions have flat roofs. Decoration centers on windows and doors, brick corbeling, and stringcourses, as was customary for a commercial structure. The main rectangular mass has yellowish-pink brick walls and a stone foundation that formed a water table. In each of the facade's five bays, windows with segmental arches above and three tiers of voussoirs create a regular pattern on the walls to the sides.

Ripley's *Believe It or Not* says that William Startup's Startup Candy Factory made the first candy bar in the United States and was one of Utah's first candy companies. Also famous for its "Magnolias," a predecessor of the breath mint with a gooey, flavored center, the Startup factory did its own printing and box production and was the state's first factory to give employees a profit-sharing bonus.[12]

Superintendent's Residence
1079 East Center Street
Utah State Hospital
1934
Public Works Administration

Utah benefited significantly from the appropriations of the New Deal's PWA program. Infrastructure projects that were more expensive than local communities could afford proceeded with the support of the federal government. Built in 1934 under the PWA, the Superintendent's Residence was part of a larger $124,000 project at the 1885 Utah State Hospital that included a remodel of the Central Administration Building and improvements to the water supply.

Rather than being designed in the era's popular modern styles, the superintendent's house is a one-and-a-half-story brick Colonial Revival house with a gabled roof, and an entrance portico offset to one side that is more PWA Moderne than Colonial. The low-pitched gabled roof makes a subtle, even abstract reference to Colonial Revival motifs. Art Deco ornamental lamps on pilaster-like panels frame the entrance, and above is a frieze and stylized cornice and a low-relief balcony.

Recreation Center
1300 East Center Street
Utah State Hospital
1936–1937
Works Progress Administration

One of the most unusual New Deal structures built with funds from the WPA is the eight-hundred-seat amphitheater at the Utah State Hospital. Built between 1936 and 1937 on a three-acre parcel of land, the amphitheater with its eighteen tiers of seats

nestles against a steep hillside at the base of the mountains that shelter Provo to the east. Constructed virtually entirely with stone, the attached rooms and two-story towers at the southeast and northwest corners have crenellations along the top like those of a fort.

Provo Tabernacle/Temple
50 South University Avenue
1883–1896
William H. Folsom

The first Provo Tabernacle was constructed from 1856 to 1867 with a seating capacity of 1,100 to 1,800 people. By 1882, the LDS Church decided to triple the size, designating a building committee to hire an architect. A 1914 description of the building emphasized the size and cost of the project: "Located in Provo, Utah and erected between 1883 and 1896, it is made of brick and stone, the superstructure being of brick. The building measures 128 by 75 feet and 40 feet to the square with a seating capacity of three thousand for a cost of between $80,000 and $90,000. There is one auditorium and a vestry. William H. Folsom was the architect. Building supervisors were Elder H. H. Cluff, and later, Elder Reed Smoot. The building was so far completed that the general conference of the Church of Jesus Christ of Latter-day Saints was held in it in April, 1897."[13]

The tabernacle was important as a community meeting place where virtually all joint meetings, special church assemblies, and the semiannual conference in October were held. This was where local Mormons received instruction from their ecclesiastical leaders at the church headquarters in Salt Lake City, unifying the Latter-day Saints of Utah Valley and connecting them to the ecclesiastical mission of the central church.

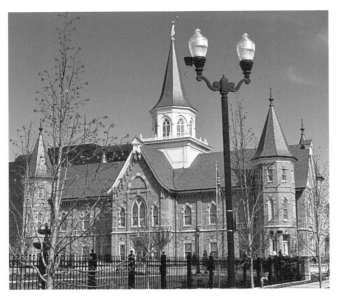

Provo Tabernacle/Temple

arches, large Gothic windows with central mullions, and a corbeled dentil run with tiny Gothic arches along the top of the gable. The building has a central tower that reaches 140 feet.

After a devastating fire on December 17, 2010, the LDS Church decided to remodel the tabernacle for use as a second temple in Provo; it opened in January 2016.

William H. Ray House
415 South University Avenue
1898

This Victorian Eclectic mansion presents an exuberant love of material, texture, and form on Provo's University Avenue. Distinguished most by the dominant round tower form to the side of the asymmetrical facade, the house has porches and entrances on both sides, topped by two rows of windows and a strong gabled element capped by a short parapet that demands attention and makes both sides read like facades. In this the tower is the turning point, orienting both sides toward the street.

Novell Campus
1800 South Novell Place
1993
Valentiner & Crane

Novell's campus in south Provo is a stunning example of the interactions between buildings and the creation of an active public space. Contrasting dramatically with the two- or three-story buildings that line Center Street in Provo's commercial district, the Novell buildings are strikingly vertical, glittering tributes to an entirely different era of economic growth. The exterior of this complex of buildings doesn't reveal the

In the hierarchy of LDS Church architecture, the tabernacle was second only to the temple. Like the other tabernacles built by the church in the last half of the nineteenth century, the Provo Tabernacle is a high-styled building constructed with the finest available materials and the highest level of local craftsmanship, and it is uniquely suited to the particular functional demands of the church. A major symbol as well of the commitment and sacrifice of the pioneer settlers of this place, it is a significant architectural landmark in Utah County.

Formed in the shape of a cross with a split-level plan and two full stories, this Gothic Revival structure best accommodated large gatherings of church members rather than small religious instruction groups or special social events and was the stage for assemblies and large-scale meetings. Gothic features in the towers include segmented bays with corbeled arches and keystones, molded cornices, and segmented, conical steeples tapering slightly at the base. There are also indented Gothic

complexity of the activities inside, and they are thoroughly modern in their anonymity and use of contemporary materials. Specialized computer research and development laboratories, communications, and data networking drove the conceptualization of the interior space.

Springville
Patrick L. and Rose O. Ward House
511 South Main Street
1900

By the turn of the twentieth century, the railroad had come to Springville, accompanied by a wave of prosperity. Patrick Ward was a superintendent and stationmaster for the Denver and Rio Grande Western Railroad in Springville. The home he built for his family exemplifies the economic success the railroad brought to the county. Beyond the simple utilitarianism of earlier buildings, this house has fired brick in multiple colors, elaborate woodwork, and a more complex plan. The railroad brought greater exposure to the outside world, new

materials and technologies for building, and a more stratified local economy. This generation of houses is the by-product of that change.

This well-preserved Victorian Eclectic home is one and a half stories and has a central block with projecting bays. At the center, the roof rises in a pyramidal shape and a bracketed frieze divides the walls and roof. Flaring eaves at the edges of the roof also add interest, as does a large wood-shingled dormer window on the front elevation. A one-story porch has Tuscan order columns, a gabled roof, and carved wooden swag decoration on the cornice.

Springville High School Mechanical Arts Building
443 South 200 East
1909
Ashton & Evans Architects

The Springville Mechanical Arts Building is part of the original complex of buildings at Springville High School after 1909. The first building was a two-story

Springville High School Mechanical Arts Building

classroom (which has since been demolished), followed by a building twice as large
in 1914. The Mechanical Arts Building
was equipped to handle auto mechanics,
woodwork, hot and cold metal work, and
other vocational courses of study. Salt
Lake architects Ashton & Evans designed
the building. When it was finished, the
first class included 190 boys in the various departments. It was used until 1960,
when the high school was replaced. Since
1986 it has been used by the city's arts
commission.

The Springville High School Mechanical Arts Building is a one-story, horizontal
three-part building measuring one hundred
by sixty-five feet, with a flat roof. Light-
colored, precast concrete elements in the
Neoclassical style accent the entrance, and
heavy, textured brick is used for exterior
walls laid in a running bond pattern. The
horizontal lines of the building are emphasized by light-colored, precast coping cap-
ping the parapet walls, and a continuous
cornice that wraps around the front and

sides of the building about two feet below
the parapet cap.

Springville Carnegie Library
175 South Main Street
1932
Ware and Treganza

Springville's club women envisioned the
creation of a free public library for their
town, promoting literacy, civility, and
culture. Laying the groundwork for the
construction of a new library in 1916, these
women set a room aside at the Mendenhall
Bank and began a serious book and mag-
azine drive, storing the donations in the
bank. Before they had a professional librarian, club members took turns checking
out books and lobbied for a bond election
to be held in the summer of 1920 to raise
funds to match the $10,000 Carnegie grant
given to partially fund the construction of a
town library. They hired some of the most
talented architects in the state. Salt Lake
architects Ware and Treganza drew up the
plans, the town bought a site for $2,000,

Springville Carnegie Library

and construction began. Under the direction of librarian Louisa Rowland, by 1932, the library had a circulation of 25,418 items, an increase of 328 percent from 1916, the year it operated out of the bank.

Springville Art Museum
126 East 400 South
1936
Claude Ashworth

Springville artist John Hafen gave the high school his painting *Mountain Stream* and launched the local art collection, which by the 1930s had grown to 150 paintings. Starting in 1921, the high school sponsored annual art exhibits with 200–300 paintings from Utah, national, and international artists. Within a decade the collection had outgrown its home at the high school and construction of a new home was planned.

WPA programs supported this type of project, which was completed for $100,000. Built entirely of reinforced concrete, the building was located on land owned by Nebo School District next to the high

school and was designed by architect Claude Ashworth. Springville sculptor Cyrus E. Dallin said at the dedication that art is "a divine thing. There is no other community in the United States which has done more per capita for art."[14]

This two-story stucco Spanish Colonial Revival building is distinguished by an irregular, asymmetrical plan, with walls finished with gunite (concrete applied with a pressure hose), a red-tiled roof, round-arched openings, and a decorative tower. The inside continues the Spanish Colonial theme with hand-troweled stucco walls, arched windows, fired red-tiled floors, and heavy red oak doors.

Springville Presbyterian Church
251 South 200 East
1892

Springville's first Protestant church, the Presbyterian Church of Springville, was built in 1892–93 and was the sponsor of the Hungerford Academy. Reverend George Leonard first came to Springville in 1877 to

Springville Art Museum

Springville Presbyterian Church

establish a mission school in a leased two-room adobe house and hired Anna Noble as the first teacher.

They built the academy with funds donated by Mrs. M. P. Hungerford of Westfield, New York, who sponsored the first high school education in town. Along with other Presbyterian schools, the academy helped encourage the territorial legislature to mandate public education at the turn of the century.

Although small, this compact wooden church features ambitious Gothic Revival details and a Romanesque Revival bell tower, complete with the following inscription: "by the Buckeye Bell Foundry 1885; Van Dozen and Toft, Cincinnati; In memory of Enos Palmer, M.D.; Artimitia Otis Palmer, his wife; Cuba, New York; Christ the Light of the World." There

is a high-pitched roof, and fish-scale and weatherboard siding. A rose window is on the wall at the back of the chapel and Moorish windows run along the sides.

Spanish Fork

Spanish Fork High School Gymnasium
300 South Main Street
1935
Public Works Administration

Perhaps an Art Deco building seems highly unlikely for a small town like Spanish Fork, but it was an incidental benefit of the New Deal's PWA programs. Modern buildings built throughout the state during this period exhibit the most contemporary styles from across the country. Like similar structures in Logan and Millard, the building has two main parts—a three-story gabled block that houses the gymnasium itself, and a smaller one- or two-story entrance/office complex with a flat roof that launches the stylistic motifs carried throughout the building.

Stylized capitals with low-relief, plant-like carvings top pilasters that break up the wall surface of the four-story facade into narrow vertical panels projecting through the molding coping at the edge of the roof and emphasizing the verticality of the building.

Spanish Fork Sugar Beet Factory
West of Spanish Fork near where Highway 6 and Highway 89 overlap
1916

The sugar beet industry was a significant economic venture in Utah, second only to mining and metal manufacturing. Sugar beets were first grown in Lehi in the 1880s with irrigation, and the Lehi factory was one of the most important sugar factory facilities in Utah. Built in the early 1900s and dependent on a "pipeline" of beets from Lehi, the Spanish Fork Sugar Factory operations were moved from Nampa, Idaho. The facility was completed in 1916 and owned by the Utah-Idaho Sugar Company, a commercial enterprise run by LDS Church leaders. In 1911, more than 2,300 acres were devoted to sugar beets in Spanish Fork, the largest acreage in any Utah town. The Spanish Fork facility was a beet slicing factory that processed 450 to 500 tons of beets daily, which were then shipped to Lehi to produce beet pulp. Rail lines were important for the transportation of beets, and other factories nearby in Payson, Springville, and Provo were also connected by rail. Some of these factories closed in the 1920s because of antitrust laws, and the Spanish Fork Sugar Factory closed in 1952 as sugar beets gave way to sugarcane, a more inexpensive source of sugar.

This early twentieth-century industrial complex included two-story wings on both sides of a central mass that was broken up into three main masses: two four-story wings with gabled roofs face the street (to the north), with subtle parapets at the roofline and shallow engaged pilasters interrupting the brick wall surface; and connecting the two masses on each side is a two-and-a-half-story section with the broadside of the rectangular mass facing the street.

Sri Radha Krishna Temple / Lotus Temple
8628 South State Road (311 West 8500 South, Spanish Fork)
1998

The most spectacular aspect of the Sri Radha Krishna Temple is the way it is situated on a small hill in the countryside outside Spanish Fork, Utah. When you approach it, you are startled by the appearance of it amid a traditional rural Utah landscape. Its brilliant white color and transparent structure set it apart and challenge your sense of solidity and permanence. Reflecting the onion domes, arcuate structure, and central dome of buildings in the Middle East, it was originally built to serve the devoted members of the International Society for Krishna Consciousness under the leadership of Charu Das (formerly Christopher Warden). Besides the building, a natural amphitheater is the scene of mass ceremonies and festivals that attract thousands of people, such as the Holi festival, often called the Festival of Colors, and a gala pageant of the epic Ramayana.

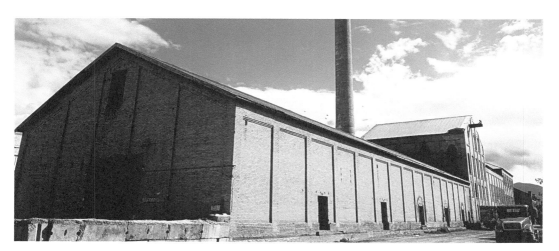

Spanish Fork Sugar Beet Factory.
Photograph by Sterling Brinkerhoff Own work, CC A-SA 4.0.

Sri Radha Krishna Temple / Lotus Temple

Payson
Payson Presbyterian Church
160 South Main Street
1882

Protestant missionaries came here from the 1870s to 1890s to operate schools and make converts among the dominant LDS culture. When the railroad came to Utah in 1869 non-Mormons began flooding into the state seeking mining opportunities in the state's mountains, establishing businesses, or claiming farmland. Several evangelical sects came as well—Baptists, Congregationalists, Methodists, and Presbyterians—all determined to find converts in the Great Basin kingdom. The Presbyterian missionaries came to Payson in the summer of 1877 and began worship services and a day school in a hall known as "Charlie Long's" or Independence Hall. The day school had forty-five students by 1881 and the Sabbath School thirty-nine.

The *Rocky Mountain Christian Advocate* ran a story about the dedication of the new church on November 2, 1882. "On the 2d inst. a new church was dedicated at Payson. The edifice is said to be one of the neatest and handsomest in Utah; it is built of brick, has gothic windows, and is divided into two departments by hoisting partitions, and will be used for church and school purposes. By the side of the church is a pleasant and convenient parsonage just finished. Rev. J. A. Smith, the pastor, is to be congratulated upon his success in pushing this enterprise to completion."[15] The familiar forms of the Gothic Revival were used for the Payson Presbyterian Church, constructed in 1882 in the midst of a Mormon-dominated town. This one-story brick building has a rectangular plan and a steeply pitched gabled roof with a bell tower.

Peteetneet School
10 South 600 East
1902
Richard C. Watkins

The Peteetneet School sits on one of the most imposing sites in the state—a bluff overlooking a field that stretches toward the center of town. This three-story stone building is distinctive in style, massing, and

Peteetneet School

site. Responding to the call for the state-wide consolidation of schools at the turn of the century, Payson raised enough money through a bond election to pay the $22,000 required to build a new school and completed construction in 1902. It was named for a chief of the Ute Indians who had historically inhabited the site before Mormon settlement.

An extraordinarily colorful building, the Peteetneet School has walls of rough, rich red sandstone and cream-colored brick, with hipped and gabled roofs, main entrances on both the west and east ends, and four classrooms on each floor. Each room has ceilings that rise as tall as twelve feet, with stained pine trim running along the doors, floors, and around the windows, creating a lofty space that surely must have inspired the students who sat quietly at their desks in the classrooms. Romanesque details include the use of massive rusticated reddish-brown sandstone, rounded arches, carved entablatures, and heavy rusticated stone sills. An unusual tower at the top has a pyramidal roof and Roman arches on each side.

Santaquin

Santaquin Junior High School
75 West 100 South
1935
Public Works Administration

Santaquin benefited from Franklin Roosevelt's New Deal PWA, a program that directed federal funds toward local public building projects. The Santaquin Junior High School building was constructed in 1935 in the PWA Moderne architectural style. As was typical of the buildings erected during this period, it exhibited abstract Classicism in a three-part symmetrical facade, with Classical pilasters and a corbeled frieze with pointed geometric figures. The facade includes a centrally placed double door entrance with a large transom window above.

Goshen

Old Goshen
1850s

Goshen was settled in the marshy alluvial plain on the edge of a lake near the foothills of a mountain range and was challenging land to farm. The Old Fort, called Sodom, was built in the spring of 1857 and covered two acres, with two rows of cedar posts filled with sod. Called by church headquarters, the Goshen pioneers were faithful and obedient, but challenged. Two years after they first came to the spot, they moved to higher land because their orchards and gardens were struggling, and once again in 1860 to the current location of Goshen proper—a town site that included forty square blocks measuring thirty square rods, with four families per block. The settlers built dugout homes, then log or adobe cabins with stone foundations. They abandoned their town in 1868, leaving behind the remnants of primitive dugouts and the stone foundations of their earliest homes.

Region B

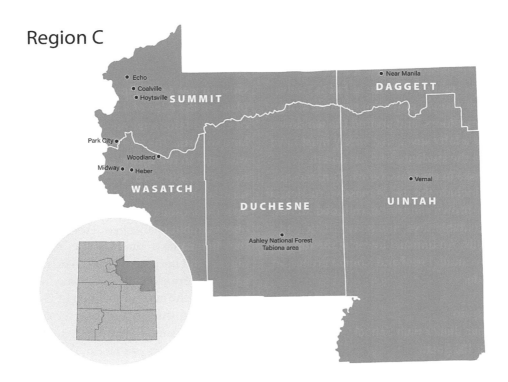

Region C

REGION C — Summit, Duchesne, Uintah, Daggett, and Wasatch Counties

Introduction

The Northern Shoshones inhabited the area that would become Summit County before white settlers came into the region. First Spanish explorers worked their way through the valleys between mountain ranges in the eighteenth century, bringing their new knowledge back with them to Spain. The Latter-day Saints struggled with the last part of their journey west into the Salt Lake Valley through Summit County and within five years came back to start settlements along the Weber River and along transportation routes through the region.

The Latter-day Saints entered the county through Echo Canyon, traveling along the Weber River, then over what would eventually be called Parley's Summit and down Parley's Canyon into Salt Lake Valley. Parley P. Pratt identified the tremendous value in the east-west route this path provided; it is now Interstate-80 and traverses the country from coast to coast.

White settlers founded towns in the county after 1859, on land that native peoples had navigated as they hunted hundreds of years before. The second wave of settlement outside Salt Lake City occurred next to the Weber River, which supplied water for irrigation and culinary purposes, promising a propitious future. Much of the county's history is the story of farming and stock raising.[1] But in the late nineteenth century, the area's economy diversified through mining opportunities, the discovery of oil resources in the 1870s, and eventually the storage of water.

During the mining boom of the 1870s and 1880s thousands of miners flooded into Park City hoping to strike it rich and extract wealth from area mines that produced silver, gold, lead, and zinc. In the first decade after the Mormon settlement of the region, Brigham Young favored settlement of agricultural communities throughout the territory rather than prospecting. When Colonel Patrick Edward Connor came to Utah with federal troops in 1862, he did the opposite and encouraged his men to use their extra time exploring mining opportunities. It is likely that his soldiers made the first discovery of silver in the mountains near Park City in 1868.[2] The most important breakthrough happened four years later with the discovery of a significant vein of silver, eventually known as the Ontario Mine. Many miners came from the West Coast and as far away as Wales, but the draw was the same: the promise of quick profits and sure wealth. Wealthy mining entrepreneurs built mansions along South Temple in Salt Lake City, but mining complexes, boardinghouses, saloons, and other service businesses lined Park City's streets, which clung to the bottom of the foothills and reflected geography rather than the orthogonal lines of Mormon villages in Summit County such as Coalville, Hoytsville, and Henefer.

In the mid-twentieth century, the same mountains that produced the original draw for mining attracted skiing enthusiasts from around the world, drawn by the variety of runs, the quality of powder, and the vast beauty of the Wasatch Range. Treasure Mountain, Park City Resort, and Deer Valley are international ski destinations.

Summit County

Echo
Echo School
3441 South Echo Road
1914

The town of Echo built this modest schoolhouse at a critical connecting hub of the Union Pacific Railroad. Used between 1914 and 1940, this rectangular two-story building has an entrance on the broadside facing the street and running parallel to the rail line, more like a house than a public building in Utah, but typical of railroad depot design of the period. The building transitioned between the consolidated schools of the early twentieth century and the one-room schoolhouses more typically built by the previous generation. Before the Echo School, students traveled to school at Coalville, the county seat.

Echo Canyon Breastworks
Off Interstate 80 near Echo
1857

The Echo Canyon Breastworks indicate the Mormons' anxiety over the advancement of Albert Sidney Johnston and his army of 2,500. President James Buchanan directed Johnston to bring the Mormon kingdom under federal control. General Daniel H. Wells organized the Mormon response, with 1,200 men who constructed the Echo Canyon Breastworks, including walls made of rocks of random sizes and shapes and laid irregularly without mortar, which rambled along the edge of Echo Canyon for 1.2 miles. The men also dammed the creek to direct the movement of troops as they proceeded through the canyon, and dug trenches that they hoped would stop them altogether.

Coalville
Summit County Courthouse
60 North Main Street
1903–1904
F. C. Woods and Company

This Romanesque Revival courthouse built in 1903–04 exhibits rough-textured, rock-faced coursed ashlars typical of the style; a two-and-a-half-story rectangular structure with a broad hipped roof; and a centrally located cross gable facing west. The main entry features a segmentally arched entry arcade with colonettes protruding from the wall, and deep-set double-hung windows with transoms on the second level. A square, slightly projecting tower rises from the second entry to the south, where there is a flat, three-story recession. Overall, the building creates an imposing fortress-like impression.

Partly in a political move to secure Coalville as the county seat, Summit County commissioners voted in May 1903 to build a new county building in Coalville and purchased a lot north of the LDS Stake House for $1,500. F. C. Woods and Company of Ogden designed the building and chose white sandstone from Summit County for the construction. Local workers

Summit County Courthouse

Region C

began work in August 1903 and continued until the weather became too severe, commencing again in the spring of 1904.

John Boyden House
47 West Center Street
1866

Nineteenth-century pattern books and carpenter guides helped perpetuate the shapes, details, and floor plans of the Victorian style. This two-story brick home known as the John Boyden House highlights familiar pattern-book design elements. The *T* cottage was a simple variation of the *I* house; it was one of the most popular housing types in nineteenth-century Utah and is found throughout the state. In this T-shaped plan, the main entrance and central passageway are at the front of the house next to the point where the side wing meets the main rectangular body of the house.

A projecting gable faces the street. Because of these steeply pitched gables and other decorative elements consistent with the style, the house would be considered Gothic Revival. One distinctive detail is the bracketed bay windows on both the north and east elevations, with relieved arches formed with stone and pronounced keystones at the top. Overall, it is an impressive statement of importance and prestige.

Local dignitary John Boyden achieved his wealth through the Coalville Co-op Store and owned Coalville's first pharmacy in the 1890s. He was known for both his public and private service as a county assessor, school board member, county recorder, three-term mayor, and bishop of the LDS ward, and he contributed to the county's coal industry as the secretary of the Park City Railroad Company.

John Boyden House

Hoytsville
Samuel P. Hoyt House
Interstate 80 and Creamery Lane
1863–1866

One of the most dignified pioneer-era houses in the state is the Samuel P. Hoyt House in Hoytsville, located a few miles south of Coalville in a picturesque spot along the Weber River.

This three-story house is made of carefully cut sandstone. It was clear from both the exterior and interior of the Hoyt House that it was the home of an important man during the 1860s: the house had thirteen rooms and nine fireplaces, three times what other houses nearby might have had. Considered an amenity at the time, the basement included a well that provided fresh water for the family. Special touches made the interior more elegant than was usual; some walls featured murals, and faux

painting on the staircase walls made them look like wood.

Samuel Hoyt was one of the first generation of converts who joined the LDS Church during Joseph Smith's time. Born in Chester, New Hampshire, Hoyt served a mission in Massachusetts before he immigrated to Utah in 1851, first settling in Fillmore, the territorial capital. Hoyt helped build the Territorial Capitol building. With the authority of a religious calling, Brigham Young chose him to settle the Weber River valley, and Hoytsville was named in his honor.

Besides his family's home, on this site Hoyt also built the county's first flour and grist mill, industries particularly important to a community in its formative stage. Always the entrepreneur, he also began a carding mill and a grocery store and eventually became a cattle rancher. Hoyt built

Samuel P. Hoyt House

a rock wall around his property, as tall as seven feet in places, during the perceived threat of the Black Hawk War (1866–67).

Park City
Kimball Hotel and Stage Stop
1 mile west of Silver Creek Junction, 3 miles east of Kimball Junction
1862

Immigrants, pioneers, and travelers on the way to somewhere else often moved through Echo and then Parley's Canyon before they descended into Salt Lake Valley. Weary from the long, arduous journey, many decided to stay for the night at a hotel and stage stop built by William Kimball in 1862. Luminaries such as Mark Twain, Walt Whitman, and Horace Greeley found lodging there.

The two-story stone hotel looked like houses in the area; it is a central-passage house with a front porch running the full length of the facade, which faces Highway 40. A side addition extended the interior space to provide food and housing for travelers.

Glenwood Cemetery
End of Silver King Drive, north of Park City Ski Resort
1885

A cemetery is almost always a place within a place, intentionally a place apart from the life of a town. The Glenwood Cemetery gives a glimpse into another era when miners, Odd Fellows, Masons, and lumbermen crowded into Park City and life in this mining town was colorful, diverse, and filled with drama. Walking through the ornate cast-iron gate with the name "Glenwood" formed in the arch overhead, one moves through a maze of marble and stone headstones fashioned between the mid-1880s and the 1920s. Unique in size, shape, and sculptural embellishments, the headstones tell the story of a town, the men and women who lived here, and the things they most valued.

After 1885, the Glenwood Cemetery was designated a private burial site. Tucked into the foothills one and a half miles northwest of Park City's Main Street, the five-acre space of gently curving land is heavily landscaped with native vegetation. Like many cemeteries, it feels like a park or a forest, a sort of sanctuary from the life of the town. Like the gridded cities throughout Utah, the cemetery is divided into four large squares, then further into blocks, and finally into lots that measure thirteen by eight feet. Two main roads, each twenty-five feet wide, run through the site. Even street names familiar to a town are used here—"Main Avenue" runs east and west and is crossed by "Center Avenue," which

Region C

Glenwood Cemetery

runs north and south. Smaller paths run between them and to the various lots. All the walkways are unpaved and are either dirt or native meadow grass.

The cemetery is a surprisingly pleasant, natural environment. But it is, after all, the headstones that are most interesting and suggestive of the stories of the individuals who once lived here. Unlike the regular, more homogeneous modern headstones, nineteenth-century examples are highly creative, unusual in shape and design, and informative. Carved in the form of tree stumps, abstract logs stacked with a globe on top, a logging tool on top of logs, or a weeping willow, they portray an open book of life and tell stories about the lives of people, what they dreamed of and cared about most. As a group they suggest social patterns—the large number of Masons or fraternal orders in town, and the different occupational groups, artisans, and religious beliefs that were present.

The importance of fraternal orders to Park City's community development is particularly evident here. Fraternal groups provided members with social, political, and religious support. Some orders offered health care, life insurance, burial, and family benefits. Perhaps more important, the cemetery speaks to Park City's distinctive and significant diversity of people, religions, and community organizations. Representatives from most European countries as well as the Far East played a role in this community, working in the mines and service industries, building homes, and in some cases raising families.

George S. and Dolores Doré Eccles Center for the Performing Arts
1750 Kearns Blvd
1998

Park City High School students and the arts community benefit from this collaboration with the George S. and Dolores Doré Eccles Foundation—a center for the performing arts built next door to the high school. Despite the growth of Park City, the population had not been sufficient to support a conference center or performing arts center in town. When the school district and the community joined forces, this center was the result. Now the Performing Arts Center offers programs ranging from dancers from Harlem to string musicians from Boston, and, importantly, many programs include a student component—master classes, lectures, or demonstrations. The Eccles Center is the anchor facility for the Sundance Film Festival.

Park City Miners Hospital
1354 Park Avenue
1904
Harry Campbell

The Park City Miners Hospital has not always been surrounded by rugby fields and picnic pavilions but was originally located on a hill closer to the mines to serve injured miners. Because its location was prime Park City property in the late 1970s, its future was in peril. Seeing its distinctive place in Park City history, the city and community rallied to move rather than destroy it, voting in support of a $750,000 bond issue to restore it for use as a public library.

The Miners Hospital functioned as a medical facility

between 1904 and the 1950s. For a period in the 1970s, the historic property was used as a boardinghouse, and eventually as a youth hostel. The city transported the Miners Hospital (which weighed four hundred tons) from a location adjacent to the Park City Mountain Resort to City Park, more conveniently adjacent to Main Street. Through a sensitive adaptive reuse process, the hospital retained its historic character and became a community asset.

Park City High School / Carl Winter School
1233 Park Avenue
1917

Virtually from the first, Park City had its own library, but long before the library had its own building, it loaned books out of the basement of the Congregational Church at 402 Park Avenue. The *Park Record* reported in September 1888: "Miss Lizzie Barbee

Park City Miners Hospital

Park City High School / Carl Winter School

has been appointed librarian for the Ladies Library Association library." The next year, in February, the *Park Record* published a list of the eighty-two books in the collection and estimated that it had "cost the ladies upwards of $75." Eventually it would include more than five thousand books. The *Park Record* announced "A Public Library for Park City" in its August 3, 1917, edition.[3] The mayor and City Council approved a tax levy to fund the library, which would be housed in the City Hall, built not long after the fire of 1898.

In the same way that community enthusiasm motivated the organization of the first library, the community mobilized for this successful adaptive reuse project of the Carl Winter School for the new city library. The school had been closed for five years when in 1986 the Park City Municipal Corporation bought it as part of the settlement of a lawsuit with the school district and began

to negotiate with a New York–based developer who saw the potential for development of the property as a cultural arts center and two-hundred-room hotel. Nearby residents opposed this effort because of the challenge to their sense of community and place and formed the Park City Community Coalition to oppose the sale of the school and its grounds. Instead, the city decided to move the city library to the Carl Winter School from the old Miners Hospital because it had outgrown its home, and it authorized $2.7 million for the renovations.

Park City High School Mechanical Arts Building
1167 Woodside
1936
Scott and Welch, Works Progress Administration
Park City High School's 1936 Mechanical Arts Building was built under the auspices

of the Works Progress Administration and conforms to the PWA Moderne style. Used for technical and industrial education by the Park City School District, this building with its sleek, unadorned, and modernist lines reflected a machine aesthetic revered in the world that emerged in the wake of World War I and the Depression that challenged the country during the 1930s.

Although Franklin Roosevelt never visited Park City, his vision for the recovery of the United States from the devastation of the Depression years impacted this mining town north of Salt Lake City. The same year Roosevelt became president, in March 1933, the Federal Emergency Relief Act passed through Congress, the first of the alphabet agencies set up by the New Deal. Offering immediate relief, opportunities for jobs, and funding for public architecture, support came in the form of loans and grants to benefit local communities. Utah would receive more per capita aid than most other states.

Kimball's Garage / Kimball Art Center (since 1976)
638 Park Avenue
1929

Marking a different time from the first wave of mining that brought settlers to Park City, Kimball's Garage in 1929 replaced a historic livery stable with a facility designed to house the newest technology in transportation—automobiles. Historically the site of a barn, Kimball's Garage had 8,000-gallon gas tanks instead of straw and grain to feed animals. A basement, entered from the side, served as storage for cars during the winter. Eventually, a local named Fred Eley purchased the business. Although Park City's economy declined in the 1950s, the Eley Garage stayed in business until 1972. This simple, flat-roofed brick building follows

the slope of the hill. Since the 1970s, the Kimball Art Center, a community institution of an entirely different sort, has occupied the space at this key location where Main Street zigzags to the east.

Park City Main Street
1880s–early 1900s

Utah's mining towns conform to the land in a way that is significantly different from the rural village settlement pattern. Hugging the sides of a narrow canyon, Park City's Main Street illustrates the uniquely symbiotic relationship between buildings and the land that exists in mining environments. Situated between the steep rock walls and shelves that distinguish the mountain range on the west from the meadows beyond in Wasatch County, Park City's buildings cling to the side of the mountain in proximity to its mines, ski resorts, and service industries.

Main Street, a long, narrow street running north and south, was the center of it all and was where most critical service businesses—saloons, boardinghouses, dry goods stores, and mining enterprises—were found. After Park City was destroyed by a cataclysmic fire that swept through town in 1898, it was rebuilt at the turn of the century, and most historic structures date from that period. In the 1970s, the National Register of Historic Places designated Park City's Main Street as a historic district, including sixty-four contributing buildings (forty-seven commercial structures), most of them one-story, frame Victorian-style buildings with shed roofs and false fronts, as well as two-story frame structures with first-floor business space and recessed entrances with display windows on either side, and offices, social halls, or residences on the upper levels. Cast-iron piers and doors with transoms above were common features of facades along Main Street and of

Park City Main Street

an interior ceiling with a series of barrel vaults.

During the peak of Park City mining activity in the late nineteenth century, commercial activity boomed on Main Street and included saloons, dry goods stores, restaurants, and boardinghouses, all businesses that catered to the needs of the transient mining population. Some mining towns in the state became ghost towns after the mining boom, but Park City redefined itself in the 1970s and became a destination recreation center, with winter sports also focusing on the moutains' resources.

Union Pacific Depot
660 Main Street
1886

Coal fuled much of the work in Park City mines and was transported there from distant locales; a predictable source of coal was critical to the success of mining enterprises. Railroad entrepreneurs made their wealth on the backs of mining developments. The Utah Eastern Railroad announced its plan to build a narrow-gauge rail line in 1879 from Salt Lake City to Park City to Coalville to compete with the Union Pacific's Summit County Railroad, which built a standard-gauge line to Park City in 1880. Competition created greater efficiency, although eventually the Union Pacific assumed control of the Utah Eastern and closed it down.

The railroad depot was an important community institution—the point of arrival and departure for goods and people, the point of export of mining products to market. Originally painted a bright yellow, this Victorian-style building, built in 1886 for $5,000, has a picturesque combination of varying roof pitches and shapes. Contrasting wooden wall surfaces and wooden moldings created a building that had a

more substantial commercial structures in larger towns.

One distinctive characteristic of Park City, in contrast to most Utah towns, is the significant number of frame buildings, suggesting the transitory nature of the town's population of miners and service workers. The group of brick structures along Park City's Main Street is impressive, with continuity in terms of scale, design, and Victorian-style elements—segmental arches, keyways, columns, bracketed cornices, and decorative Queen Anne brickwork. There is a uniformity of scale and compatibility of design on the street as a whole.

Utah's most prominent nineteenth-century architects designed structures for Park City enterprises. Frederick A. Hale designed the brick First National Bank of Park City and the Silver King Mining Company office; and Richard K. A. Kletting designed the Rocky Mountain Bell Company and Utah Independent Telephone Company building, a Mission-style structure with a curvilinear parapet roof and

Union Pacific Depot

certain charm as well as practicality about it. As was typically the case, on the main level the depot included a ticket office, freight office, and waiting room. The station master's quarters were upstairs.

Utah Coal & Lumber Company
201 Heber Avenue
1925

Critical to the rapid construction of housing and structures for the mining industry was a lumberyard. Frills and architectural style were less important than convenience, practicality, and location. After 1925, the Morrison & Merrill Lumber Yard operated out of this one-story frame building strategically located at the intersection between Main Street and Heber Avenue and near the scene of rapid growth. Historically, in front were massive scales to weigh lumber, and a watering trough where locals and the teams that traveled through town could water their horses. Morrison & Merrill sold the building to Albert Smith in 1948. Smith changed

the name to Utah Coal & Lumber Company; the name proudly painted across the top of the frame facade was preserved for decades afterward but was later removed.

Gateway Center
136 Heber Avenue, corner of Swede Alley
1996
Cooper/Roberts

Maximizing the square footage provided by a triangular lot just behind Main Street and at the intersection of Heber Avenue and Swede Alley, Park City's Gateway Center is a three-level commercial and office building on top of a two-story parking garage. The architect had to deal with the unique restrictions of the project—a tight budget; city ordinances determining size, setback, and height restrictions; and the existing parking garage as well as the Historic District Commission's requirement that the project reflect the historical commercial and industrial architecture of the area. The building was designed to look like eight individual commercial structures, the same pattern stretching up Main Street itself. The structure has two entrances and steps back toward the upper level. Each facade is slightly different in materials and design details. As a result, the building exemplifies compatible, contextual architecture that relates to its historic neighbors and reflects the quality work Cooper/Roberts built its reputation on.

George Washington School/Inn
543 Park Avenue
1889

Even though most newcomers who made their homes in Park City were men, some of the supervisors or managers of miners had families, including children who needed to be educated. The company or the church felt obligated to educate the community's young people, and before the mid-1880s Park City's children were learning at the school run by the Ontario Mine or at St. Mary's of the Assumption. Institutionally accommodating this responsibility to the youngest citizens in town, the city in 1885 levied a 1 percent property tax that generated $10,555 for the construction of a school. The 1886–89 Central School or George Washington School differed from the neighboring frame buildings and was constructed with sandstone quarried in nearby Peoa (it survived the fire of 1898). Children of all ages gathered in the same spaces in this T-shaped structure, which had three classrooms and a spacious two-story foyer. A school bell sat near the intersection of the two wings. The school grew in 1910 with additional classrooms and offices. After it stopped being used as a school in 1936, the Veterans of Foreign Wars bought the building for $200 and met there until the 1950s. Later it became a bed-and-breakfast, the Washington School Inn.

St. Luke's Episcopal Church
525 Park Avenue
1890

In the nineteenth century Park City had significant religious diversity. A series of modest-sized churches served the needs of the miners and those who lived in town. Most referenced the Gothic Revival style; the frame St. Luke's Episcopal Church is similar to other wooden churches in Park City. Its distinctive porch features the same pitch and form as the building itself, jutting out from the front wall with doors headed by a pointed Gothic arch and sweeping lines to the sides. Highly original and charming, it shows evidence of the creative and playful spirit of its vernacular designer.

Bishop Daniel Tuttle, an Episcopalian priest, organized and helped secure funding for St. Luke's Mission for Park City by 1889,

George Washington School/Inn

twenty-two years after he had first arrived in Utah. Besides gathering for worship in the building, the congregation held dances, staged plays, and a hosted a range of parties.

There was a substantial population of Episcopalians in town and by 1896, they had their own auxiliary for young girls—the Junior Girl Guild—along with a boys' choir and a rectory for their own minister. The 1898 fire destroyed the church, but the members dug in and rebuilt it in three years, preserving certain design elements such as the original fixtures, wooden moldings, altar, and brass cross.

Elks Hall
550 Main Street
1922

Fraternal orders provided men who were far away from their families with a sense of connection and community. The Benevolent and Protective Order of Elks Lodge No. 734 first organized in 1902 and has been active in Park City ever since. Besides providing members the chance to associate with other men, the Elks have a strong tradition of community service and have made

St. Luke's Episcopal Church.
Photograph by Tricia Simpson, CC A-SA.3.0.

a substantial and enduring difference in this community for the past century.

The Elks first met in the Sutton Building and at Rasband's Hall, adapting their rituals and meetings to spaces they could use, and eventually built their own three-story concrete building, with "B.P.O.E." embedded in the parapeted facade, announcing its use and proud owners. A prominent stringcourse separating the various levels constitutes the primary decoration of the simple facade. The building includes a basement-level gymnasium, which was the only one in town.

Community activities such as the Miners' and Muckers' Ball, the Ancient Order of Hibernians' St. Patrick's Day Ball, and big band dances during the 1930s and 1940s were also held in the building, which was also the scene of funerals and political meetings.

Masonic Hall
540 Main Street
1908

Unlike the more substantial brick buildings on Park City's Main Street, this simple vernacular building is constructed of wood with modest trim and a flat roof. Unusually placed and shaped central windows have two diamond-shaped openings on each side. Historically, the Masonic symbol was over the middle window. For the men of the Masonic order, what the building looked like on the exterior was less important than the rituals that were performed within its walls.

During Park City's mining boom, several Masonic orders were active in town and provided meaningful ritual, social association, and networking opportunities. The 1878 Park City Order of Freemasons met first in the Ontario Schoolhouse and a variety of other locations, including Lawrence

Hall over a store, and the E. P. Sutton & Company building. They built their three-story hall for a total cost of $6,088.88 and included donated furnishings from Ontario Mine miners.

City Hall
528 Main Street
1899

Miners flooded into Park City in the late 1860s and 1870s, bringing with them the social issues typical of mining towns—drunkenness, prostitution, and theft. The city incorporated in March 1884. The first city hall was destroyed in the 1898 fire, and the city built this two-story brick and masonry building in its place, complete with a facade with ornamental brickwork, as was typical of Victorian commercial architecture, and windows flanked by pilasters. On each of the three levels, segmental arches top the windows. In 1901, a few years after the fire that devastated much of the town, the city added a distinctive tower complete with a 1,500-pound bell to sound the alarm in the event of another fire. After a while, the "Ten O'Clock Whistle" replaced the bell, reminding children to return home at the end of the day and acting as an alarm in times of crisis. For a while, City Hall served as the Utah Territorial Prison, with three solitary cells in the basement and a common cell where a prisoner could be chained to the thick stone walls. Someone burned the emblem of the Industrial Workers of the World into the wall when the Wobblies were jailed after a 1916 demonstration.

447 Main Street
1903

There is a regularity of size and form in the buildings on Park City's Main Street. They tend to be one- or two-story commercial

City Hall

blocks with larger windows on the main level than above. On this structure, the elaborate corbeled brickwork so typical of Queen Anne–inspired commercial architecture from the late nineteenth century is easily the most interesting feature. Even though it is modest in size, the building compensates with a complex facade. Segmental arches over the two windows flank the entrance door, and there are rows of corbeled brick and a zigzag variation on a stringcourse to the parapet outlined with stone; combined they create a varied and intricate exercise in Victorian excess. A building such as this speaks volumes about the aspirations of a mining town like Park City. Long before wealth had guaranteed the town's future after the first mining boom, merchants, bankers, and those willing to provide just about any service to the mining population exhibited hope, optimism, and a sure bet on the prosperity flowing out of Utah mines.

Rocky Mountain Bell Telephone Company
434 Main Street
1898
Richard K. A. Kletting

The Rocky Mountain Bell Telephone Company hired the state's premier architect, Richard K. A. Kletting, the designer of the Utah State Capitol, to build its Main Street home in 1898. Kletting already had a significant portfolio of well-known designs including the original Saltair Pavilion, the Salt Palace, and homes of wealthy individuals in Salt Lake City. The Mountain States Telephone and Telegraph Company took over the company and the building in 1911. Over time a series of businesses have been located in this single-block, two-story brick building. Like many other commercial blocks, it is a narrow rectangle with the short end facing the street, a parapet at the

top, and an entrance door and large-paned display window to one side.

Marsac Elementary School / City Hall
431 Marsac
1936
Public Works Administration
Scott and Welsh

Park City built the Marsac School in 1936 to consolidate schools located throughout town in a single location. Marsac had more than three hundred students until 1979, when it closed. Park City housed its city offices in the Marsac School building after a 1983 adaptive reuse.

Salt Lake architects Carl W. Scott and George W. Welch designed the building, a New Deal PWA project. Scott and Welch's reputation was enhanced by the design of the Masonic Temple in Salt Lake City, Copperton's company houses, and countless schools throughout the state. The Public Works Administration greatly served the needs of small-town America, employed out-of-work men, and bolstered the infrastructure and public architecture of towns that had widespread poverty and unemployment.

Blue Church
421 Park Avenue
1897

Although there was overt animosity toward Mormons in Park City (the *Park Record* announced the organization of a Mormon "branch" in an article titled "A Branch of the Octopus Is Planted in Our Midst"[4]), there were nonetheless Latter-day Saints in town. It was not until 1886 that a branch of the church was established in Park City, with Gad Davis and P. W. Timms as leaders. The small congregation held its first meetings on Park Avenue in the back of what the *Park Record* described as "Hop Chong's

Region C

Marsac Elementary School / City Hall

washee." The year before the fire, the Latter-day Saints built their own church, which was completely destroyed except for the stone foundation. Mormons used the rebuilt building until it underwent an extensive renovation in 1975.

The Blue Church is a plain frame structure with clapboard siding painted blue. At one side of the asymmetrical facade is a tower, with the entrance at the base. Gothic elements include pointed window openings and a relatively steeply pitched main roof.

Park City Community Church
402 Park Avenue
1899

In the 1880s, the Congregational Church was the first non-Mormon church to arrive in Park City. The *Park Record* frequently mentioned the congregation's contributions to the community, their religious activities, and the engagements of some of the prominent members. As with many other first-generation church buildings in town, the great fire of 1898 destroyed their first church, but they rebuilt, using the extant exterior walls of the old structure. Mirroring the same configuration as the Blue Church, the single-story brick Community Church has an engaged tower on the side, a simple rectangular plan, a moderately pitched roof, and Gothic arches familiar on parish churches throughout America.

Raddon House
325 Park Avenue
1901
Peter Anderson

Several men became wealthy off the Park City mines either because of lucky investments or because they provided a service the miners needed. Samuel L. Raddon was such a man. As the owner, publisher, and editor of the *Park Record* for sixty-five years, he lived in this house for almost five decades. Moving quickly up the ranks, Raddon began as a reporter and before long owned the paper. He made his presence felt with his spirited and biting editorials, and the state felt his influence as the president of the Utah State Press Association. We know much of what we know about Park City's early years from his reporting.

Raddon's two-and-a-half-story Victorian mansion includes the charming excesses so typical of the style: a strong emphasis on wooden decorative trim, a double porch with lathe-turned piers, leaded-glass windows, and a truncated hipped roof. The white trim forms an interesting contrast with the color of the walls, extenuating in spindles, brackets, and balusters among other wooden elements.

St. John's Lutheran Church
323 Park Avenue
1907

Reflecting the cultural diversity so typical of a mining town, this small frame church speaks volumes about the determination of a Lutheran congregation to worship in their own way and with like-minded believers. Park City's Lutheran community was first organized in 1902 by the Reverend O. H. Elmquist, a minister who traveled to Park City from Ogden with a congregation that included about three dozen Finns and Swedes who met in private homes and for a time in the Methodist Episcopal Church. Elmquist bought the property for this church in 1906. They embarked on a three-month blitz, erecting the building for $2,197.54 and holding their first service on August 25. Traveling ministers continued to preach at the church because there was not sufficient population to warrant or fund a permanent preacher.

In terms of shape and design, the building is a simple frame temple-form building with a portico that juts out from the facade, echoing the same shape and with the same gabled roof form as the building itself. The walls are sheathed with clapboard siding.

Egyptian Theatre
328 Main Street
1926

Theaters were an incredibly important component of a culturally enriched town, gathering strangers together for entertainment and providing escape from the drudgery of daily life. One of the most unusual revival styles to be popular at the turn of the century was Egyptian Revival. The typical flat surfaces of the style vocabulary invited bas-relief sculpture or elaborate decoration and intricate design. Fully in line

Egyptian Theatre

Region C

with the style, Park City's Egyptian Theatre featured replicas of busts of pharaohs and the images of Thoth, Anubis, Amenhotep, Horus, Hathor, and Nestor. Surfaces of walls, pillars, and arches were decorated with symbols and hieroglyphics that held mysterious secrets. The distinctively flared columns, symmetrical facade, and polychromatic surface created a building that stood out in Park City's Main Street commercial district and that duplicated one designed by Egyptologist C. R. Berg for Pasadena, California—Warner's Egyptian Theatre. Historically, the Dewey Theater was located on the site until it crumpled under the weight of one of Park City's record-breaking snowstorms.

Besides movies and vaudeville shows, the theater was often the backdrop for popular melodramas. Today Sundance films are viewed by audiences from around the world. When it opened on Christmas Eve 1926, it featured Zane Grey's movie *Man of the Forest*. The name changed throughout its history, but since 1981, it has been known as the Egyptian Theatre. There are only two other Egyptian Revival theaters in the state.

Park Tavern
320 Main Street
1900

The Park Tavern represents another type of community institution, a place men exhausted from the difficult work in the mines would have come to unwind and let loose, a place they would play cards or gamble, where they might eat or talk. A tavern was as important to community building as a lodge or church. This simple commercial building has a shed roof that slopes toward the back. Allegedly, the Park Tavern had its own slot machines in a room at the back of the building and gambling

that continued until the mid-1950s, when a police raid closed it down. In 1963, a family operation—the Red Banjo Pizza Parlor—renovated the space, complete with a second-story porch and fancy wooden cornice with six thin wooden arches attached to the plain wooden surface that had existed before.

St. Mary's of the Assumption Catholic Church
121 Park Avenue
1884

Park City's population was religiously and ethnically diverse from the start. Not surprisingly, there was a substantial population of Catholics in town, particularly after Patrick Connor's troops came to Utah and established Fort Douglas. As the local leader of the Catholic Church, Lawrence Scanlan visited many of the communities in the region and made an assessment about which congregations needed their own church. He saw the need for a congregation in Park City. The town's Catholics had been meeting in Simon's Hall, and mission priests who traveled through town led religious services. By 1881, they built a frame church and a schoolhouse that provided education for the children of the few miners with families. The school closed in 1933 when the number of students had slumped to fifty-seven. The church, however, is the oldest Catholic church to still be in use in Utah.

These simple masonry buildings are rectangular in shape but domestic in scale, with the gabled end facing the street. A bell tower on the roof of the church and the Gothic pointed arch over the entrance door signify the religious identity of the building as well. As is true of most buildings at this end of town, the two structures cling to the hill and overlook buildings on Main Street below.

St. Mary's of the Assumption Catholic Church

Duchesne County

Ashley National Forest (Tabiona Area)
Stockmore Ranger Station
Duchesne Ranger District
1914
U.S. Forest Service

When Theodore Roosevelt helped usher in the twentieth century, his vision of the American Dream shaped land use policies that would preserve wilderness and protect forestland for future generations. Forest rangers, the first stewards of our national forests, housed their activities in ranger stations like that at Stockmore in isolated environs, establishing a federal presence in the most remote areas of our country after the Forest Reserve Act of 1891. The U.S. Forest Service was officially established by President Theodore Roosevelt on July 1, 1905, and placed under the jurisdiction of the Department of Agriculture.

The site of the Stockmore Ranger Station was withdrawn from the Uintah and Ouray Indian Reservation and approved for a ranger station in 1908, the year the government established the Ashley National Forest, and it became a living and social center for forest rangers as well as sheepherders and miners who worked in the vicinity. The principal building, built in 1914, is a one-story cross-wing building sitting on a fieldstone foundation, with a wooden frame and drop siding with wooden shingles in the gabled ends. The facade has a full-width covered porch abutting the projecting cross wing, and a wooden frame.

Additional outbuildings speak to the range of activities that engaged the time of forest rangers. The buildings were originally painted "cinnamon brown," a color listed in a 1936 Forest Service Descriptive Sheet, with mustard gold accents.

Region C

Indian Canyon Ranger Station
Duchesne Ranger District
1914
U.S. Forest Service

One of the lasting legacies of President Theodore Roosevelt's great love of the natural environment is the U.S. Forest Service, established on July 1, 1905, under the jurisdiction of the Department of Agriculture. The ranger stations built to house activities of the federal government in remote areas helped protect the country's great natural resources. The Indian Canyon Ranger Station is the earliest remaining ranger station in the Ashley National Forest.

Until midcentury, the Indian Canyon Ranger Station was central to the district, part of the Uinta Forest Reserve and near a stage stop on the route between Duchesne and the rail station at Kyune, Utah. President Grover Cleveland created forest reserves on February 22, 1897, upon the recommendation of Gifford Pinchot, who would later become Roosevelt's key adviser on forest policies. Pinchot maintained that government stewardship of forestlands was necessary if the forests were to survive. In 1905 the forest reserves were placed under the jurisdiction of the Forest Service.

The ranger station was first built in 1914 on a ridge high above Mill Hollow and Indian

Uintah Stake Tabernacle / Vernal Temple.
Photograph by Mooncowboy, public domain.

Canyon. It is a simple rectangular structure on a fieldstone and mortar foundation, with sawed log siding and a covered porch.

Uintah County

Vernal

Uintah Stake Tabernacle / Vernal Temple
Northeast corner of 500 West and 200 South intersection
1900–1907
FFKR, Richard Jackson (rehabilitation)

Certainly one of the most distinctive and monumental buildings in the Uinta Basin, the Uintah Stake Tabernacle is a poignant symbol of the settlement efforts of the Mormon pioneers. Tabernacles were always evidence of regional solidarity; they were high-styled buildings made with the finest materials and craftsmanship available in the area. Distinguished mostly by a large, elaborately decorated assembly room, tabernacles were no longer built by the church after 1915. Only twenty of the forty originally built are still extant.

Uintah Stake organized in 1886. Because the stake relied on donations of money and labor from members, the building took longer to complete than was originally planned. Unlike many other tabernacles, the Uintah Stake Tabernacle does not rely on the Gothic Revival style but is instead a simplified and almost secular variation of the Georgian New England church form. Greek Revival stylistic elements include a pedimented facade, a three-part, round-headed window, and an octagonal belfry. This distinctive building is stately, formal, and simple and addressed perfectly the programmatic needs of the church.

Mormon president Joseph F. Smith dedicated the Uintah Stake Tabernacle on August 24, 1907. It provided the backdrop for large gatherings of Mormons from across the county: stake conferences, patriotic meetings and bond drives during war years, and high school graduations and concerts. In 1994, the First Presidency of the LDS Church made a startling but exciting announcement—the building would be remodeled into a temple, the first such adaptive reuse project for the LDS Church.

As a temple, the Uintah Stake Tabernacle added another tower and includes an addition, a newly excavated basement beneath the original building for the baptismal font, and a reconfigured interior for the new use. A statue of the angel Moroni covered in gold leaf signals the shift from a tabernacle to the most sacred LDS building, the temple, which was intended to benefit the forty-two thousand church members in eastern Utah, western Colorado, and southwestern Wyoming.

Fenn/Bullock House
388 West 100 North
1901

The range of housing styles, types, and scales reveals social realities—the presence of wealth or poverty, social class, and other distinctions. The Fenn/Bullock House is Vernal's finest example of Victorian architecture. This one-and-a-half-story side-passage wooden-frame building with drop siding sits on a stone foundation and has an asymmetrical facade, various projecting bays, and decorative wooden trim and embellishment. As is typical of Eastlake or Queen Anne detailing, the house has a spindled porch frieze, decoratively sawed

Fenn/Bullock House.
Photograph by Ntsimp Own work, public domain.

and chamfered porch columns, lathe-turned balusters, brackets on either side of the upper-story windows, a dentil molding on the front bay window, roof pitches of varying sizes and shapes, wooden lattice work in the corners of the pediment, and octagonal shingles in the upper portion of the gable.

The original owners, Lorenzo R. Fenn and his son Richard Fenn, were carpenters who worked on the Salt Lake Temple and Provo Tabernacle before Lorenzo moved to Vernal from Provo. John Bullock was the most famous owner of the house. Also from Provo, Bullock moved in 1895 to Vernal, where he was the treasurer for the Vernal Milling and Light Company flour mill and

helped establish the Uintah State Bank in 1910. Bullock was also a prominent member of fraternal organizations such as the Vernal Lodge of the Independent Order of Odd Fellows; he was the oldest living member of the Storey Lodge, and mayor of Vernal between 1908 and 1909.

St. Paul's Episcopal Church and Lodge
226 West Main Street
1909
John P. Hill

St. Paul's Episcopal Church is the second oldest church in Uintah County. Built in the familiar Gothic style, it includes a large, pointed-arched window centered in the gabled end wall, which faces the

St. Paul's Episcopal Church and Lodge.
Photograph by Ntsimp Own work, public domain.

street. Ornate stained-glass windows, with flanking decorative buttresses and wooden shingle siding, are on the back wall. Five buttresses run along the sidewalls. Reverend O. E. Ostensen first arrived in September 1900 and held services in Jake Workman's Opera House and later in the Odd Fellows Lodge Room.

In contrast, St. Paul's Lodge is domestic in scale and is a two-story brick Craftsman-style house that looks more like a bungalow you would see in neighborhoods throughout the state. A one-story porch extends along the entire length of the facade of the gable-roofed structure. The broad gabled roof, half-timbering in the upper gabled end, and exposed rafters and purlins of the porch and dormers above continue the Craftsman motif. The lodge or parish house was used by the Girls' Friendly Society of New York as a boardinghouse for girls who traveled to Vernal to work or go to school, as well as for social events and civic or club meetings. After it was sold in 1932 it was used as a hospital.

Vernal Tithing Office
Northwest corner of 500 West and 200 South
1887
Harley Mowery

Although a simple rectangular structure was familiar throughout Utah Territory, the gabled end or the short end of this temple form faces the street as was typical of tithing offices of the era. Constructed with coursed cut stone, it has a moderately pitched roof, boxed cornice, and wide fascia, and the symmetrical facade consists of windows on each side of a central door.

A religious leader was always the administrator of a tithing office. Samuel R. Bennion, stake president of the Uintah Stake of the LDS Church, directed construction of the Vernal Tithing Office in 1887 with local men. Stonemason Harley Mowery, a British convert to the LDS Church from Vernal, cut and laid the stone. The tithing office was important to the town's economic survival and was filled with eggs and milk, homemade brooms, clothing, and other handmade products or in-kind donations, which

Vernal Tithing Office.
Photograph by Tricia Simpson, CC A-SA 3.0.

Region C

were stored in the tithing office itself as well as in the granary, barn, and corrals on the site.

Daggett County

Near Manila
Flaming Gorge Dam
Utah Highway 43
Early 1960s

Besides storing water for the region, Flaming Gorge Dam created a popular recreational destination managed by the U.S. Forest Service for people to enjoy boating, fishing, paddleboarding, and other water sports. It was named by Major John Wesley Powell, who traveled with his party through the area in May 1869, for the point where the Green River moves through the Uinta Mountains. Construction on the thin-arched concrete dam commenced

in 1958 and concluded in 1963. The dam stretches 502 feet vertically and 1,285 feet horizontally and has a capacity of 3.7 million acre-feet of water. Besides water storage in Flaming Gorge Reservoir, the dam produces hydroelectricity, plays a role in flood control for the Green River system, and is one of six dams in the Colorado River Storage Project.

Wasatch County

Midway
Watkins-Coleman House
5 East Main Street
John Watkins
1869

One of the most original and distinctive houses in the state, the Watkins-Coleman House, built by architect John Watkins, set the standard for other Gothic Revival

Watkins-Coleman House

cottages in Midway. The charming two-story house includes a partial basement and a pot-rock foundation. The walls are formed of hand-pressed brick, with white sandstone quoins marking both ends of the facade. As is true of the other Watkins houses in town, the bricks were eventually painted red, which accentuated the contrast between the decorative and structural elements.

Watkins built this home for his plural family. Trained in architecture in England before he immigrated to the United States and converted to Mormonism in 1856, he would be well known for his house designs and the design of several distinctive religious buildings.

Although it is not characteristic of a cross-wing cottage, the Watkins-Coleman House is virtually symmetrical. A variation on the traditional *T* or *L* shape of this housing type, this example has wings on both ends of the central rectangular mass, which contains a long parlor. Gabled ends on both wings face the street and are adorned with cut ornamental wood; there is a small decorative balcony over the main entrance at the center of the facade, and a classical porch running between the two wings. Distinctive cresting runs along the ridgeline of the roof, which concludes in simple finials and is interpreted by two chimney stacks with corbeled brickwork and an upper portion twisted on a diagonal.

George Bonner Jr. House
90 East Main Street
1877
John Watkins

Like his father's house and John Watkins's family house across the street, George Bonner Jr.'s house is a celebration of form, contrast, and line. A simple cross-wing type, it nevertheless makes a strong impression.

George Bonner Jr. House

Region C

The L-form plan of this one-and-a-half-story brick house includes a projecting wing with a relatively steeply pitched roof gable at the top, and a rectangular mass moving to the east that features a Classical porch with an ornamented gable above. A diminutive balcony includes lathe-turned porch rails, a wooden pedimented window, and wooden decoration along the edges of the gable.

Although the elaborate wooden decoration most distinguishes this house, as in the decorative bracketed bay windows, strong white sandstone quoins at the far ends of the facade and at the edge of the projecting wing create a dramatic contrast in color and texture in this version of the Gothic Revival style.

Watkins's broad experience in architecture gave him a particularly rich toolbox of pattern-book designs, decoration, familiarity with the picturesque, and building techniques. He was skilled as an architect before he immigrated to Utah, and his talents and buildings were welcomed in Provo, where he worked on the LDS tabernacle (1856), among other significant projects.

George Bonner Sr. House
55 North 300 East
John Watkins
1876

George Bonner Sr. hired John Watkins in 1876 to design a home for his family after he had seen the one Watkins had built for his own family. The Watkins-Coleman House at 5 East Main Street set the standard for a group of houses Watkins would design in Midway reflecting a similar aesthetic. Besides George Sr., Watkins built houses for George Jr. and William the next year across Main Street and farther south from their father's. George Sr.'s house was a two-story Gothic Revival house best known for the significant amount of decorative

woodwork. He started a grocery with his sons, first in his front room and then in a separate building also on Main Street, also designed by Watkins.

Bonner's house is a one-and-a-half-story brick house that varies the basic cross-wing type, with wings on both ends of the central rectangular space and the entrance at the center. In this example, a parlor is found at the center, with bedrooms to one side and the kitchen to the other. The building celebrates materiality, ornament, contrast, and almost a sort of playfulness toward decoration. White sandstone quoins contrast with the brick of the walls, and cut bargeboards and finials embellish the gables over the two wings and facing the street; on one side is a bay window on the main floor. Dormers and elaborate decorated porch balconies continue the theme throughout, and the wooden crest defining the ridge of the roof and the diagonally placed chimneys produce an element of surprise and delight.

Midway Social Hall
71 East Main Street
1898

This simple Greek Revival one-story stone building was the center of Midway's community life for decades after it was built in 1898. Constructed with pot rock, a local limestone, with a rubble ashlar masonry pattern in walls that are twenty-one inches thick, this sturdy single-block building claims a position of centrality in its placement on Main Street. The gabled end of the rectangular plan faces the street and is reminiscent of the triangular pediment of a Greek temple. Two tall double-hung windows with wooden pedimented lentils at the top flank a central door on the facade. The building interior included a large assembly room with an entrance area at one end and a stage at the other.

Midway Social Hall

Between 1898 and 1940, the Midway Social Hall was the scene of most cultural and community events in town and continued a tradition that started in Salt Lake City and spread throughout Utah. Theatricals, dances, and musical performances balanced out the everyday reality of working farms and running businesses. When the new Midway Town Hall was built in 1940, the Midway Social Hall was used for a range of different purposes, including a bishop's storehouse, a cannery, and welfare storage.

Midway Town Hall
120 West Main Street
1941
Claude Shepherd Ashworth

The Midway Town Hall made evident the impact of financial support from the Works Progress Administration in putting unemployed local men to work. Constructed out of the locally popular pot-rock limestone,

the building is a uniquely conceived and built Arts and Crafts and Tudor Revival–style structure that also reflects the influence of the Swiss immigrants who settled in this mountain town.

This large two-and-a-half-story town hall has been the principal center of recreation, civic, and cultural activities since it was built in 1941, replacing the longtime sentimental center of community activities in the Midway Social Hall. This WPA project included a gymnasium, a kitchen, a post office, and offices of local government. The walls are nineteen to twenty inches thick, with ashlar masonry and scribed mortar joints. Steel windows reflect improvements in materials available for construction during the mid-twentieth century.

The exterior takes advantage of revival styles, imitating the look of a Tudor building's half-timber construction with stucco filling the spaces in between. Large wooden

Midway Town Hall

rakes, projecting brackets, and steeply pitched gables continue the theme. The emphasis on the rich color of the stone wall, the heavy wooden timbers, and the cream of the stucco infill evoke the richness of the Arts and Crafts style of the early twentieth century and a Scandinavian influence as well. In 1987, a glockenspiel was added to the gabled area of the facade, emphasizing the heritage of Midway's Swiss population.

Schneitter Hotel
700 North Homestead Drive
1886

The historic Schneitter Hotel building is still extant on the grounds of what is now known as the Homestead Resort. This two-story central-passage building is virtually as deep as it is wide and has a square plan with symmetrical elevations on each of the four sides. The facade, the elevation to the north, is organized into five bays, with a central door framed by windows on both sides. The building speaks of dignity; its allegiance to the Federal style and all its formality is a reference to the Classical world and order, complete with a low-pitched hipped roof topped by a widow's walk so reminiscent of the East Coast, and with woodwork that resembles that of the porch. The building's brick walls sit on a pot-rock stone foundation. The two-story porch has been restored since it was first built in 1886, but it features square columns with corner brackets, and a gabled roof at the top of the second level. The hotel's interior central hallway and staircase connect the four rooms on each floor.

Schneitter's Hot Pot Resort capitalized on the nearby hot springs surrounded by conical mineral deposits that provided easy access to the healing powers of the warm water. One was two hundred feet in diameter. Simon Schneitter, his wife, Maria, and their twenty-three-year-old son, Simon J., built their resort in 1886–91, with swimming and soaking as the main attraction at this "bathing resort" that also featured horse races, abundant food, and other entertainments.

Wilson House and Farmstead
94 East 250 North
1894

Local farmer and cattleman Wilson W. Wilson built this simple one-and-a-half-story Victorian cross-wing brick house in 1894 for his first wife, Elizabeth Bailey Coleman. After Elizabeth died, Wilson married Bertha Sonderegger, the daughter of Swiss immigrants, in 1903. As was common at the time, Wilson went on a mission five years later, between 1908 and 1910, despite his familial responsibilities. Wilson and Bertha had nine children between 1904 and 1925. Wilson added an addition in 1915, rebuilt the roof structure, and expanded space in the attic to make room for his growing family. The simple gable of the main rectangular mass spans the area on one side above a porch, with the entrance to the house and a room on the side. Chiseled shingles enliven the wall space in the gable, and square-butt shingles cover the wall surface to the south and east. Other decoration includes transoms over the doors and stone lintels over the windows.

There are a number of simple stone buildings in this part of Midway. The granary on the Wilson farmstead is a rectangular gable-roofed building made of pot rock, and it has a root cellar.

The property includes the house itself, a stone granary from around 1894, and a 1915 wooden shed.

Attewall Wootton Jr. House
270 East Main Street
Midway, Utah
1888

This simple rectangular hall-parlor house feels grander than its form or size would suggest. Wooden trim reflecting the Eastlake style and including decorative brackets at the top of the columns is found along the lines of the roof of the porch running across the front of the house and the main rectangular mass, creating a lively contrast with the brick of the main walls. The walls and white decoration couldn't create a more pleasing difference. Segmental arched windows as well as dentils along the cornice continue the theme of mixed stylistic elements that together create a sense of abundance.

Attewall Wootton Jr. built this house for his family in 1888. Wootton was raised in Midway and completed eighth grade at the school where his father, Attewall Wootton Sr., was superintendent. After teaching at the Wallsburg School briefly, Attewall attended Brigham Young Academy in Provo for one year. Afterward he came back to teach school in Midway, where he taught for the next forty-seven years. Like many men in the valley, Attewall worked at a variety of other jobs to provide for his family when school was out. He and his wife, Margaret Elizabeth, lived there until 1905, when they moved to Heber City.

Snake Creek Hydroelectric Power Plant Historic District
Utah Highway 224
James E. Allen
1909

Every once in a while, when you are driving around in Utah searching for hints to the state's history, you come upon a place like this, a cluster of structures and built elements that promise a story larger than what is apparent at first glance. Built between 1909 and 1910, the Snake Creek Power Plant includes a complex of buildings—a powerhouse, transformer house, and the diversion dams—and conduits related to the creation of power from the movement of water. It includes built features that divert and deliver water, and structures that house the generation of power. Power plants typically also included housing for operators, in this case two residences and five other ancillary structures. The complex lies along the south side of Snake Creek near Wasatch Mountain State Park and golf course.

The most significant structure on the site is the brick powerhouse, built in 1909. This T-shaped building sits on a concrete foundation and includes gabled ends that culminate in a concrete-capped parapet wall. Identified as the Snake Creek Plant of the Utah Power and Light Company, the building pushes beyond mere practicality, with the three gabled ends of the building featuring semicircular corbeled brick lintels and semicircular arched transom windows. James E. Allen designed the powerhouse and transformer house using elements from the Italian Renaissance style.

This hydroelectric power plant was built to provide nearby mining districts and cities throughout the area with electricity and was built by the Snake Creek Power Company, controlled by mining, agriculture, and power entrepreneur Jesse Knight. Knight's company was part of the 1913 organization of Utah Power and Light, a merger of smaller power operations.

Heber
Wasatch Stake Tabernacle and Heber Amusement Hall
Main Street and corner of 100 North and 100 West
1887–1889
President Abram Hatch, superintendent

For the Mormon settlers of Heber Valley, the building of a tabernacle was a sign of their regional importance. Second in the hierarchy of LDS religious buildings next to the temple, tabernacles were the stage for large-scale instructional meetings where church leaders transmitted church doctrine from the center of the church in Salt Lake City. Not used for Sunday School or sacrament meetings, the tabernacle's main assembly room was the key focus of activity and included a three-part stand on the west where church leaders arranged themselves according to their priesthood and leadership positions. The sandstone Heber City Amusement Hall was built jointly by three local wards in 1906–08 on the same site. A one-of-a-kind building in Heber Valley, the tabernacle epitomizes the attention to style, extravagance of materials, and central location of this type of building throughout Utah.

The Wasatch Stake Tabernacle was built between 1887 and 1889 with sandstone quarried by local men east of Heber

Wasatch Stake Tabernacle and Heber Amusement Hall

at Lake Creek. Stake president Abram Hatch was the local ecclesiastical leader and superintendent of the construction of this fifty-by-ninety-foot building. A fourteen-foot-square sandstone tower rises ten feet beyond the roof and continues another twenty-five feet in a combination of red wood and metal, with a weathervane on top.

Joseph S. Murdock House
115 East 300 North
c. 1865

For more than twenty years before he built this house in Heber City for his family, Joseph Murdock had been a member of the Church of Jesus Christ of Latter-day Saints. Murdock converted to the church in 1836, just six years after it was organized, and was a friend and personal bodyguard to Mormon prophet Joseph Smith. His first wife was converted by Wilford Woodruff, the LDS Church president in the 1890s. He married two other women in 1854—Jane Sharp and Elizabeth Hunter.

Brigham Young chose Murdock to lead the Mormon settlement of the upper Provo River valley. His family lived in Midway for two years before moving to Heber City. Murdock was a well-known and respected church leader and a member of the territorial legislature. Perhaps best remembered for his role during the Black Hawk War in the 1860s, Murdock gained the respect of local native people and married a member of the Ute/Shoshone Tribe, Pernetta (Nettie) Murdock. Brigham Young called Murdock to go to Nevada and lead settlement along the Muddy River.

When Murdock built this house, he had four wives. The property included small buildings when he purchased the land—a log cabin, and a frame house occupied by two of his wives, Elizabeth and Jane.

The large stone house, constructed with local pot rock, was built in 1865. Eliza and Nettie lived with Murdock and their children in the house. Local tradition suggested that the house was divided into two levels, each used by a different wife and family.

During the 1880s when the Edmunds-Tucker Act prohibiting the practice of polygamy was enforced, Murdock stood trial and was convicted.

The two-story house is a double-cell type built of red sandstone in random rubble ashlar masonry. The symmetrical facade facing the street includes a central door and windows on both sides with bush-hammered sandstone lintels, and chiseled margins above. The two ends of the building have clipped or "jerkin-head" gables with red brick chimneys. On this relatively simple, straightforward, practical design the recessed semicircular motifs that appear on the gabled ends are a welcome relief.

Abram Hatch House
81 East Center Street
1892

The Abram Hatch House speaks to the prestige and wealth of a successful businessman and a religious and political leader.

As is sometimes true of a grand Victorian house, the Hatch House combines an eclectic list of elements that conform to or contrast with those of other homes of the late nineteenth century, such that it does not fall easily into one box or another. Built with regional red sandstone, the house has a symmetrical facade reminiscent of the regularity and order of pioneer-era architecture common throughout the Heber Valley and other parts of the state. There is an irresistible tendency toward balance, organized around a central entrance framed by a three-sided porch and topped by a triangular pediment, with a wall surface lined with shingles. Gingerbread wooden decoration lines the top. At the center of the house and atop the roof is a tower with a subtly spiked roof. To both sides on the main level are half-octagonal wings with windows headed by stone-pedimented arches. Small triangular pediments jut out from the roof above. Decoration ranges from lathe-turned posts and elaborate balustrades to a variety of patterns in shingles on both the tower roof and small gables. Corbeled brickwork on the chimneys and ornate metalwork on the finial on top of the tower together create an impression of wealth and importance. In a beautiful rural valley like Heber, a house like this stands out and suggests a story about the growth and development of this place.

Hatch's financial success was due to wide-ranging activities. Besides running a store, a ranch, and a farm, Hatch served in the territorial legislature. A longtime faithful member of the LDS Church, Hatch came to Utah in 1850 and first settled in Lehi. Like many Mormon men, he was a missionary to England between 1864 and 1867. Between 1877 and 1901 Hatch was president of the Wasatch Stake, best known for his leadership of the construction of the Wasatch Stake Tabernacle.

Heber Second Ward Meetinghouse
100 West Center Street
Joseph Nelson
1913–1915

For a short time, in the wake of the rectangular Classical Revival meetinghouses of the first generation of Mormon builders, the LDS Church built a number of revival buildings that referenced church architecture in more direct ways, particularly between 1905 and 1915. This example uses the vocabulary of the English Gothic Revival with its asymmetry, buttressed and crenellated tower, and distinctive wooden trim and is the oldest extant LDS meetinghouse in the valley. Overall, the proportions and treatment of the walls of the Heber Second Ward Meetinghouse are relatively heavy and dark. Stone ornament contrasts with the dark brick of the walls, which is corbeled in places, forming pointed Gothic arches in the tower and over the entrance, and stringcourses that define the change in elevations. Dark brown wooden trim accents the edges of the steeply pitched gables and the cornice that juts out from the top of the tower wall. Hammer and collar beams seem to brace the front gable. Stained-glass windows appear on the north gable in recessed arches along the side walls. The wall is modulated by this series of recessed panels or buttresses. The crenellations on the top of the tower link the style to its English antecedents. Architect Joseph Nelson of Provo designed the church for the Heber Second Ward. Nelson had designed other Gothic-style churches during the 1910s and was known for the design of Provo's City and County Building. He was also a popular designer of houses, apartment buildings, and schools.

Local men built the church, which cost $19,251. The Heber Second Ward used the meetinghouse for more than fifty years before the Catholic Church bought the building and a stake center was built for the Second and Fifth Wards.

Woodland

Bernard J. Stewart Ranch House
Near the Diamond Bar X Ranch
1911

When William Stewart and his brothers began buying acreage in the northern end of Pine Valley in 1900, they began what would eventually become a "recreational ranch" that would include 2,262 acres. They raised sheep and cattle on the land as well as the hay and grain required to keep them fed, on what was truly a working ranch that provided summer recreation for the Stewart brothers—William, Samuel, Charles, and Bernard—and their friends.

Bernard practiced law in Salt Lake City and assumed sole ownership of the Stewart Ranch in the 1920s. He built what became known as the Bernard J. Stewart Ranch House in 1911. The one-and-a-half-story log house sits on a stone foundation with a porch that wraps around two sides. A cobblestone wall topped with concrete coping defines the edge of the porch. The front of the building includes a central door topped by a transom window and two windows to the sides. Also on the site are a woodshed and two large "three-seater" outhouses made of rough-sawed planks rather than logs like the main house. A modest addition in 1967 added modern conveniences to the house, including two additional bathrooms and a laundry room.

Region C

Region D

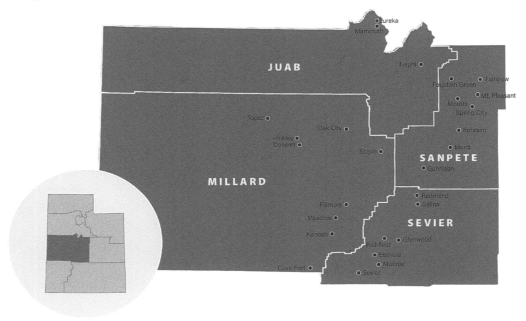

Juab, Millard, Sanpete, and Sevier Counties

Introduction

In some ways, these counties have been constructed through migrations— of ancient peoples and Native Americans building, planting, and traveling in search of food, security, and a healthy life; of Spanish explorers traveling to map and identify resources, to convert and engage; of Mormon pioneers settling towns for their church and their own futures; and of the railroad providing new opportunities for the transportation of goods and services in and out of the area.

Anthropologists have identified Paleo, Archaic, and Fremont culture sites in central Utah and in Sevier County; this part of the state is rich with opportunities for exploring remnants of ancient cultures. According to M. Guy Bishop, by 1984, thirty-nine Fremont sites had been discovered near Salina that suggested that these ancient peoples grew corn, beans, and squash and had some domestic animals.[1] The Southern Paiute Indians were in the area when Catholic priests Francisco Atanasio Domínguez and Silvestre Vélez de Escalante came through in October 1776.

When white settlers moved into the county in the 1860s, they competed with Native Americans for land and other resources. A series of treaties over the next several years moved some of the native peoples northeast to the Uintah Valley Reservation, but some clung to their historic homes and resisted removal.

As part of the second wave of white settlement, Mormon pioneers moved into central Utah, settling what would become Emery, Sanpete, and Sevier Counties. Sevier's principal town is Richfield, first settled in 1871 by eight families and twelve single men. The railroad moved through the county, to Salina in 1891 and to Richfield in 1896, connecting the county to national markets for the shipment of agricultural products.

The Utah Southern Railroad came to Juab Valley in 1874 but did not reach the Tintic mines until 1883. According to historian Tom Alexander, more than ten thousand Chinese worked on the railroad; they came to Utah with the Central Pacific, and some stayed and worked in mining, started their own businesses, or worked in restaurants or laundries, following employment opportunities through the West.[2]

By the time the railroad came to Utah, many of the key mining districts had been discovered, although the Ophir and Tintic mines were not established until 1882. The railroad was key for successful mining, transporting mineral wealth to smelters and to distant markets beyond.

The Tintic Mining District began operation on December 13, 1869, and quickly became one of the top three producers in the territory. A hundred years later the mines had produced $570 million in mineral wealth. Located eighty-five miles south of Salt Lake City, the district was on the western end of the Tintic Valley, where peaks stand 5,600 feet tall. Tintic was one of the first mining districts in Utah, along with Bingham, Little Cottonwood Canyon, and Rush Valley. Like the streets of Park City, Eureka's meandering streets hugged the base of the Tintic Mountains and were lined with frame houses, saloons, dry goods stores, and other service industries.

Beyond Eureka, other mining towns included Bullion Beck, Blue Rock, and Gemini, all of which peaked and failed.

Although the Mormon Church had branches for a while in Park City, Eureka, and Frisco, most of the workers in the mines were non-Mormons. The first wave of miners in the 1860s and 1870s came primarily from other mining districts in the West, but starting in the 1880s and continuing through the 1890s, immigrants from Italy, Greece, and other countries in eastern Europe came to the United States and worked in Utah mines. The vast majority of immigrant miners ended up at Carbon County coal mines or at Bingham Canyon mines. Local institutions and service businesses reflected this ethnic makeup; a Greek Orthodox church in Price exemplified greater social and cultural diversity than existed in the typical Utah town.

The Union Pacific constructed the Utah Southern Railroad to Frisco in 1880, bypassing Fillmore and Cedar City. Eventually spurs connected these towns to the line as well. New technologies facilitated the expansion of Utah mines, increased capital investment from outside the territory, and

Eureka Main Post Office.
Photograph by HABS Utah,12-Eur,2-2, public domain.

enabled a symbiotic relationship with the existing Mormon towns, which helped supply food and other supplies to the mining towns.[3] Before smelters and other processing plants were built locally, ore was transported to San Francisco, Baltimore, and other locations nationally for processing. Dynamite, mechanized drills, and other modern technologies advanced mining, creating greater efficiency and boosts in production. According to Tom Alexander, other technologies included "railways, trams, cable systems, concentrators, electric power plants, and smelters."[4]

Juab County

Eureka
Eureka Main Post Office
Main and Wallace Streets
1923
Federal government

The United States built fifty-six post offices between 1920 and 1926, including four in Utah. Although each was grounded in the Beaux Arts tradition, they were simpler in design and decoration, classically proportioned, and symmetrical, with flat unadorned facades. Exterior material was most often stucco rather than brick or stone and conveyed an overall economy of design and materiality.

Although the symmetrical, one-story Eureka Post Office is a simple building constructed with terra-cotta block faced with stucco, the elevation facing the street has a central arched entry bay with two bays to each side. The building sits on a raised, reinforced-concrete basement.

The main entry stairs and retaining walls are also concrete. The bays are embellished with agricultural images on terra-cotta panels placed over them, and Spanish tile coping makes a subtle reference to the Spanish Colonial style.

Mammoth
Mammoth Historic District
1870

Mammoth City benefited from the same prosperity Eureka generated during the mining boom days, sharing resources and services. Centered on one long street leading to the Mammoth Mine and a few smaller streets branching off from this main route, the extant buildings are only shadows of the past. They are vivid reminders of a better time and the town's peak as a mining community, when Mammoth was known across the world. Mammoth-Copperopolis Ltd. was a British mining venture. Today fewer than forty people live in town, but once it was packed with miners, merchants, and boardinghouse owners ready to become wealthy off the business associated

Mammoth Historic District.
Photograph by HABS, public domain, National Park Service.

with the mines. The buildings that cluster along these remaining streets are primarily residential or industrial structures built between 1892 and 1910, although some were built at the time of the initial strike in the area in 1870.

As a group the buildings are typical of mining towns, for the most part small frame structures with little ornamentation or detailing; they were raised quickly and just as rapidly left and unsentimentally deserted as miners moved on to other mines.

Nephi
Tintic Mining District
1869

The Tintic Mining District comprises an area about eight miles square in both Juab and Utah Counties and runs along the western and eastern slopes of the central portion of the East Tintic Mountains.

Between 1890 and 1926 Tintic was one of the largest mining districts in the state, feeding off strikes in Centennial-Eureka, Gemini, Mammoth, Chief, Plutus, Godiva, and the Iron Blossom Ore Run. Remnants of the nineteenth-century mining landscape are visible throughout the district. Massive head frames, or gallows frames, are found throughout the area, as are timber-framed and steel-framed structures that were used to lower and raise men and equipment in cages in and out of mining shafts. Slag dumps as well form tangible physical memories of days gone by.

The architecture of the Tintic Mining District is typical of mining towns—because of a scarcity of land, there is little wasted space. Houses dating from the 1880s to the 1920s were built in a variety of styles, and wooden frame houses were the most popular, providing shelter and not much else. With two rooms and an entrance on

the pitch side of the roof rather than the gable end, they were built on the sides of mountain streets that stretched through narrow gullies or canyons. Walls were covered with plank siding, clapboards, horizontal overlapping wooden boards, or sometimes even vertical board and batten. The managers of the mines, entrepreneurs or foremen, built more architecturally distinctive homes in revival styles, the Prairie style, or bungalows.

Typically, commercial buildings lined a single main road that snaked through town and had a variety of styles, materials, and designs. Simple frame structures with false-front facades were sometimes covered with corrugated iron or tin sheeting to protect them against fire. Stone or brick commercial-style buildings emerged after the mines began to make a profit, with a range of stylistic details ranging from Classical Revival to Italianate. Churches tended to be Gothic Revival, such as the wood-frame gabled St. Patrick's Church and the Eureka Ward Meetinghouse of the LDS Church.

Juab County Jail
45 West Center
1892

For more than eighty years after it was built in 1892, the Juab County Jail was an important center of county law enforcement activities until 1974. Located next to the county courthouse in Nephi, the Juab County seat, the two-story Juab County Jail is virtually intact, one of the largest and most well-preserved jails in the state.

The jail is a rectangular brick building with a sandstone foundation, a hipped roof, and a single solid metal door facing the adjacent courthouse. Three bays divide the facade and back of the building, and two bays run down both sides. Virtually the only

Juab County Jail

leader. He played a role in the organization of several key community institutions: the First National Bank of Nephi, the State Bank of Payson, the Fillmore Commercial and Savings Bank, and the Fountain Green State Bank. Also a politician, he was a member of the Utah State Senate between 1900 and 1908, and a delegate to the Democratic National Convention in 1904 and 1912.

This elaborate home embodied Whitmore's wealth and notoriety and was designed and built by Oscar Booth, a local architect. A well-known landmark in the area, the house is a three-story Eastlake/Queen Anne–style building with all the typical Victorian excesses in ornamentation, shingles, finials, moldings, lattices, carved panels, friezes, balustrades, and other elements that characterize the style. All visible wall surfaces are richly detailed with varied materials, textures, and colors. The porch also has a projecting pediment with carved wood ornamentation and sandstone steps with the words "Colonial Villa" chiseled into their surface. Leaded windows and woodwork on the interior create a luxurious, elegant ambience of wealth and material success.

architectural details are the brick segmental arches over the windows and doors and the bands of corbeled brick just below the eaves. The interior features four cells on the main floor and four on the second level. Each space is constructed with metal bars and sheet metal.

George Carter Whitmore Mansion / Colonial Villa
106 South Main
1898–1900
Oscar Booth

The railroad first came to Nephi to haul coal from Wales, a small Sanpete County town on the western edge of the Sanpete Valley, and Nephi became an important transportation hub, the center of four highways and the terminus of two railroads. Merchant George Carter Whitmore, the co-owner of the Hyde and Whitmore Mercantile Establishment, benefited by this growth.

Whitmore was a well-known and respected philanthropic and business

Nephi Main Post Office
10 North Main Street
1933
Federal government

With all the sturdy practicality imaginable, the Nephi Main Post Office is a one-story cream-colored rectangular brick block sitting on a raised basement platform using the most up-to-date technology; reinforced

Nephi Main Post Office

concrete is used for the footings, basement walls, and floor slabs, and steel framing for structural support. The relatively flat, symmetrical facade is classically proportioned and symmetrical and has evenly placed narrow windows covered with ornate iron grilles on both sides of the central entrance, with a slightly projecting center section topped by a compound sandstone arch. Rich sandstone detailing is continued throughout in the round-arched window bays, facing on basement walls, water table, belt course, bracketed cornice, coping, and delineation of the building's corners. Instead of sandstone, granite is used for the entry stairs and the landing. Circular sandstone bas-relief medallions are located over each window, one depicting an eagle and the other the head of Mercury. The words "United States Post Office" are incised over the entrance. The style of the building does not fit nicely in either the Beaux Arts tradition common during the early 1900s in Utah, or the simplified modern design of the Depression era, but forms a transition between the two.

Millard County

Topaz
Topaz War Relocation Center
16 miles northwest of Delta
1942

The few remaining traces of the Topaz War Relocation Center near Delta bitterly remind us of a dark episode in American history. In the wake of the bombing of Pearl Harbor, a tide of racial hatred and fear was directed against Japanese Americans. When President Franklin D. Roosevelt signed Executive Order 9066, he gave the army under the War Relocation Act blanket power to deal with the "enemy" alien problem. In what was perhaps the worst example of nativism in our country's history, a single ethnic racial group was identified as dangerous and foreign and was subjected to offenses against civil rights in the name of national security. The policy was activated with Public Proclamation No. 1, which announced that all persons of Japanese ancestry would eventually be removed from the West Coast "as a matter of military necessity."[5] Topaz is one of the ten internment camps that together imprisoned more than 120,000 Japanese Americans during World War II.

Topaz was officially known as the Central Utah War Relocation Center and opened on September 11, 1942. Taking its name from nearby Topaz Mountain, the camp included 19,800 acres and was designed to provide shelter for 9,000 individuals. More than 8,500 Japanese Americans lived in quickly and cheaply constructed barracks.

Internees occupied the site throughout this period, and conditions in the residential structures were abysmal. Buildings included forty-two blocks of residence units, each of which was designed to house 250–300 people and was constructed with simple pine planks. For insulation, tar paper and Sheetrock blocked out the winter air. When the first fall temperatures dropped below freezing in September and October, many of the units still had no windows. Each single-story barrack had six rooms that ranged from sixteen by twenty feet to twenty by twenty-five feet. Residents shared a central dining hall, recreation hall, combination washroom/toilet/laundry building, and outdoor clotheslines. The government supplied pot-bellied stoves, cots, mattress covers, and blankets, but evacuees had to make their own benches, tables, shelves, closets, storage chests, and other furniture.

The camp operated for about three years. Residents kept occupied with agriculture, furniture making, brick making, sheet metal manufacturing, and other jobs and services. Children attended the Topaz School, and the camp produced its own newspaper—the *Topaz Times.* When Topaz closed in October 1945, the federal

government sold both the land and the buildings—several of the latter were moved to various locations throughout the state. Visible traces of the lives of men, women, and children are still in evidence—pieces of discarded or forgotten toys, combs, and other personal objects lie around the site in the dust.

Deseret
Deseret Relief Society Hall
4365 South 4000 West
Utah Highway 257
1906

When Relief Societies were reorganized for Mormon women in the 1860s in Utah Territory, they were given incredible autonomy in their organization. Basically given the commission to give care and assistance to the poor and needy, each separate Relief Society group identified needs in its own area and addressed them as best it could, providing nursing, organizing donations, and delivering immediate relief. Others organized the equivalent of business enterprises to earn money by investing in real estate, opening Relief Society stores, or other entrepreneurial activities that required a central physical facility and were in many cases important to the local economy. The Deseret Relief Society Hall, built in 1906, is just such an entity. This building measuring twenty-four by thirty-eight feet is on the main road that runs through Deseret, Utah Highway 257. The women of the Deseret Ward saved funds for the building for more than a decade after 1894 under the leadership of Relief Society president Amelia Cahoon.

The Deseret Relief Society Hall is a simple rectangular structure with a distinctive Victorian Eclectic entrance porch on the gabled end of the building facing the street, which includes cornice returns

Region D

Deseret Relief Society Hall

typical of the Classical Revival style, but Queen Anne details in the lathe-turned columns of the porch, with spindled brackets. All exterior walls have novelty siding with corner boards.

The flexible space of the interior includes a small stage on the east end. The women of the Relief Society met there until 1934, when LDS auxiliary functions were consolidated into a single ward meetinghouse across the street.

Hinckley
Millard Academy
Off U.S. Highway 650
1908
Samuel T. Whitaker

The Mormon Church established academies to provide balanced secular and religious education for high school students in various areas of the region, beginning with Brigham Young Academy in Provo in 1875, Brigham Young College in Logan in 1877, and the Millard Academy in 1908. By 1905 more than 60 percent of Utah's high school

students and many from bordering states were enrolled in Mormon academies. The academy offered a combination of courses in both technical education and teacher preparation, including normal (teacher training), domestic arts, and manual training.

The Millard Academy is a sturdy two-and-a-half-story brick centralized block. Exhibiting at once naivete and enthusiastic confidence, the building has elements of both Craftsman and Romanesque Revival design, which were both in vogue at the time. Samuel T. Whitaker of Ogden was the architect.

Craftsman elements include the wide overhang of the roof supported by large wooden brackets, and the half-timbering of the gable sections on the north and south ends. Romanesque Revival details consist of the rounded arch at the entrance, the textural richness of the wall surface, a rusticated stone basement level, and raised bands and decorative corbeling that contrast with the rough-faced brick.

Millard Academy

Oak City

Oak City Tithing Granary
Off Utah Highway 125
1905

The Oak City Tithing Granary is one of twenty-eight tithing buildings in the state built between 1850 and 1910. In the nineteenth century, LDS tithing buildings functioned as a sort of social service center where members made in-kind donations, and newcomers or those in need could find welfare assistance. The tithing granary was key for collecting, storing, and distributing grain to those struggling for survival in a time of general privation.

This interesting building type features an inventive, tightly built chamber for the storage of grain, with an "inside-out" construction. The Oak City Tithing Granary has an exposed balloon frame structure, an interior wall of tongue-and-groove siding, large corner posts (measuring four by six inches), and two-by-four studs. One-by-twelve-inch vertical boards cover the upper walls of the building. A single door is centered on

the east wall, and a square opening on the second level above it provides access to the interior space of this one-and-a-half-story rectangular-frame gable-roofed building, which sits on a stone foundation.

Scipio

Thuesen-Peterson House
260 West Center Street
1870

There are subtle hints on the exterior of this building about the ethnicity of its pioneer builders. The pair house, or parstuga, was a preferred building type of Scandinavian immigrants, who were accustomed to low-profile homes built to conserve heat. The pair house has three main rooms—a principal central room that can be kept warm in the severe winter months, and equally sized rooms on both sides. The home is entered through a centrally located door.

This pair house has an indented porch on the facade in the center. It is built of locally produced yellow brick in walls laid with common bond. When it was first built it was one story and had a gabled roof and two chimneys—one on both sides of the central room. From this point these chimneys could add warmth to both the central room and the rooms on the sides. The home was later expanded to include a second level. The symmetry and regularity of the placement of windows and other openings conforms to the Classical style, but the pitch of the roof over the porch is more in line with the Victorian.

Danish immigrant John Thuesen built the home for his family around 1870. Settling first in Gunnison with his wife in 1866, he later moved over the mountain to Scipio. Within a decade he uprooted his family again and moved to Sevier County.

Scipio Town Hall
Utah Highway 63
1935
Public Works Administration
When the Scipio Town Hall was built in 1935 it was the largest building in town, as was true of many structures constructed with funds from the Public Works Administration program of Franklin Roosevelt's New Deal. Familiar in terms of style and massing, the town hall is a one-story brick building with stylized Classical detailing, or PWA Moderne. Rather than the strict austerity of the International style, PWA Moderne includes veiled references to the familiar detailing of the Classical style, expressed here in large piers with jagged fluted panels at each corner and running around the building, with the same vertical regularity as a colonnade. The flat parapeted roof was constructed in two sections. At the front the parapet is slightly stepped.

Below the water table line is unusual rustic rock facing, and similar rock occurs on a small flat-roofed bay that projects to the side. Probably five years after the building was completed, a brick entrance pavilion was added to the front with a parapeted flat roof, mirroring the design motifs of the rest of the building.

When it was built, the building was to be used for both a town hall and a general meeting place for all civic and social groups in town. But several years after it was built, a sloping floor was added to the interior so that it could be used as a motion picture studio on Friday and Saturday nights. In 1985–86 it was renovated for use as a senior citizen center.

Fillmore
Peter and Jessie Huntsman House
155–175 West Center Street
1871
Hans Hanson
The Huntsman House is an excellent example of Classical elements—symmetrical facade, side gables, low-pitched roof, and lintel-type window heads—a style vocabulary much preferred locally between 1847 and 1900. Altogether, the house's formality and symmetrical organization relate it to countless other similar buildings built along the path of immigration into the West. Representing what was left behind, a physical memory of sorts and a positive assertion of what was to come, the Huntsman House established its owner as a man of means and culture. This two-story central-passage house is a vernacular interpretation of the Federal style. Now painted green, the red brick of this house was laid three layers thick in a common bond pattern for extra insulation. Many of the materials are indigenous to the area. The house has a sandstone foundation, and floor joists rest on native, hand-hewn logs. The facade to the north has a full-width two-story porch, rebuilt in 1960 with fixed-sash multilight transoms over the doors.

In the late 1950s, again reflecting the times, the owner of the house converted the root cellar into a bomb shelter, which features built-in bunks, a fruit cellar, and a concrete deck on top that serves as a patio area in the backyard. Perhaps a more powerful cultural icon than the house itself, the combination forms a marked contrast between the pioneer frame of mind and the hysteria of the postwar decade.

Territorial Capitol
Center Street between Main Street and
100 West
1852–1855
Truman O. Angell Sr.

The first territorial legislature laid out the boundaries of counties, including Millard County, and designated Fillmore as the capital because of its central location in the region. Mormon church architect Truman O. Angell Sr. designed this Classically detailed capitol building, funded with a congressional appropriation of $20,000. Construction was limited by the available tools and technologies of the 1850s and the few available skilled craftsmen, and all of the structure's red sandstone and timbers from the hills nearby were hand fashioned. Because of the lack of funding, only one wing of the projected capitol structure was ever completed. This part of the building was three stories high, with eight rooms on the first and second floors, and a large legislative chamber measuring fifty-seven by thirty-seven feet that was fashioned after the room used for the Constitutional Convention in Philadelphia.

In 1855, the capitol was a rectangular structure rising forty-three feet to the top

Territorial Capitol

Region D

of a hipped roof. Only one full session was held in Fillmore—the Fifth Legislative Assembly. The next year, the legislature designated Salt Lake City as the territorial capital, and government offices, both executive and judicial, traveled north. Despite Brigham Young's ambitions for central Utah, population growth and development there languished, and it never became a prosperous center of agriculture or industry. Eventually the building became the property of Fillmore City and locals used it as a school, jail, and office building and eventually for religious services. Since 1927 it has been a historic site, reminiscent of the state's pioneer history.

Edward and Elizabeth Partridge House
10 South 200 West
1871
Lewis Tarbuck

Stonemason and bricklayer Lewis Tarbuck built this house for Edward Partridge Jr. and his wife, Elizabeth, in 1871, an excellent example of pioneer craftsmanship. The walls are two feet thick at the basement level and eighteen inches above. Some of the rich red sandstone has "desert varnish," or a natural patina. Stones throughout are carefully cut and laid. Chimney stacks demonstrate another type of work—paired and rotated on a forty-five-degree angle, they are capped with corbeled dogtooth brickwork. A two-story porch with a hipped roof runs across the front of the house. In an unusual move, the balcony level rises eighteen feet higher than that of the main house.

Edward Partridge was the son of Edward Partridge Sr., the first bishop of the LDS Church, and Lydia Clisbee. He lived through the expulsion from Missouri and Nauvoo and came to Utah with his mother and family in October 1848. Edward and his first wife, Sarah Lucretia Clayton, lived first in Farmington, where they saw many beautiful stone houses and hoped that one day they would have one of their own. Edward married his second wife, Elizabeth Buxton, on February 16, 1862, before the family moved to Fillmore, where he built his stone house.

Fillmore Tithing Office
40 West Center Street
1880

This temple-form tithing office is one of ten extant structures from the period between 1850 and 1910 when the LDS Church was collecting tithing in goods and distributing relief to the poor. This two-story rectangular brick building has a gabled roof facing the street and a boxed cornice that returns at the wall level. This along with the pedimented gabled facade refers to the Greek Revival style, by far the most popular style for religious buildings in Utah Territory. A pulley and projecting shaft above the entrance door suggest that this door was most likely used for loading and unloading tithing goods from the second story. The Fillmore Tithing Office is larger than many others, suggesting that it was a regional office and most likely would have had corrals, a barn, a granary, or other auxiliary buildings. The building was also used for meetings of the Millard Academy and possibly for the women's Relief Society, the Young Men's Mutual Improvement Association, and maybe even for prayer circles, as were other tithing offices in Lewiston, American Fork, and Panguitch.

In 1920, T. Clark Callister bought the building and turned it into a local telephone office. Callister played a role in bringing telephone service to Fillmore and

Millard County at the end of the nineteenth century.

Fillmore Rock Schoolhouse
100 West and 100 South
1867

Fillmore's first school after 1851 was a log room with a dirt floor in the original fort, complete with split-log seats. Three years later the community built an adobe church, which was also used as the local school for students of every age and level. This rock schoolhouse was built in 1867 with ashlar masonry and with the simple symmetry and formality of a Greek temple. Edward Milo Webb taught at this school before he moved to Salt Lake City, where he became a student himself at Deseret University. When it was constructed, this schoolhouse was one of three, but today it is the only one remaining and is one of a complex of buildings on the site of the Territorial Capitol in Fillmore.

Meadow
Meadow Tithing Granary
50 North 100 West
1900

Although we don't know the exact date of the construction of the Meadow Tithing Office, it was most likely built around 1900. Its construction method was commonly used for tithing granaries during this period, and it was located on the same lot as the tithing office and other related structures on the site. During the nineteenth century and early decades of the twentieth, tithing was important to local rural economies where many were cash poor and donations typically in-kind: farm produce, domestic animals, and donated labor. Donations came in and went out to those in need. Grain storage was critical to the

Fillmore Rock Schoolhouse

ebb and flow of the harvest and was a key part of the tithing system. Tithing granaries speak to the cooperation and sacrifice that marked the pioneering generations' efforts at survival and community building.

The Meadow Tithing Granary is a one-and-a-half-story square frame building with a gable roof. Like other Utah granaries, it has an exposed balloon frame that was constructed with two-by-four studs with interior horizontal siding, a building type called "inside out." This type of interior wall creates a sort of crib for the storage of grain or corn. The east entrance to the granary has a second-level door above, facilitating transportation of grain in and out of the building.

Not long after it was built, grain bins were installed on the interior. When in-kind tithing donations ceased after 1910, the building was still used as a granary and storage shed.

Kanosh
Kanosh Tithing Office
Off U.S. Highway 91
1870

More permanent than frame tithing offices, this one-and-a-half-story rectangular brick

Region D

temple form might be mistaken for an early Mormon meetinghouse. As was typical of Greek Revival temple-form buildings, the tithing office is oriented with its gabled end facing the street, where a pedimented gabled roof imitates that of well-known Greek temples. A central door with a window on each side created a symmetrical facade, dignified and quietly elegant.

Bishop Culbert King of the Kanosh Ward oversaw construction of the Kanosh Tithing Office in 1870 with the same care he might have shown for the meetinghouse, as a center for the collection and distribution of in-kind tithing contributions. Very little cash circulated in this small agricultural community. Eggs, milk, livestock, and chickens were more common than coins. After the 1920s, when cash was more plentiful, tithing was more typically given in cash and the building sat vacant. Sometimes the Mutual Improvement Association would hold meetings in the old tithing house, and eventually, in 1952, the church gave it to the local chapter of the Daughters of Utah Pioneers, which used it for meetings and as a relic hall.

Cove Fort

Cove Fort
Between Fillmore and Beaver on I-15
1867

At Brigham Young's instruction, Parley P. Pratt's exploration party identified Cove Creek as a favorable place for settlement in the fall of 1849. For years, travelers to the south went through Cove Creek on their way to California, southern Utah, and Arizona. Young wrote a letter to Ira Hinckley on April 12, 1867, asking him to "take charge" of building a fort on Cove Creek, which was a day's journey from Fillmore and a day's journey from Beaver to the south. Between Logan and St. George, towns were spaced about thirty-five miles apart, or a day's journey, making travel between them reasonable and efficient. Because water was scarce at Cove Creek, Young believed a way station would be preferable to a town. Quarrymen, stonemasons, and carpenters from all over central Utah came together to construct the fort with indigenous materials: black volcanic rock and dark limestone quarried in the hills nearby. The men used cedar and pine for

Cove Fort.
Photograph by Jllm06, CC A-SA 4.0.

the roof, twelve interior rooms, and densely built doors at the east and west ends of the fort. The fort is one hundred feet long and eighteen feet high.

Hinckley's daughter Luna described the lively activity that centered on the fort. "In those early days it was not isolation to be at the Fort. The news of the great, growing West throbbed over the lines into the telegraph office at the Fort and through [the] post office passed the news of the new western empire," delivered by Pony Express riders.[6] Children played in the inner courtyard, each day two-stage coaches brought tired journeyers and their baggage to the fort, and cowboys watched the tithing herds or horses in fields to the rear.

Sanpete County

Introduction

The central area of Sanpete County is the Sanpete Valley, a long, narrow valley dissected by the San Pitch River. Highway 89 runs through the valley as well, parallel to I-15 but far enough apart that it has preserved the nineteenth-century rural culture distinctive to the area. Each of the county's largest towns is tied to a particular identity or activity. Ephraim, the county's largest city, is home to Snow College, a two-year state institution with more than three thousand students. Manti is the center of county government and religious activity, with the Manti Temple and Sanpete County Courthouse. Moroni's turkey industry provides jobs for local residents, as does Gunnison's state prison to the south. Chiefs Walker and Sowiette invited Mormon settlement of the area in a visit on November 19, 1849, to church president Brigham Young, who sent 220 settlers to the site, 125 miles from Salt Lake City. Led by Isaac Morley and

George Washington Bradley, they founded towns from Gunnison in the south to Fairview in the north. Sanpete's agricultural economy has been sustained by an area surrounded by the Wasatch Plateau to the east and the San Pitch Mountains to the west. Until after the 1890s, more than 70 percent of the county's residents were Scandinavian—immigrants from Norway, Sweden, and Denmark who came to the United States under the auspices of the Perpetual Emigration Fund. A prominent exception to this largely LDS-convert population was the settlement of Clarion in 1911, a Jewish agricultural colony founded a few miles away from Gunnison. A local example of an international "back to the soil movement" that brought families out of urban environments and gave them the chance to work on farms, Clarion was a short-lived experiment that ended in 1916 but brought twenty-three families from the East Coast to this western landscape in the beautiful Sanpete Valley.

Fountain Green
Fountain Green Tithing Office
Southwest corner of 100 South and Main Street
1906

The LDS Church built the Fountain Green Tithing Office using a standard plan developed at church headquarters around 1905 that was also used for tithing offices in Spring City, Garland, Ephraim, and Fairview. The plan was referred to as "tithing office no. 2" in official correspondence, and the blueprints, lists of materials, and specifications came down from the church offices. Not long after it was completed, the bishop allowed the Relief Society to use some of the space as long as it did not interfere with the operations of the tithing program. During the 1950s it was abandoned

Fountain Green Tithing Office

for a time and turned over the Daughters of Utah Pioneers.

Any structure would struggle to compete with the beautiful pioneer brick buildings found throughout Fountain Green, but this one does so handily. In contrast with many of the multilevel brick or adobe houses along Fountain Green's Main Street, the tithing office is a tightly designed and constructed one-story square building of red brick, with a coursed sandstone foundation and a pyramidal roof. This particular standard plan is typified by an asymmetrical facade divided into equal halves by a simple buttress. The entrance is framed by an arched porch set in the northeast corner that forms half of the facade. The other half has three double-hung sash windows. A large sandstone block over the buttresses announces the building's name.

Fountain Green Hydroelectric Plant Historic District
Utah Highway 89
1922–1923

Located in a clearing in the foothills of the San Pitch Mountains, the Fountain Green

Hydroelectric Plant consists of a powerhouse, earthen dam, steel conduit, switchyard, and ancillary structures—a sort of industrial, hydroelectric power landscape critical to the growth and expansion of a rural area like this one capitalizing on water power from Big Springs. The plant served numerous communities in Sanpete County, facilitating the electrification of this rural area. Construction on the powerhouse began in 1902 and electricity was produced the next year. By the 1920s, it was clear that the plant was too small to satisfy demand and the firm built a new plant with two generators about 1,500 feet southeast of the first, and an earthen dam. A steel pipeline carried water 6,000 feet along a 500-foot drop to the generating station.

The powerhouse is a small building with a subtle reference to the Art Moderne, with its rectangular mass, concrete-capped parapet wall above a flat roof, and plain brick walls. The foundation is made with slightly flaring concrete, and a prominent concrete coursing wraps around the building. The entrance is identified by a centrally located brick pavilion and a sign that reads "Telluride Power Co./Ft. Green Hydro Plant."

Andrew M. Barentsen House
Utah Highway 30
1874

Much of Sanpete County was settled by Scandinavians, an ethnic and cultural presence hinted at in the pair house, or parstuga, which was greatly favored by these immigrants who were familiar with the difficulties of keeping their home warm during severe winter months. The Andrew M. Barentsen House is a one-and-a-half-story brick home built in 1874 with a large central chamber and a pair of equal-sized rooms to the sides, typical of the style. On this house, an addition built to the rear

Moroni ZCMI Cooperative

creates a T-shaped plan. Distinguishing features include windows topped by smooth stone pediments and a stone over the front door that reads "1874."

The house suggests the ethnicity of its first owner and builder, Andrew Marcus Barentsen, a forty-one-year-old Mormon convert from Bovsthoue, Ribe, Grimstrup Parish, Denmark, who immigrated to Utah in 1863 and located in Pleasant Grove, then Richfield, and by 1867, Fountain Green with his two wives and their children.

Moroni
Moroni ZCMI Cooperative
22 West Main Street
1902

When the Moroni Cooperative building was first constructed in 1902, it was known as A. K. A. Consolidated Mercantile, purveyor of general merchandise. Sold in 1925, the business became the Moroni Mercantile hardware store and remained a ZCMI cooperative until 1932, when it was again sold. As is the case with other historic cooperative buildings, the original ZCMI logo was painted on the side of the building, advertising ZCMI All Overs, the cooperative's unique brand of overalls (the historic sign can still be seen).

Moroni Opera House
Approximately 325 West Main Street
1891
Mons Monson, T. J. Morley

The earliest opera houses in the state were simple, unostentatious rectangular blocks with only Classical details that provided a wholesome environment for theatricals, musicals, and vaudeville troupes traveling the West. When built in 1891, the Moroni Opera House was the best-equipped opera house in Sanpete County. Mons Monson, the county treasurer, and T. J. Morley, a local musician, joined to fund, build, and manage the institution.

Built between 1890 and 1891 on the south side of the far west end of Main Street, this stone and brick building had a rectangular plan that measured approximately fifty-one feet by thirty-five feet, with the short end of the rectangle facing the street. The

Region D

Moroni Opera House

workers constructed the walls with local cut, coursed limestone on the first story and red brick above on the exterior of walls constructed with adobe. A slightly pitched gabled roof was eventually covered with corrugated iron. The facade originally had a single-step horizontal parapet on the gabled end.

The interior includes a large, tall room with a wooden floor and plastered walls and ceiling. The proscenium stage at the south wall measured thirty-five by twenty-five feet and had an elaborate Classically detailed front piece surrounding the arched opening to the stage, with trompe l'oeil paintings on each side. Lavish scenery was imported from Chicago and autographed by traveling performers, and sets were produced by local artists. The actors wore authentic costumes and used props provided by Moroni businesses.

The Opera House stayed open between 1891 and 1915, when what was then known as the Kozy Theater became Moroni's most popular movie house. In 1930, the Moroni Opera House was reconstructed to become the Monson Flour Mill to mill and store grain and flour. The Moroni Feed Company stored feed there between the 1940s and 1960s.

Moroni High School Mechanical Arts Building
350 North Center Street
1936
Works Progress Administration

The Moroni High School Mechanical Arts Building mirrors those built in Mount Pleasant and Ephraim between 1936 and 1937 as a Federal Emergency Relief Administration project, becoming a type of standard plan for this use. The straightforward

Moroni High School Mechanical Arts Building

and simple concept and design addressed programmatic considerations without frills or added expenses. This large, two-story box has a rectangular plan and a centrally placed two-story entrance portico. The beautiful cream-colored oolite limestone quarried in the Sanpete area was also used for many of the historic landmarks in the valley. The low-pitched hipped roof, heavy cornice returns, round-arched upper-story window, and molded cornice over the front door are the principal points of decoration on this otherwise quite plain building. Quoins at the corners make a faint reference to historical styles.

Fairview

Fairview City Hall
85 South State Street
1936
Hugh Anderson

The *Mount Pleasant Pyramid* announced the construction of the Fairview City Hall in its January 31, 1936, edition, what was considered a gift from the federal government. It described designer Hugh Anderson's Fairview plans: "It will be a two-story building and will be constructed of sawed native rock, known as blue sandstone. The building will be erected on Main Street on the corner lot south of the amusement hall and will have accommodations for city hall, library, jail, Legion hall, kitchen and serving room and two rest rooms."[7] Thirteen men from Fairview would work on the building starting that month and continuing through summer.

The New Deal had an important impact on Sanpete County in the 1930s. The Fairview City Hall is a one-story rectangular building with a raised basement and a flat roof designed with the stark, abstract Classicism so popular during the period, or the PWA Moderne style. The facade is divided into three sections—a smaller center section with the entrance, and two large Palladian windows on both sides topped by arched, elliptical fanlights. The oolite limestone is from local quarries and is familiar to lovers of Sanpete architecture; here it is

Fairview City Hall
Photograph by Cory Stokes. Used with permission of photographer.

finely cut to a smooth ashlar surface. A low-relief band of dentils runs beneath the cement coping at the roof edge.

Fairview Tithing Office
60 West 100 South
1908

Like the tithing offices in other Sanpete County towns—Ephraim, Spring City, and Fountain Green—this brick example is an LDS standard plan referred to as type 2, which has an asymmetrical front with an arched porch on one side and three windows on the other. A buttress running up the center has a large sandstone block announcing the name of the institution and the date of construction. Sandstone contrasts with the brick wall on the foundation level and is

used for sills and lintels for all windows and doors. Deviating from the standard plan, dormers may have been a later addition to the house.

Fairview is known for the excellence of its nineteenth-century brickwork. It is fitting that the tithing office was a perfect

Fairview Tithing Office

example of the transition away from the strict symmetry of pioneer buildings to balanced asymmetry. The LDS Church built the Fairview Tithing Office in 1908 along with a barn, granaries, and other facilities to keep farm products and livestock donated as tithing. Although none of these auxiliary structures are extant, they were likely part of the original complex of buildings. The Fairview Ward received approval from the presiding bishopric's office for the building project in March 1908 and completed the building for about $2,000 in 1908.

Mount Pleasant
Mount Pleasant Historic Commercial District
Main Street and Center Street
1870s

Mount Pleasant's commercial zone developed along Main Street, the town's major east-west axis, which intersected with the old state road, Utah's principal thoroughfare, at the center of town. Commercial buildings in Mount Pleasant face either Main Street or State Street and were built in clusters sharing contiguous walls or up against each other so tightly that there was no passageway between. The storefronts form a corridor for a block to the south and two blocks to the west. Despite some variation in style, material, and height, the district reads as a whole, a part of town distinguished by function, public life, and activity. Residential neighborhoods stretch in each direction from this central point.

Mount Pleasant's first commercial structure was a small log building that housed a cooperative store built in 1867. The Gentile Co-op, a non-Mormon store also built in 1871, was built on Main Street not far away. In the 1870s, the post office, the Liberal Hall, and Rolph Dry Goods Store filled out a growing Main Street cluster of public buildings, extending even farther in the 1880s with the Peel House hotel, Rosenlof's Carpentry Shop, the Sanpete County Co-op, the Lundberg Block, and several other new stores after the railroad came to Mount Pleasant in 1890. The same type of expansion occurred along State Street, with the Zion's Cooperative Mercantile Institution (1869), the Telegraph and Photograph Office, and other businesses and hotels.

Other local industries impacted Main Street development. Brick making, timber milling, stone quarrying, and mining affected the shape and materiality of local

Mount Pleasant Historic Commercial District

commercial architecture. Many of these buildings were architect designed—Richard Watkins and James Hansen, among others, designed houses for locals as well as public buildings for the downtown district. Between the 1880s and the first decade of the twentieth century, Mount Pleasant's commercial district rivaled those in much larger towns to the north and south. Exhibiting the range of available services and resources, the buildings on State Street reveal the stratification of Mount Pleasant society.

Mount Pleasant's City Hall is located at 115 West Main Street and is a rare example of the International style in Sanpete County. Built with Works Progress Administration (WPA) funds, the building has simple, strong, rectangular massing; metal frame windows; and the minimal decoration typical of the style. The brickwork on the Mount Pleasant Commercial and Savings Bank, at 146 West Main, illustrates local craftsmanship. The entire surface of the facade is modulated and given heightened interest through brick corbeling and other fancy brickwork. The entrance is recessed and highlighted by a rusticated stone arch in the belt course dividing the first-floor row of windows from the wall above. Brick dentils and corbeling run to the parapet wall, which is headed by a stone plaque with the inscription "19 BANK 01." At 160 West Main, the Sanpete County Co-op building housed a mercantile group organized by Neils S. Neilsen and brothers Andrew and Hans, first known as the Lower Store, Swedish Store, or Gentile Store, largely because it competed with ZCMI. An impressive two-story, three-bay brick commercial building with a recessed entrance on the first floor, it features extensive fancy brickwork and stonework on window arches and pilasters.

William Stuart Seeley House
U.S. Highway 89
1860

Prominent Mormon pioneer and bishop William Seeley was instrumental in the construction of Fort Mount Pleasant in 1859 when hostilities with the Native Americans increased and surrounding communities clustered together for safety. Although not every area of Utah Territory was impacted by conflict with Native Americans, Sanpete County was.

Seeley built this house in 1860 or 1861 for his third wife, Ann Watkins. More ample than the more typical hall-parlor house, the Seeley House has a central-passage plan and is built with two-foot adobe walls covered with stucco. This vernacular house exhibits a high level of craftsmanship and reflects the Greek Revival in its symmetrical facade, formality, and regular placement of windows and doors. The house is one room deep and is capped by a gabled roof.

Twenty years after the first section was constructed, a one-and-a-half-story wing was built to the west, making the plan a *T*. Similar in terms of materials and style to the original portion of the house, an entrance porch was added at this time that had a flat roof, full entablature, and two Tuscan columns. In 1910 additional rooms were built to the southwest in a one-story brick addition, topped by a hipped roof and surrounded by a covered porch with turned wooden columns that are more like the Victorian.

Mount Pleasant High School Mechanical Arts Building
150 North State Street
1935–1936
Public Works Administration

Mount Pleasant benefited from federal and national programs supporting construction of large-scale public buildings—a Carnegie library, the National Guard Armory, and the Mount Pleasant High School Mechanical Arts Building—during the first three decades of the twentieth century, an important period of growth and expansion for rural Utah. It was a duplicate of the Moroni High School Mechanical Arts Building, which was also constructed in the county between 1935 and 1936 under the auspices of the Federal Emergency Relief Administration.

Mount Pleasant National Guard Armory
Photograph by Cory Stokes. Used with permission of photographer.

The Mount Pleasant High School Mechanical Arts Building has a straightforward attitude toward design and function: it has a two-story rectangular plan, a two-story entrance portico, cream-colored limestone, and a low-pitched hipped roof. Emphasizing its formality, the facade is balanced with windows on both sides of the door, a round-arched upper-story window, and a molded cornice over the door. Other details include heavy cornice returns and low-relief quoins at the corners that link the building with historically traditional Classical designs.

Mount Pleasant National Guard Armory
10 North State Street
1936–1937
Niels P. Larsen

G. W. Brand of Mount Pleasant directed the construction in 1936–37 of the WPA Mount Pleasant National Guard Armory. Architect Niels P. Larsen of Salt Lake City designed the building as well as other armories in Nephi, Fillmore, Manti, and Spanish Fork that all look much the same. The building's second floor had offices for the county courthouse and city council, and an ample

hall, perfect for large meetings—political rallies, plays, and dances. For years, the building was the social center of town.

Like many buildings of the period, the Mount Pleasant National Guard Armory was designed in the PWA Moderne style, a sleek and streamlined style of the 1930s. This two-story flat-roofed rectangular block has the entrance in the center of the long side of the building that faces the street, and this is divided into three sections by flat pilasters that hug the building. Side wings have taller, stepped parapets and symmetrical vertical window panels.

Mount Pleasant Carnegie Library
24 East Main Street
1917
Ware and Treganza

When Andrew Carnegie began his program to fund libraries in America's small towns, he might have had Mount Pleasant in mind. This small agricultural community valued education and had already begun efforts to start a small library. In 1912, a local organization, the Home Culture and Twentieth

Region D

Mount Pleasant Carnegie Library.
Photograph by Cory Stokes. Used with permission of photographer.

Century Ladies' Club, began a small library with about fifty donated books and a small traveling collection. They used the old Armory Hall for their space until about 1915. That year it was combined with the public school library and relocated to the Hamilton School.

The well-known Salt Lake City architectural firm of Ware and Treganza designed the library, and local builders and contractors built it. The city dedicated the building on February 15, 1917. Like many other Ware and Treganza buildings, the Mount Pleasant Carnegie Library is designed in the Prairie style and epitomizes the style's core elements. It is a one-story rectangular building with a raised basement for extra space, and Classical Revival decoration. Band windows, a low-pitched hipped roof with a wide overhang, and a concrete band three-quarters of the way up the walls are all Prairie-style elements used on public buildings. The entrance is to the side of the central bay and projects slightly from the center of the facade. The geometric decorative elements are arranged symmetrically on the building just below the concrete band dividing the long window segments from the short window segments, and mullions between windows on all sides of the building terminate in capital-like elements at the cornice level.

Wasatch Academy
120 South 100 West
1888

Wasatch Academy was the most successful effort of the Reverend Duncan J. McMillan to establish a free Presbyterian school in Utah Territory. It is the oldest continuously running high school in the state and resembles a small New England liberal arts college, with a central green surrounded by impressive school buildings. Mount Pleasant's Mormon ward was divided over issues around church authority, which made the field ripe for Presbyterian missionary work and the establishment of a church school. McMillan purchased the building the Mormons had been meeting in—Liberal

Wasatch Academy

Hall—set up his offices, and perpetuated his strong ideas about education. McMillan's plan was to offer free education with properly trained teachers operating on a nine-month school year.

Within a year after the school first opened in 1875, it had one hundred pupils. Over the next several decades generous benefactors donated funds for a series of buildings that filled out the school campus: Mrs. Charles F. Darlington from New York donated funds in 1916 for a boys' dormitory, and church friends in Passaic, New Jersey, built the Frances Thompson Memorial Infirmary in 1921–22. Clearly, the venture had friends across the country who were watching the school's success.

Today, the Wasatch Academy welcomes students from a variety of religious, racial, cultural, and economic backgrounds. It includes some new buildings and historic restorations.

Spring City
Spring City School
Off Utah Highway 117
1899
Richard C. Watkins

Public education was a particular focus during the Progressive Era as the key to the moral redemption of society, the effort to make the world anew, and certainly the desire to maintain a well-informed citizenry. At the same time, church-supported education in Utah transitioned to public education with the Free Public School Act of 1890, which made it mandatory for local school districts to make free public education available to the state's children from kindergarten age to high school. Towns and regions throughout the state consolidated small one-room schools into distinctive four-square multilevel school buildings. Architect Richard Watkins designed this school for Spring City in 1899.

Spring City School.
Photograph by Cory Maylett, CC A-SA 3.0.

The Spring City School is one of the most impressive landmark buildings in town. Brick walls stretch two and a half stories, with wings that jut both forward and backward to form an *H* floor plan with a hipped roof. The lively wall surface of the facade exhibits the textural diversity typical of the Victorian Eclectic style and is richly colorful. Perhaps the most interesting detailing occurs in the brickwork itself, which creates the greatest appeal; patterned brick details around the doors and windows as well as at the cornice create surface richness and interest. The roof over the projecting round-arched entrance canopy creates a second-floor balcony with curved corners, round-arched windows appear in the stepped parapet, and a small bell tower caps the roof framed by two corbeled and patterned brick chimneys, all Romanesque details.

Spring City Historic District
1860s

There is something about Spring City that carries you away to another century. Perhaps it's the order implied by wide streets that meet each other at right angles, or the preponderance of pioneer buildings made of adobe, stone, or logs. Maybe it's the historic landscape—shade trees towering over fruit trees and fields of hay or corn, clustered around historic homesteads like sacred circles protecting home and hearth. Whatever it is, Spring City is special. Designated

Spring City Tithing Office

against a ridge called Horseshoe Mountain

Spring City Tabernacle

James Allred Schoolhouse / Endowment House

as a historic district, this small rural town gives you a sense of what life must have looked like in the last century, when it was slower paced and more intimate, with homes surrounded by trees rather than parking lots, and irrigation canals instead of curbs and gutters running along the streets.

Spring City is one of eleven towns in the upper Sanpete Valley that began in the mid-nineteenth century. Part of the regional plan for colonization directed by LDS Church headquarters, these towns reflect in form and substance a religious ideal and the Mormon effort to impose what they considered order and civility upon this western landscape. Spring City is tucked up

that rises dramatically to the east, and it depends on the springs that flow from the mountains into the valley below.

The boundaries of the historic district are coincident with the city limits, and are therefore easily marked. It includes about 95 blocks and 306 buildings, of which 76 percent suggest the character of a nineteenth-century village. The essence of the Mormon rural village was its orientation toward community and religion. In Spring City, the LDS Meetinghouse is the most significant figure on the landscape. Visible from virtually every corner of town, it is a beautiful reminder of what held the original settlers of this place together and what gave their efforts at community building meaning.

Region D

Besides exhibiting all the basic elements of the rural Utah village, the town also has a textbook lineup of nineteenth-century building types—the LDS Meetinghouse, the Spring City School, the Tithing Office, the City Hall, the Relief Society Granary, and the unusual James Allred Schoolhouse (sometimes known as the Endowment House), besides most of the housing types typical of the period. Many used the warm, rich oolite limestone quarried nearby; these homes are at once typical of the region and indigenous to the area. Significant and extant examples of adobe, frame, brick, and stone vernacular buildings line Spring City's streets, surrounded by historic landscaping and irrigation canals that weave along streets and through fields, dividing city blocks.

As was true of Utah Territory's other towns, Brigham Young called a group of settlers to settle Spring City, providing religious instruction as well the practical consideration of finding homes for the immigrants who followed him to Utah. In Spring City these included Latter-day Saints William Black, J. T. Ellis, and the family of James Allred, who moved from the Manti fort in the summer of 1859.

Sanpete County attracted so many Danish converts to the Mormon Church that the town was sometimes called Little Denmark. Inhabitants included Scandinavian craftsmen—blacksmiths, bakers, wheelwrights, shoemakers, carpenters, masons, and builders who brought their traditional crafts and skills to aid their settlement efforts.

Ephraim
Ephraim Carnegie Library
30 South Main
1935
Watkins, Birch & Wright
Unlike most other Carnegie libraries in Sanpete County, which are in the PWA

Moderne or Prairie style, Ephraim's library has Classical Revival motifs such as the prominent cornice running around the building, and the pilasters moving in regular intervals across the facade. But in terms of shape, size, and elevation, the building is fully in line with the approach to building and style of this group of public buildings. This single-story rectangular yellow brick building has a raised basement, a flat roof, and a brick parapet.

Modern glass doors have replaced the building's original doors, but they are still topped by a projecting sill and transom. Unlike other Carnegie libraries in the state that have pilasters across the facade only, this one has pilasters that run around the entire building.

Andrew Carnegie gave Ephraim a grant of $10,000 to build this new library in 1914, supporting the town's long tradition of valuing education and literacy. Mayor P. D. Jensen managed the project and hired the architectural firm of Watkins, Birch & Wright to design and manage construction of the building. Ephraim celebrated both the library's opening and the community's commitment to education with a parade, band concert, benefit dance, and series of speeches that brought the townspeople together. Professor John Widstoe of Salt

Ephraim Carnegie Library

Lake City and state superintendent of public education Dr. Ephraim G. Gowans gave enthusiastic speeches on the subject of "prevention," suggesting that libraries were valuable community agents in what Gowans called "preventive moral training for young people."[8]

Ephraim United Order Cooperative Building
Corner of Main Street and 100 North
1871–1872

Brigham Young worked to combat the growing power of the non-Mormon business class through Zion's Cooperative Mercantile Institution, a regional network of local cooperatives connected to a parent store and wholesale operation in Salt Lake City in 1868. Within a decade, more than 150 cooperatives organized by local stockholders appeared in cities throughout Utah Territory. The Ephraim United Order Cooperative Building is possibly the most beautiful extant structure of the group. Built between 1871 and 1872 with native oolite limestone, it has a symmetrical and formal facade that establishes the store

as a Mormon store with the iconographic inscriptions "Ephraim U.O. Mercantile Institution," "Holiness to the Lord," and the familiar beehive symbol. These were more than logos; they were symbols of loyalty, association with the group, and a united economic front.

Ephraim Granary

Ephraim United Order Cooperative

Ephraim Wooden Granary

Mormon historian Leonard Arrington emphasized the centrality of the cooperative ideal to the Mormon way of life. "Cooperation, it was believed, would increase production, cut down costs, and make possible a superior organization of resources. It was also calculated to heighten the spirit of unity and 'temporal oneness' of the Saints and promote the kind of brotherhood without which the Kingdom could not be built."[9]

The two-story co-op is a substantial rectangular temple-form building with the gabled end facing the street. Windows and doors around the building have a formal rhythm and regularity. The main level was used for the store and the second floor as a recreation hall and Relief Society meeting hall. Restored as part of a county-wide economic redevelopment effort, the building benefited from the Sanpete Trade Association, which saw the value in historic

properties in preserving history, attracting tourists, and leading to economic recovery.

Ephraim Tithing Office and Bishop's Storehouse
64 North Main Street
1906

In some ways the Ephraim Tithing Office and Bishop's Storehouse looks more like a tightly built residence than a public building. But it is, in fact, one of three standard plans used by the LDS Church in the early twentieth century for tithing house designs. This building type was believed to efficiently and practically satisfy the programmatic demands of the tithing program, and the plans, specifications, and lists of materials were available upon demand from the office of the presiding bishop at church headquarters in Salt Lake City. When built in 1906, the Ephraim Tithing

Ephraim Tithing Office and Bishop's Storehouse

Office replaced earlier, historic structures. The site also included corrals, a barn, a root cellar, and a Relief Society granary where Ephraim's women stored grain for distribution to the poor.

The plan for this building is described as type no. 2, the same as those built in Spring City and Fountain Green. It is a one-story square building of red brick with a coursed sandstone foundation and a pyramidal roof. One enters the building through an entrance on the southwest corner in an arched porch separated from the other side by a

Snow Academy Building / Noyes Building

simple buttress, with three windows on the other side. When it was built in the early twentieth century, the tithing office would have played a vital role in helping to locate newcomers in town and assist the poor, evidence of the willingness of church members to sacrifice for the common good.

Snow College
150 East College Avenue
1888

Snow College was founded twelve years after the first major LDS school in the region—Brigham Young Academy in Provo—and was known as the Sanpete Stake Academy. Classes were held in the second-story space of the Ephraim Co-operative Building at 100 North Main Street. Newton E. Noyes was the academy's principal for twenty-nine years, advocating for the school's students at church headquarters. Lorenzo Snow was president of the Church of Jesus Christ of Latter-day Saints at the time, and he gave the academy $2,000 in November 1909. Recognizing this important support, the school changed its name to Snow Junior College, and then

in 1923 to Snow College, in his honor. The LDS Church turned over many of its educational enterprises in the 1930s, including Snow College, which became a state school in 1932–33. Between 1951 and 1969, Snow College functioned as an extension of Utah State University. Expansion has resulted in greater diversity in school programs and structures, an energetic athletic program, and cultural activities that are impressive for a school of its size.

Snow Academy Building / Noyes Building
150 College Avenue
1898
Richard C. Watkins

Richard C. Watkins, the premier school designer of his day, proposed this impressive and commanding brick and stone building ten years after the school was first organized. Watkins designed more than ninety-five schools during his career, many in Sanpete County and other central Utah towns. In fact, in 1911 he was appointed architect for state schools. The building was built with local labor, donated materials, and $7,500 the town raised itself. The

Region D

people of Ephraim held "Sunday Eggs" and "Nickel Sunday" drives and delivered truckloads of oolite limestone and sand to the building site.

This two-story rectangular building has brick walls and a stone foundation. Classical Revival details include an overall sense of formality, symmetry, and dignity, round-arched stone openings, a triangular pediment on the projecting pavilion that announces the entrance, and dentils and modillions running along the cornice level. Until 1904, when the building was completed, classes were held at the co-op building. But from that time to the present, classrooms and offices have enlivened the building.

Manti

Manti Temple
U.S. Highway 89, north edge of Manti
1877–1888
William H. Folsom

The Manti Temple, designed by William Folsom, is one of the most beautiful buildings in Utah. Located on a butte eighty feet above the highway overlooking Manti, it is visible for miles throughout Sanpete County. Surrounded by sloping lawns, beautiful flowers, and shade trees, its twenty-seven-acre site, or "temple hill," seems a place apart in this rural Utah town.

The temple measures 171 feet by 95 feet and has walls built with the beautiful warm cream-colored oolite limestone native to the area. William Folsom was one of the key LDS Church architects. He chose mansard roofs typical of the French Empire style for the top of the towers, which reach 179 feet. The east facade of the temple faces the mountains, and the west faces the highway below. The interior space is simple and elegant and conforms to domestic standards of excellence in decoration and craftsmanship. The high level of local craftsmanship is particularly evident in the interior woodwork with its graceful arches, heavy doors, and finely cut moldings. In the basement, the life-sized oxen holding the baptismal font on their backs also suggest local talent in

Manti Temple

craftsmanship. As was customary for a nineteenth-century Mormon temple, a series of ceremonial rooms were located on the main floors and an assembly room on the upper level, which held 1,500 members for the temple's dedication in 1888. Movement from the basement baptismal area to the upper level passes through spiral staircases in the two corner towers that extend from the basement to the roof without any supporting columns, and the walnut railings and balusters wind up through five stories, forming a symmetrical coil.

Manti City Hall

Manti City Hall
191 North Main Street
1873–1882
A. E. Merriam

Two years after the pioneers first arrived in Salt Lake Valley, Brigham Young sent explorers to Sanpete Valley to identify opportunities for settlement there. Manti would be the first town to be settled outside the Wasatch Front and would hold its city meetings in the Council Hall, a multipurpose building raised during the 1850s. The Manti City Hall was constructed between 1873 and 1882 and is one of the oldest remaining city halls in the state. It was designed by a local man, A. E. Merriam, whose principal experience was building houses. Although it was not the most popular style, there are good examples like this one of the Italianate in Sanpete County and along the Wasatch Front, built in the 1870s.

Although it is a public building, the Manti City Hall resembles a double-pile central-passage house plan, with four roughly equal-sized rooms separated by a central passageway and a staircase leading to the second level. Merriam's unique contribution was his application of Italianate details to this familiar form and its use for a public building. Boxlike massing, a low-pitched hipped roof, bracketed eaves, and the decorative cornice are fully in line with the principles of the Italianate design.

Sanpete County Courthouse
160 North Main Street
1935–1937
Federal government

Sanpete County's builders capitalized on the gently sloping foothills to perfectly site its most distinctive buildings. Creating a sense of monumentality and emphasizing its importance to the community, the Sanpete County Courthouse sits on a slight rise on the east side of Main Street in downtown Manti. Stretching long and horizontally along the landscape, this two-story rectangular block is a modern building, but the symmetry of its form and veiled

Region D

Sanpete County Courthouse

references to other details of Classicism combine in a style termed PWA Moderne, one of the best examples in the state. The building has a large two-story central block with narrow, vertical window panels that are flanked by smaller two-story side wings with horizontal windows. Locally quarried oolite limestone, the county's indigenous building material, creates a smooth monochromatic surface. Flat bas-relief sculptural detail is found at the top of the windows in the center section, and large lanterns hanging on either side of the entrance are supported by iron rods; these design motifs are common to the PWA Moderne.

Manti Tithing Office
Southeast corner of 100 North and Main Street
1905

The Manti Tithing Office was the first tithing office constructed with a standard plan out of LDS Church headquarters. It was one of three standard plans designed in 1905 for a very particular purpose—to gather and distribute tithing donations in a structure that was aesthetically pleasing and economically constructed. This building is important as the first evidence of the LDS use of standard plans, which would become the basic approach to church buildings in the mid-twentieth century.

The Manti Tithing Office is a one-story square building of yellow brick topped by a pyramidal roof, sitting on a sandstone foundation with a projecting gabled pavilion on the symmetrical facade. An inset rectangular panel is located above the round-arched opening, and above that is a semicircular vent. A wide frieze wraps around the building below the line of the cornice, formed with brick that projects at different levels. For textural relief and decoration, rock-faced brick was used for the arches over the windows and in the pavilion. The tithing office is still used by the LDS Church as a bishop's storehouse where welfare donations are stored for distribution to the needy.

Manti Tithing Office

Manti National Guard Armory
50 East 100 North
1930s
Niels P. Larsen

Manti benefited from the New Deal funding for infrastructure and public projects in rural America. Architect Niels P. Larsen designed a series of similar National Guard armories during this period under the auspices of the WPA: two-story, flat-roofed PWA Moderne buildings.

As was typical of the style, the armory building is a long, rectangular block with a central principal entrance and flanking side wings divided by low-relief pilasters. The entrance is announced with three recessed door panels and a slightly raised parapet, and taller stepped parapets on both sides. The ends of the two wings feature vertical window panels. Oolite limestone finished with cement plaster places the structure in the material context of Sanpete County.

When the United States entered World War II, the armory was occupied by the

Parachute Company of Utah; after 1944 by the Reliance Manufacturing Company, which continued the production of parachutes and employed two hundred men and women; and eventually by the Carlisle Manufacturing Company, which produced military uniforms for the federal government and had more than three hundred workers by the 1950s, when it claimed to be one of the largest and most modern plants west of the Mississippi.

Manti Carnegie Library
12 South Main Street
1912
Richard C. Watkins

The Manti Carnegie Library is a one-story box with Classical Revival detailing and is more square than rectangular, as was the norm. The library features brick the same color as the native limestone so common to the area, a raised basement, and a flat roof. It has a symmetrical facade with a projecting pedimented portico and a monumental

Manti Carnegie Library.
Photograph by Cory Stokes. Used with permission of photographer.

arched opening; it is framed by a pair of pilasters that hold up a large semicircular arch. Each window also has a projecting concrete sill made with light brown concrete that contrasts with the tan brick. Other Classical details include brick piers and pilasters topped by simple geometric capitals, a Classical cornice with dentils and modillions on the frieze, and a crowning parapet.

Andrew Carnegie gave Manti $10,000 to help fund construction of a local library. It is one of twenty-three built in the state. The city appointed a special library committee to manage the project, which would be built on the site of the old Council Hall. The group inspected other Carnegie libraries in Eureka and Ogden in 1910, preferring the Eureka library, designed by popular architect Richard C. Watkins of Watkins & Birch, the designers of at least five other Carnegie libraries in Utah, more than any other architectural firm.

Hans Ottesen House
202 South 200 West
1865

The subtle shadow of Scandinavian roots is best seen in the parstuga house form, or pair house. The Hans Ottesen House is a one-and-a-half-story example, with the kitchen at the center and two smaller rooms on both sides. Like many other buildings in the county, this gable-roofed house was built with oolite limestone in a coursed rubble pattern covered with plaster to finish it off in a way common for domestic structures. Details of the house fall into the Greek Revival–style repertoire—fine limestone sills and pedimented lintels compliment the windows. During the 1920s a bungalow-like porch was added to the front.

Otteson, a stonemason, farmer, and Mormon convert, came to Utah in the 1850s. Born in Aalborg, Denmark, he would have brought with him an understanding of the advantages of the parstuga house. Robbers attempted to break into his home on November 2, 1884, and he was murdered.

Manti Presbyterian Church
185 South Main Street
1881
Peter Van Houghton, Jenson Brothers

Salt Lake City architect Peter Van Houghton designed Manti's First Presbyterian Church, built in the 1880s under Reverend Melancthon Hughes's direction and one in a chain of towns, including Manti, Gunnison, Salina, Richfield, and Monroe, in which buildings of native stone are linked stylistically. Competing with the

LDS temple of the same decade, the Manti Presbyterian Church stands out from the others and is the most architecturally sophisticated. Completed in 1881, this Gothic Revival church faces the street and is a tall, one-story gable-roofed structure built with the familiar oolite limestone of Sanpete County. A stone tower dominates the facade, and there is a wooden belfry at the southwest corner of the front facade and a wood-paneled door at the first-story level, along with a pair of Gothic arched openings on the second. The wooden belfry at the top has three parts: the base is a steep-sided truncated pyramid covered with wooden shingles; the next is a series of open arches supported by simple rectangular columns, with a strip of molding at the top; and at the top a tall, steep, flared hipped roof is covered with wooden shingles. The church's window and door openings are pointed Gothic arches formed with stone.

Peter Hansen House
247 South 200 East
1865
Peter Hansen

This one-story pair house has three rooms—a larger central room with smaller equal-sized rooms on both sides—and a more unusual configuration of openings on the facade than is usual. The house has a limestone foundation supporting walls of yellow brick produced in Manti. A vernacular house that makes no reference to a particular style, it has a matter-of-fact and pragmatic approach to shelter. Chimneys on both sides of the

Manti Presbyterian Church

central room provided heat for exterior rooms as well. The pair house plan was particularly good for conserving heat in the central room. In dreadfully cold winters, a family could huddle together for warmth in this single chamber and make the most efficient use of the heat generated by the dual fireplaces.

Manti Tabernacle
100 South Main Street
1877–1882
Dedicated 1903

The construction of the Manti Tabernacle took place over a twenty-six-year period. This beautiful stone building was constructed with the indigenous oolite limestone so characteristic of the Sanpete Valley. Stonemasons laid carefully cut stones between 1877 and 1882. Over the next two decades the steeple, finials, and other decorative details were added to the original structure. LDS Church president Joseph F. Smith dedicated the building in 1903, and it was rededicated in 1930 by President Heber J. Grant after some major interior remodeling, which resulted in multiple levels rather than the single large assembly room so typical of LDS tabernacles, with classrooms down below. The Manti Tabernacle was restored in 2014–15, with remortared stonework bringing the steeple back to its original beauty. This evolution of the interior space mirrored changes in LDS liturgical requirements. Originally the tabernacle was the scene of large-scale regional instructional meetings. After the 1930s it was used more in the ways a traditional LDS meetinghouse was used, with sacrament meeting, Sunday School, and a variety of auxiliary meetings throughout the week.

Gunnison
Casino Theater
78 South Main Street
1913

The Beaux Arts style of the Casino Theater announces its prominence on Gunnison's Main Street. This two-story, two-part commercial block is distinguished from other buildings nearby in style and function. In terms of mass, the building is a rectangular structure, with the short end facing the street and sidewalls formed with common brick. Its facade is symmetrically organized and includes large fluted columns that support arched pediments, a heavy cornice with modillions and dentils, flower decorations and cherubs, and a large rounded arch over

Manti Tabernacle.
Photograph by Cory Stokes. Used with permission of photographer.

Casino Theater

the central entrance, flanked by round-arched windows on the second story. As is common for a theater, the central entrance is deeply recessed and flanked by small windows that open up commercial space. The auditorium has a stage at the front, and a four-room apartment and projection room upstairs. Dressing rooms were in the basement.

Sims M. Duggins bought Main Street property in June 1912 for an opera house, tearing down an old adobe building to make way for the new one. His goal was to create the most beautiful amusement halls outside Salt Lake City. After January 1913, this building was used primarily as a movie theater for eighty years, but also as a residence, and at various times it housed a barbershop, grocery store, confectionery, brokerage office, and millinery shop. Thanks to the dedicated efforts of local advocates of historic preservation and lovers of theater, the building was mostly restored by 2014.

Sevier County

Redmond
Redmond Town Hall
18 West Main Street
1881 (abode structure); 1890s

In many ways, the Redmond Town Hall is the quintessential example of a vernacular pioneer structure. The original adobe building measured twenty-four by thirty-six

Salina Municipal Building and Library.
Photograph by Cory Stokes. Used with permission of photographer.

feet and had a gabled roof. A stove heated
the single multipurpose interior chamber
and was connected to a chimney on the
north end of the building. Long after it was
built, the city sheathed the adobe walls
with stucco to protect it from the weather.
As is usually true of vernacular buildings,
ornamentation is minimal and restricted
to Classical lintels, corbeled brickwork on
the chimney, a plain frieze, and a mod-
estly adorned box cornice. After the town
stopped using it as a meeting hall, it was
used as a jail.

The 1891–97 addition had more style
elements. Light-colored limestone quarried
east of Redmond was carefully cut, squared
off, made slightly rock faced, and laid in a
plain ashlar pattern. A hipped roof has a
belfry on the ridge and a simple boxed cornice. Interior moldings around the windows
and door have a post-Eastlake feel.

Redmond Hotel
15 East Main Street
1879–1904
Jacob Nielsen, James Frandsen
After 1879, the Redmond Hotel was
expanded in a series of stages as the community grew. At first a single story with a
symmetrical organization, a rectangular
shape forming a *T* plan, a gabled roof, and
end chimneys, the three-room house was
sometimes used by travelers coming to
Redmond on the Denver and Rio Grande
Western Railroad. In 1904, to expand the
number of rooms for boarders, an adobe
second story and hipped roof were added,
as well as a two-story front portico with
a gabled pediment in the middle. Tuscan
columns support the portico and a western
shed-roofed porch, all characteristics more
in line with Victorian styles than the pioneer vernacular.

It is optimistic at best to describe this rural public boardinghouse as a hotel, but that is how it was used in the past. The house was sold after World War I to Ada Nielsen, the granddaughter of one of the original inhabitants, Jacob Nielsen, who started calling it the Redmond Hotel and rented rooms during the Depression years. After 1951, the house became a private residence again.

Salina
Salina Municipal Building and Library
90 West Main Street
1936–1937
Public Works Administration

Salina's first city hall was built in 1897 but was replaced in 1936–37 because it "lacks

Salina Presbyterian Church

modernized equipment and style."[10] The modern building housed the administrative offices of the WPA for a period. Here "zone five" of the Works Progress Administration oversaw programs in a six-county region in south-central Utah from offices in the large basement.

The Salina Municipal Building and Library is a single-story brick building that exhibits blended elements of the Prairie and Art Deco styles. Demonstrating the eclecticism in public architecture of the 1930s, the building has a symmetrical rectangular plan, a flat roof, a full basement, and a polychromatic surface; the deep brown of the brick and the cream color of the plastered panels enrich the wall surface. The building has abstract geometric stickwork at the corner, above the main entrance, and below the roof edge, a feature that breaks up the strict formality of the building's design.

Salina Presbyterian Church
204 South 100 East
1884
Mathias Andreason (stonework)

When the Reverend Duncan McMillan began a mission in the Sanpete and Sevier Valleys in the 1880s, he established small congregations in a series of Mormon-dominated towns, sometimes with only a few members. As they grew, each built a church of its own, proud testaments to religious diversity and the determination to worship as one chooses. The congregation built the Salina Presbyterian Church with native stone in the Gothic Revival style. Like similar churches in Manti, Gunnison, and Monroe, it is a single-story, gable-roofed stone building with a wooden belfry atop an asymmetrical front gabled end.

Stone on the Salina Presbyterian Church is rough faced and laid in coursed ashlar

Region D

bond, with mortar oozing out above the plane of the wall. It is likely that the same stonemason—Mathias Andreason—worked on each of these churches. The wooden belfry at the top of the church, like that at Manti, designed by Peter Van Houghton, has three parts—a base that is a truncated pyramid covered by wooden shingles, a center section consisting of wooden arches resting on eight columns, and a top with a tall, steep, flared hipped roof covered with wooden shingles. A shed-roofed frame addition moves to the rear and once housed the schoolteacher who taught in the building.

The church was first used as a school and never had a permanent minister, although the circuit-riding Reverend G. W. Martin from Manti visited the congregation upon occasion. More important to the town, however, were the resident Presbyterian teachers—at once teachers, missionaries, nurses, and benevolent aides, these women made a mark on these small towns.

Peterson/Burr House
190 West Main Street
1900
P. J. Peterson

This substantial late Victorian, Queen Anne house has two stories, frame construction, and a stone foundation. In terms of mass, the house is a central block with projecting bays with drop siding on the walls and decorative leaded-glass transoms within the larger windows of the bays. The house is entered through a double-tiered veranda wrapping around to the northwest. Lathe-turned columns with bargeboard detailing support the porch roof. The house's roof is the most elaborate and varied example of Victorian excess and includes a seemingly endless number of pitches and roof planes: a central pyramid with a gabled roof over

the front bay, a segmental hipped roof over the west bay, a hipped roof over the east bay, a conical roof over the veranda tower, a segmented conical roof over the cupola, a shed roof on the northeast, and a hipped roof over the back of the house.

Salina Hospital
330 West Main Street
1917

With an unusual style for a hospital, the Salina Hospital is a Prairie-style brick structure with stucco trim. The two-story portion of the front of the building has a low-hipped roof extending from the flat-roofed central mass. Horizontal lines are emphasized throughout the exterior design. This is accomplished by a cornice running around the entire building, windows arranged in horizontal groupings, and a wide overhanging roof. Four brick piers on the main elevation terminate in decorative corbeled and stuccoed capitals. In terms of materiality, the building sits comfortably in the group of Prairie-style buildings constructed throughout the state. Segmental arches are found over windows on the side elevations.

This modern building was one of the first medical facilities to provide health care for a rural farming town and was important throughout the 1920s and 1930s. The use of the Prairie style in this isolated central Utah town shows the popularity and significant diffusion of the style into virtually every part of the state.

Richfield

Richfield Carnegie Library
83 East Center Street
1913–1914
Archibald G. Young

At the turn of the century, most Americans still believed they had a chance at the American Dream. The popular

Richfield Carnegie Library

rags-to-riches stories of men like Andrew Carnegie seemed to prove that anything was possible. Carnegie, himself an Irish immigrant and child of poverty, believed that the key to success in life was education and that it should be available to everyone. His commitment to free libraries that would be available to all Americans was exemplified in his program to fund small-town libraries.

Andrew Carnegie gave the central Utah town of Richfield a grant of $10,000 to fund the construction of a local library. A year later the mayor and city council passed a resolution authorizing the purchase of grounds for the library and maintenance fees.

The Richfield Carnegie Library is distinguished by its Craftsman style. It is a one-story rectangular building like most of Utah's other Carnegie libraries, with a raised basement. The gracefully pitched gable roof of the main block, the use of yellow clinker brick as the primary building material, half-timbering in the gabled ends of the building, window bands, and stick-work in the front and side entrance gables and over the small dormers are familiar Craftsman elements more commonly seen in residential examples.

The horizontality of the design is emphasized by the contrast between the concrete and brick of the main wall, the window bands, and the roofline supported by monumental brackets. At the center, a pair of double doors is set into an ogee-shaped opening and flanked by sidelights, an unusual motif repeated in stickwork up above.

Young Block
3–17 South Main Street
1907
Archibald G. Young

The two-story brick Young Block occupies a corner lot on Richfield's Main and Center Streets. The entrance to the building is indented from the sidewalk, framed by

Region D

Young Block

Classically derived pilasters, and topped by a square corner tower. Pilasters on the side of the building lead to upper-level apartments. On the street level, the windows are large and inviting for display space. A cornice separating the first and second stories wraps around the prominent corner tower. Large stone lintels and continuous sills form a stringcourse on the second level. A corbeled cornice and an applied pressed-metal cornice cap off the building.

Archibald Graham Young, a carpenter and the building's original owner, immigrated to Richfield from Scotland in the 1870s. Young worked on the Sevier County Courthouse, a new jail, the Richfield elementary school, the Fillmore School, and the post office and library in Richfield. Young purchased this lot with Morten Jensen for what would be Richfield's most architecturally significant commercial building. Many local businesses have at one time or another been located in the Young Block.

Richfield Main Post Office
93 North Main Street
1919
Federal government
The Neoclassical Richfield Post Office building is a good example of a combined town post office and federal building. This two-story brick building rests on a raised basement platform made with reinforced concrete footings and steel framing. Symmetrically organized and proportioned according to Classical styles, the facade is divided into five bays, with a central entry and flanking Palladian windows. There is only moderate decoration: a horizontal water table, sandstone belt and coping courses, paired windows in the center, single windows on the ends, and main entry stairs and a landing made of granite. Overall the building is compact, formal, and minimal in its approach to decoration and mass.

The local newspaper, the *Richfield Reaper*, was vocal in its disappointment

Richfield Main Post Office

with the post office design, saying on March 9, 1918, "Honestly, good people, doesn't that square, unadorned pile of masonry form a blot on the landscape."[11]

Richfield Tabernacle
200 West Center Street
1929–1930
Joseph Don Carlos Young

The LDS religious building with the most status was the Mormon temple, but a region that had a sufficient population base and wanted to build a permanent and important religious landmark might choose to build a tabernacle instead, a decision made locally rather than by church headquarters in Salt Lake City. The building of a tabernacle was a signal that a community had matured and had enough regional significance for large-scale meetings of the church for both instruction and celebration throughout Utah. The Richfield Tabernacle was both a place for religious services and

a community center, a use that continues to the present day, with performances ranging from the Utah Symphony orchestra to local theatricals.

The design of the Richfield Tabernacle is provincial in that it is a slightly awkward combination of a portico with six Corinthian columns running across the facade, elevated on a podium base and topped by a triangular pediment. The main rectangular building mass rises two and a half levels to a hipped roof behind. Red brick walls contrast with the butter-yellow plaster on the walls in the central bay of the facade. Clearly meant to impress and to celebrate religious and cultural life in this town at the heart of "Panoramaland," this building is a stark contrast to the smaller-scale buildings in downtown Richfield. President Heber J. Grant officiated at the dedication of the Richfield Tabernacle, the last designed by architect Joseph Don Carlos Young, on September 13, 1936, at 1:00 p.m.

Region D

Richfield Tabernacle

Jens Larson Jenson Lime Kiln
About two miles north of Richfield
1903
J. H. Kyhl

The Jens Larson Jenson Lime Kiln is carved into a red-rock hill two miles north of Richfield. The kiln itself is twenty feet high and about twenty feet in diameter, with thick eight-foot walls forming a rectangle and a large semicircular fireplace opening centered at the base. Iron bars once spanned the opening at the top, preventing rocks from tumbling down into the fire in the kiln.

Swedish immigrant Jens Larson Jenson cured lime used for the mortar on the exterior of many of the area's rock and brick structures; the lime was also used for the production of whitewash for the interior walls of local houses and public buildings. The process included men hauling limestone to the site and dumping it into the top of the kiln, where the rocks were burned or cured for three to five days. Afterward the stone cooled for three days before it was taken to market in wagons, where Jenson sold three bushels for a dollar.

Andrew Petersen House
92 East 200 South
1870s

Danish immigrant Andrew Petersen built this house in the early 1870s after the people of Richfield moved back to their homes following the Black Hawk War. Petersen's ideas were colored by what he had experienced in his homeland, where the parstuga house, or pair house, was a common vernacular type. It would be easy to guess that this was a hall-parlor house with two rooms on the main floor. But instead it has three, behind the symmetrical facade and centrally located door, as well as chimneys on both edges of the larger central room. The house is a one-and-a-half-story sandstone building with smoothly finished stone quoins at the corners and smooth stone courses surrounding the windows and the door on the facade. Details like gable returns, entablature, and entrance transoms are reflective of the Greek Revival.

Glenwood
Glenwood Cooperative Store
15 West Center Street
1874
United Order Building Board

The United Order Building Board built the Glenwood Cooperative Store in 1874 to house the retail operations of the order, with the "all-seeing eye" and the inscription "More Holiness to the Lord" above the entrance in an alcove establishing its link to ZCMI and the centralized mercantile system of the LDS Church. Participating members exchanged property for shares in the company. A committee of stockholders

established prices they deemed fair in terms of the local economy. The bishop and president of the Glenwood United Order, Archibald Oldroyd, ran the store, which stayed in business until 1882, when it became privately owned.

The Glenwood Cooperative Store is a two-story commercial block built with coursed, rough-faced ashlar masonry with the short end of the rectangle facing the street. Pressed-tin pilasters on each side of the facade, a tin cornice above the first level, a carved wooden cornice at the top, and a recessed double-door entrance put the best face forward for this pioneer enterprise.

Joseph Wall Gristmill
355 South 250 East
1874

The year 1874 was an important one for Glenwood; three years after settlement it built its first gristmill and started a United Order. Before that time, the closest mill for processing wheat into flour was sixty miles away in Manti. Water from Glenwood Spring ran down a hill into a pond, cascaded through a mill chute, and ended up on an overshot wheel.

The mill was built in two phases with stone gathered from nearby fields. One section housed the gristmill, the large overshot waterwheel, the millpond, the mill chute, and the wheel buckets where flour was first produced by grinding wheat between a fixed stone and a rotating grooved stone that cut and ventilated the meal as it traveled outward from the center. On the exterior walls, corner quoins formed with rough

Glenwood Cooperative Store

ashlars contrast with the stone of the walls, and lintels are made of massive wooden beams instead of stone. When the mill was modernized around 1900, a two-and-a-half-story addition was built to the east. Also with a rectangular plan, this fieldstone section has a mansard roof.

Elsinore
Elsinore White Rock Schoolhouse
25 South 100 East
1896
T. T. Davis

Most buildings constructed during the first decades of settlement, unlike the Elsinore White Rock Schoolhouse, were simple rectangles made with indigenous material, in this case native white limestone. This building includes two and a half stories and a full-height basement that is partly aboveground to provide ample natural light; it measures thirty-five by seventy-six feet. There are three interior spaces: classrooms on each end and a foyer, closets, and restrooms in the middle. Topped by a deep pediment and gable that mirror the pitch of the main roof, the entrance section is twenty-one feet wide. The bell in the rooftop belfry was produced by Thomas Christian Jensen at a foundry on the canal behind Elsinore bishop J. I. Jensen's home.

Square notches in the corners, the cornice, and a double hipped roof create interest and movement through the mass and its surface. Large brackets at two-foot intervals highlight the cornice. The stonework demonstrates the high level of craftsmanship of the local rock masons. John Marinus Johnson, a stonecutter and mason, directed the construction following plans drawn up by architect T. T. Davis. For the most part Scandinavians or the children of

Elsinore White Rock Schoolhouse

Scandinavian immigrants, the community worked cooperatively to raise this public building twenty-three years after the town was founded. The schoolhouse was an important gathering place, used for just about any type of public event.

Elsinore Sugar Factory
87 North 100 East
1911–1928
E. H. Dyer and Sons Construction Company

One consistent theme running through the settlement history of Utah was the drive for self-sufficiency. The production of sugar beets was first attempted in the 1850s under the auspices of the Deseret Manufacturing Company, and sugar beets were processed in both Provo and Sugar House. Sugar beets were first grown in Sevier County in 1878 because of favorable soil conditions and irrigation. As technology improved and demand increased, the industry stayed healthy and markets were consistently good. In 1907, the Utah-Idaho Sugar Company resulted when the Utah Sugar, Idaho Sugar, and Western Idaho Sugar companies merged, depending on a promise from Sevier County farmers to raise at least six thousand tons of sugar beets. E. H. Dyer and Sons Construction Company built a sugar beet plant near Frogs Jump north of Monroe. Enlarged in 1916 and again in 1925, the plant could produce 1.9 million 100-pound bags of good-quality sugar at capacity. It was closed in 1928.

Two of the original buildings in the factory complex are extant: the warehouse, and the factory office and rooming house, which were both rectangular structures. The warehouse is constructed of brick with a gabled roof. Symmetrically arranged piers divided the different levels into bays. Brick corbeling at the roofline provides a decorative allusion to a more finished cornice. The one-and-a-half-story factory office and rooming house has a frame upper level with shingle siding instead of brick.

Monroe
Monroe Presbyterian Church
20 East 100 North
1884
Mathias Andreason (stonework)

Reverend Duncan McMillan, mission superintendent of Utah, managed the construction of five Gothic Revival, native-stone Presbyterian churches in the 1880s in central Utah's Sanpete and Sevier Valleys in Manti, Gunnison, Salina, Richfield, and Monroe (all small towns with populations of less than five thousand).

Monroe Presbyterian Church

The Monroe Presbyterian Church was one story and had a wooden belfry on the peak of the gabled roof. The rough-faced stone walls have courses of random width, and mortar projecting slightly beyond the wall plane. Mathias Andreason was most likely the stonemason for both the Monroe and Manti churches. Both churches have similar belfry designs created by Peter Van Hougton, the architect of the Manti Church: the belfries sit on a truncated pyramidal base covered by wooden shingles; they rise with a series of wooden arches resting on eight rectangular columns and are topped by a flared hipped roof also covered with shingles.

Monroe City Hall and Library
10 North Main Street
1934
Public Works Administration
Despite the climatic similarities of New Mexico and Utah, the Spanish Colonial Revival style was rarely built in Utah. Those rare buildings that were designed with this style vocabulary are particularly noteworthy. The single-story Monroe City Hall building is square, with a parapeted flat roof with a curvilinear gable and ornate carving in the center of the symmetrical facade. Low-relief carving also enlivens round arches over the windows on the principal facade. White stucco walls (now painted pale green), typical of the style, formed a stark contrast with the sky and mountain range beyond.

The Monroe City Hall was built in 1934 as a Federal Emergency Relief Administration project. When it was completed it had city offices, a courtroom, a city jail, a public library, an assembly room, a kitchen for the American Legion, and a heating plant and storerooms in the basement. Today, the building functions as Monroe's city library.

Monroe City Hall and Library

Martin Johnson House
45 West 400 South
1880

This building is evidence of the creativity expressed in vernacular architecture; it combines a variety of influences and is a curious variant of the pair house or parstuga form. It appears that the original intent was to build the three rooms typical of the pair house, but only two were built. Additionally, in a variation on the pair house theme, this house is two rooms deep and has a gabled *T* section moving perpendicular to the main house. Popular in the late nineteenth century, the *T* house or cross-wing form undoubtedly influenced Johnson's design decisions. A Gothic Revival cross gable positioned asymmetrically over the facade, and other decorative features such as Doric porch columns, plain gable cornice returns, scroll-cut bargeboards, and pedimented window heads create a highly individual vernacular house, with a mixture of style and type elements that shows the determination of its builder and owner—Danish immigrant Martin Johnson.

Sevier
Sevier Ward Church
3001–3039 U.S. Highway 89
1928–1929
John Marius Johnson

Farmers settled in Sevier Valley, with mountains on three sides containing uncovered riches in terms of mining opportunities. But the Mormon pioneers were more concerned with the richness of the soil and the potential for grazing livestock in their fields. When they built the Sevier Ward House in 1928–29, they chose the Classical Revival vocabulary. Similar to the New England meetinghouse in terms of detail, proportions, and overall formality and popular during the 1920s and 1930s, Mormon church buildings throughout the state were usually built of brick. This example is composed of rough-faced ashlar masonry quarried locally, which makes it relatively unique, with contrasting granite decorative elements such as quoins, sills, and lintels. In 1947 the walls were plastered and painted white. The mass of the building includes a split level with a podium ground floor and a full basement. The rectangular form of the main part of the church has a gabled roof and temple-form front, complete with cornice returns and Classical pediments. A gabled pavilion projects out from the facade.

Region D

Region E

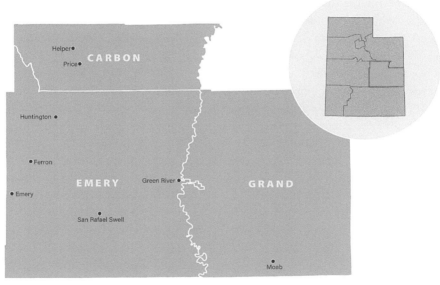

Carbon, Emery, and Grand Counties

Introduction

Price is the county seat and cultural and economic center of Carbon County. Population density is greatest in the Price River valley, defined by the prominent landforms of the Book Cliffs to the east and the Wasatch Plateau to the north and west. The rock art of Nine Mile Canyon and at other sites throughout the area attests to the presence of ancient Fremont peoples. After the late 1870s, Mormon settlers moved into the valley and began farming and stock raising. It was not until the Denver and Rio Grande Western Railroad carved out a route between Denver and Salt Lake City in the 1880s that the extensive coal fields of Carbon County inspired economic development that would change the fabric of the community. Between 1890 and 1945 a steady stream of immigrants came to Carbon County, lured by the possibilities of working in the mines and striking it rich. Immigrants came from eastern Europe—from Greece, Italy, Slovenia, Croatia, Serbia, Armenia, and Austria—as well as from China and Japan in the Far East, and still others came from Mexico and Finland. Men were recruited to Utah's mines by labor agents who published the opportunities, arranged for transportation, and ultimately, once the men arrived in Utah, helped them

secure jobs. By the time of the 1910 census, at least 4,000 Greeks and 3,116 Italians had immigrated to Utah.[1] Towns such as Helper and Price were marked by significant ethnic and cultural diversity, and this was expressed in architecture, such as the Greek Orthodox church and the Catholic church, and in the number of ethnic restaurants and coffeehouses that served particular immigrant groups and created a sense of community for men so far away from home. These structures signify in material terms the significant difference between these towns and the typical villages across Utah. Because the coal mines were in steep, narrow canyons, the coal companies sometimes built company towns, which were inhabited largely by groups of immigrants. These towns, such as Wellington, Sunnyside, and East Carbon, typically included simple structures for mine managers, apartments or small structures to house the miners, and a common hall for meals and social gatherings. Royal, Utah, for example, was a company town (named for the Royal Coal Company) in the early 1900s that originally included fewer than ten buildings and was deserted when the mine shut down.

After a period of strikes in response to dangerous working conditions, mine workers joined the United Mine Workers of America in 1933 to collectively work for safer working conditions, fair wages, and fair treatment and to create another type of community that crossed ethnic boundaries. The explosion of the Castle Gate Mine Number 2 in 1924, which killed 172 men and left 417 dependents behind, was an image that was hard to forget.[2] Greek or Italian labor agents, or padrones, would also provide strikebreakers during these confrontations, but the steady stream of unemployed immigrants made it difficult for this pressure to have its intended impact, and violent confrontations erupted between management, the strikers, and the strikebreakers.[3] These men laid rail lines, worked in the mines, and worked on other infrastructure projects. They arrived in Utah at the Union Pacific or Rio Grande railroad depots and found their way to ethnic neighborhoods that helped them get oriented. Greek Town, Little Italy, and Japan Town were critical in helping immigrants find work and connect with others who spoke the same language, ate the same food, and shared the same religion or cultural traditions. Greek men dominated mining towns and were the single largest immigrant population to contribute to Utah's economy through the mining industry. When Italian immigrants came to Carbon County, they would find their way to a mining camp, possibly Castle Gate or Sunnyside, secure a job, and live in company housing.

After 1937, the College of Eastern Utah in Price began offering classes, and more recently it has functioned as a branch campus of Utah State University, providing an important source of higher education for the county's young people and acting as an economic driver.

Running along the Colorado-Utah border in central Utah, Grand County is located on the Colorado Plateau. In this area once occupied by the Ancestral Puebloans, cliff houses and rock art are evocative of a life carved out of the land and intimately impacted by the capriciousness of nature. Spanish explorers traveled through this region of vast sandstone and limestone canyons on a route that became known as the Spanish Trail. Although the first effort at Mormon settlement was in 1855, it was not until the 1870s and 1880s that more permanent settlements were founded. The history of this agricultural landscape with family farms and livestock ranching, as well as tourism related to Arches National Monument (after 1929), has attracted visitors from around the world. The extraction of resources such as uranium and potash has also stimulated population growth in this remote part of the state.

Carbon County

Helper
Helper Main Post Office
45 South Main Street
1900
Federal government

Like much of rural Utah, Helper benefited from the programs sponsored by the New Deal. The Helper Post Office is one of only three Utah post offices with artwork commissioned by the Treasury Department's Section of Painting and Sculpture, established in 1934 to provide direct aid, jobs, and cultural amenities to small-town America. Artists had a difficult time finding employment during the Depression. The Section of Painting and Sculpture dealt directly with local artists through national and regional design competitions to find the highest-quality art for federal buildings, particularly art that reflected the American scene, in the hope that this would stimulate

Helper Main Post Office

a positive response among local audiences. Sometimes the result was local narratives. The 1941 mural at the Helper Post Office, *A Typical Western Town*, was painted by Jenne Magafan. Measuring five by twelve feet, it hangs over the postmaster's door. Magafan won the state competition sponsored by the Section of Painting and Sculpture, later known as the Fine Arts Section.

The mural depicts a typical dusty main street lined with false-front frame buildings—a post office, general store, saloon, blacksmith shop, and various other buildings. A town marshal and blacksmith stand on one side of the street watching two men on horseback ride through town.

Helper benefited significantly from the program during those years and secured at least sixteen other pieces of art from Utah artists that impacted its future development. In fact, in 1939 it built a fine arts center to house the collection. Helper is now known for its arts festival, held each August.

Overshadowed by the interest in the interior murals, the building itself is typical of PWA Moderne buildings—a single story, with red brick and reinforced concrete, and a raised basement platform. The building's surface is relatively unmodulated, with flat fluted pilasters, entablature, arched bays, and overall symmetry.

Helper Historic Commercial District
1900s

Helper's Historic Commercial District reads like a newsreel about the life of an immigrant in this railroad and mining town, with buildings narrating the ways people in the early twentieth century lived—how they spent their money, how they played and worshipped, how they made their homes—a sort of microcosm of the experience of a diverse ethnic population. When the Denver and Rio Grande Western Railroad came to Helper in the early twentieth century and mining became important in the surrounding bituminous coal fields, Helper became a significant service center, and home to hundreds of immigrants of various nationalities who came to Carbon County to work in the mines. Helper's

Helper Historic Commercial District

Helper Civic Auditorium

buildings express the ethnic heritage of its inhabitants. Local businesses offered a wide range of services and goods—grocery stores, furniture stores, laundries, clothing stores, general mercantile stores, banks, and other businesses were built in downtown Helper to serve a diverse and varied group of residents. Louis Fossat, a first-generation Italian immigrant, operated the Helper Bakery, Meat, and Grocery from 1913 to 1940, a market that sold Italian food products hard to find in rural Utah. Kay and Masa Amano, part of a first-generation Issei Japanese family, ran the Helper Fish Market between 1922 and 1954, where they lived upstairs and rented out rooms to itinerant workers from Japan. The market also sold specialty foods, trucked produce, and other food products to the coal camps. Not necessarily examples of high-style architecture, the buildings in Helper's Historic Commercial District are nevertheless important and illustrate the evolution of early twentieth-century building types. Small wooden-frame buildings were the first to be built but were later destroyed by fire. The second round of commercial structures were built with hand-hewn native stone by immigrant stonemasons, including the Ricci Market Building, built in 1924.

By the late 1920s, new prosperity was stimulating a building boom and the construction of more standard commercial-style buildings. Two significant public buildings in particular were also built during this period—the City Hall and the Civic Auditorium. Well-known Salt Lake architect Walter E. Ware designed the City Hall in 1927. Scott and Welch, also of Salt Lake City, designed the International Streamline–style Civic Auditorium, a PWA

project designed to ease local unemployment as well as provide significant public architecture for this rural area of the state.

Three churches reflect diversity in religious activity as well. The nondenominational Railroad Chapel was used by a variety of different sects, and St. Anthony's Parish served Catholics among the Italians, Slovenians, and Croatians. Besides coming together to worship, Helper's diverse ethnic groups gathered at theaters and coffeehouses.

Price
Hellenic Orthodox Church of the Assumption
61 South 200 East
1916

At the turn of the nineteenth century there were only three Greeks in all of Utah. But during the Carbon County coal miners' strike between 1903 and 1904, mining companies recruited Greek men from Europe as strikebreakers. Within a decade three thousand Greek men were working in Carbon County coal mines, and very few women. The county's architecture hints at that ethnic diversity. Immediate outsiders, they clashed in just about every way with

Hellenic Orthodox Church of the Assumption

the resident Mormon population—they were clannish but didn't bring their families because they weren't sure they were there to stay, and they brought their own religion. The Hellenic Orthodox Church of the Assumption built in Price in 1916 embodied their beliefs and traditions, their history and values in a sacred place. Perhaps more importantly it helped make Price their home, a place where they could work and worship and raise their families.

The church provided the Greeks with a sense of stability and security in this foreign place. It offered refuge, a place apart from the intolerance of the mainstream population toward their foreign ways and the drudgery of work in the coal mines. It created a sense of permanence in a transitory immigrant world.

As is typical of Orthodox churches in America, and like those built elsewhere in the American West, the building conforms to the Byzantine style, with an onion-shaped dome sitting on a square tower supported by four pillars, walls of yellow brick, and a concrete foundation. The plan of the building is the Greek cross. The congregation added two towers in 1940–41 to the outside front, and a balcony was built on the inside, expanding the building's seating capacity. Cast Corinthian columns replaced the original wooden columns. The original icons burned during a fire in 1945 and were repainted by the Reverend Zoygraphos of Texas, an artist who was a Greek priest and iconographer.

Student Center
Utah State University Eastern
Brixen & Christopher

At the heart of Utah State University Eastern is a two-story commons designed by Brixen and Christopher Architects of Salt Lake City. The 49,500-square-foot building houses a bookstore, snack bar, dining hall, ballroom, lounges, and administrative services. The Deer Crest Gate House designed by the Richardson Design Partnership is a much smaller building, only 1,730 square feet, but it is recognized by the Utah AIA for its distinctive design reflective of the client's interest in the historic architecture of the national parks of the West. Massive raw and unpeeled log trusses, stone columns, and a porte cochere integrate the building into the surrounding environment.

Notre Dame de Lourdes Catholic Church
200 North Carbon Avenue
1919

The Notre Dame de Lourdes Catholic Church is distinctive as a bungalow church, a one-and-a-half-story rectangular brick building with a podium basement, an unusual choice for a church. Instead of the horizontal orientation of bungalow windows, arched Gothic stained-glass windows run along the sides and across the back of the building and contain memorial inscriptions—the names of immigrants from Italy, France, and Ireland who formed the first congregation. But the feature that most distinguishes it and sets it apart from other Catholic churches in the region is the symmetrical facade. A wide flight of stairs runs across the front of the building, leading to a recessed porch with a gabled roof that also spans the entire facade. Above that is a second porch, supported by four thick, square brick pillars on pedestals, and simple banding at the capitals.

The entrance door has high, wide, stained-glass triple windows on both sides. A small cupola stands at the peak of the roof, and a round rose stained-glass window is at the center of the gabled end. As is typical of the bungalow style, the roof has projecting eaves and exposed rafters.

Notre Dame de Lourdes Catholic Church

cornice lines, the central parapet, the geometric quality of the main block mass of the building, and the characteristic geometric ornamentation. It is a significant example of the early twentieth-century commercial development that occurred in Price.

Immigrants Harry Mahleres and Sam Siampenos were brothers-in-law who came from mountainous central Greece, where most men earned their living herding sheep. Convinced that the American West promised the American dream, Harry and Sam arrived in America in the early 1900s, worked at odd jobs, and eventually tried their hand at sheepherding, saving enough money to start this store.

Like many of the buildings on Main Street, this one has seen a variety of different businesses over time—a bar, restaurants, and a Bureau of Land Management office during the 1940s. For several decades the upper floor was used as a boarding-house or hotel, and the basement for meetings of numerous local clubs—Rotarians, Kiwanis, and the American Legion.

The interior of the building was dictated by Catholic liturgy rather than the confines of the bungalow style—walls are plastered and space is arranged according to ritual requirements. The rectangular sanctuary has a semicircular niche at the nave end opposite the main door.

The church was built because of the devotion of Italian monsignor Alfredo F. Giovanni, the area's first Catholic resident priest, who also established a Catholic school. The church and school created a community for the displaced ethnic population of Carbon County.

Parker and Weeter Block / Mahleres-Siampenos Building
85 West Main Street
1913
A great example of a Prairie-style commercial building is the two-story brick Mahleres-Siampenos Building. The typical horizontality of the Prairie style is emphasized here by window bands accented with

Price Main Post Office
95 South Carbon Avenue
1930s
Federal government
Like most federal buildings, the Price Main Post Office was proof of the community's regional significance, linking this local area with the federal government. When Utah congressman Don B. Colton laid the building's cornerstone, he reminded the crowd gathered for the event of the enthusiastic and untiring efforts of countless volunteers to secure the building for Price—the Price

Region E

Price Municipal Building

Chamber of Commerce, civic clubs, treasury officials, and town citizens. Price is the county seat of Carbon County, with an economy based primarily on mining, government, and trade.

Perhaps most popular for small-town public buildings was the Classical Revival style, and this one is strongly rooted in the Beaux Arts tradition popular in the early twentieth century. The richly ornamented building preceded the massive public works projects of the New Deal years that were designed to pump money and infrastructure into small towns in America. An ornate entrance, arched window bays, and limestone detailing exemplify the use of quality materials and fine craftsmanship. Classical design motifs continue throughout the building.

The building has a relatively flat, symmetrically organized facade, a central entrance bay, and arched bays on both sides with Palladian windows. Limestone is also used for the raised basement wall, the water table, and the belt course that divides the top of the first story and the parapet and cornice. Cast-iron lanterns are mounted on the wall on either side of the entry. Steps and a landing with buttresses, all made of

granite, lead to the entrance. An architrave consisting of half-round fluted pilasters with palm leaf capitals surrounds the double aluminum-framed glass panel doors.

Price Municipal Building
Corner of 200 East and Main Street
1938
Fausett and Pessetto

Capitalizing on available funds for local infrastructure projects, the Price City Council secured funding for the Price Municipal Building from the Works Progress Administration on June 8, 1936. WPA requirements stipulated that local expenditures had to be at least 55 percent of the total cost. Price raised $85,000 from a bond election.

A local firm, Fausett and Pessetto, received the contract for $139,936, and the council hired Lynn Fausett to paint a mural in the building. The council accepted the proposal and designated $350 to initiate the project. The city dedicated the building on February 22, 1939.

The Price Municipal Building is a modern structure in terms of its massing and lack of exterior ornamentation, as well as in its flat roof, reinforced concrete, light-colored brick, and expression of International characteristics. The building houses the offices of the city, an auditorium, a handball court, and a gymnasium (which has been converted into a museum). The building is similar to other municipal buildings built during the 1930s. Perhaps, however, the most distinctive element here is the foyer mural located to the east. The mural is only four feet high and moves through quite a narrow area in a low-ceilinged space. Nevertheless, Fausett effectively narrates the color and flavor of the region's history, and the mural is a great source of local pride.

The mural reads like a comic strip, with panels narrating separate stories from Utah history: Abram Powell and Caleb Rhodes's entrance into the area as fur trappers in 1877, shown with W. H. Branch surveying the Price Canal in 1884; freighters camping near the rail yards; the completion of the Denver and Rio Grande Western Railroad in 1883 when Price became the railhead for shipping goods into the vast Uinta Basin to the north and east; Price's Main Street with the Price Trading Company at the center, with Fausett's own mother, Josephine Bryner Fausett, standing in the doorway of the store wearing a white apron; Mrs. Bryner holding up a petition to incorporate the city of Price (Bryner, a widow homesteader, obtained the land used for the original town site); J. M. Whitmore, a prominent early rancher and first president of the town board, standing in front of the town hall;

a group portrait including Catholic bishop Lawrence Scanlan, Greek Orthodox priest Mark Petrakis, and Methodist minister R. P. Nichols surrounded by illustrations of Notre Dame de Lourdes, the Price Academy Building, and the Greek Orthodox Church of the Assumption. The remaining six scenes include panels on local education and government, other stores and the post office, and the coal mining industry and cultural life.

Star Theater / Carbon Theater
20 East Main Street
1923–1924
J. A. Headlund
Five Greek brothers—Pete, Angelo, Charlie, George, and Harry Georgedes—started the Star Theater in 1923–24, two decades after

Star Theater / Carbon Theater

they arrived in Carbon County, providing Greek drama and other theatricals for the immigrant population. Evidence of their material success as well as the cultural aspirations of the local population, the building has an impressive facade that speaks to their love of their homeland and traditions as well as their belief that this was a place they would stay.

The Georgedes family had been in Carbon County for only two decades when they began building this theater, choosing the Classical Revival style. Father Smyrnopoulos, the Greek Orthodox priest and leader of the Greek community who recommended the name "Star" for the theater, said that everyone saw the stars in the sky at night, so it would appeal to all people.

Only the second theater in town, the Star presented both live theater and motion pictures. Traveling burlesque and theatrical companies as well as local productions performed in the Star. The brothers fully equipped the stage for virtually any type of performance with a fancy drop curtain and pair of heavy drapes, as well as scenery for an extravagant living room, a rustic family kitchen, a garden, a forest and other landscape scenes, and a commercial street, in addition to the screen for the motion pictures.

Decorative elements include fluted pilasters with Corinthian capitals, bands of round-arched windows, an elaborate entablature with modillions on the cornice, egg-and-dart molding and dentils on the frieze, and an architrave and parapet. Vertically the building is divided into three sections, like the Greek column—a main level, a second section, and a broad cornice at the top. Three round-arched windows are in each second-level bay, with concrete moldings contrasting with the plum-colored brick of the theater. Cast masks of figures in Greek drama are set into panels below each window and between pilasters on the second-story level.

Emery County

Huntington
Huntington Roller Mill and Miller's House
400 North Street
1896
Oliver J. Harmon, William Hunter

The Huntington Roller Mill first provided flour and feed for farmers and townspeople in Carbon and Emery Counties in 1896. Several local men worked as carpenters on the mill and were also shareholders in the corporation. For a time, the same steam engine that powered the sawmill was used to power the roller mill, with inconsistent results. Instead, a flume and penstock were built from the town ditch a few yards to the south, diverting water to a wheelhouse on the south side of the mill. A Pelton metal undershot wheel was used inside the wheelhouse to generate power with water that flowed through the flume. The huge wheel, eight feet in diameter, was set six feet into the ground to increase the force of the water flowing under it. After the grinding was done each fall, the ditch clogged up with leaves, killing the waterpower. In the winter it was even worse because the water froze up altogether, causing work to stop completely.

The mill itself was a simple structure—a two-story frame building built with wooden tongue-and-groove boards, a gabled roof, and simple triangular pediments above the windows. A second wing was built in 1918 with one-by-twos laid on top of each other and braced horizontally, vertically, and on the diagonal to compensate for the vibrations of the milling machinery.

A house for the miller is also located on the site. This is a one-and-a-half-story stuccoed frame building with a U-shaped plan.

Huntington Tithing Granary
65 West 300 North
1904

Bishop James W. Nixon of the Huntington Ward directed construction of a brick tithing office, a frame tithing granary, and a large hay barn, root cellar, and corrals, all built between 1902 and 1906, exemplifying typical Mormon cooperation, or the Latter-day Saint version of communalism. Used to store and manage the agricultural donations given by ward members as tithing for the LDS Church, these facilities were important in cash-poor communities where in-kind tithing donations were more common than cash. The only remaining structure from this original group is the granary, and it was moved in the early 1940s to its current location two blocks north of the historic tithing lot.

The Huntington Tithing Granary is a one–and-a-half-story rectangular frame building with a gabled roof. It was constructed with a balloon frame with two-by-four studs and a wall of horizontal siding on the interior, except in the rear of the building, where rough planks were used instead. The inside-out construction created a sort of crib for the storage of grain or corn. At the east end is a central door situated beneath a small window with a pedimented window head.

Ferron
Ferron Presbyterian Church and Cottage
Northwest corner of Mill Road and 300 West
1911
Tom Jones and Mac McKenzie

Presbyterian missionaries first came to Utah hoping to infiltrate the Mormon hegemony in June 1869, when Reverend Melanchton Hughes first preached in Corinne, Utah. Between 1869 and 1883 the Presbyterians pushed through the territory, establishing thirty-three different "stations," with forty-one buildings valued at $65,000 according to a Utah Presbytery report. As many as sixty-six teachers taught in these schools, with 1,789 students. In 1883 there were 350 members and thirteen ministers. The most effective missionary tool used by the Presbyterians in Utah was the church school. Utah schools were seriously deficient during the last decades of the nineteenth century, and schools established by the Catholics, Presbyterians, and other Protestant groups were the only alternative to LDS schools. By 1887, some fifty thousand children had been enrolled in Presbyterian schools in thirty-three different Utah towns.

The Ferron Presbyterian Church and Cottage were built after the period of missionary expansion in an area where public education was quite successful. Nevertheless, on February 15, 1908, the First Presbyterian Church of Ferron bought two lots of land for a church and residence for the clergy. Funding proved to be more difficult than anticipated, so the building was not completed until 1911. For the next thirty years it was the scene of religious services, elementary school for grades one through eight, and a lending library.

Locally quarried stone and brick produced at the nearby Molen brickworks were the materials used for this two-story Gothic Revival–style building. About half of the first story is below ground level, and the floor plan forms a *T*, with a bell tower at the intersection of the two main building masses. A roof covered with wooden shingles and gables with gingerbread ornamentation continue the Gothic style.

Region E

The minister and teachers lived in a 1908 residence built on the site. The minister resided with his family on the first floor, and unmarried female missionary schoolteachers lived on the second floor. Also two stories, the cottage is constructed with brick walls and walls covered with shingles on the upper level, overall creating a charmingly simple and straightforward building.

Emery
Emery LDS Church
Off Utah Highway 10
1898–1900

The Emery LDS Church was the first religious building to be constructed in town after settlement in the 1880s. Work began on the church in 1898 with local lumber. The chapel measured thirty-six by eighty-four feet and seated five hundred people. It has a wooden frame with non-load-bearing adobe walls sheathed by clapboards and rests on a stone foundation. Emery County's alkaline soil was not ideal for heavier stone or brick buildings. Lighter frame construction was a better solution. As in many churches, the principal east-facing facade features a tower topped by a belfry with a mansard roof with a metal and wooden railing. Both the north and south elevations have central projecting bays that jut out to the north and south as well as side entrances and transom lights. On the west elevation a small room projects out from the wall that originally housed the presiding bishop's office. There are boxed cornices with plain returns on the roof gables.

The main interior space is a long meeting hall oriented to the podium and a small foyer area. The chapel's walls are plastered, painted white, and have board wainscoting.

San Rafael Swell
Denver and Rio Grande Lime Kiln / Buckhorn Flat Lime Kiln
Buckhorn Flat
1881–1882

Since the turn of the nineteenth century, historians of the American West have struggled to find paradigms that explain the meaning of the steady progression of settlement in the frontier. If you read Frederick Jackson Turner's frontier thesis and its description of the people who inhabited the West—fur trappers and miners, frontiersmen and farmers, merchants and community builders—you might assume settlement was a process not all that different from evolution. Growth was the result of accumulation of population, land, and resources. Significant technological advancements had a dramatic impact on the steady movement of settlement. In Utah the coming of the railroad ended the period of isolation, exposed the Mormon empire to outside forces, brought state goods into the area, and linked the territory with markets, society, and politics in the world outside. Its importance cannot be overestimated. Moreover, the railroad stimulated the local economy by providing a means for the easy transportation of natural resources to distant markets. For years the Denver and Rio Grande Western Railroad proposed building a route across Utah that would connect Denver with Salt Lake City and ultimately with Los Angeles and Old Mexico.

The railroad companies built routes with local resources whenever possible. The Buckhorn Flat Lime Kiln produced lime for the grading of the track bed and for building bridges or damming up washes; both types of construction involved the use of cement or mortar that contained lime, which was produced in a furnace or kiln where the desired temperature could

Denver and Rio Grande Lime Kiln / Buckhorn Flat Lime Kiln.
Photograph by Trisha Simpson, GNU Free Documentation License, 1.2, CC BY SA 3.0, Wiki Commons.

be reached and maintained. The Buckhorn Flat Lime Kiln was built in 1881–82 for the Denver and Rio Grande Western's proposed route through the area, a route that was abandoned late in 1882.

Nevertheless, this nineteenth-century lime kiln is still of interest. It is a round structure of uncoursed rubble twelve to sixteen feet high, with a conical roof that has since caved in. Air moved through the space through an arched doorway on the southwest side and a hole in the roof.

Green River
Green River Presbyterian Church
134 West Third Avenue
1906
Ware and Treganza
This picturesque Victorian Gothic wooden church is a good example of the determination of the Presbyterian Church to maintain a presence in rural Utah. But perhaps more important, this is evidence of the early "community church" phase of Protestant church activity in Mormon Utah. Typically, only small congregations of the various denominations persisted in rural Utah. At the turn of the century many would band together to build a "community church." Willing to put sectarian considerations aside for worship space, diverse church members came together for ecumenical Sunday worship services. The Green River Presbyterian Church was an example of this interdenominational cooperation.

A Presbyterian pastor, Reverend J. K. McGillivray, established the church in 1906. Of the twenty-nine original members of the congregation, eight came from different denominations. Later that year, Reverend McLain W. Davis became pastor and proposed that the congregation construct a building for worship. The Green River Land and Townsite Company donated five $1,000 lots for the church site and the church raised $2,200 in donations.

Green River elected its first town council the same year the church organized, laid out a new town site, and incorporated in 1910. The town entered a period of municipal growth corresponding with a boom in the peach industry.

The church is a small Victorian Gothic building with one and a half intersecting wings and an entrance that meets the two-story main building mass at an angle. The tower roof is clipped at each corner by square battlements protruding upward to a point just below the apex of the hip. Large Gothic-arched stained-glass windows with wooden tracery are located in each wing. A flared hipped roof canopy placed over the tower's front door has a wooden frame covered by clapboard siding and sits on a rusticated stone foundation. In 1963 a four-room addition was constructed to the west to create new space for Sunday School classes and storage.

Grand County

Moab
Grand County High School
608 South 400 East
1990s

Amid the primal grandeur of the Arches and Canyonlands region of the state, Grand County High School holds its own with simplicity in form, material, and detail. Located in Moab, the school sits on a particularly remarkable site and provides beautiful views of the surrounding environment.

Interiors are filled with natural light, transporting the outer landscape into the built and relating the two in an implicit and natural way.

Colored concrete in the form of both cast-in-place elements and tilt-up wall panels blends naturally with the surrounding landscape. Lightly sandblasted concrete creates a subtle play of color and texture when the sun moves across the sky and clouds obscure the light. The Utah AIA acknowledged the sensitive relationship between the school and the surrounding terrain with a 1998 Award for Excellence.

The school administration wanted a centralized student hub or commons at the heart of the school. The relationship between the common space and the academic, athletic, and fine arts areas of the building reflects a holistic approach to high school education. Because of the way the building spaces are organized, primarily in a linear pattern, the central commons divides the academic classrooms, perhaps the quieter areas, from the more energized sections of the school.

Elk Mountain Mission Fort Site
47 North 200 East
1855

The Elk Mountain Mission Fort was the first Mormon settlement in southeastern Utah. Established in the summer of 1855, the mission had a dual purpose: first, to teach Mormon doctrine to the Indians, and second, to prevent future conflict like that of the Walker War of 1853. William Huntington Jr. first explored the area during the summer of 1854 and followed the Spanish Trail to the Colorado River, where it was necessary to lower wagons down a steep slope to make the crossing. Based on their report, the following April at General Conference, Alfred N. Billings and forty other men were called to establish a mission at the foot of the Elk Mountains, now called the La Sal Mountains, a strategic point that further solidified Young's control over the territory. With a similar settlement in Limhi, the settlement of Las Vegas, the establishment of Fort Supply, and the purchase of Fort Bridger, the church had created a nucleus for settlements that facilitated colonization, helped control Native Americans, and provided safe haven for Mormons from the rest of the United States.

The fort provided temporary housing for newcomers to Moab for several decades. All that remains of the original fort is ruins of the stone wall and the spring that flowed through the space. The fort was sixty-four feet square, with walls constructed of rock quarried in the hills half a mile away. For greater stability, tapered walls were four feet thick at the base and one and a half feet at the cap. Single cells housed individuals or families around the periphery of the fort and shared contiguous walls. Horses and cattle grazed in a corral nearby. The isolated location and traces of the original fort speak volumes about the sacrifices required of the Elk Mountain missionaries to establish a home in the desert environment. Conflict with the native inhabitants of this land was only one of the challenges they faced—dry land, limited water, and harsh weather challenged their commitment and ability to survive. A monument on the site commemorates the sacrifice of the pioneers who settled the area.

Orlando W. Warner House
1010 E. Mill Creek Road
1890
Orlando W. Warner

This sturdy adobe brick house makes ample testimony of the determination of the Mormons to establish permanent homes

in Utah's isolated desert landscape. Clearly building it to last, Orlando W. Warner constructed this two-story central-passage house in 1890, ten years after he arrived in Moab. Warner was born in New York in 1839 and came to Utah with his family in 1851. He learned to run a gristmill in Fillmore and established his own sawmill and later a gristmill in Moab after his arrival. Before he built this house, his family lived first in a dugout and then in a log cabin. He planted orchards on his property that produced apples, peaches, and pears to help feed his family.

Central-passage houses are less common in Utah than the hall-parlor type. This example has an ample two-story, four-column porch extending the length of the entire facade. The gabled end of the building has cornice returns, a moderately pitched roof, and an addition to the rear. On both levels of the rear section are large rooms—the upper one was used as a parlor and the lower one as a kitchen, dining, and living area. Warner also built a fruit warehouse, a one-and-a-half-story rectangular brick building on a stone foundation composed of random rubble.

Moab LDS Church
195 East Center
1889

Not looking much different from the typical I-form house, the Moab LDS Church is a one-story building with a gabled roof. It was originally a simple rectangle, but a later addition turned the floor plan into a *T*. Walls are constructed with adobe bricks that were made cooperatively by members of the congregation and then laid on a stone foundation and covered with stucco. The main distinguishing feature of this and other homes built with the same approach in Moab was that the gabled end

Region E

faced the street. Here, simple Greek Revival decoration includes cornice returns on the gabled ends, a triangular pediment over the entrance door, and a belfry on the roof ridge over the facade. On the addition, slender chimneys with decorative brick coursing are located on each end.

Similar buildings were built in virtually every Mormon town during the first period of settlement. Conforming to the same basic floor plan and mass, and reflecting the same level of building expertise and design, they were one of the key features of the Mormon village and visual evidence of the centralized nature of colonization efforts in the region. Even more important, these buildings speak to the place they were built and use local materials—the adobe bricks used for the Moab Church match the hue and chemistry of the soil in the fields that stretched in every direction. This Greek Revival vernacular church shows the Mormon effort to build beautiful structures with what was at hand.

Moab Cabin
100 East St. 56 S.
1893
John Jackson

We usually think of log cabins as temporary structures, thrown up rapidly to provide shelter in the initial weeks of settlement, but this one-story log cabin proved to be incredibly durable and is still intact after 120 years. Constructed with rough-hewn log walls sealed tightly with mud chinking and unevenly notched at the corners, the cabin has a flat roof of parallel logs covered with branches and mud, and usually a fine layer of growing plants.

Marietta, the third wife of Randolph Hockaday Stewart, the first bishop of Moab, owned the cabin. In the spring of 1881 Stewart and his three wives and children came to Moab, where he built three log cabins to accommodate his family. After her death, Marietta's children leased the cabin to Texas cowboy John Jackson, a colorful storyteller who entertained his audiences with stories about the Wild West. Jackson often took his family with him when he worked on the range, but when they were in town they occupied this cabin.

Turnbow Cabin or John Wolfe Ranch
13½ miles north of Arches National Park Visitor Center, at Delicate Arch trailhead
1907

A historic homestead's footprint maps the way men and women lived on the land in the past. It is hard to imagine that they could survive and eke out a living in the harsh environment of southeastern Utah. Yet many did, and sites like the Turnbow Cabin and the Wolfe Ranch are proof of their efforts. The settlers confronted Native people who proceeded them, the unforgiving terrain, and scarce water supplies, but the structures they built reflect an ingenious use of the limited available building materials. Although no two logs were consistent in size or shape, which created a challenge for traditional construction techniques, the resulting buildings provided shelter and refuge from the harsh sun of this desert landscape. John Wesley Wolfe, his son Fred, and his son-in-law Ed Stanley built this cabin and cellar in 1907.

The extant structures of what is called the Wolfe Ranch include a small cabin measuring fifteen by seventeen feet and constructed with unhewn notched cottonwood and juniper logs; a twelve-by-twelve-foot dugout cellar with a roof made of logs, with shale and juniper bark on top and filling the cracks, a creative solution to the problem of sealing the building at the top; and a corral.

After a series of owners, Marvin Turnbow bought the property in the early twentieth century.

Moab Information Center
22 East Center Street
1996

Located on a one-and-a-half-acre site on the corner of Main and Center Streets in downtown Moab, the Information Center includes a 3,000-square-foot building and a plaza. Five governmental agencies—the Grand County Travel Council, the Canyonlands Natural History Association, the National Park Service, the U.S. Forest Service, and the Bureau of Land Management—joined forces in creating the Information Center displays to promote the natural wonders of the area. For a long time, Moab's architecture in general felt more like a hodgepodge than an accurate reflection of local values or even distinctive treasures. Overrun by franchise America

and its garishly innocuous buildings, the town accommodated crowds of tourists long before it developed a strong sense of what types of buildings were appropriate for the area. This facility moves the city in a different direction and relies on a striking twenty-seven-foot cantilevered roof to stand out. Visible from U.S. Highway 91, the triangular roof contrasts with the irregular stone and stucco masses of the base structure. In this way it creates a tangible, understandable relationship between the forms and materials of the natural world and the human-created environment.

The plaza also abstracts the geography of Canyonlands. The architect created the curvilinear shape by digitally transferring freehand sketches directly to the surveyor's "total station" laser surveying equipment. Native materials and plants were used to create an environment conducive to rest and relaxation.

Region E

Region F

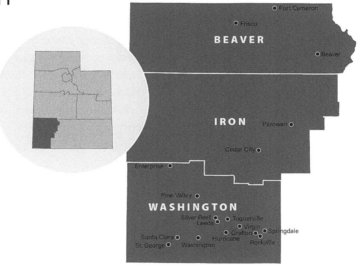

Beaver, Iron, and Washington Counties

Introduction

One way to arrive at a sense of the Mormon pioneers' orderly colonization of what became the state of Utah in 1896 is to recognize the design motif established through the Plat of the City of Zion. While mining towns cling to the sides of mountains and respond to geography in the effort to survive, Mormon villages seem to defy the constraints of geography and superimpose a pattern for settlement on the land: a grid plan, a strong central square, and farm lots. Several towns throughout Utah reflected the prototype constructed by Salt Lake City in other ways. The territory's capital city had large-scale religious, governmental, and cultural buildings that told the story of the life that played out there. Reflecting this strong example of the physical and social components of the Mormon version of the good life, Beaver City built its own county courthouse, opera house, and LDS stake tabernacle with local materials but with style elements that yearned toward something grand, impressive, and permanent.

The colonization effort that was centered at LDS Church headquarters but extended both north and south was designed to maximize the opportunities provided by the natural landscape, create regional independence and self-sufficiency, and allow for easy travel between communities in a single day's wagon ride. When you visit cities in this region—Beaver, Milford, St. George, Bunkerville, Toquerville, or Santa Clara—it is hard to imagine the privations experienced by the first wave of settlers. It is a harsh but sublime landscape with scarce water and challenging conditions for agriculture or home building. In southern Utah, the Mormons tried to grow cotton, and in some places sugar beets or even grapes in the 1860s. Brigham Young called more than one thousand members of the church to settle in this desert landscape, which would become a regional religious center and a way station on the route to Southern California. The Washington Cotton Mill is a physical reminder of this moment in time and of the fleeting experiment with industries that would benefit church members throughout the territory. Besides subsistence farming, stock raising became an important part of the local economy. Cattle and sheep ranching was a good use of land that proved lacking for agriculture, and some local economies such as that of Kanab were heavily dependent on livestock raising and, eventually, tourism related to the national parks and the motion picture industry. George A. Smith led the Iron Mission colony, which arrived in Parowan, 250 miles south of Salt Lake City, on January 13,

1851. Young personally called a group of about 120 men, many with iron manufacturing experience, many also from the British Isles, to set up and run an iron manufacturing enterprise in this part of southern Utah. Iron had been identified near Cedar City by early explorers, and in 1852, Brigham Young asked Franklin E. Richards and Erastus Snow to raise funds and even recruit church converts from England who had manufacturing experience. They identified iron at the Muddy River and built an ironworks near Coal Creek, forming the Deseret Iron Company with an initial capitalization of $5 million. After meeting with success the first year, they confronted a series of challenges, and in 1858 with the coming of Johnston's Army to Utah, they closed down the iron project altogether. Other iron companies formed over the years. The next decade, the railroad brought iron more readily into the territory. The Iron County mining district was three miles wide and twenty-three miles long and was the richest iron-ore body in the West, according to historian Janet Seegmiller.[1]

Mining is part of the story of southern Utah as well. Mining and the railroad helped diversify Utah's economy, extracting mineral resources from area mountain ranges and exporting them to distant markets. Railroad spur lines connected mining towns to the main rail lines that traversed the territory. Mining towns attracted an ethnically and culturally diverse group of people. The Horn Silver Mine in the San Francisco Mountains in Beaver County was the richest silver producer of the day. In eastern Washington County, the Silver Reef District also produced silver-lead ores. The railroad connected to Beaver's mines but did not reach as far as St. George, a fact that impacted the shape of the economies and histories of these counties.

Much of the story of the settlement of this part of the state is the effort to diversify Utah's economy and promote home manufacturing. These entrepreneurial activities confronted challenges, and most failed within decades of beginning, but colonization efforts in southern Utah were successful. Brigham Young sent talented LDS leaders to the colonies outside Salt Lake City, men such as Lorenzo Snow, Orson Hyde, Ezra T. Benson, and other apostles who helped build communities, religious centers like that established at St. George, and a series of community institutions—the St. George Temple, the St. George Tabernacle, the Dixie Academy, and the Washington County Courthouse.

Washington County was always isolated from the rest of the state and was challenged severely in terms of water, but it featured a dramatic natural landscape that would in the twentieth century draw tourists from around the world with the creation of Zion National Park in 1909, and with the spectacular red-rock cliffs and sweeping plateaus in an environment that was at once severe and sublime.

Beaver County

Frisco

Frisco Charcoal Kilns
Approximately 16 miles west of Milford, north of Utah Highway 21
1877

Frisco was a boomtown where prosperity and growth seemed unlimited, a town inspired by the dream of immense wealth—and a town that declined when that dream dissipated. The Frisco smelters and the five beehive charcoal kilns were built to supply fuel for the smelter.

Frisco Charcoal Kilns.
HAER UT-25-3, public domain.

The smelting process was critical to the production of refined minerals and depended on charcoal for fuel. Before the construction of the kilns, charcoal was produced in conical pits lined with bricks. Workers would fill the pit with wood, light a fire, and cover it up with earth and sod, allowing it to smolder for fifteen to twenty days until it burned itself out. The result was a porous black residue of wood with all the organic matter removed, almost pure carbon. This material would burn in a smelter furnace without smoke and produce an intense heat.

The five Frisco charcoal kilns were built in 1877 on a hill adjacent to the site of the smelter, and they are the best surviving charcoal kilns in the state. The Frisco kilns are built of a granite composite with a lime mortar in a random rubble construction. All the kilns have arched front openings at the ground level as well as arched openings on the other side about two-thirds of the distance to the apex. Iron doors originally sealed up these entrances. Each has three rows of vent holes, in some cases with logs used in the vents as stops. It usually took from three to five days for the fire to burn down, and three more to cool off.

Beaver
Beaver Main Post Office
20 South Main Street
1941
Federal government

The mural in the lobby of the 1941 Beaver Main Post Office represents the government's best efforts at giving rural America a boost during the years of privation during the Depression era, a project supported by Utah congressman Abe Murdock from Beaver. It is one of three post office murals in the state that narrate the social history of the community and contemporary values and mores.

Unlike other Classical Revival buildings, the post office has virtually no ornamentation except in the ornate grille and low-relief eagle sculpture above the entry doors. The hipped roof and cupola are traditional elements from American Colonial styles.

Region F

Beaver Main Post Office.
Photograph by Tricia Simpson, GNU Free Documentation License 1.2, CC A-SA 3.0.

This subtle mixture of old and new is typical of the design of public buildings during this transitional period. During the 1930s and 1940s more-modern austerity and simplicity became common. This building forms a transition between the two with its symmetry, formality, and traditional detailing but overall simplicity and more unmodulated facade.

The post office mural was funded through the Section of Painting and Sculpture established by the Treasury Department on October 14, 1934. The section dealt directly with local artists and selected them for work through national and regional design competitions, seeking the best decorative art possible for designated federal buildings. No Utah artist received a commission under this program, and none participated in the Treasury Relief Art Project, which was initiated in July 1935.

This twelve-by-six-foot oil mural, *Life on the Plains*, was painted by John W. Beauchamp of Marion, Indiana, and hangs on the lobby wall over the postmaster's door. The mural depicts various elements of the local economy—prospectors panning for gold, wranglers rounding up a steer for branding, and local Indians trading with merchants—illustrating mining, stock raising, and commerce.

Beaver County Courthouse
Southwest corner of Center Street and
100 East
1885
Even though Beaver is a modest-sized community far from denser population

Beaver County Courthouse

William Stokes, a U.S. Army soldier and one-time U.S. marshal of Beaver, was superintendent of construction. The contrasts between building materials create a lively, rich, and colorful exterior: a full basement of black basalt, a main superstructure of red brick, white wood trim, and a four-sided clock tower above. Different floors held the multiple functions of the building: county offices on the first, a large second-level courtroom, and rooms for officials and juries on the third floor. Like many pioneer-era buildings, the courthouse was partially destroyed by a fire; this one burned in 1889, but it was immediately rebuilt and improved, with the addition of a tower to house the town clock as well as a bell. The building saw many of Beaver's historical high points—the polygamy trials of the late nineteenth century and the trial of John D. Lee—and legend suggests that Butch Cassidy stayed in the jail for a time.

Beaver Opera House
55 East Center Street
1908–1909
Liljenberg and Maeser

By the end of the nineteenth century, Beaver had many of the same cultural amenities as Salt Lake City, although more modest in scale and style—large public and religious buildings; significant residences built of stone, adobe, and brick; and commercial blocks that lined Main Street. The Beaver Opera House, erected in 1909,

centers, it has a veritable treasure trove of architecturally significant buildings, especially rich in its variety of materials, styles, and early Mormon house types. One of the state's most spectacular historic brick buildings is the Territorial Court House— the eventual county courthouse. Beaver City's officials petitioned the territorial governor and legislature in 1876 for support for the construction of a courthouse that would house the Second Judicial District Court. Built between the mid-1870s and 1885, the three-story Victorian building is one of the finest historic courthouses in Utah. Its architect is unknown, but

Beaver Opera House

speaks to more than the fight for survival but also to the importance of cultural life in Beaver. The building was constructed of rough-faced tuff, the pink stone used in so many Beaver residences and quarried in the hills nearby.

The architectural firm Liljenberg and Maeser designed the building, which had a seating capacity of one thousand, a third-floor balcony, an auditorium on the second floor, and a dance pavilion on the first. The auditorium was also used for dances and as a gymnasium and theater, and later for movies. Between 1929 and 1955 the building was used for offices and as storage for the Utah National Guard.

This Classical Revival building has rectangular massing, a prominent entablature supported by massive piers, and pilasters flanking the monumental round-arched openings on the facade, similar to the Salt Lake Theater, the opera house prototype to the north that features smoother stonework. A pressed-tin cornice has block modillions capped by a decorative band of simple geometric ornamentation. The building sits on a low base that emphasizes its weight.

Duckworth Grimshaw House
95 North 400 West
1877
Thomas Fraser

This house is tied to both the unusual history of Mormon polygamy and the distinctiveness of local craftsmanship. The Duckworth Grimshaw House is an excellent example of the stonework of Thomas Fraser. British convert Grimshaw was a polygamist who was convicted for "unlawful cohabitation" and sent for a period to the Utah Territorial Penitentiary. He lived

Duckworth Grimshaw House.
Photograph by Scurry1515, CC A-SA 4.0.

in this house with one of his wives and five of her children.

The one-and-a-half-story house (a basic hall-parlor plan with two rooms on each floor and measuring thirty-six by twenty feet) was constructed with black basalt rock from a quarry four miles east of Beaver, and lime mortar from west of town in the Mineral Mountains. Lumber used in the building is from the nearby Tushar Mountains.

Like many other buildings in town, the house has walls eighteen inches thick. It has two cut-rock facades on both the front and rear, with white mortar joints. The central entrance door has two windows on each side, and on the upper level a central gable is flanked by dormer windows. The symmetry, the proportions of the windows and doors, and the contrast of the black stone and white trim create a sense of formality and care.

Fort Cameron
Fort Cameron Barracks
State Route 153, 1½ miles east of Beaver
1879

Two events motivated the U.S. government to build a fort near Beaver City—the Black Hawk War and the Mountain Meadows Massacre. Cyrus M. Hawley, associate justice of the Utah Supreme Court, recommended to the federal government that a military force of at least five companies be sent to Beaver to provide protection. In response, Secretary of War William W. Belknap recommended a governmental appropriation of $120,000 to construct a military post near Beaver. Colonel John D.

Wilkins and four companies of troops, about 181 men, came to Utah to establish the post in 1872.

The rectangular fort site measured 700 by 620 feet, with a parade ground in the center and buildings around the periphery—two barracks to both the east and west, and officers' quarters to the south. A hospital, headquarters building, and store were to the north, and outside the fort were stables. The buildings were constructed with the same black stone used for houses and public buildings in town. Buildings were roughly plastered. Of the original barracks buildings, one remains. A basic rectangular plan, it is thirty-one by fifty-seven feet, with a gabled roof, three chimneys at both ends and in the center, and eight rooms on each level.

Fort Cameron was closed on May 1, 1883, and the troops removed to Fort Douglas in Salt Lake City. Buildings once used as barracks became dormitories for Mormon students from across the territory until 1922, when the Beaver Branch of the Brigham Young Academy closed its doors and the

school equipment was donated to Beaver High School. During the New Deal era, men of the Civilian Conservation Corps inhabited Fort Cameron.

Iron County

Parowan
Parowan Third Ward Meetinghouse
90 South Main Street
1916
Miles Miller

The Parowan Third Ward building contrasts dramatically with the nearby old rock church in form and demeanor and speaks to the continuity and stability of Mormon worship in this southern Utah town. The surprisingly sophisticated Parowan Third Ward building is on the same block as the rock church and reflects the influence of Frank Lloyd Wright. Designed in 1916 by architect Miles Miller and completed two years later, it is one of the most impressive Prairie-style buildings in the state. It physically symbolized the end of the pioneer era

Parowan Third Ward Meetinghouse

and a reaching out to progressive national styles. Entered on the north, it emphasizes massive geometric forms, band windows, and details. The building features the geometric massing and decorative detailing typical of the style, with exposed orange-red bricks on the interior, and is reminiscent of the Unity Temple in Oak Park, Illinois, one of Wright's masterpieces.

William and Julia Lyman House
191 South Main Street
1895

William Lyman most likely built this house for his family in 1895, the year he returned from a missionary trip to London, bringing home sketches of houses he most admired. He built this soft-fired brick house upon his return. William was the son of Amasa Lyman, an apostle in the LDS Church. One of four remaining central-passage houses in Parowan, this is the only one built of brick and the only one that is one and a half stories.

In some ways, the form of the central-passage house can track the movement of the Mormons through the Midwest. Called the *I* house because of its widespread occurrence in Indiana, Illinois, and Iowa, it became a symbol of sorts of economic success in the nineteenth century. Related to its smaller relative, the hall-parlor house, the central passage was often the choice of local elites and was more frequently built after the 1880s in Utah. A hallway that could be entered from the main entrance separated public from private spaces.

The Lyman House's walls are fourteen inches thick and formed with brick. When the family first built the house, a two-story porch ran along the symmetrical facade, with modified Ionic columns on the corners and a white balustrade around the top. The moderately pitched roof has cornice returns

and dentil molding. The house combines elements from both the Classical and Revival styles, typical of a Victorian Eclectic building. Perhaps hinting at the connections between LDS blue bloods, a fireplace mantle removed from the home of Mormon president John Taylor's Salt Lake home is in the parlor.

Parowan Rock Church
Center of block on west side of Main Street between Center and 100 South
1862–1866
Ebenezer Hanks, Edward Dalton, William A. Warren

Parowan was settled in 1851 and was the first Mormon settlement in southern Utah, an important hub of the LDS Church's colonization efforts in the region. Built between 1862 and 1866, the Parowan Rock Church was the first permanent and substantial meetinghouse in south-central Utah. Although it is vernacular in style, its scale and materiality are impressive. It was

Parowan Rock Church

used as a tabernacle or stake center for large-scale meetings, seating eight hundred comfortably. The three architects/builders were also important religious leaders in the community—Ebenezer Hanks, Edward Dalton, and William A. Warren.

This charming rock building is one of the best early examples of Mormon pioneer ecclesiastical architecture. The church's split-level entry, typical of many other church buildings, leads to a chapel and gallery upstairs and six smaller classrooms downstairs. During the early years there were separate entries for men and women, reflecting the congregational traditions of New England but not a tradition that took hold in Utah. The four main exterior walls are made with orange-brown sandstone laid in coursed rubble. The simple gabled roof has a modest, awkwardly proportioned belfry. Because glass was scarce in the 1850s, the windows are constructed with sixteen-by-sixteen-inch squares. The simple molded cornice is boxed and has a plain frieze.

At the heart of the pioneer community and central to the town, the Parowan Rock Church stands in the town green with two other generations of Mormon churches, a block that gives a visual parade through LDS meetinghouse types through history. The Daughters of Utah Pioneers operates a museum in the building today and holds public meetings there when needed.

Meeks/Green Farmstead
40 North 400 West
1853

The pioneers first came to Parowan after the discovery of iron ore deposits nearby. Apostle George A. Smith was the leader of the Iron Mission, which established Parowan. Priddy Meeks arrived in Parowan on May 8, 1851, with a large

group sent from Salt Lake City to bolster the five-month-old village. The home on this pioneer farmstead was built no later than 1853, the year it first showed up on a map of the town. The other buildings in the farming complex were built after Meeks and his family left Parowan for Kane County in 1861 and provide us a picture of a working homestead in a rural Utah village. James Green purchased the farm in June 1904 and later added the existing agricultural elements—the outbuildings, barn, granary, rail fence, and freestanding lean-to. As a group they suggest the working and living patterns of a family running a subsistence farm.

Not all of those who lived in Parowan were farmers or ranchers. Meeks was a prominent civic leader who was well known for his medical skills. A Thomsonian medical practitioner, or herbalist, Dr. Priddy Meeks used his home for his office and for storage of the herbs and instruments he used in his practice. Meeks's journals help us understand botanical treatments for common medical complaints including ulcers, black canker, various skin diseases, intestinal disorders, dropsy, rheumatism, and accidental amputations. Until the end of the century, folk medicine was the preferred medical treatment in these small towns; it was given the blessing of LDS president Joseph Smith, who described it as inspired by God.

The Meeks/Green Farmstead is about four miles west of Main Street and includes four extant structures. One is a hewn-log cabin measuring twenty by sixteen feet, with dovetail notching, chinking, and filler strips of wood; it sits on stone and wooden piers that create a small crawl space under the cabin. At one time vertical planks dressed the structure up some, covering its log walls.

A frame granary is to the north of the cabin, probably built in 1910. It was constructed inside-out; the walls have sawed planks nailed horizontally on the inside of exposed vertical studs. It is connected by round wooden post-and-rail or post-and-wire fences to a small freestanding shed-roofed structure that opens to the south. This outbuilding, also constructed with sawed planks, was built in the 1930s and was most likely used as a feed house and shelter. A 1910 barn, measuring twenty-four by twenty-one and a half feet, was built with widely spaced round logs that were saddle notched at the corners.

Parowan Tithing Office
21 North 100 West
1880s
William Adams

Cash was scarce in pioneer agricultural areas. As a result, tithing contributions were usually in-kind products of the farm—fruits or vegetables, livestock, or handmade baskets or brooms—but they nevertheless demonstrated the selflessness of the faithful. Bishops in virtually every community typically collected donations and then distributed them to the poor, centering their work out of the tithing office. The Parowan Tithing Office is one of twenty-eight well-preserved tithing offices extant in Utah, all part of the tithing system run by the LDS Church between the 1850s and 1910. A tithing office typically included a barn and other outbuildings as well as a corral to accommodate the range of donations.

The Parowan Tithing Office was probably erected in the 1880s by William Adams, a local stonemason who helped build the St. George, Manti, and Salt Lake Temples as well as the old rock church in Parowan. It is a one-and-a-half-story rectangle with a gabled roof and a chimney at the west end.

Perhaps the only distinctive element of its construction is the temple-form detailing of the roof. Commonly used for religious, educational, commercial, and residential buildings, the temple form was dignified, symmetrical or formal, and clean. As is typical of vernacular temple-form public buildings, the short end of the rectangle faces the street and forms the facade, and cornice returns are on the gabled end. Because the stone was random ashlar, it was originally covered with plaster and painted.

Jesse N. Smith House
45 West 100 South
1856

In Utah, the Youngs, Smiths, and Kimballs were the equivalent of Utah aristocracy, known for their connection to the prophets and general authorities of the LDS Church. Jesse N. Smith, the youngest cousin of Joseph Smith, was one of southern Utah's most prominent pioneers, who traveled to Utah in Parley P. Pratt's company, arriving on September 25, 1847. Four days later, Brigham Young called Jesse Smith to work in the Iron Mission. He began building his home in 1856, resourcefully baking the adobe bricks himself, plastering them over for a more finished look, and cutting the wood for the framing and details. The house was simple—two rooms on the first floor and two above, sitting on a rock basement. It was easy to add on to such a house, and Smith did in 1865, giving the house the familiar saltbox outline along with four additional rooms. The front of the symmetrical house is a large porch that runs across the facade, and two windows on each side flank a central door on the main floor and three windows on the second. A simple molded cornice provides additional decorative detail.

Jesse married five wives and had a total of forty-four children.

Cedar City
Adams Memorial Theatre
Southern Utah University
1977

It is impossible to separate Professor Fred Adams from the history of the Utah Shakespeare Festival. His vision, teaching, devotion, and experience brought the festival from a small group of students and volunteers in 1962 to one of the state's most popular cultural events today. Each summer thousands attend three or four Shakespearean plays, works by other playwrights, and other events throughout the warm summer months. Lectures, backstage tours, meals, Renaissance fairs, and seminars enrich the experience. Students at Southern Utah University can read a common play and then have the chance to see it performed in the replica of the Globe Theatre at the heart of the festival grounds. The annual Utah Shakespeare Festival, recognized in 2000 with a Tony Award, brings visitors from across the state and the nation.

Hunter House
86 East Center Street
1866–1924

This two-story red brick house, which was built in 1866 and added to in 1924, is at the center of town across the street from the well-known historic rock church in Cedar City and is similar in terms of mass, materiality, and vernacular style to other homes in the region. Joseph S. Hunter was a Scottish immigrant who came to Utah to be with the Mormons in 1849. During the journey west,

First Ward Meetinghouse / Old Rock Church

he lost most of his family—his wife and two of his five children perished. In Cedar City, Hunter became a prominent farmer and livestock man. In 1865 he remarried an English immigrant, Elizabeth Catherine Pinnock, and had ten more children.

First Ward Meetinghouse / Old Rock Church
Center Street between Main Street and 100 East
1920s

In contrast to the austerity more typical of Depression-era buildings, the Old Rock Church is colorful, textural, and richly varied. Near the corner of Main and Center, it is an imposing example of varicolored native stone in a distinguished steepled church building. Members of the congregation gathered the rocks used in its construction; local red cedar or juniper from the surrounding mountains was used for interior finishing; and local wool was used in rugs and draperies. The colorful rocks in the exterior walls include iron, copper ore, gold ore, petrified wood, limestone, sandstone, and different varieties of quartz. Salvaged items such as Cedar City's old town clock and bricks from an earlier Mormon tabernacle (which was razed for a federal building) were used in the construction.

Old Main
351 West University Boulevard
Southern Utah University
1898

What is today known as Southern Utah University was first established as a branch normal school in 1897. It became the Branch Agricultural College in 1913,

Old Main

Region F

the College of Southern Utah in 1953, and Southern Utah State College in 1971. In 1992, the college became a four-year university.

At the end of the nineteenth century, when Utah became a state, there were no state-sponsored institutions of higher education in southern Utah. The LDS Church founded the Parowan Stake Academy in Cedar City in 1888 as part of the system of local academies in towns in outlying areas of the territory.

Resembling an Ivy League college in a New England state, SUU has spaces evocative of the long history of public education in the United States. At the center is Old Main, a building constructed with the help of an entire community who worked through the winter, hauling logs from Cedar Mountain and raising money, materials, and labor so that the institution could meet the construction schedule imposed by the state. This tree-lined campus is in a sense like an oasis in the midst of an arid desert. The campus includes about twenty-five buildings, which range from the traditional formal structures of the historic quad—Old Main, the Braithwaite Liberal Arts Center (1899)—to the Centrum, the special events center completed in 1987.

Old Main is a three-story brick building with a low-pitched hipped roof and a central octagonal bell tower with a tent roof. The Second Renaissance style is reflected in the three-part division of the exterior, the arched entrance, and the particular use of materials. Horizontal divisions are accentuated with belt courses and different materials and textures. The building's first level is constructed with stone and the second two with brick, with levels distinguished by a belt course. It is topped by a projecting cornice decorated by large modillions. At the center of the facade is

a stone pavilion jutting out from the main wall. An arched opening is crowned with a transom fanlight, double glass doors are flanked by sidelights, and at the top a large molded stone with Roman numerals gives the date of the building.

Old Main is situated on a slight rise in an open space that moves to the east, surrounded by a vertical wall of historic trees. It went through a significant adaptive reuse project in 1976–77, when the interior was completely gutted and reconfigured and the exterior was restored.

Old Science Building
351 West University Boulevard
Southern Utah University
1904

The Old Science Building was the second building on campus, built with local labor and locally produced bricks and lumber. Like Old Main, the Old Science Building has three stories and a low-pitched hipped roof, reflecting its predecessor in many ways. However, rather than an elaborate bell tower, this building has a small cupola on the roof ridge. Also a Second Renaissance Revival–style building, it divides its elevations horizontally by changes in material, detail, and color: stone on the basement level, brick above, and belt courses showing where floors begin and end. Other details consistent with the style include a projecting cornice with modillions, an arched entrance, and varied window headers. A two-story central pavilion has a flat roof topped by a balustrade leading to a second-level door. Stairs mark the entrance along with an arch over the doorway and a fanlight transom. Together, the two buildings make a unified visual statement about the importance of education in nineteenth-century Utah. In 1974–75 the Old Science Building underwent restoration.

Cedar City Railroad Depot / Union Pacific
Railroad Depot
220 North Main Street
1923
Union Pacific Railroad Company

Cedar City's iron-manufacturing enterprises were finally connected with more accessible markets when the railroad came to Iron County in 1905. Even then the first depot was thirty miles northwest of the city, at Lund. For the next twenty years wagons freighted between Lund and Cedar City, but when the Cedar City Union Pacific Railroad Depot was built in 1923, it was tourism, not iron, that secured the deal. The Union Pacific Railroad helped promote tourism by purchasing the El Escalante Hotel, starting a large bus station in town, and buying the Wylie Tourist Camp interests in Zion Canyon and the Parry Transportation Route from Cedar City to Zion. When automobile traffic became markedly more efficient than railroads, the company closed the depot in 1959.

Plans for the building were reviewed by the chief engineer's office of the Union Pacific System in Los Angeles and the Salt Lake Railroad Company and were signed by architect W. T. Wellman. Accommodating the platform for arrivals and departures, the main mass of the single-story depot building is a long, rectangular brick structure with a gabled roof and stone foundation and no particular reference to style. An L-shaped waiting area and bus shelter is connected to the building on the south end with a low-pitched hipped roof, supported on massive brick piers with stone foundations, and a porch is attached on the north end.

Cedar City Main Post Office
10 North Main Street
1933
Lewis Telle Cannon and John Fetzer

The Cedar City Main Post Office is made of brick, as are most of the town's public buildings. Classically proportioned and symmetrically organized, this building creates a sense of monumentality. Strong horizontal accents modulate the wall surface and create greater interest. Modern elements include reinforced-concrete walls and floor slabs as well as a steel frame

Cedar City Railroad Depot / Union Pacific Railroad Depot

Region F

structure. Granite faces the basement-level walls, with rough tapestry brick on the first and second stories. The facade is subtly modulated with five central recessed bays, and six engaged terra-cotta columns with Ionic capitals create a colonnaded portico topped by a slightly projecting cornice extending above. Materials include a combination of old and new: aluminum-framed entrance doors with glass, a leaded-glass transom window, and terra-cotta frames around the flat-arched bays. A terra-cotta entablature runs across the entire facade and includes an architrave, frieze, and projecting cornice with dentils. A brick parapet wall includes the words "United States Post Office" carved into the frieze.

This building's size and imposing Neoclassical design distinguish it architecturally, but the post office is also the first and only federal government building in town, a legacy of the public works programs of the New Deal's response to the Great Depression. Salt Lake architects Cannon and Fetzer designed the building.

Washington County

Enterprise
Enterprise Meetinghouse
Approximately 24 South Center Street
1899

Establishing the centrality of religion to the community, the 1899 Enterprise Meetinghouse is at the intersection of Main and Center Streets and is positioned about fifty feet back from both roads at Public Square, a block that historically contained two subsequent LDS meetinghouses, built in 1913 and 1952, to the south of the earlier structure.

The building is small, only twenty-four by thirty-eight feet, with the short end of the rectangle facing east toward Center Street. The walls are made of locally produced reddish-brown brick and rise from a foundation built from local igneous rubble. A shallow segmental arch frames the single door, with unusually shaped bricks at the base of the arch. A single horizontal diamond brick is found over the door. Reddish-brown stucco was once applied to the south side of the building, perhaps to retard deterioration of the brick, but echoing the earth tones of the surrounding environs. The moderately pitched roof has fairly shallow painted eaves and a simply detailed frieze that runs around the entire building. The meetinghouse interior was always modest in design and included not much more than a tall wainscot painted on plaster walls and a painted headboard ceiling. For years there was a slightly raised platform at the west end.

Pine Valley
Pine Valley Meetinghouse
30 miles north of St. George on Utah Highway 18, to Forest Road 35, east
1859
Ebenezer Bryce

Legend has it that when Isaac Riddle and William Hamblin were herding cattle about fifteen miles north of Santa Clara in the summer of 1855, they were surprised to come across a secluded verdant valley. Pine Valley had a lush green carpet of thick grass and hills covered with pine, aspen, and thick undergrowth. In an area marked by scarce timber, news of Pine Valley spread quickly and by 1855 Robert Richey, Lorenzo Roundy, and Jehu Blackburn had built a sawmill and farmers had begun agriculture in the beautiful valley. It eventually became home to more than three hundred people.

It is fitting that one of the state's most beautiful buildings is found in such a

Pine Valley Meetinghouse

a building much like a ship, Bryce allegedly said, "If the floods come, it will float. And if the winds blow, it may roll over but it will never crash."[2]

The two-story building has a gabled attic containing a small prayer room over the sitting area down below. The building is set up on a podium foundation to create well-lit rooms in the basement and under the chapel above, proudly presenting the building as worthy of respect. A grand baroque wooden staircase leads to the entrance, a pair of double stairs with a landing halfway up.

Also on the site and to the east of the building is a small tithing office built of soft red brick in the 1880s. It is one story and measures only sixteen by twenty-seven feet, with a warehouse door on the side. The tithing office is all about business and was left undecorated, with a simple gabled roof, cornices, and eaves. Interior flooring is five-inch ponderosa pine. Still in use, a reconstructed and scaled-down version of the Pine Valley Meetinghouse is in This Is the Place Heritage Park in Salt Lake City.

Santa Clara
Santa Clara Relief Society Hall
3036 West Santa Clara Drive
1908

During the nineteenth century, women of the Relief Society purchased property and managed businesses from a modest-sized building usually located near the ward meetinghouse or tithing office. The Santa Clara Relief Society first organized in 1868 with sixty-four women; two years later they purchased this lot for $150 as a site for mulberry trees and a sericulture project. The earliest building was constructed with locally produced adobe bricks, with the upstairs devoted to silk production and the main level to grain storage through the General Relief Society Grain Storage

remarkable place. Modest in size and materials, it is nevertheless a little gem. Folklore suggests that Ebenezer Bryce designed the church, which was constructed in 1859, based on what he knew about boat building. A British convert, Ebenezer Bryce oversaw construction and conceived of the unusual truss system. If you climb to the top of the winding staircase to the attic level, you can see that the interior resembles an upside-down ship and is curved like a hull. Bryce erected it in the same way one would a ship—the wooden frame walls were assembled on the ground and raised into position, and then joined with wooden pegs and rawhide. Basically, the frame stands independently, with walls and partitions hanging on the basic structure. Poking fun at his own effort to build

Santa Clara Relief Society Hall

Santa Clara Tithing Granary
3105 West Santa Clara Drive
1902

The Santa Clara Tithing Granary is a one-story sandstone building with a raised sandstone foundation and a corrugated-steel gabled roof, originally built to house donations from Latter-day Saints in the area. As is true of many of the region's pioneer-era buildings, the design is vernacular, with no pretense to style or distinction. This sturdy stone building is the size of a modern master bedroom, only eighteen by twenty feet, with walls one and a half feet thick made of limestone laid in a random ashlar pattern. Over time a store was also built on the site as well as a residence, and the original tithing barn was torn down.

The tithing lot was of critical importance in a fledgling community struggling to survive, with a constant influx of newcomers and the challenges of settling in a remote, challenging environment. Besides the storehouse itself, there was usually a barn and chicken coops for keeping animals given in place of cash, a granary and cellar for storage of grains and produce, and sometimes an office where the local bishop transacted business.

Jacob Hamblin House
Approximately 3400 West Hamblin Drive
1862

Jacob Hamblin was a frontiersman who played a pivotal role in negotiating with the native inhabitants of the region, exploring the Arizona Strip country, and organizing colonization of the area. When Hamblin arrived in Santa Clara in 1854, he saw it as

program. The second building was only twenty by twenty-five feet and had the gabled end of the rectangle facing the street. A masonry false front with a rounded parapet top corbeled with a row of dentils was attached to the facade. A slightly recessed rectangular panel possibly used for signage is formed in the south end, resulting in a Victorian Eclectic look. As in many of the other public and residential buildings in town, the walls are built with multiple layers of locally produced reddish-brown brick laid in a stretcher or running bond and sitting on a stone foundation. The single chamber formed by the building is also modest in design, with painted plaster walls, ceiling, and window and door casings. Long after the Relief Society stopped managing its activities in this building, the hall was used as a school, a post office, and even for a time as a makeshift clinic.

a proselytizing opportunity. Known as the "buckskin apostle," Hamblin was appointed by Brigham Young in 1857 to be president of the Southern Indian Mission, which required frequent travel away from his family. In 1862 some of the local missionaries, with the expert guidance of stonemasons Elias Morris and the Averett brothers, constructed a sandstone home for his family. Made with red rock quarried nearby, it was carved into the hillside and permitted entrance into the second floor from the ground level.

The Hamblin home has porches on two sides to maximize shade during the hot summer months. Hamblin's plural families used the two separate sides of the house, each with its own fireplace and staircase to the upper level. The house was also used for public, religious, and social events and had a staircase leading directly to the outside as well. The children slept in two

small rooms, also on the upper level. The house was usually filled with children and family members: Hamblin's wives Rachel Judd and Priscilla Leavitt had eight children between them and helped raise the children Jacob had had with an earlier wife. While he lived there, he married a young Native American girl as well as another wife, Louisa Bonelli. At one time the house was home to as many as fifteen children. In 1871 the family uprooted and moved to help settle Kanab.

Hamblin scouted for Major John Wesley Powell, who described the Mormon leader as "a silent, reserved man, and when he speaks, it is in a slow, quiet way, that inspires great awe. His talk is so low that they must listen attentively to hear, and they sit around him in a death-like silence. When he finishes a measured sentence, the chief repeats it, and they give a solemn grunt."[3]

Jacob Hamblin House

St. George
Addie Price House
185 West Diagonal Street
Late 1800s

The charming Addie Price House deviates somewhat from the typical rectangularity of pioneer-era homes in St. George. As was true of many other homes in town, the foundation material was basalt rock, and double-thick adobe was used for the walls, illustrating the versatility of the material, which could be used to produce homes of virtually any style. This home shows the influence of the Carpenter Gothic with its graceful porch, gingerbread at the gable, and bay window. Fireplaces kept each room warm in winter. This simple detail added to the basic geometry of the house—a main rectangular form and a single wing—which created a house that was at once picturesque yet sturdy and anchored into the earth. Although Addie Price was a widow with three dependent children, she was financially secure and according to her neighbors had "considerable means," spending freely on detailing the house.[4]

On the house's south elevation, the first floor was constructed slightly below ground level. Price ran a millinery shop out of this space, advertising in the *Southern Utah Star* on July 20, 1895, that she had the largest supply of millinery south of Provo, offering lovely hats and dry goods in a convenient location.

Thurston House
270 West 200 North
1880s

Across from the Catholic church is the Thurston House, built in the early 1880s, a simple *I* house that looks like those built throughout New England. Originally from Vermont before he converted to the Mormon Church, Thomas Thurston used wood that he hauled from Pine Valley for his family's home. He chose to build low ceilings, hoping to preserve heat in winter, with three windows on both the ground floor and the upstairs. Unfortunately, he died before he completed the house, but his widow and family finished it and lived there for the next fifty years. It was briefly used as a taxidermy shop.

Whitehead House
241 North 100 West
1883
George F. Whitehead

For an individual or family, the home is the center of the world—the place where they spend their most meaningful time and the center of economic and social life. George F. Whitehead built this home in 1883 for his wife, Esther Jane Morris, and poured the finest craftsmanship into its construction. First he built the foundation and let it settle for a year before he raised the walls, which he eventually covered with stucco. Then he added a frame porch with a balustraded second level supported by thin wooden posts and simple wooden trim.

George F. Whitehead was a local dignitary—a counselor in the St. George Stake presidency for twenty-five years and later the president of the St. George Temple. Church leaders from across the territory stayed in his home when they traveled through town or he and his wife entertained. After their deaths, the family sold the building and it was divided into apartments. In 1988, Jay and Donna Curtis and Jon and Alison Bowcutt bought the home and restored it.

Woolley-Foster House
217 North 100 West
1870s

The Edwin G. Woolley house would have been considered grand regardless of where in the territory it was built, but in St. George, it was a significant piece of architecture. Woolley was well known and respected as both a judge and a member of a prosperous law firm—Woolley, Lund, and Judd. Woolley's education and sense of culture were reflected in his home, which also witnessed key moments in Utah and Mormon history: the coming of the railroad, the underground period, and the shift from a time when home manufacture and self-sufficiency were highly valued to one when state goods reflected wealth and prestige. The house's fifteen rooms were extravagantly furnished with woodwork, art glass, and imported furnishings. Local lore suggested that the unfinished attic was often used as a hiding place for polygamists on the run from federal marshals.

Woolley's family lived in the house between the 1870s and 1907, when they moved to Salt Lake City. Charles F. Foster, a pioneer stockman, merchant, and banker, bought the house and filled it with his nine daughters, one son, two orphaned nieces, and an orphaned boy his family had sheltered. Although the house had ample space, the family needed more and expanded into the attic. The frequent scene of parties and other social events, the Woolley-Foster House was a grand reminder that despite the widespread privation of settlers in the area, some wealthy individuals also lived in St. George.

Brigham Young Winter Home and Office
Corner of 200 North and 100 West
1874
Miles Romney Sr. and Miles Romney Jr.

As LDS Church president, territorial leader, and husband to dozens of wives, Brigham Young had homes throughout the territory, including in St. George, and frequently

Brigham Young Winter Home and Office

traveled throughout the Great Basin kingdom. Missionaries were in the area as early as 1856, and he often visited the Dixie Mission, building a home in 1874 where he spent his winters until his death in 1877, the same year the St. George Temple was completed.

Always wanting to demonstrate the versatility of adobe bricks for construction, Brigham Young opted to have the house constructed with locally produced adobe bricks covered with stucco rather than a fancier material. Miles Romney, architect of the temple and tabernacle, worked with his son Miles P. Romney on the structure for their church president. Black rock was used for the foundation, sandstone for the basement level, and adobe bricks above. Reminiscent of New England Colonial-style homes or the homes built by the Mormons in Nauvoo and elsewhere in Utah, this central-passage house has basic rectangular massing and a gabled roof covered with wooden shingles, bracketed cornices, and a symmetrical facade. From above, you would see that a wing moves toward the back, creating a T-shaped plan.

Adobe walls provided efficient insulation for a home. Even so, four fireplaces heated this home during the few months of winter. Throughout the house pine was refashioned to look like oak, locally called "Brigham Oak." Brigham's personal one-room office is east of the main home, a chamber measuring eighteen by twenty-two feet. Here adobe walls sit on stuccoed sandstone foundations.

After Young's death his family sold the home to Dr. Judd Gates, a local dentist who used the upstairs rooms for his offices. During the 1940s the home was badly in need of repair. Young's grandson Georgius Cannon Young, an architect, helped plan restoration of this important site. In 1959 the property was deeded to Utah State Parks and Recreation, and the church donated funds for reshingling the roof. It is now a popular tourist destination and is managed by the Historic Sites Department of the LDS Church.

St. George Opera House
212 North Main Street
1875

The Mormon pioneers struggled with taming the land, weathering the severe climate, and building a whole new world, but they balanced their efforts with play. They loved to come together for dances, theatricals, and other social activities. The people of St. George built an opera house in 1875 to house traveling troupes of musicians and actors, as well as local performances.

The Gardeners' Club erected the first building on the site it called St. George Hall. It used the lower level for storage and production and the upper level for social events. That same year, it turned the building into a store and decided to build a larger building purely for recreation.

Instead, in 1880 the club doubled the square footage of the building by adding a wing that met the main rectangle in the middle. And like its equivalent in Salt Lake City, it became known as the Social Hall

and was used only for social and cultural rather than religious activities. It was a perfect space for theater—the stage was in the older part of the building and seating in the new wing. Going to the theater helped the pioneers escape the drudgery of their difficult lives—the elegant backdrops, scenery, and costumes enhanced the otherworldliness of the performances. Dozens of plays and musicals were performed here in the nineteenth century. Patrons paid for their tickets with goods, not unlike tithing barter, buying their way with vegetables, eggs, and flour.

The Utah-Idaho Sugar Company bought the opera house in 1936 for use as a sugar beet and seed cleaning plant. By that time motion pictures were popular and live theater had lost its original appeal. After sitting vacant for decades, it was restored for a new use.

The restoration of the opera house in 1995 was the first step in the development of a complex called the Pioneer Center for the Arts. It includes two large warehouses built by Utah-Idaho Sugar located next to the opera house, a log cabin brought onto the property, and a plaza and fountain, an eloquent testimonial to the dedication of the inhabitants of St. George to the preservation of pioneer heritage.

Anthony Ivins / Bessie Gardner House
165 North 100 West
1880s

Anthony W. Ivins was a Mormon apostle who spent most of the last few decades of his life exploring southern Utah and becoming familiar with the ways of Native Americans, people in the Mexican colonies, and the people of Washington County. He was very influential because of what he knew, what he made happen, and his loyalty to the church. He helped orchestrate the denouement of polygamy in the post-Manifesto era.

Built in the 1880s as the southern Utah home for Ivins's family, this home is interesting in the way it deviates from more traditional pioneer home design but uses the same basic architectural vocabulary. Rather than a simple *I*, the plan is shaped like a *U*—a double cross-wing type—formed with two gabled wings with eight rooms each connected by a basic single-story rectangle. The house sits on a basalt rock foundation with adobe walls four layers thick that are covered with white stucco. Pine floors are still extant, and the square nails used for construction can be seen around the house, giving a glimpse into pioneer-era technologies. When built, the house had a front porch and a rear sleeping deck that no longer exist. Deviating from the recommendation of the Plat of the City of Zion to place a home twenty-five feet back from the street, this house is set back much farther than its neighbors.

Moses Andrus House
125 North 100 West
Late 1800s

Besides the basic *I* house, another preferred building type was the cross wing or *T* cottage. It was asymmetrical, with the entrance door off center at the intersection of the two wings. Variations included changes in the number of stories in the wings and the overall square footage, but regardless the gabled roofs were still simple and moderately pitched. Moses Andrus was an active cattleman who built this house for his wife, Orpha Morris, the daughter of a pioneer merchant. This charming *T* cottage has two stories in each wing, a black basalt rock foundation with four rooms on the first level, and bedrooms upstairs. The Andrus family lived in the house for fifty years.

Gardeners' Club
48 West St. George Boulevard
1867

Clubs and fraternal orders were particularly popular during the second half of the nineteenth century. The common thread for members of St. George's Gardeners' Club was a great love of natural environments and gardening. In contrast to the modern environmentalist devotion to the land, gardening in the 1860s in this desert landscape sought to tame or civilize the land rather than preserve it intact. The group built a club building in 1867 on a site donated by Joseph E. Johnson, a nearby neighbor. Club members came together for an adobe-making party to form their own bricks for construction and to haul lumber from the Pine Valley sawmill. When Brigham Young first sent settlers to St. George, he solicited the help of well-known horticulturist Walter E. Dodge of Santa Clara along with Luther Hemingway and J. E. Johnson to come up with better ways of planting in this arid landscape. Johnson published a newspaper, *The Pomologist*, which promoted more effective means of agriculture in dry environments like this one. The club furthered these ends by sponsoring competitions and displaying agricultural products, not all that different from a county fair. In many ways, the Gardeners' Club was the center of the town's social and cultural life in the early years before the Social Hall was completed. Besides agricultural events, the club building hosted plays, dances, receptions, and meetings.

This temple-front building has a rectangular plan with the short, gabled end facing the street and heavy cornice moldings. As in many other buildings from the period in St. George, the basalt foundation is topped by adobe walls covered with white stucco. Today the Gardeners' Club building is part of the complex of Ancestor Square.

Orson Pratt / Bentley House
Tabernacle Street and 100 West
1862

Brigham Young handpicked longtime Latter-day Saint Orson Pratt to preside over the Cotton Mission. The rectangular massing, arrangement of windows, and pitch of the roof of this two-story house were repeated in countless houses constructed before the turn of the century in virtually every community in Utah Territory. This one was made with hand-mixed adobe bricks that were fashioned into molds and then dried in the hot desert sun. Respite from the heat of summer as well as warmth during the winter was guaranteed by the double-thick adobe walls, which worked as excellent insulators. Pratt opened a dry goods store on the main floor level and St. George's first post office. Pratt eventually returned to Salt Lake City and served a mission to Europe in 1864. But before he left, he sold his property to Richard Bentley, whose family continued to operate a store out of the home. Elizabeth Bentley was involved in sericulture, or the production of silk, organized by the Relief Society. The family devoted a separate room upstairs to this unusual enterprise. Contemporary accounts suggest that one could hear the silkworms as they wiggled in the trays laid out across a room. Bentley's son W. O. Bentley lived in the home until the early 1920s, when he built a more contemporary home nearby.

Bentley House
76 West Tabernacle Street
1870s

The Bentley House was built in the 1870s by William Oscar Bentley as a wedding present for his wife. But William sold the house to his brother Richard instead. The entrance to this simple *T* cottage is under a single-story porch with a wooden balustrade, posts, and moderate wood decoration at the intersection of the wing with the main section of the house. The house was constructed with two layers of adobe bricks.

Richard Bentley sold the house in 1908 to pioneer businessman Thomas Judd, who ran a store out of the home's dining room and rented out the remainder. Thomas's son Joseph Judd assumed management after his father and continued to run the single commercial-block store but left the rest of the home vacant. Today it is part of Greene Gate Village, owned and operated by Dr. Mark Greene and Barbara Greene.

A Washington County landmark, Judd's Store has been in continuous operation since Richard Bentley opened it in 1870. Thomas Judd capitalized on the number of stock raisers who had moved into town at the turn of the century. His children had better access to schools in St. George than in La Verkin, where they had lived before, and the family moved into the home attached to the store.

Hardy House
46 West St. George Boulevard
1870s

Brigham Young gave Augustus P. Hardy the calling of working with the Native Americans of southern Utah. Hardy was known for his facility with languages and often interpreted for LDS Church leaders and Native American groups. For a while in the 1870s, Hardy served as the sheriff of Washington County, a job made more challenging because of the mining population at Silver Reef.

Hardy built this house with the most readily available materials: black basalt left over from the construction of the tabernacle, and adobe bricks made by locals. Also on the site is a small rock building he used for a time as a jail, with stuccoed walls that helped prevent deterioration. The house was a simple hall-parlor plan, with one and a half stories, two rooms on the main floor, and sleeping quarters in the half story above, with little more than dormer windows and a more elaborate lintel over the entrance door for decoration.

St. George Tabernacle
Tabernacle Street and Main Street
1863–1881
Miles Romney

During their first year of struggling to master nature in a battle for survival, the pioneers suffered greatly. Dams built on the Virgin River had repeatedly washed out when water was needed most desperately. Food was scarce. The intense summer sun beat down on them and shelter was limited. Despite these privations and trials, St. George's Mormon pioneers raised a landmark building, truly one of the most beautiful in the state—the St. George Tabernacle. Built between 1863 and 1881, it was financed by tithing donations paid in labor or in produce that was stored in a tithing office on the corner of north Main Street. For their work, laborers were paid with tithing script, exchangeable for goods.

Set against St. George's clear brilliant blue sky, the stately tower on the facade of the building forms a striking figure on the landscape, much like New England Congregational churches or those of Sir Christopher Wren in London. Limestone for the three-foot-thick basement walls was hand quarried and hauled from the foothills north of the city. The red sandstone blocks for the two-and-a-half-foot-thick walls were also hand quarried, in a site nearby. Miles

St. George Tabernacle

Romney fashioned the twin spiral staircases of the interior, complete with balustrades and railings. A plaster of paris ceiling and cornice work was locally cast. Some decorative items were shipped around Cape Horn and freighted to St. George by ox teams from San Diego. Local men worked on the construction.

Architect Miles Romney designed the building and oversaw the carpentry work. The tabernacle measures 106 feet long and 56 feet wide. The tower rises 140 feet at the east end of the gabled roof. The interior space has ceilings that rise 29 feet from the floor. A 10-foot-high gallery extends along the north, east, and south walls. The

Dixie Academy

Because of the similarity in the stylistic detailing and massing of public buildings built during these years, the style of this building is called PWA Moderne, although this example also includes Colonial Revival details. The main form of the building is a long, rectangular plan with a low-hipped roof and a slightly recessed central entrance bay. A series of low-relief stringcourse bands create surface rhythm and definition between stories. First-story windows have vertical pink stucco panels reflecting the warm rich tones of the surrounding landscape.

Dixie Academy
Main Street between Tabernacle Street and 100 South
1911
Richard C. Watkins

Schools were always present in St. George, but it was not until the first of the twentieth century that a normal school was established in town. Funded by both the LDS Church and local donations, the Dixie Academy became part of the church educational system in 1911. Located near the St. George Tabernacle, this substantial three-story sandstone building sits on a black lava rock foundation and holds a commanding presence near St. George's central space. Materials for the building, as for so many important early structures, were indigenous: stones for the building were cut by hand and transported to St. George in wagons along rutted roads and then hand dressed on the site. Beautiful pine paneling adorns many rooms on the interior. As in other square-plan schools built during the first decades of the twentieth century, the basement and ground-floor levels have six classrooms each. The upper level is one large room that was used for

focal point of the interior is at the west end—a choir loft, a three-level speakers' stand, and the inscription "More Holiness to the Lord" on the wall at the back remind viewers that the important work of the tabernacle is the message of God.

St. George Elementary School
30 South 100 West
1935–1936
Public Works Administration

Many New Deal programs built amenities in southern Utah's national parks, pouring money and other resources into rural Utah towns and building infrastructure that had not moved ahead for decades. Such was the case with St. George. The St. George Elementary School was one of 233 public works buildings built in Utah during the 1930s and 1940s under these programs; 10 were in Washington County. Of the 233, 43 were elementary schools, and only 19 are extant.

physical education, town meetings, and performances of student groups.

In terms of mass, style, plan, and materiality, the academy building resembles those designed by Richard Watkins (1858–1914), who was the architect of between two hundred and three hundred school buildings in Utah that are markedly similar in concept and design. In terms of national styles, they are reminiscent of Richardsonian Romanesque architecture; the heavy local sandstone was perfect for this style. The building is symmetrically arranged, with a hipped roof, and a projecting bay in the center of the facade. Besides its location, the entrance is identified by a significant round arch and pavilion, and above the arch is a tripartite window arrangement, and a deeply recessed double transom window so characteristic of Richardsonian buildings.

Since it opened in 1911, it has been known by a series of names: St. George Academy, Dixie Normal School, and Dixie Junior College. During the Depression, the LDS Church discontinued its support and it became a publicly run school.

Bradshaw House
190 South 300 West
1875

Because wood was scarce and there was no brickyard, adobe bricks were a frequent choice for the first wave of houses built throughout Utah Territory. Adobe was economical, readily available, and used by all social classes regardless of wealth. This example is typical of an adobe house built in a style familiar throughout the country—a simple rectangular plan. The Bradshaw House is one of the oldest extant homes of any type in St. George, first recorded in 1875 by William Butler. The house is a small hall-parlor structure

with two rooms in the original portion and a fireplace in the wall dividing the two, and two rooms in the later addition. The house is heated by wood stoves built by its second owner, Casper Bryner. The thick adobe walls kept the home toasty warm in the winter and cool throughout the long hot summer.

The home is also identified with Bert and Hazel Bradshaw, who lived in it from 1921 to 1945. Hazel Bradshaw finished the granary at the back of the lot and furnished it to house students. While they lived in the house, Bert and Hazel stored meat, vegetables, and milk in the underground cellar and did laundry and made soap in a blackened kettle in the yard.

St. George Temple
Block bounded by 200 East, 300 East, 400 South, and 500 South
1871
Truman O. Angell

The St. George Temple's stark white plaster exterior formed a striking contrast with the red rock of the surrounding hillsides, the blue of the sky, and the plainer adobe and brick houses that moved in every direction from its base as it loomed tall above them. But most distinctive was its location. Rather than being centered at the nexus of the street grid laid out in St. George, the temple is southeast of the center. Regardless, view lines from across the valley emphasize its centrality to the religious enterprise launched by the pioneers in this town surrounded by breathtakingly beautiful red-rock formations.

The St. George Temple was the first to be dedicated by the Mormons in the Great Basin, forming a tangible spiritual claim to their new home. Finally, the Mormons had a temple, a backdrop for special ordinances

Region F

St. George Temple

such as marriages, baptisms for the dead, and the special temple endowment that could not be performed elsewhere. It proved to be an economic boon to the area, providing jobs and stimulating the local economy.

Construction was funded by the Latter-day Saints themselves through money raised in tithing funds, donated labor, and other resourceful methods of utilizing the talents of members. A huge crew worked on the temple—workers at the Navajo sandstone quarries north of St. George; rock dressers on the temple site; road building crews near the sawmills on Mount Trumbull; water haulers supplying water from the infrequent springs on the Arizona Strip; and mill workers producing the floor joists,

studs, pillars, window frames, doors, steps, stairways, and baseboards.

Plans for the temple were produced by Truman O. Angell, Mormon Church architect, and Miles Romney, who directed construction. Linked to the two earlier Mormon temples in Kirtland and Nauvoo, the building style is called variously Castellated Gothic or English Norman. Of the four early Utah temples, the St. George Temple is the only one to have a single attenuated tower and a whitewashed finish, although because of its fortified or bastion-like appearance it resembles the others.

The temple measures 141 feet, 8 inches in length; 93 feet, 4 inches in width; and 175 feet to the peak of the tower.

Sacred rituals are performed in each of the temple's three levels. In the basement is a baptismal font resting upon the backs of twelve oxen cast of iron, filling a slight depression in the floor for the ritual of baptism of the dead. Above this level are two stories that each originally contained one main room measuring seventy-eight by ninety-nine feet, with an elliptically vaulted ceiling seventy feet from the floor. The most sacred space is the large chamber on the center floor, which features pulpits on each end—the east for the Melchizedek Priesthood (the higher) and the west for the Aaronic Priesthood (the lesser). The temple endowment ceremony proceeds through a series of rooms and culminates in the Celestial room.

The decorative vocabulary of the exterior includes Roman-arched bays and a window pattern also featured on the Manti and Logan Temples. Window and door bays emphasize the depth of the exterior walls, with buttresses alternating with windows; a crenellated parapet wall runs around the top of the building, with squared pinnacles rising directly over stepped buttresses. Together these features create a sense of strength, permanence, and monumentality. The corners of the front facade are segmented in a semioctagonal manner, breaking up the regularity of the building's design.

Dixie College / Dixie State University
Blocks between 100 South, 300 South, 700 East, and 1000 East
1960s–1970s

Between 1933, when the LDS Church pulled out of what had been called the St. George Stake Academy, and 1965, what was then called Dixie College expanded from its St. George city square location to include five buildings. In 1951, the Dixie Education Association purchased four blocks of land on the east side of town after the state legislature gave the school money to build a new gymnasium and gave the land to the state in return for a promise to move the school to this new site. A Fine Arts Center and a heating plant were built in 1963, and in the 1970s buildings to support a new vocational education program were added to the growing base. Today, besides its goal of becoming an excellent regional college, Dixie has a successful continuing education program, is home to the Southwest Symphony, and has dozens of certificate, associate, and bachelor's degree programs.

Washington
Washington County Courthouse
85 East 100 North
1866

While he was county probate judge between 1859 and 1870, James D. McCulloch decided St. George needed a courthouse. Rather than starting a subscription campaign as was customary, the Washington County Court proposed a tax increase of two and a half mills, an idea approved by a majority vote on August 5, 1867. Washington County was cash poor, so raising money was difficult. A special session of the court in October 1869 set the following values for donated goods, a strategy that proved effective: $1.25 per gallon of molasses, $1.50 per bushel of corn, $2.50 per yard of cotton, and $8.00 per load of flour.

The building project provided jobs and taxed already limited resources, but it was evidence of the settlers' dedication to making this place a permanent home. Despite the local enthusiasm for the project, multiple large-scale construction projects were proceeding in parallel, and it took ten years to complete.

The same workmen who built the tabernacle erected this three-story building, which measured thirty-six by forty feet and was built with a basalt foundation and eighteen-inch-thick walls of red sandstone quarried to the north of the city. Miles Romney's expert carpentry skills shaped the wood—ponderosa pine from the Pine Valley Mountains thirty-five miles to the north—demonstrated in details like the curb railing leading to the second level. Precious glass was transported in wagons from Salt Lake City to St. George for the construction of this important building.

The actual courtroom was upstairs from the main-level city offices. The judge had chambers in a room behind the bench, and prisoners were housed in one of the three jail cells in the basement, each constructed for a different level of security. The "Black Hole" cell was reserved for murderers and thieves, the worst of the bunch.

In terms of its massing, the courthouse resembles the Council Hall built in Salt Lake City during the same period, or even the statehouse in Fillmore. Square buildings, sometimes with domes at the top,

Washington County Courthouse

were standard courthouse fare. This building vocabulary linked the pioneer builders of southern Utah with the builders of America in rural counties throughout the country.

Washington Cotton Factory
U.S. Highway 91, Frontage Road West
1865
Appleton Harmon (superintendent of construction); Elijah and Elisha Averett (stonemasons); John P. Chidester (chief carpenter)

When Samuel Adair, Robert Covington, and thirty-eight other families came to settle the Cotton Mission in 1857, they found a challenging landscape—barren flats that stretched to black lava formations and red sandstone. As was true throughout Utah, it was clear that water would be the key to their survival in this desert landscape. At lower elevations, alkali encrusted the surface in white ridges. The first year, less than a third of the crop germinated, and alkali killed most of the plants that did. The settlers were there to grow cotton and enhance the self-sufficiency and independence of the territory. Water flow was erratic—floods washed out their dams year after year. The settlers even had to deal with the chills and fevers of malaria, spread by mosquitoes hatched in springs along the creek banks. Poverty, drought, grasshoppers, and other animals plagued their fledgling settlements. Four years after they had first arrived, only twenty families remained.

In 1865, Brigham Young sent the millworks from a dismantled mill in Salt Lake to Washington. The cotton factory depended on water from springs feeding the steam, stored in a reservoir west of the mill.

The Washington Cotton Mill is a substantial two-story sandstone structure, one hundred by forty-four feet wide, built with lumber from Cedar Mountain. By 1867, one story was completed and the machinery was in operation for the mill. Subsequent growth in the area and expanding demand that eventually included processed woolen goods led to the construction of two additional stories. When it was operating at peak capacity the mill produced five hundred yards of cloth each day, as well as cotton bats, mattresses, quilts, blankets, jeans, denims, broadcloth, flannels, and gingham.

Washington Cotton Factory.
Photograph by Delos H. Smith, HABS UTAH,27-WASH,3-2, public domain.

On behalf of the LDS Church, Brigham Young sold the factory in 1870 to the Rio Virgin Manufacturing Company. During this second period of operation the Mormons organized into a United Order, a communal economic system, and grew their cotton and processed it together. In 1890, Thomas Judd leased the factory and was able to operate it at a profit for a time, but by 1898 it was once again idle. Important as a symbol of industry and enterprise for this region, the cotton factory had only mixed success as an actual business. Scarce cash, difficulty in shipping supplies in and products out, limited availability of cotton, and perpetual employment problems prevented its success. Supplies to run the mill always had to be shipped a great distance at a great expense and were unpredictable. Debts had to be paid in cash, which was always in short supply in the county. Evidence of Young's desire to produce territorial self-sufficiency, the Iron Mission, the Cotton Mission, and others diversified Utah's economy and put settlers to work.

Covington House
181 East 200 North
1859
Elijah and Elisha Averett

Stonemasons Elijah and Elisha Averett built this red sandstone house with Robert D. Covington in 1859. The two men also built Windsor Castle at Pipe Springs and worked on the cotton mill. This substantial central-passage house measures twenty-one by thirty-nine feet and has two stories, a central hallway, a staircase basement, and walls sixteen inches thick. A two-story wood porch with a balustrade wraps around the entire facade on both sides. The moderately pitched roof has a carefully molded wooden cornice, a slight entablature, and a temple-front configuration at the sides. Although none of these features are unique, in combination they imply that this is the home of an important man.

Region F

One large room upstairs was used for housework such as drying fruit, quilting, weaving, and other activities. But an outside entrance to the same space created access for public events such as community meetings, plays, and dances without interrupting the family space.

Robert Covington's family came to Washington in 1857, and he served as bishop of the Washington Ward until October 1869, when he went on a six-month mission to the southern states. Covington led the residents of this small desert community through a particularly challenging time when their crops died, their fields flooded, and they struggled to produce enough food. Covington was a member of the territorial legislature between 1858 and 1859 and a vice president of the Washington United Order.

Washington Relief Society Hall
100 West Telegraph Street
1875

When Washington City established its own ward, it also organized its own Relief Society for the town's women in 1868. In 1875, the ward constructed a small adobe Relief Society hall and rented it to the Washington Cooperative Association. The post office, sometimes located in the home of the postmaster, operated out of the co-op store for several years before World War I.

This building is the oldest Relief Society hall in Washington County, a simple Greek Revival adobe building that required enormous sacrifice to build when the settlers were struggling to survive in 1875. Although it is a vernacular structure with Classical elements, the small rectangular mass, low gabled roofs, gabled-end street facade, symmetrical facade piercing, and molded cornice aspire to something grander.

Silver Reef
Wells Fargo Building
2000 Silver Reef Road
1877

The Wells Fargo Building is the only original structure left in this southern Utah ghost town. Silver Reef was once the largest town in Washington County and certainly the most diversified and perhaps lively; it had a dozen mines and six ore-processing plants. Established in 1886 when John Kemple accidentally discovered silver while working a reef of sandstone, Silver Reef furnished much-needed wealth that helped the Mormons raise their temple. Regardless of countless sermons exhorting the Mormons to avoid the mines, and Brigham Young's constant criticism of the mining industry in general, many locals worked in the mines, but others found that the miners were ready customers for the produce they had to sell.

In total, more than $10 million in ore was transported to Salt Lake, contracted primarily through Wells Fargo. Woolley, Lund, and Judd had a contract with the company in St. George and opened a branch of their mercantile business. Eventually the mines closed and the service businesses that fed off the mining population followed in their wake.

Leeds
Leeds CCC Camp Historic District
96 West Mulberry
1933
Federal government, Civilian
Conservation Corps

Rural Utah suffered dramatically during the Depression, with more than 36 percent unemployment and federal spending during the 1930s that was ninth among the forty-eight states. Even so, the number of local men who became workers in the Civilian Conservation Corps was far above the national average. CCC programs were a boost to the reclamation of the state's arid lands.

The Leeds CCC Camp was one of the first to be established in Utah. During its operation about 250 men were housed at the camp. Typically, unmarried men enrolled in the CCC for six months, and married men sometimes for nine to twelve months. In addition to regular recruits, in Utah 1,300 other workers such as lumbermen and miners worked for the government as project leaders and benefited from this New Deal program. Crews were managed by several different federal agencies including the Forest Service, the Soil Conservation Service, and the Division of Grazing. More than one hundred CCC camps were established in Utah during the 1930s.

The men housed at the camp often went into Leeds for dances, activities at the LDS church, or other social events. They had their own band, the "585 Ramblers," which presented a radio show on KSUB in Cedar City—and they had their own gourmet chef. The Leeds CCC Camp includes four separate buildings and other extant structures such as stone retaining walls and stairs. Several buildings were razed for the construction of I-15 and others moved when the camp closed in the 1940s. The remaining buildings are typical of CCC camps that were built on concrete foundations with walls of coursed rubble masonry and concrete. Local red-orange sandstone was used for all the buildings and retaining walls. Buildings that remain include an infirmary, a dispensary and supply facility, and a blacksmith shop. Building 4, on top of the hill southwest of the promontory, was the commander's headquarters. It is about 496 feet square, and the main entrance faced southwest toward the rest of the camp. CCC workers also installed prominent stone

pillars on each side of the camp's entrance, stone terracing, a frame horse barn, and other substantial features on the site.

Toquerville
Thomas Forsythe House
111 North Toquerville Boulevard
1870s
Thomas Forsythe

When Thomas Forsythe first came to southern Utah in 1861, he arrived in Santa Clara but moved to Pine Valley the next year to build a sawmill, capitalizing on what appeared to be an abundant source of pine and a surge of settlers coming to the area. Forsythe built not only a mill but also a house for his family. The opportunities were not as limitless as he had hoped—five other mills were already operating there and it was doubtful that available water resources would sustain another business. Instead he regrouped and chose to move to Toquerville, where he made his name as a capable business, civic, and church leader.

Forsythe was resourceful and an excellent craftsman, as is evident from this house that he built in the 1870s with local rock and lumber produced in his own mill. Even today, more than one hundred years later, it remains in good condition. Rock walls and a rock foundation created a house that was tight and sturdy. Forsythe located a wine cellar in his basement and arranged windows in an unpredictable way according to his preference rather than the dictates of style.

Hurricane
Hurricane Historic District
1900s

The town of Hurricane is in some ways a dramatic entrance into nearby national parks—surrounded by red and black rock formations and fields of sage and sand—a place of contrasts between nature and human-created environments. The Hurricane Canal, which made settlement possible in this extreme environment, runs along the side of a ridge and provides a visual boundary to the district. As was always true in settlement of the West, water was the key, and here is a visible reminder of that fact. Hurricane is eighteen miles away from the Washington County seat at St. George and in the mid-1990s had a population of about 4,500.

The Hurricane Historic District includes twelve square blocks, with 121 primary buildings and 24 outbuildings at the center of town. Blocks in Hurricane typically have four lots and ample space between buildings—of which there were twelve to fifteen per block. The houses on these blocks are for the most part Victorian Eclectic cross wings, single-story Foursquare cottages, bungalows, and Period Revival cottages built between 1908 and 1940. These single-family houses are modest in size, with one or one and a half stories, and have moderate decoration. By far the most typical building material is red brick, regardless of style, and as many as 10 percent of the buildings have been covered with stucco. The first brick was produced locally in 1908.

Main Street is lined with commercial buildings typical for a town this size—one- or two-part brick commercial blocks built between 1911 and 1922. In 1913, Hurricane had four mercantile stores, an ice supply operation, a planing mill, and long-distance phone service; by the next year it had a moving picture house, and by 1915 three hotels. These buildings are decorated primarily with Victorian Eclectic details— decorative brick patterns, some covered with stucco, with large display windows and recessed entries. The two principal New Deal buildings are also in this historic district.

Hurricane High School
34 South 100 West
1935–1936
Public Works Administration

The Hurricane High School is a good example of the PWA Moderne style in Utah, built between 1935 and 1936. This substantial two-story red-brick building blends Moderne elements with Prairie-style features. It was built under the auspices of the Public Works Administration for $110,000, 45 percent of which came from the federal government. It was one of three schools built in Washington County with Works Progress Administration funds (the other two were in St. George and Enterprise).

Overall, the composition of the building is symmetrical, with a centrally placed entrance bay, and a flat parapet projecting through the line of the eaves. Modern interpretations of Classical elements include a heavy cornice, applied terra-cotta decoration in the shape of the school crest over the entrance, and a pediment above with fluted pilasters to the sides. Prairie elements include horizontal bands of upper- and lower-story windows interrupted by brick piers. Stuccoed spandrels connect windows that are pierced in the center by short vertical lines of red brick.

The building combined a middle school and high school, both with eight classrooms, two large halls, a principal's office and supply room, a kitchen, a dining and sewing room, and a gymnasium that some considered to be the finest south of Provo.

Hurricane Library / City Hall
35 West State Street
1938–40
Public Works Administration

Perhaps the most significant public building in town is another public works project under the auspices of the WPA, the Hurricane Library / City Hall, a one-story sandstone building with a raised basement and concrete foundation built in 1938–40. The library has a hipped roof and large multipane sash windows, all of which are functional but have no particular reference to style.

Rock for the building was hauled to the site from the banks of Berry Springs, a few miles west of Hurricane. In fact, much of the construction was done by local men— Harvey Dalton served as general contractor. Leo A. Snow, the county surveyor, helped design the building, according to the *Washington County News*. Twenty men worked on the building.

Virgin
Isom/Semmens House
Across from Virgin's LDS meetinghouse
1865

George Isom built a home for his wife, Alice Parker, in Virgin, Utah, in 1865. It was challenging to find arable land in the area around Zion Canyon. Nephi Johnson founded this location in a narrow canyon in the Hurricane Fault in 1858, and Virgin City is situated on the edge of the river where it makes a wide loop and is joined by North Creek. Although the Native Americans called the place "Pockkitch," settlers opted to name it Virgin Creek, acknowledging the value of the river. The area attracted hardy individualists who cooperated to lay out

Hurricane Library / City Hall.
Photograph by Ntsimp, CC0 1.0, public domain.

Region F

their town in square blocks, dam the river, and build canals.

The house is a simple hall parlor, with a two-story porch, a hipped roof, a simple wood balustrade, and decorated posts similar to those you would see anywhere else in the state. The couple used a small building near their home for a store to supply farmers and ranchers living in the isolated settlement near Zion. In 1907, when a different kind of opportunity hit Virgin, Alice opened her home as a boardinghouse, decades after George's death from a poisoned arrow wound during the Black Hawk War.

Grafton
Grafton Adobe Church
1888
Miles Romney

For anyone interested in sleuthing out ghost towns, Grafton is a perfect hunt, a fleeting reminder of what life looked like in the past. The harsh, yet beautiful, land surrounding the few remaining buildings of Grafton illuminates the challenges that settlers confronted there. Record rains in January 1862 lifted towns off their tentative foundations and washed them away completely. It is said that the settlers of Virgin, five miles downriver, watched remnants of Grafton's houses float on by. By 1864, the town had been rebuilt one mile upriver, and twenty-eight families started life again, growing cotton, corn, fruit, and other crops. During the years of the Black Hawk War, the settlers experienced conflict with earlier inhabitants, again forcing them to abandon their homes and move north of the river. By 1868, most had given up and deserted the town, although a few remained until 1900. Clearly, Grafton was founded in a severely challenging spot on the river.

Grafton Adobe Church

By the 1930s most people had moved out of town permanently, and all that remains are reminders of the efforts of a group of disappointed town builders. The setting has since become a backdrop of the imagination—several movies, including *Butch Cassidy and the Sundance Kid*, have been filmed in Grafton.

Organized in the late 1990s, the Grafton Heritage Partnership Project began preservation of Grafton's historic landscape. It states two ambitious objectives—"to stabilize the town's historic and prehistoric structures with some limited rehabilitation, 1) to protect them from further deterioration and 2) to restore the Virgin River near the town site to a more natural condition by returning more native willow plants and shade-giving cottonwood trees to its banks."

The Grafton Adobe Church and the cemetery nearby are all that remains of this small agricultural town. Miles Romney, the architect of the St. George Temple, was sent by Brigham Young for a short period to stay in Grafton before the temple project began. He was somehow immune to the grandeur of the surrounding red-rock country and wrote in his diary: "When I studied Milton's Paradise Lost in school I never intended to spend the last part of my life in it." Regardless, a small group of families planted homes and built this church as a monument to their faith in 1888. The church was everything to the people who lived there—the scene of educational activities, weekly dances, and socials as well as religious services. In a wonderful show of cooperation, the community gathered on the building site to mash the muddy soil into adobe for the church's walls; it was then dried in the sun, placed in forms, and formed into walls.

Rockville
Deseret Telegraph and Post Office
91 West Main Street
1864

The transcontinental telegraph line reached Salt Lake City on October 23, 1861, and the pioneers finally had contact with the world outside and with each other. The telegraph line built from Logan in the north to St. George in the south was partially funded by the federal government with war surplus materials, and it created critical communication between the different outposts of the territory. Although it was a public good, cash tithing helped purchase wire and insulators for the five hundred miles of line, and a telegrapher's school, taught by John C. Clawes, was held in Salt Lake City to train operators. Each area along the line sent men or women to the school to receive instruction. Because it was so important, some local ecclesiastical leaders called workers to perform the job, which lent religious significance to the effort, and others received salaries from donations. Even so, local church leader Erastus Snow was discouraged by his people's limited willingness to

donate goods or funds for the construction of the line south. So instead, to finance construction the church organized the Deseret Telegraph Company on March 21, 1867, with a stock issue of $100,000. Volunteer workers cut poles and hauled and set them so that when the lines arrived in October 1866 they were ready. The St. George office opened on January 10, 1867, not long after the Rockville station, becoming an important link in the system extending service east to Pipe Springs and Kanab. Edward Huber built a stone house near the Rockville station a few years afterward near the small frame clapboard office with a shed roof, which was built in the mid-1870s and served as a telegraph office and post office for a number of years.

Rockville Meetinghouse
43 East Main Street
1870s

Rockville's first meetinghouse was destroyed in April 1869, and ward members immediately made plans to erect a new one. This simple temple-form church is set up on a podium base with a staircase

Rockville Meetinghouse

Region F

leading to the entrance and parapet walls to each side. Round-headed windows run down both sides and over the entrance, which is framed by two columns and a triangular pediment above. A modest-sized tower at the end of the roof peak is topped by a pyramidal roof. Overall a quiet atmosphere of solemnity and formality is evoked through these modest references to the Classical Revival style. This orderliness belies the tempestuous history of this small town at the base of Zion Canyon, where federal marshals pursued polygamists, and conflict with Native Americans and the daily struggle for survival made life difficult. It made resilient and resourceful settlers more determined to stay in this desert landscape marked by extremes.

Springdale
Ruesch House
729 National Park Road
1880
John Jacob Ruesch

John Jacob Ruesch, a master carpenter and coffin maker, built this showcase home for his family despite the considerable difficulties of erecting a house in the area around Zion Canyon. Ruesch converted to Mormonism while he was in Germany and immigrated to Utah in the 1840s. Brigham Young called him to help settle Toquerville and eventually Springdale. It is not known exactly when the building was constructed, but family diaries record that the family was in the building by the time of the birth of their third child in 1880. Although the house was relatively small for a central-passage house, it had the requisite four rooms on each floor, a central hall, and a steep staircase to the second level. Local tradition suggests that a store was managed

from a main floor room for a time, to generate revenue for the family. The house is built with pine from nearby mountain forests and has a two-story porch running across the facade with a hand-fashioned balustrade and wooden posts. Fireplaces on both ends of the building hint at the interior configuration of rooms.

Cable Mountain Draw Works
Top of Cable Mountain, east side of Zion Canyon
1904
David Flanagan

Every now and then visitors to Utah's canyon lands or mountainous areas come across obscure evidence of pioneer industries—an old mining shaft, a deserted wagon, or other machinery or technology that lies partially in ruin. The Cable Mountain Draw Works was devoted to extracting timber from the mountain.

Springdale's David Flanagan saw a serious need for lumber for the people living in the towns at the base of the canyons around Zion National Park, and abundant timber at the top of Cable Mountain. He devised an ingenious system of cable works running from the mountaintop to the bottom of the canyon to transport lumber down the mountainside. This could quickly accomplish what had taken ten days of transportation before.

Old-timers questioned the viability of the plan, but Flanagan kept at it, refining his idea, working through failures, and eventually by 1904 meeting with success. He operated the cable works until 1906, when he sold it to Alfred Stout and O. D. Gifford of Springdale. The Cable Mountain Draw Works operated from time to time until 1926, and it was abandoned all together and the cable removed in 1930.

Cable Mountain Draw Works.
National Park Service, public domain.

Region F

Region G

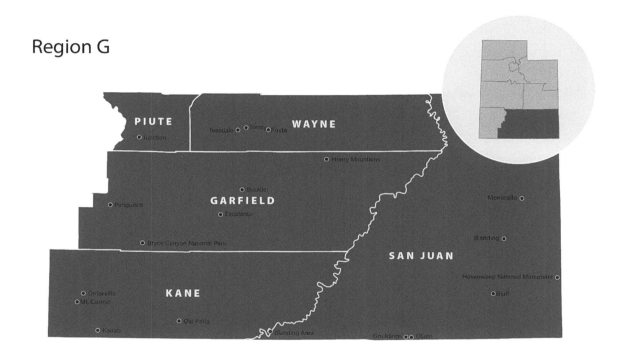

Wayne, Piute, Garfield, Kane, and San Juan Counties

Introduction

When Wallace Stegner visited Kane County in 1942, he was struck by its vastness and the extremes of its colors, textures, and space:

> The tiny oases huddle in their pockets in the rock, surrounded on all sides by as terrible and beautiful wasteland as the world can show, colored every color of the spectrum even to blue and green, sculptured by sand-blast winds, fretted by meandering lines of cliffs hundreds of miles long and often several thousand feet high, carved and broken and split by canyons so deep and narrow that the rivers run in sunless depths and cannot be approached for miles. Man is an interloper in that country.[1]

Although counties in southern and southeastern Utah have small towns with histories similar to those in other parts of the state, it is the landscape itself that is the main actor in this story.

The backdrop to this region, the canyon lands, includes some of the most spectacular geography in the state—the Colorado Plateau, Arches and Capitol Reef National Parks, Fishlake National Forest, the Henry Mountains, and the Green, Fremont, and Colorado Rivers. In the twentieth century these wild canyon landscapes would attract tourists from around the world, but in the nineteenth century they challenged white settlers with limited water and arable soil in vast areas of rock and sand. While conditions were not the most ideal for agriculture, after the 1860s, cattle and sheep ranching seemed an ideal use of this land. Cattle had always been a viable means of exchange in Utah, according to historian Charles Peterson, who says that more than thirty thousand head of cattle came with the Mormon pioneers from Nauvoo.[2] By the turn of the century, the livestock industry had grown significantly, and grazing land was at a premium. According to Peterson, the Deseret Land and Livestock Company ran 65,000 head of sheep and controlled 220,000 acres of land, or a total of 3.7 percent of the privately owned land in the state.[3] According to historian Bob McPherson, "truly large cattle companies" arrived in San Juan County after 1880. Favorable tax rates, abundant grazing land, and "unfenced land for general use" made a winning combination.[4] Many times the livestock ranchers lived in rural villages and drove their herds into the canyons nearby or into the desert to graze on public lands.

Two towns are of particular significance in this landscape of rock and sand—Kanab and Moab. Both started as Mormon towns at the tail end of the second wave of settlement through the region or the beginning of the third—after far more difficult areas were settled. The calling to settle in southeastern or southern Utah was not for the faint of heart. Resources were a lot more limited, the seasons more extreme, and confrontations with Native Americans pressed the issue of who had claim to the land and who did not. In Kanab, the group that came in the late 1860s started with a fort before they built houses. Many had already struggled for survival in the LDS Muddy Mission in Nevada's Moapa Valley. Farming in the desert was difficult if not impossible; many left because it was simply too hard, and others found other ways to scrape out a living in this beautiful but difficult place. The land would shape their futures in profound ways—stock raising seemed a better fit for such vast grazing lands until the federal government carved out national monuments or parks that restricted some of this public use. Estimates of as many as one hundred thousand cattle during the high point at the turn of the century were compounded by the number of sheep grazing in the area as well. The era of open land use changed in the twentieth century as the government began regulating resources such as land more closely. The debate over public versus private land use heated up in counties dependent on free use of grazing lands for their livelihood, and it was perhaps the most critical issue they faced in modern times.

The Bureau of Land Management described Kane County with the frame of wilderness recreational activity in 1967:

> Vermillion Cliffs ... Coral Pink Sand Dunes ... Kodachrome Flats ... White Cliffs ... Pink Cliffs—these names of geologic features in south central Utah give a clue to the area's principal characteristic: color. This is 'red rock' country, with a spectacular view of eroded, highly colored landscape at almost every bend in the road. This is wilderness—not densely forested and green, but stark, expansive and uninhabited.[5]

Over time, the area's small towns became access points for entrance into some of Utah's most magnificent canyon lands, national parks, and other sublime landscapes. Tourism has become increasingly integral to the local economy.

In a similar way, San Juan County's Moab is located near the Colorado River but also near the entrance to two major national parks—Arches and Canyonlands, which have some of the most diverse, harsh, chiseled landscapes in the world. River rafting, hiking, biking, and off-road vehicle use have drawn recreation enthusiasts from around the world. Besides tourism, which is profoundly important to this place, Moab's economy has depended on stock raising, mining, and agriculture. In the 1950s, the search for uranium brought new money into the county, and in 1952, Charles A. Steen mined the largest deposit of high-grade uranium ore in the nation.[6]

Finally, the southeastern corner of the state has some of the most spectacular examples of Ancestral Puebloan, Puebloan, and Native American architecture, wall art, and native traditions. Edge of the Cedars State Park is on the site of an Ancestral Puebloan village, and Hovenweep National Monument includes remnants of six Puebloan villages. The Navajo Nation reservation includes land in southeastern Utah, northwestern New Mexico, and northeastern Arizona, a total of 24,078 square miles. Canyon de Chelly National Monument, Monument Valley, and Rainbow Bridge National Monument are all contained within the nation and contain outstanding examples of ancient architecture and unique land formations carved out of the rock.

Wayne County

Fruita

Fruita Schoolhouse
North side of Utah Highway 24
Capitol Reef National Park
Early 1890s

At the beginning of the road winding though Capitol Reef, one comes across a most unlikely sight—a diminutive frame structure that speaks volumes about the pioneer determination to survive in the harsh canyon lands of the area. Niels Johnson, the first permanent settler, located a homestead near the junction of a couple of streams in 1880, in a narrow valley with only enough land to sustain eight to ten families. Even though it was unbelievably isolated from the world outside, a few brave families planted a fruit orchard and a vegetable garden and built frame homes. After the Fruita Schoolhouse was built in the 1890s, the community held classes there until 1941.

Fruita Schoolhouse.
Photograph by Staplegunther at English Wikipedia, CC A-SA 3.0.

This building is the area's earliest schoolhouse and is typical of carefully crafted log structures from the period. Its logs are squared and more regular on the facade. The spaces between the logs are filled with lime mortar; its builder also detailed windows and doors with care.

This single-story one-room building is seventeen by twenty feet, with floor sills and exterior log walls set on a foundation formed with square blocks of sandstone. Until just before World War I the building had a sod roof, which was changed to a gabled, shingled roof. The fascia trim, soffit boards, and window trim are constructed with pine. Although the interior walls were left unfinished, the tongue-and-groove wooden flooring is set on two-by-six-inch wooden joists.

Torrey

Torrey Log Church and Schoolhouse
Approximately 49 East Main Street
1898

The distinctive shape of the Torrey Log Church leaves no doubt that this building was a church—a very small version of a familiar ecclesiastical form. The weathered wood and sturdy construction of this thirty-seven-by twenty-one-foot building stakes a fervent claim to the land. Clearly, the Mormon pioneers who built it meant to stay. Completed in 1898, Torrey's first church and schoolhouse was a multipurpose structure that was the backdrop for weddings and funerals as well as recitations of the alphabet or scripture. School was held there until 1917 and church until 1928.

The building has a single room with an entrance to the south. Rough-sawed logs are joined with half-dovetail

Torrey Log Church and Schoolhouse

A modest-sized rectangular building with a gabled roof, the structure measures twenty by thirty feet. Lumber came from the Isaac Riddle and Sons steam sawmill three miles away. A door on the short end of the rectangle with a second-story door above facilitated the movement of grain in and out of the building. Extraordinarily tight construction marked this effort to store wood for the winter months. With inside-out construction, horizontal boards were attached to the inside of a lumber frame made with two-by-four timbers, which created a space for internal grain storage. The framing on the outside prevented the weight of the grain from forcing off the siding.

Piute County

Junction
Piute County Courthouse
550 North Main Street
1902–1903
Richard C. Watkins

Piute County was carved out of Beaver County in 1865, with the Tushar Mountains as its western boundary. Most of its population is concentrated in the Sevier Valley. Provo architect and British LDS convert Richard C. Watkins designed the building in the Tudor style in 1903.

The Piute County Courthouse is in a region dependent on livestock and mining, on a site surrounded by a grove of trees where visitors would sometimes camp. The county courtroom has had a colorful history, with a series of criminal cases and mining suits reflecting the area's diversity.

Watkins's imposing building includes towers and burnt-red brickwork reminiscent of English styles. Towers rise on each corner, one taller than the rest. Porticoes on both levels sit on granite from nearby

notching and white mortar chinking; the building originally sat on a stone foundation. Rising tall above the central entrance is a square bell tower covered with wooden planks and shingles. Windows on the sides are a variation on pedimented windows, basically within the Greek Revival vocabulary. The tall, steeply pitched hipped roof flares to the eaves on all four sides, and a truncated hipped roof tops the tower.

Teasdale
Teasdale Tithing Granary
Off Utah Highway 117
1895

The Teasdale Ward first held meetings in 1886 with George Coleman as bishop and Robert N. Adams and Rudolph Naser as his counselors in the bishopric.

In terms of form, the Teasdale Tithing Granary is familiar in the Utah landscape.

Piute County Courthouse.
Photograph by Tricia Simpson, CC A-SA 3.0a.

Kingston. Particularly noteworthy is the interior woodwork, which was hand turned on the site and demonstrates a high level of craftsmanship. Over time pot-bellied stoves were converted to more modern central heating systems, and eventually the courthouse was wired for electricity. Fire damaged the interior in 1943, but much of it was reconstructed and repainted.

Garfield County

Boulder
Coombs Village
Anasazi State Park
AD 1075–1150

It would be easy to speed by the Coombs Village site and miss it altogether, but it would be a huge loss. It is estimated that between AD 1075 and 1150 as many as

two hundred people lived on this site at the northern end of Boulder, in an area that forms a transition between the fairly smooth, well-watered, vegetation-clad slopes of the plateau and the rugged, severe, barren canyon lands bordering the Colorado River at an elevation of 6,700 feet. The inhabitants located their settlement near water and at the top of a hill for greater visibility. Currently the site is surrounded by agricultural land. But before the pioneers dry-farmed there and raised food in this challenging terrain during the last half of the nineteenth century, the fields were more likely filled with scattered sagebrush, greasewood, junipers, and grasses. Even so, the area offered plenty of game; building materials such as sandstone, caliche, and wood; clay for pottery; and rocks for stone tools.

Eighty-three structures were uncovered by researchers from the University of Utah,

Region G

Coombs Village.
Photograph by Nickeyrc, public domain.

including many larger multiunit structures oriented toward inner courtyards; 76 percent of them had been damaged by fire. The landscape had a diversity of structures and functions: pit structures carved into the hill were surrounded by soft, sandy deposits; storage units and homes were built with masonry and/or jacal; and there was one ramada.

Tools such as mortars and pestles, used primarily to prepare food, and mealing bins are reminiscent of the labor involved. Coombs Village is part of Anasazi State Park.

Boulder Elementary School
50 School House Lane
1935–1936
Public Works Administration
The small town of Boulder lies in some of the most spectacular scenery in the state. Isolated and remote but situated in a vast and sublime environment, the town

benefited by expanding its infrastructure under the Public Works Administration building program of the New Deal. Easily the largest building erected in town to date, the Boulder Elementary School served children bused in from the area's isolated farmsteads and became a community anchor in an area marked by individualism and independent isolationism. Built between 1935 and 1936, the Boulder Elementary School is a quintessential PWA Moderne structure built of wood and covered with clapboards, with a hipped roof and basic rectangular plan, and a blend of elements from the Moderne and Classical styles. Children entered through a projecting gabled porch with a recessed entrance and flanking windows. To the rear a long-hipped roof extension added additional classroom space to the main bulk of the building. Classical motifs include cornice returns, a pedimented head over the recessed doorway, a transom above the door, and a simple cornice and frieze. A zigzag belt course breaks up the formality of the porch and instead creates the abstract geometric quality that was part of the Moderne style.

Escalante
Escalante Tithing Office
40 South Center Street
1884
Morgan Richards

Most pioneer builders would have understood the logic behind the Classical proportions of the Escalante Tithing Office. Anyone who could first make a square in the sand could swing a rope around from one corner to the side to come up with the perfect proportions for a rectangle that corresponded with the golden mean. This familiar rectangle, based loosely on the proportions of four to nine, is found in windows and doors, floor plans and bays, on virtually every type of pioneer building throughout the state. Pioneers easily mastered and replicated the logic and rationality of this approach to design and found in it the forms that seemed to express their need to create logic and beauty in the world they built.

This example is a one-and-a-half-story rectangular stone building with a gabled roof, measuring approximately twenty-five feet by fifty feet. It has a temple form with a moderately pitched roof, and a Classical triangular pediment with the short end to the street, as would also have been true of a Greek temple. Constructed in what was easily the most popular form for public buildings in nineteenth-century Utah, temple-form buildings were made with stone and adobe bricks, or with frame and kiln-dried bricks, depending on available resources and technologies.

Stonemason Morgan Richards and volunteers from the congregation built this random ashlar masonry building in 1884. The first-story door is indented slightly into the wall, and the second-story door was later converted into a window once the original use of the building had ended.

Bryce Canyon National Park
Bryce Canyon Lodge
Bryce Canyon Lodge Historic District
1925

Besides the New Deal, the railroad and National Park System most impacted the

Bryce Canyon Lodge.
National Park Service, public domain.

physical landscape of rural Utah. The
Utah Parks Company, a division of Union
Pacific Railway, constructed this imposing
exposed-frame and log-siding structure in
1925 along with thirty-seven rectangular
exposed-frame buildings set on rubble
stone masonry foundations at the rim
of Bryce Canyon. Originally designed as
temporary structures, they have endured
because of their excellent craftsmanship
and care. The lodge is an irregularly shaped
building with a green roof and brown walls
sited in the pines near Sunset Point. At the
center of the building mass is a roughly
square core with wings that stretch to the
southeast and north. The central square
core of the building was completed in 1925
and the wings four years later.

The building's studs and diagonal braces
are exposed on the exterior. An ample
porch enclosed by logs running between
cobblestone piers welcomes visitors and
invites them to linger. Four beautiful, heavy
stone keyed fireplaces provide warmth
during the surprisingly cool winter nights.
The lobby is just one example,
with rough wooden columns,
Arts and Crafts brackets, and
massive wooden beams that
stretch across the room overhead. The theme is continued
throughout the dining room
as well, with a rubble masonry
fireplace topped by a pointed
arch. Maple parquet floors and
wrought-iron lighting fixtures
continue the sturdy yet lush
interior theme.

A group of extant cabins dating from 1929 are located southeast of the main lodge and use
the same rustic, natural materials. Cement chinking creates
an interesting contrast with the
color of the logs and the stonework. Cedar
shingles, originally painted green, are laid
in a wavy pattern across the high-pitched
gabled roofs. A National Historic Landmark, the Bryce Canyon Lodge speaks to
the importance of national parks and tourism in Utah's local economy and heritage.

Panguitch
Panguitch Tithing Office and Bishop's
Storehouse
100 East Center Street
1907

Most Mormon communities built a tithing
office as a depository and point of distribution for the tithes contributed by church
members. These storehouses were usually
part of a complex of buildings complete
with barns, granaries, cellars, storage
houses, and stores.

The Panguitch Ward secured approval
for the construction of the tithing office to
replace an earlier structure built during the
pioneer era and received an appropriation
of $2,000. The design for the building came

Panguitch Tithing Office and Bishop's Storehouse.
Photograph by Jerry Basford. Used with permission of photographer.

from church headquarters as well, standard plan type 3, which served the unique functional demands of the tithing program and streamlined the process of designing and building.

This one-story square building of red brick is topped by a pyramidal roof and stands on a sturdy coursed sandstone foundation. A boldly projecting gabled pavilion announces the entrance and dominates the symmetrical facade. A round-arched opening in the pavilion is accented by a large keystone, a rectangular panel, and a semicircular vent, as well as pilasters to the side and two doors, each of which is set at an angle into the wall. A wide frieze runs around the entire building, with a string-course of brick at the cornice level. Topping off the building is a quaint domed cupola.

The LDS Church used the building for tithing offices until the 1930s, when it became offices for church leaders. For many years it was used as a seminary for LDS instruction of high school students.

Panguitch Carnegie Library
75 East Center Street
1918
Isaac L. Wright

Of the state's Carnegie libraries, the Panguitch Carnegie Library might be the smallest. Nevertheless, it served an important public purpose as a place for city meetings, city offices, and its principal function as a library. Like many other Utah towns during this era, Panguitch received a grant of $6,000 from millionaire philanthropist Andrew Carnegie that it combined with local funds, land purchased by the city, and local labor to complete the project, designed by Isaac L. Wright of Richfield in 1918.

The Panguitch Carnegie Library is a one-story, flat-roofed, rectangular brick building with a raised basement, like other Carnegie libraries in the state, which greatly expands the interior with an open airy space. The building's symmetry is emphasized by a raised entrance centered between two

Panguitch Carnegie Library.
Photograph by Jerry Basford. Used with permission of photographer.

Region G

bands of windows. The surface is decorated with contrasting colors of brick, piers, an entablature, and dentils, familiar to Classical Revival architecture.

Panguitch Social Hall
50 East Center Street
1908

The Social Hall shows how the pioneers worked to survive in this desert basin by having fun, gathering for recreation and engaging in the community's social life in nineteenth-century Utah. Weddings and dances, theatricals and musicals, funerals and quilting bees and just about any social community activity were found here.

Between 1900 and 1918 Panguitch built a school, courthouse, library, and high school on Center Street. In a period of rapid development and progress during these same years, telephone and electrical service came to town, changing life there forevermore. A distinctive locally produced red brick was used in many houses and other buildings of the late nineteenth and early twentieth centuries, with unusual patterns and a high level of craftsmanship. Panguitch's brick buildings are worth seeing.

This two-story rectangular vernacular brick building has modest Prairie-style detailing on the stuccoed facade and slight references to the Victorian style in arched Romanesque window openings on the sides that create the impression of an arcade. A recessed entrance in the facade is framed by engaged pilasters with Prairie-style geometric designs. When built, the building seemed to local residents "like heaven with its beautiful floor, and good music and management."[7] Used at various times for contemporary recreation—dances, movies, a gymnasium and weight room, or whatever was in vogue at a given time—the building has continued to play a role in Panguitch's social life for generations.

Panguitch Social Hall.
Photograph by Jerry Basford. Used with permission of photographer.

Panguitch Victorian Brick Homes
Blocks surrounding the center of town
Late 1800s and early 1900s

One of the most distinctive aspects of the architecture of Panguitch is the nearly two dozen extant nineteenth- and early twentieth-century brick homes. This town had several of its own brick kilns that produced beautiful red bricks in a range of sizes during this period. Local tradition suggests that brick workers were often paid in bricks. These houses were typically more elaborate than the standard *I* home so typical of southern Utah towns. Instead, extravagant towers, bay windows, wraparound porches, and varied roof pitches and planes reflecting the luxuriousness of the Victorian style were more common.

Henry Mountains

Starr Ranch
Starr Springs Campground, 46 miles south of Hanksville on Utah Highway 276
1890

The setting for the Starr Ranch seems at once stark and desolate but also primal, created with massive sweeps of the earth's forces. Rolling hills and desert flats run near a large spring that was given Al Starr's name. In the earliest days of settlement in this isolated spot, the settlers' push for survival would maximize the opportunities the earth provided. In this 1890 example, the ranch house at the Starr Ranch, the first permanent ranch at the southern end of the Henry Mountains, was built into the earth. Granite rocks were shaped into an arch without any internal or external support or mortar. Instead, the builder carefully chose tight-fitting rocks and packed them with soil to create two-foot-thick walls. The smokehouse is also a simple dugout, with earthen sides and an arched roof. In the

center of the space, two pole stringers were used as meat drying racks.

Al Starr first came to the Henry Mountains in a failed prospecting effort in the early 1880s, settling instead at Starr's Spring in 1890 to try his hand at cattle raising, the first attempt in the area. Perhaps because of overgrazing, the Starr Ranch was a short-lived venture.

Kane County

Orderville

Valley School
Off U.S. Highway 89
1935
Scott and Welch

The contrast between the PWA Moderne style of the Valley School and the typical pioneer rectangularity of most of Orderville's buildings couldn't be greater. The Valley School, evidence of the federal government in this tiny town in Long Valley, was one of 233 public works buildings built during the 1930s and 1940s, with 5 in Kane County alone. Two teachers taught students from Mount Carmel, Orderville, and Glendale in the Orderville Elementary School on the upper or main floor, and the high school's home economics and shop departments used the basement.

The Salt Lake architectural firm of Scott and Welch designed the building as well as a number of other public works projects around the state. A bronze plaque advertises that the building is a PWA project and includes the names of the local school board officials, contractors, and architect.

Like other PWA buildings, the Valley School includes a basement, a single story, a flat roof, and a central entrance portico. The formal, symmetrical design emphasizes

Region G

horizontal lines. Low-relief brick piers run rhythmically around the building and alternate with more imposing pilasters with decorative cream-colored concrete capitals that project above the roof line and create an impression of crenellation.

Mount Carmel
Mount Carmel School and Church
Off U.S. Highway 89
1890; 1923–1924

The Long Valley along Highway 89 is one of the most remarkable drives through Utah's beautiful terrain. Towns such as Mount Carmel and Orderville provide wonderful glimpses into another time, with great extant examples of nineteenth-century architecture. The Mount Carmel School and Church is a Victorian T-shaped random ashlar stone building with a hipped roof and a bell tower. Symmetry is emphasized through the placement of windows and doors.

Mount Carmel has always been a small town with fewer than two hundred inhabitants who manage small businesses or family farms. This church/school replaced the pioneer-era log building that the community had used for twenty-five years. Like the earlier example, this building became the backdrop for religious, civic, social, and cultural activities until 1924, when it was used exclusively as a church. Indigenous materials were used for the construction—rock and rough pine from the nearby hills.

When the Mount Carmel School was built, Utah's educational system was in flux and free public education was becoming available for the first time. As a result, many new schools were built in the late 1890s and early 1900s, funded first by territorial and then state government. Within a couple of decades, the state consolidated its smaller schools, although Mount Carmel continued

to use its own until the 1920s. During this time, the LDS Church consolidated its religious auxiliaries into a single ward house, and in Mount Carmel it brought the Relief Society, Young Men's Mutual Improvement Association, and Primary under the same roof. The building has been in virtually continuous use since it was first built.

Kanab
Bowman-Chamberlain House / McCallister House
14 East 100 South
1892–1894

The Bowman-Chamberlain House is a relatively ambitious example of Queen Anne architecture for this remote desert location. Although more flamboyant examples of the style are common in larger cities, in Kanab it is unique. Besides the architectural significance of the house itself, the outbuildings show the way a typical turn-of-the-century family used a town lot—the equivalent of an urban homestead. A barn, chicken house, decorative picket fence, and several large shade and fruit trees encircling the house create a homestead—more than providing shelter, these features combine to form a microcosm of life in this pioneer settlement.

As is typical of the Queen Anne style, the house features a variety of different materials, details, and forms, including sandstone foundations, brick walls, and wooden shingles on the hipped and gabled roof with a spired tower. Perhaps the most endearing characteristic of the Queen Anne house, however, is its sweeping porch. Bringing living space outdoors, this porch wraps around the house to the front on both sides and to the back. The most elaborate section of the porch is on the northwest and features fancy spindlework, lathe-carved wooden posts, ball newels, and a pedimented entrance with a fan motif.

The square tower is topped by a steeply pitched hipped roof and an ornate metal finial, more familiar on a church than a home. Adding character to the house, its form adds stateliness and dignity and emphasizes a vertical sweep.

Bowman & Company Building
97 West Center Street / U.S. Highway 89
1892
H. E. Bowman & Company

One of the oldest buildings in Kanab is a commercial block. Since it was first constructed by H. E. Bowman, the building

has housed a series of different businesses: a bank, a general store (an upper story was added for additional space in the 1920s), an ice cream shop, a restaurant, and a pawn shop. The building's straightforward facade includes a door framed by windows on both sides and two windows on the second level. A shallow raised parapet crowns this elevation and produces a little dignity for this commercial institution.

H. E. Bowman graduated from the Normal School at the Brigham Young Academy and taught for four years after he and his wife, Mary Bertha Gubler, moved to Kanab and before he went into the merchandising business.

Bowman-Chamberlain House / McCallister House.
Photograph by Finetooth, CC A-SA 3.0.

Old Paria

Old Paria Townsite
Off U.S. Highway 89
Mid-1800s

A small farming community in Kane County, Pahreah was deserted by the end of the pioneer era, and all that remains is a number of abandoned buildings. The native meaning of "Pahreah" was muddy water, which suggests the challenged history of the site. But for Hollywood, this ghost town presented a special opportunity. The ruins of old houses and a few other structures were often used by twentieth-century movie makers as a set for western films like *Sergeants 3* with Frank Sinatra and Sammy Davis Jr. During the 1940s several Hollywood westerns were filmed in the area surrounding Kanab, and locals frequently acted as extras in the motion pictures. Southern Utah's landscape became a familiar element in westerns, epitomizing the challenging desert landscape of the quintessential cowboy life.

San Juan County

Blanding

Edge of the Cedars State Park Museum
¼ mile west of 400 North and 400 West
1978
Utah State Division of Parks and Recreation

Dedicated in 1978 and constructed by the Utah State Division of Parks and Recreation to preserve and interpret the cultural history of the Anasazi, Ute, and Navajo Indians and other residents of the area for the past two thousand years, this museum interprets the remains of an Ancestral Puebloan village, attesting to the remarkable architectural techniques and adaptability of this culture. It is located on the site of a pre-Columbian Puebloan site.

Monticello

Hyland Hotel
116 South 100 West
1916–1918
Joseph Henry Wood (builder); Ed Thompson (stonemason)

This Arts and Crafts bungalow was originally built as a single-family residence in 1916–18 but was adapted in 1924 as a hotel. The four spacious upstairs bedrooms became nine smaller ones. It is two stories tall, and a series of gabled roofs spread over the central rectangular mass and two small cross wings. Exposed purlins and rafters add interest to the gables, characteristic of the Arts and Crafts style, as is the wide front porch, deep overhanging eaves, exposed rafters, and leaded-glass windows that are set within segmental arched windows on the first level.

A rich, warm, spacious interior originally contained twelve rooms, two baths, and a full basement. This included two large parlors, a small office at the front, a downstairs bedroom, a kitchen, and a small workroom at the back. Beautiful California fir was used for the interior doors, panels, wooden trim, and exposed beams. When the house was used as a residence, the lot also included a dairy, barns, sheds, icehouse, orchard, and garden.

Joseph Henry Wood hauled stone from South Creek near the Abajo Mountains to create hand-hewn sandstone blocks eighteen inches thick and thirty-six inches long. Ed Thompson, also of Monticello, supervised the stone cutting, dressing, and laying. Walls on the upper level were wooden frame, with shingle siding cut in the "square-butt" pattern. Wood for the interior was shipped to Utah by rail from California and hauled from Salt Lake City by wagon to Monticello.

Hyland Hotel.
Photograph by Ntsimp Own work, public domain.

Bluff
Bluff Historic District
1880s

The bluffs bordering the narrow San Juan River valley formed a distinctive edge to this small settlement in the isolated southeastern corner of Utah. Laid out in the familiar grid pattern of the Plat of the City of Zion, Bluff is composed of a dozen or so blocks running east and west. U.S. Highway 191 runs through it like a river and defines the eastern and southern boundaries of the historic center. Bluff has a strong physical sense of edge—the three-hundred-foot sandstone bluffs to the north, desert to the west, farmland to the east, and the San Juan River to the south.

Bluff's historic district includes buildings constructed from 1880 to the mid-1940s, for the most part Victorian Eclectic or vernacular sandstone houses, but also in the original grid pattern of large square blocks with houses on lots with outbuildings, fruit trees, and vegetable gardens behind. Irrigation canals line the streets as well, the lifeblood of the town.

Although Bluff was a significant distance from the LDS Church headquarters in Salt Lake City, it was important in establishing a Mormon presence in the southeastern corner of the territory. Key to the slow and discouraging development of this town was the dedication of the Mormon pioneers to their religious ideals and their commitment to what they considered the building of the kingdom of God.

Lemuel H. Redd House
Off Utah Highway 47 (Lot 3, Block 10, Plat A)
1900
Nick Loveless and Ed Thompson (masons)

Prominent political, business, and ecclesiastical leader Lemuel H. Redd Jr. played a key role in the settlement and development

Region G

Lemuel H. Redd House.
Photograph by Jerry and Roy Klotz MD, CC BY-SA 3.0.

of agriculture in southeastern Utah during the late nineteenth and early twentieth centuries. In 1880, Bluff had a number of small log cabins and a timid economy. Stock raising helped bring prosperity to Bluff after 1885, when Redd built this substantial home for his family.

This two-story Victorian house enthusiastically affirms the future success of this small town. More than shelter, it speaks to financial and material success, social prestige and culture.

Redd made his wealth as a stockman; he was also a member of the state legislature, the superintendent of San Juan County schools, a member of the San Juan County Board of Commissioners, and the LDS bishop of the Bluff Ward.

Exploding the excesses so typical of the Victorian style, this ample house uses the style motifs of the Romanesque Revival—heavy rusticated red sandstone laid carefully in coursed ashlar bond, irregular massing, and round-arched tops on the windows. Three stone chimneys with corbeled trim and a long front dormer window with an unusual truncated hipped and gabled roof add to the variety of elevations and wall surfaces.

John Albert Scorup House
Lot 2, Plat B
1904
Nick Loveless and Ed Thompson (masons)

John Albert Scorup immigrated to Utah from Denmark in 1864 with his parents, Christian C. and Karen Hansen Scorup. As a teenager, Scorup worked for a variety of different cattlemen and the Salina Grazing Company. In 1891 Claude Sanford paid him to care for 150 cattle, one-third of the herd, in San Juan County's White Canyon. He and his brothers saved the money they earned by working for other stock raisers, but eventually they bought their own herd and formed the Scorup-Somerville Cattle Company, the largest in the state for a period.

The Scorup house is built with coursed ashlar sandstone blocks that mirror the rock walls of the natural landscape surrounding Bluff. Distinguished locally because of its size, complexity, and Victorian design, this one-and-a-half-story building has a hipped roof and strong central core with wings that project to the west, north, and east and have triangular pediments and wooden-shingled siding.

Old Fort Cabins
Off Utah Highway 47
1880s
Bluff was rugged and isolated when the first white settlers arrived in 1880 in this extraordinarily challenging part of Utah Territory. A sort of transitional area at the base of the Great Basin and Snake River drainage areas, this settlement was connected to the Colorado Plateau and was located on the edge of the Navajo Reservation. Bluff was a refuge for outlaws passing through to somewhere else and for cattlemen pushing west into the San Juan River region from Texas and Colorado. Part of the original fort still exists, a series of log cabins built with uneven and twisted cottonwood logs, log and willow ceilings, and dirt floors and muslin curtains. They make a poignant statement about the sacrifice required of the pioneering generation.

The fort was constructed with a cluster of log cabins that had contiguous walls along two sides of a square stockade. The back walls of the cabins were the wall of the fort itself. A log building sat in the center, with forked tree branches used as vertical supports. The lack of pine in Bluff was a

challenge for the construction of buildings. Cottonwood didn't work as well. The logs used for these cabins are round, with saddle notches at the corners, and wood chips and mud chinking in the interstices. Historically, roofs were formed with willow branches and covered with sod.

James Bean Decker House
Lot 3, Block 8, Plat A
1898
LDS Church president John Taylor called James Bean Decker to settle the Bluff area in 1879. In the spirit of a religious assignment, Decker willingly traveled with the exploration expedition that followed the San Juan River in the summer of 1879 by way of northern Arizona to Parowan along the Old Spanish Trail through eastern and central Utah. Afterward, Decker moved his family to the area and was one of the original settlers who traveled the difficult terrain across the Hole-in-the-Rock Trail from Escalante to Bluff in 1879–80.

Decker was a prominent figure in Bluff—he was San Juan County's first sheriff, a member of the school board, and a cattle and sheep man. He was a member of the "Bluff Pool," a cooperative organization of Mormon livestock men who challenged the non-Mormon dominance of the cattle industry. Many members benefited from this association and became wealthy in the process.

The two-story brick Decker House is larger than other houses nearby. It has a cross-wing plan, common at the end of the nineteenth century, with the gabled end facing the street, a chimney in the center with corbeled brickwork, cornice returns on the gable, patterned shingle siding, and an arched attic window. The roof of the main section flares slightly at the eaves and adds a unique flourish to the house.

St. Christopher Episcopal Mission
1.7 miles east of Bluff on Utah
Highway 162
1943

The St. Christopher Episcopal
Mission includes two rectangular
wings, connected by a central or
common space, that face each
other across a central courtyard
and are constructed with sandstone blocks from the surrounding landscape in a rubble pattern.
An arcade runs across the elevations facing the interior space,
small chambers run along the
west wing, and the east wing was
used as a chapel. In 1956, another
building was built as a clinic/
hospital, where approximately five hundred
babies were delivered. The clinic had four
patient rooms, lab space, and an examina-
tion room. Currently, St. Christopher's is
operated by the Episcopal Church on the
Navajo Reservation.

H. Baxter Liebler founded the mission
in 1943 to serve the Navajos, naming it
St. Christopher's for the patron saint of
travelers. He had with him five others who
lived in tents as the slow construction of
the building proceeded. In the meantime,
Liebler learned to speak the Navajo language, found water, and offered medical
assistance to the people they served. A year
later he began a school for the Navajos
living nearby, although the state took it
over a number of years later. A vernacular Mission-style building that features
shallow-pitched shed roofs covered with
boards and asphalt roofing material stands
on the site. A log addition provided more
space for a dining hall. Besides the main
Mission structures and the clinic, there are
as many as eight other stone buildings on
the site.

St. Christopher Episcopal Mission.
Photograph by Jimmy Emerson Own work, CC BY-NC-ND 2.0.

Goulding

Goulding's Trading Post
About 70 miles southwest of Blanding
1923
Harry Goulding

The trading post in the Navajo world was
more a community center than strictly a
commercial endeavor, providing a commercial venue for craftspeople who worked out
of their homes. Goulding's Trading Post is
a great example of a small building erected
to house trade activities but also to distribute aid, information, and announcements
about social or community activities. Harry
Goulding and his wife, "Mike," started the
post in 1923 and owned it for the next forty
years.

When the Gouldings first arrived in
1923 they homesteaded 640 acres on the
Utah side of Monument Valley. Drawn to
the austere and stark beauty of the desert,
they centered their business on trade with
Native Americans and boarding tourists
visiting the area.

Goulding promoted area businesses
by contacting movie companies that were

Goulding's Trading Post.
Photograph by Bernard Gagnon, GNU Free Documentation License, 1.2, CC BY-SA 3.0.

filming westerns in Utah's canyonlands: John Ford came to Monument Valley to film *Stagecoach*, *My Darling Clementine*, and *War Party*. When a film crew came into the area, Goulding provided housing and supplies, and Native Americans earned income as extras in the movies.

Goulding's Trading Post is a two-story, flat-roofed building made of locally quarried, coursed sandstone. A porch stretching across the facade from side to side created a welcoming social space. Behind the building is a more modern motel and dining room.

Oljato
Oljato Trading Post
About 75 miles southwest of Blanding
1921
The Oljato Trading Post is at the Four Corners intersection of Utah, New Mexico, Colorado, and Arizona. Built in 1921

approximately one mile west of the ruins of the Wetherill Trading Post (1906–10), it was the first trading post to be established in the northwestern part of Navajo country. Displaying an eclectic collection of Navajo artifacts, the post is also important as a communications center.

Trading first began on the reservation in the 1880s and continues to the present. Between 1887 and 1890 the number of traders increased from six to nine, and as many as thirty others came to trade at the reservation periodically. More than just salespeople, they were also interpreters, guides, and explorers, exploiting the opportunity to make a connection between those who lived on the reservation and those in the outside world. When World War II ended, many of the old traders left and were replaced by commercial businessmen.

The post is a rectangular, single-story adobe building with a flat or slightly sloping

Region G

roof. The original section had a log and branch roof covered with dirt and sod. In terms of materiality, the building was in line with Navajo building traditions.

Hovenweep National Monument
Ancestral Puebloan Sites
15 miles south of Blanding on Utah Highway 191, east on Highway 262 to Hatch Trading Post, then 16 miles east
AD 1200s

Hovenweep National Monument stretches from southwestern Colorado to southeastern Utah—between Cortez, Colorado, and Blanding, Utah, on the Cajon Mesa of the Great Sage Plain. The monument includes the remnants of six villages between Montezuma and McElmo Creeks constructed by Ancestral Puebloans in the late thirteenth

Hovenweep National Monument.
Photograph by Greg Willis, CC BY-SA 2.0, Wiki Commons.

century, where they planted corn, beans, and squash and in some places built terraced gardens, catch basins, and dams. The Square Tower Village was occupied by several hundred people around AD 1270, where they built residences, granaries, dams, and water storage facilities and planted fields. According to the National Park Service, more than 2,500 people lived in the Hovenweep villages. Because of a major drought that swept through the region, they vacated the settlements around AD 1200. Best known for the Square Tower and Hovenweep Castle, the various communities built oval, circular, and square towers as well as D-shaped and oval structures including kivas. The towers might have been built for defensive purposes or for tracking the movement of the sun and the night sky. The federal government designated Hovenweep a national monument in 1923, and it is managed by Mesa Verde National Park.

Blanding Area
Monarch Cave
Comb Ridge, an 80-mile-long formation in southeastern Utah near Blanding and northeastern Arizona, moving toward the San Juan River
Approximately AD1250

Monarch Cave is located on Comb Ridge, an eighty-mile-long formation in southeastern Utah near Blanding and in northeastern Arizona, moving toward the San Juan River. Monarch Cave is in Butler Wash on the east side of Comb Ridge near Bluff, Utah. The canyon itself is about half a mile long. There, cottonwood trees, flowering plants, and shrubs contrast with the more desolate mesa and valley beyond. The walls were formed with a combination of adobe bricks, random-sized stones, and sand.

The Monarch Cave ruins are the remnants of an Ancestral Puebloan cliff dwelling in an alcove on a vertical canyon wall with a desert pool of water below. The cliff house included eleven rooms on the ground floor, one reaching two stories high. Inhabitants climbed to the site by way of footholds cut into the sandstone cliff. Warren K. Moorehead led an expedition there in 1892, mapping, surveying, and photographing the area. His comments are recorded on a marker at the site:

> About two miles south of Eagle Nest Cave, we discovered one of the most picturesque series of ruins that we had yet seen. It is situated in a beautiful box canyon in the rocky divide between Butler's Wash and Comb Wash, about nine miles south of the Rio San Juan.... Directly to the west end of the canyon, the high sandstone cliffs, with a graceful and undulating curve on their weathered surfaces, close together abruptly, forming a large cavern about one hundred feet from the bottom of the canyon. In this cave are

the ruins we are about to describe. From their prominent position they command the valley, and their curved fronts, cut with dozens of loopholes, give the effect of a modern fortress. We named it Monarch's Cave, for it must have been monarch of all it surveyed.[8]

The federal government designated Comb Ridge as a National Natural Landmark in 1976 because of its significance as the only North American location of tritylodont fossils.

Lake Powell
Glen Canyon Dam
Glen Canyon Dam is eight miles into Arizona, but Lake Powell is accessible from Hite Marina off Utah Highway 95; from Bullfrog Marina on the west side of the lake; and from Wahweap Marina off U.S. Highway 89
Early 1960s
One of two massive hydroelectric dams built after World War II, the

Glen Canyon Dam.
Photograph by Adbar Own work, CC BY-SA 3.0.

concrete-arched Glen Canyon Dam brought jobs, provided power, stored water, and created recreational opportunities for the region. Lake Powell, the resulting reservoir named for John Wesley Powell, is one of the nation's largest human-made lakes. As part of the U.S. Bureau of Reclamation's Colorado River Storage Project, Glen Canyon Dam was constructed between 1956 and 1966, with the intent of regulating the flow of water from the upper Colorado River Basin (Colorado, New Mexico, Utah, and Wyoming) to states lower in the system (California and Nevada).

Notes

PREFACE

1. Dolores Hayden, *The Power of Place* (Cambridge: MIT Press, 1997), 9.
2. Leonard J. Arrington, *Great Basin Kingdom: An Economic History of the Latter-day Saints, 1830–1900* (Cambridge: Harvard University Press, 1958).

UTAH'S ARCHITECTURAL HISTORY

1. Leon Sidney Pitman, "A Survey of Nineteenth Century Folk Housing in the Mormon Culture Region" (PhD diss., Louisiana State University, 1973), 115.
2. These pair houses were originally built in Sweden and then spread to Denmark.
3. Jacob Heinrich Wilhelm Schiel, quoted in Michael W. Homer, *On the Way to Somewhere Else: European Sojourners in the Mormon West, 1834–1930* (Norman: University of Oklahoma Press, 2006), 62.
4. Horace Greeley, quoted in Samuel Adams Drake, *The Making of the Great West: Illustrated History of the American Frontier, 1512–1883* (Madison & Adams Press, 2018).
5. Richard Burton, *City of Saints* (New York: Harper & Brothers, 1862), 197.
6. Pitman, "Survey of Nineteenth Century Folk Housing," 83.
7. Brigham Young, quoted in *Journal of Discourses*, vol. 1–2 (May 27, 1855), 284.
8. Thomas Carter, *Building Zion: The Material World of Mormon Settlement* (Minneapolis: University of Minnesota Press, 2015), 95.
9. Florence Hall, quoted in *Through the Eyes of Many Faiths* (Salt Lake City: Utah Heritage Foundation, 1983), 14.
10. Thomas Alexander, *The Americanization of Utah for Statehood* (San Marino, CA: Huntington Library, 1971).

CONTEXT FOR THE GUIDE

1. Glen M. Leonard, *Nauvoo: A Place of Peace, a People of Promise* (Salt Lake City: Shadow Mountain Press, 2002); David E. Miller and Della S. Miller, *Nauvoo: The City of Joseph* (Santa Barbara, CA: Peregrine Smith, 1974).
2. Arrington, *Great Basin Kingdom*; Lowry Nelson, *The Mormon Village* (Salt Lake City: University of Utah Press, 1952).
3. Nelson, *Mormon Village*.
4. Becky Bartholomew, "New Deal Agencies Built 233 Buildings in Utah," *History Blazer*, June 1996, http://historytogo.utah.gov.
5. Leonard Arrington, "Sagebrush Resurrection: New Deal Expenditures in the Western States, 1933–1939," *Pacific Historical Review* 52 (February 1983): 1–15; Arrington, "The New Deal in the West: A Preliminary Statistical Inquiry," *Pacific Historical Review* 8 (August 1969): 311–16.
6. Brian Q. Cannon and Jessie Embry, *Utah in the Twentieth Century* (Boulder: University Press of Colorado, 2009); Arrington, "Sagebrush Resurrection"; Arrington, "New Deal in the West."
7. Bartholomew, "New Deal Agencies," 1996.
8. Jasen Lee, "Utah Sets State Record for Tourist Visits in 2012," *Deseret News*, September 17, 2013; http://www.deseretnews.com.
9. Richard Jackson, *Places of Worship: 150 Years of Latter-day Saint Architecture*, vol. 13, Occasional Papers Series (Provo, UT: Religious Studies Center, Brigham Young University, 2003); Thomas Carter, *Building Zion: The Material World of Mormon Settlement* (Minneapolis: University of Minnesota Press, 2015); Thomas Carter and Peter Goss, *Utah's Historic Architecture, 1847–1940* (Salt Lake City: University of Utah Press, 1988); Allen D. Roberts, *Salt Lake City's Historic Architecture* (Mount Pleasant, SC, Arcadia Publishing, 2012).

10. John McCormick, *The Historic Buildings of Downtown Salt Lake City* (Salt Lake City: Utah State Historical Society, 1982); Karl T. Haglund and Philip F. Notarianni, *The Avenues of Salt Lake City* (Salt Lake City: Utah State Historical Society, 1980), rev. 2nd ed. by Cevan J. LeSieur (Salt Lake City: University of Utah Press, 2012).

SALT LAKE CITY

1. John N. Berry III, quoting Nancy Tessman, "Gale/LJ Library of the Year 2006: Salt Lake City Public Library—Where Democracy Happens," *Library Journal*, June 15, 2006, http://web.archive.org.
2. Jon M. Huntsman, quoted in "Most Outstanding Healthcare Project," *Utah Construction & Design*, January 24, 2018, accessed October 4, 2019, utahcdmag.com.
3. *Salt Lake Tribune*, November 8, 1908, and April 11, 1909, accessed October 4, 2019, http://npgallery.nps.gov.
4. Elaine Jarvik, "A New Downtown Salt Lake City?," *Deseret News*, November 6, 1991, accessed October 4, 2019, http://deseret.com.
5. Philip F. Notarianni and Karl Haglund, "Chapman Public Library," National Register Nomination, January 16, 1980, http:npgallery.nps.gov.
6. 1 Corinthians 15:40–41.
7. Revelation 14:6.
8. W. Knight Sturges, "Cast in Iron: New York's Structural Heritage," *Architectural Review*, October 26, 2015, accessed October 4, 2019, http://architectural-review.com.
9. Rebecca Green, *Fox News*, "New 'You Are Here' Art Installation Unveiled in Downtown Salt Lake City," August 3, 2016, accessed October 4, 2019, http://fox13now.com.
10. Whitney Butters, "Capitol Theatre Serves as a 'Memory Builder' 101 Years after Its Construction," *Deseret News*, August 23, 2014 accessed October 4, 2019, http://deseret.com.
11. "Kazuo Matsubayashi, Asteroid Landing Softly, 1994," Public Art Collection, accessed October 4, 2019, http://saltlakepublicart.org.
12. "Kazuo Matsubayashi."
13. Jared Page, "Odd Fellows Hall Packing Up and Moving," *Deseret News*, March 22, 2008, accessed October 4, 2019, http://deseret.com.
14. John Smith, quoted in the *Salt Lake Tribune* in B'Nai Israel Temple, National Register Nomination, June 21, 1978, 2.

REGION A

1. Richard D. Poll, Thomas G. Alexander, Eugene E. Campbell, and David E. Miller, *Utah's History* (Logan: Utah State University Press, 1989), 220.

2. F. Ross Peterson, *A History of Cache County* (Salt Lake City: Utah State Historical Society, 1997), 6.
3. Daniel Potts, quoted in Peterson, *History of Cache County*, 13.
4. Benson and Hyde, quoted in Peterson, *History of Cache County*, 37.
5. *Twenty-First Report of the Superintendent of Public Instruction of the State of Utah for the Biennial Period ending June 30, 1936* (n.p., n.d.), 140, quoted in John McCormick, Logan High School Gymnasium, National Register Nomination, August 7, 1985, 3.
6. Gary Forbush, Old Main, National Register Nomination, February 23, 1972, 3, 5.
7. John McCormick, Home Economics Building, Utah State University, National Register Nomination, 1984, 4.

REGION B

1. Glen M. Leonard, *A History of Davis County* (Salt Lake City: Utah State Historical Society, 1999), 6.
2. Richard Neitzel Holzapfel, *A History of Utah County* (Salt Lake City: Utah State Historical Society, 1999), 28.
3. Holzapfel, *History of Utah County*, 40.
4. "Frank Lloyd Wright Quotes," AZ Quotes, accessed October 4, 2019, http://azquotes.com.
5. Roger Roper, Farmington Tithing Office, National Register Nomination, March 28, 1985, 2, accessed October 4, 2019, http//npgallery.nps.gov.
6. Becky Bartholomew, "Charcoal Kilns and Early Smelting in Utah," *History Blazer*, May 1996, accessed October 4, 2019, www.historytogo.utah.gov.
7. Kent Powell, Camp Floyd, National Register Nomination, January 11, 1974, 2, accessed October 5, 2019, http://npgallery.nps.gov.
8. John C. McCormick, Lehi City Hall, National Register Nomination, March 1, 1982, 5, accessed October 5, 2019, http://npgallery.nps.gov.
9. Brigham Young Academy, National Register Nomination, January 11, 1974, accessed October 5, 2019, http://npgallery.nps.gov.
10. Jesse Knight House, National Register of Historic Places, 1975, 2, accessed October 6, 2019, http://npgallery.nps.gov.
11. Deborah Temme, Maeser School, National Register Nomination, May 26, 1983, accessed October 8, 2019, http://npgallery.nps.gov.
12. Cheryl Hartman, Ripley's quoted in Startup Candy Factory, National Register Nomination, December 3, 1984, 6.
13. Allen D. Roberts, Provo Tabernacle, National Register Nomination, September 9, 1975, 2, accessed October 13, 2019, http://npgallery.nps.gov.

14. John McCormick, Springville High School Art Gallery, National Register Nomination, April 26, 1986, 3, accessed October 6, 2019, http://npgallery.nps.gov.

15. Roger Roper, Payson Presbyterian Church, National Register Nomination, March 27, 1986, 3, accessed October 6, 2019, http://npgallery.nps .gov.

REGION C

1. A good reference for this period is Leonard J. Arrington, *Great Basin Kingdom: An Economic History of the Latter-day Saints, 1830–1900* (Cambridge, MA: Harvard University Press, 1958).

2. David Hampshire, Martha Sonntag Bradley, and Allen D. Roberts, *A History of Summit County* (Salt Lake City: Utah State Historical Society, 1998), 95.

3. "Park City Library: Heart of the Community since 1888," Park City Library, accessed October 13, 2019, http://parkcitylibrary.org.

4. *Park Record*, September 1888, quoted in Hampshire, Bradley, and Roberts, *History of Summit County*, 107.

REGION D

1. M. Guy Bishop, *A History of Sevier County* (Salt Lake City: Utah State Historical Society, 1997), 38.

2. Tom G. Alexander, *Utah: The Right Place* (Layton, UT: Gibbs Smith Peregrine Press, 1995), 164.

3. Alexander, *Utah: The Right Place*, 161.

4. Tom Alexander, "Generating Wealth from the Earth, 1847–2000," in *From the Ground Up: The History of Mining in Utah*, ed. Colleen Whitley (Logan: Utah State University Press, 2006), 41.

5. Kent Powell, Topaz Relocation Center, National Register Nomination, January 2, 1974, 4, accessed October 13, 2019, http://npgallery.nps.gov.

6. Luna Hinckley, quoted in "Cove Fort," accessed October 13, 2019, www.utah.com.

7. Roger Roper, Fairview City Hall, National Register Nomination, February 26, 1986, accessed October 13, 2019, http://npgallery.nps.gov.

8. Roger Roper, Ephraim Carnegie Library, National Register Nomination, n.d., 4, accessed October 13, 2019, http://npgallery.nps.gov.

9. Leonard Arrington, quoted by Kent Powell, Ephraim United Order Cooperative Building, National Register Nomination, March 20, 1973, 4, accessed October 13, 2019, http://npgallery.nps .gov.

10. Salina Municipal Building and Library, National Register Nomination, April 9, 1986, 4, accessed October 13, 2019, http://npgallery.nps.gov.

11. Jim Kolva, Richfield Main Post Office, National Register Nomination, November 15, 1988, 5, accessed October 13, 2019, http://npgallery.nps .gov.

REGION E

1. Helen Papinikolas, quoted in Richard D. Poll, Thomas G. Alexander, Eugene E. Campbell, and David E. Miller, *Utah's History* (Logan: Utah State University Press, 1989), 448.

2. Helen Papinikolas, *Peoples of Utah* (Salt Lake City: Utah State Historical Society, 1976), 429.

3. Papinikolas, *Peoples of Utah*, 419.

REGION F

1. Janet Seegmiller, "Iron County," in *From the Ground Up: The History of Mining in Utah*, ed. Colleen Whitley (Logan: Utah State University Press, 2006), 197.

2. Pine Valley Meetinghouse, National Register Nomination, April 16, 1971, accessed October 5, 2019, http://npgallery.nps.gov.

3. James H. McClintock, *Mormon Settlement in Arizona* (Phoenix: Arizona Historian Office, 1921; Bristol, UK: Archive Publishers, 2000), 65.

4. "Addie Price Home," Washington County Historical Society, accessed October 5, 2019, http://wchsutah.org/homes/addie-price-home .php.

REGION G

1. Wallace Stegner, quoted in Martha Sonntag Bradley, *A History of Kane County* (Salt Lake City: Utah State Historical Society, 1999), 1–2.

2. Charles Peterson, quoted in Richard D. Poll, Thomas G. Alexander, Eugene E. Campbell, and David E. Miller, *Utah's History* (Logan: Utah State University Press, 1989), 61.

3. Peterson, quoted in Poll et al., *Utah's History*, 124.

4. Bob McPherson, *A History of San Juan County* (Salt Lake City: Utah State Centennial County History Series, 1995), 173.

5. Bureau of Land Management, quoted in Bradley, *History of Kane County*, 10.

6. Kent Powell, *The Utah Guide*, 2nd ed. (Golden, CO: Fulcrum, 1998), 442.

7. "Golden Nuggets of Pioneer Days: A History of Garfield County," *Garfield County News*, 1949, 196.

8. "Monarch Cave Anasazi Ruins," Climb-Utah .com, accessed October 4, 2019, http://www .climb-utah.com/CM/monarch.htm.